THE
GREAT
GERMAN
FILMS

THE GREAT GERMAN FILMS

FREDERICK W. OTT

CITADEL PRESS   SECAUCUS, N.J.

Published by Citadel Press
A division of Lyle Stuart Inc.
120 Enterprise Ave., Secaucus, N.J. 07094
In Canada: Musson Book Company
A division of General Publishing Co. Limited
Don Mills, Ontario

Queries regarding rights and permissions should be
addressed to: Lyle Stuart, 120 Enterprise Avenue,
Secaucus, N.J. 07094

Designed by Christopher Simon
Manufactured in the United States of America

Library of Congress Cataloging-in-Publication Data

Ott, Frederick W.
    The great German films.

    1. Moving-pictures—Germany—History.   2. Moving-
picture industry—Germany—History.   I. Title.
PN1993.5.G3088   1986   791.43′75′0943   85-29068
ISBN 0-8065-0961-9

Acknowledgements

I wish to express gratitude to the Deutsches Institut für Filmkunde, Weisbaden-Beibrich, for courtesies extended to me in 1974 and 1979. Dr. Theo Furstenau, director of the Institut für Filmkunde, and his deputy, Eberhard Spiess, were always helpful.

I am also indebted to individuals and staffs at the Photo and Film Division of the Stadtmuseum, Munich; Hauptstaatsarchiv Stuttgart; Anthology Film Archives, New York; The Academy of Motion Picture Arts and Sciences, Los Angeles; the Cinema Library, University of Southern California; the National Film Archive, London; the New York Public Library; Department of Film, Museum of Modern Art; the Los Angeles Public Library; and the Goethe-Institute, Los Angeles.

Appreciation is also expressed to John Pommer, Carl Junghans, Dr. Enno Patalas, Percy Adlon, Dr. Peter Bucher, Wolfgang Lies, Stefan Dolezel, Willy Otto Zielke, Robert A. Haller, Dr. Viege Traub, Marta Feuchtwanger, Donald Deschner, Luis Trenker, Gerard Notzon, Clemis Martin, Georgio Moroder, Werner Mayer, Lutz Becker, Irene Fischer-Uhrig, Colin Hall, Herman Millakowsky and Ria Wenzel. Dr. Arnold Fanck, Lil Dagover and Mia May, now deceased, were most helpful and provided me with a living link with the early German film.

I must also mention, with gratitude, Gertrude Zeisl and Sylvia Benjamin who translated the German references, and Margaret Thomlinson who typed the manuscript.

Photographs were provided courtesy of the Cinémathèque Royale de Belgique, Brussels; Det Danske Filmmuseum, Copenhagen; Staatliches Filmarchive der D.D.R., Berlin; Ullstein GmbH, Berlin; Werner Herzog Filmproduktion, Munich; Franz Seitz Filmproduktion, Munich; Neue Constantin Film, GmbH, Munich; Export-Union des Deutschen Films, Munich; Landesbildstelle, Center for Audio-Visual Media, Berlin; TMS Film-Gesellschaft GmbH, Munich; Road Movies, Berlin; National Film Archive, London; Nederlands Filmmuseum, Amsterdam; National Archives, Washington, D.C.; Library of Congress, Prints and Photographs Division, Washington, D.C.; The Academy of Motion Picture Arts and Sciences, Los Angeles; Dr. Viege Traub Photo Archive, Los Angeles; The Museum of Modern Art Film Library, New York; Cinema Library, University of Southern California; The Wisconsin Center for Film and Theater Research, University of Wisconsin; Larry Edmunds Cinema Book Store, Hollywood; Collection of Eddie Brandt, North Hollywood; Sterling W. Smith (deceased); Film Corp Distribution, Inc., Los Angeles; and Cinema Entertainment Ltd., Los Angeles.

Acknowledgment is made to publishers for permission to quote short passages from the following works: *Archaeology of the Cinema*, C. W. Ceram (Harcourt, Brace and World, New York, 1965); *Art and Politics in the Weimar Period*, John Willett (Pantheon, New York, 1978); *Fifty Years of the German Film*, H. H. Wollenberg (Falcon Press, London, 1948); *Final Entries, 1945, The Diaries of Joseph Goebbels*, edited by H. R. Trevor-Roper (G. P. Putnam's, New York, 1978); *From Caligari to Hitler*, Siegfried Kracauer (Princeton University, Princeton, 1947); *Fun in a Chinese Laundry*, Josef von Sternberg (Macmillan, New York, 1965); *German Newsreels, 1933-1947*, Stefan Dolezel (Goethe-Institute, Munich, 1984); *Goebbels—The Man Next to Hitler*, Rudolf Semmler (Westhouse, London, 1947); *The Goebbels Diaries, 1939-1941*, translated and edited by Fred Taylor (G. P. Putnam's, New York, 1983); *The Goebbels Diaries, 1942-1943*, translated and edited by Louis Lochner (Doubleday, Garden City, 1948); *The Haunted Screen*, Lotte H. Eisner (University of California, Berkeley and Los Angeles, 1969); *Hitler Was My Friend*, Heinrich Hoffmann (Burke, London, 1955): *Hitler's Secret Conversations 1941-1944*, translated by Norman Cameron and R. H. Stevens (Farrar, Strauss and Young, New York, 1953); *Inside the Third Reich*, Albert Speer (Macmillan, New York, 1970); *Murnau*, Lotte H. Eisner (University of California, Berkeley and Los Angeles, 1964); *Politics and Film*, Lief Furhammer and Folke Isaksson (Studio Vista, London, 1971); *Sergei M. Eisenstein*, Marie Seton (Grove Press, New York, 1960).

Contents

Preface

The Great German Films presents an overview of the German cinema from its origins in the last decade of the nineteenth century to the present. The book is divided into eight sections: the formative years, 1895-1913; the period of the First World War, 1914-1918; the "Golden Age" of the German film, 1920-1929; the development of the sound film in the closing years of the Weimar Republic, 1930-1933; film in the Third Reich, 1933-1938; the war years, 1939-1945; the postwar period, 1945-1962; and finally, the emergence of the new German cinema. Forty-five notable films, from *The Cabinet of Dr. Caligari* to *Céleste*, have been singled out for special study in the context of Germany's cultural and political history. This group has been designated great in the sense that they are "worthy of preservation and study," although some may additionally possess the attributes of "noble simplicity and quiet grandeur," as Winckelmann defined the word more than two centuries ago. While the book is comprehensive, certain editorial decisions were necessary, especially in the treatment accorded the two Germanys and Austria.

Believing that the study of film cannot be divorced from the larger context of history, this writer has chosen to regard the cinema of the German Democratic Republic (East Germany) as a unique development. *The Great German Films*, therefore, deals exclusively with the cinema of the German Federal Republic (West Germany) in the section since 1949. This is not to denigrate the cinematic achievements of the German Democratic Republic or to suggest that the GDR has not produced meritable or even classic films, but to recognize the reality of its independent political status. In recent years a degree of cooperation has marked the relationship between East and West, even to the point of exchanging films, but unification remains a distant prospect. According to the East German leader Erich Honecker, it would be as impossible to combine the two Germanys as it would be to combine "flame and ice." Honecker's blunt simile may be all too true and as applicable to the cultural sphere as to the political. The film industry of the GDR, then, shaped as it has been by Marxist ideology and the political and social exigencies of a totalitarian state, is deserving of a separate study reflective of that nation's thirty-five-year history in close alliance with the Soviet Union.

The exclusion of Austria is less disputable, although Austrians have contributed substantially to the development of the German film since at least World War I. Such Austrians as Erich Pommer, Joe May, Fritz Lang, Willi Forst, G. W. Pabst, Billy Wilder and Walter Reisch enriched the German film immeasurably. But this German-speaking realm, albeit allied with Germany at various points in history and briefly united with the Reich between 1938 and 1945, possesses a unique cultural identity. It should be noted that since the 1970s, Austria has experienced a cinematic renaissance not unlike its German neighbor, but one which has unfolded along lines distinctively Austrian, owing more to France and Italy in terms of influence than to Germany. Rather than consider the Austrian cinema as an appendage of the German, a separate study, as in the case of the GDR, seems warranted.

It is to be hoped that *The Great German Films* will stimulate interest among English language readers whose curiosity may have been aroused by the viewing of *Das Kabinette des Dr. Caligari (The Cabinet of Dr. Caligari), Der letze Mann (Last Laugh), Metropolis,* and *Aguirre, der Zorn Gottes (Aguirre, the Wrath of God)* but are unfamiliar with works no less astonishing: *Hintertreppe (Backstairs), Die Büchse der Pandora (Pandora's Box), Fährmann Maria (Ferryboat Pilot Maria), Münchhausen, In Jenen Tagen (Seven Journeys),* and *Die Kinder aus No. 67 (The Children of No. 67).* If this book should contribute to a deeper study and appreciation of the German film, it will have served its purpose.

1

The Formative Years

1895-1913

Anschütz *Schnellseher.*

The origins of the German film stem from the experiments of Ottomar Anschütz in the late nineteenth century. A photographer in Lissa, Prussia, Anschütz had studied the experiments of Eadweard Muybridge and John D. Isaacs who had used a battery of twenty-four cameras to photograph Leland Stanford's race horse. In 1884 Anschütz presented pictures of good quality in a series, having photographed animals in a wilderness reserve adjoining his estate. Notable in this regard was a series of 120 pictures illustrating the life of a family of storks. "People were delighted to see close-ups of the parent storks standing in the nest and of the different stages of development of the young," historian Gernsheim wrote, "while particular interest was aroused by photographs of the stork alighting and 'taking off' from the nest, for such pictures had not hitherto been taken." As C. W. Ceram noted in his *Archaeology of the Cinema*, Anschütz's "pictures compared to those of Muybridge as, to use a modern analogy, a Leica's to a box camera." Like Muybridge, Anschütz used a series of cameras, twelve to fourteen, contained in a single apparatus, to photograph flying birds, galloping horses and jumping men. He also devised the slot shutter and created a viewing apparatus called the Tachyscope. The improved electrical Tachyscope built in 1887 to the order of the Prussian war minister "intermittently illuminated each transparent positive as it moved past a slit" with a Geissler vacuum tube and a steel stroboscopic disc mounted on a stand. The device was shown to audiences in Berlin and Vienna.

Siemens built seventy-eight Tachyscopes between 1892 and 1895. The images Tachyscope produced could be seen by only a few viewers, but in the early 1890s Anschütz built an apparatus for public screenings, and on November 25, 1894, he gave the first public demonstration of his projection apparatus at the General Post Office in Berlin. Using a double projector system, which cast images on a screen 6 × 8 meters, Anschütz entertained viewers with a variety of humorous scenes, including a barber soaping a man's face. Ceram observed that "While Muybridge had only improved the Phenakisticope for his projections, Anschütz with his double projector [Tachyscope] set out on a new—though wrong—road."

In this same period, Max and Emil Skladanowsky, the sons of a Berlin magic lanternist, perfected their Bioscope apparatus which made series photographs on Eastman Kodak celluloid film. The Skladanowsky projection system projected two strips of film simultaneously through two objectives which were alternatively covered by a shutter to follow each other in logical sequence. The rolls were shown at eight frames per second, producing when combined a frequency of sixteen frames per second.

When Max Skladanowsky patented his gear mechanism, he wrote that his machine had been "manufactured, on the basis of my drawings, for 150.25 marks in 258 hours of labor . . . by the Berlin firm of Mehr and Schäfer from high-quality special steel. . . ." The brothers recognized the commercial potential of motion pictures and on November 1, 1895, presented their Bioscope pictures at the Berlin Wintergarten. Although the Lumières had shown their films privately, the first public performance of their pictures did not occur until December 28 at the Grand Café, Boulevard des Capuchines. The Skladanowsky Wintergarten films were preceded by a live variety program after which the lights dimmed to present "The Bioscope, the most interesting and amusing invention of modern times." The program commenced with two children performing a peasant dance, followed by a pair of gymnasts working on a horizontal bar, gloved kangaroos engaged in a boxing match, a juggler demonstrating his skill, and a boxing match. The Bioscope concluded with the performance of a family of gymnasts. The Skladanowskys gave further performances in Germany, Holland and Scandinavia, although the double projector system was abandoned after 1896.

Ottomar Anschütz, 1846-1907.

Oskar Meester was the third and perhaps the most important of the German film pioneers. Born in 1866, the son of a Berlin mechanic turned optical maker, Meester entered his father's firm and assumed control of the business at the age of twenty-six. Fascinated by the "dissolving view devices" and other magic lantern apparatuses which proliferated in the last decade of the nineteenth century, Meester studied the possibilities of motion picture projection, having made a careful study of Anschütz's Tachyscope and Edison's Kinetoscope. In April, 1896, Meester saw his first cinematographic projections in Berlin. Two months later he created a projector system which substituted the Maltese Cross for the claw movement of the Lumières. Meester recalled that after he had constructed a camera he "assembled the necessary equipment for the developing and copying of the films. That done, by the end of 1896 we had the basis for building a cinema and film industry in Germany which would operate entirely with German apparatus."

Meester continued to perfect his equipment, developing seventeen improved versions of his projector between 1896 and 1913. In 1902 he established Meester's Projektion Gmbh and produced all his own films until 1913. Having established a studio on the Friedrichstrasse, Meester recruited talent from the music halls, cabarets

Oskar Messter, 1866-1943.

A Messter program for Berlin's *Biophon-Theater*.

Advertisement for Messter-Film

Messter's *Kinetographen*.

Max Sklandanowsky's *Bioscop*, a double projection system demonstrated at the Berlin Wintergarten, February 1, 1895.

and the theater. Some of the most notable of Germany's future film stars, including Lil Dagover, Ossi Oswalda, Emil Jannings, Harry Liedtke and Conrad Veidt, were to make their debut under his aegis. Not the least of his remarkable achievements was the creation of the *Meester-Woche* (Meester Week) newsreel which debuted on October 1, 1914, and was distributed through Europe, the United States, Latin America, Japan and the Dutch East Indies. In January 1920, the *Meester-Woche* was absorbed by the *Deulig-Woche*.

The first Meester catalogue, issued in October, 1897, suggests that he understood the vast potential of the motion picture. "By its means historical events can henceforth be preserved just as they happened," he wrote, "and brought to view again not only now, but also for the benefit of future generations." Meester's inaugural catalogue offered to sell eighty-four films which included Berlin street scenes, the arrival and departure of locomotives, sporting events, parades, ceremonials, short films of the Emperor William's visit to Stettin and scenes of the aged Bismarck in retirement at Friedrichsruh. Some of the titles in the 1897 catalogue are of particular note for their innovative cinematic effects: Number four, *Vom Ernst zum Lachen: Die Mimik des Gesangskomikers Franz Amon* contained the first close-ups; Number five, *Schnellmaler Clown Jigg*, the first animation effects; and *Flower Arrangement*, the first speeded-up motion effect.

In August, 1903, Meester issued the first *Biophonton-bild* or sound film, *Der Specht*, synchronized with a gramaphone recording of a Polka-Mazurka. And the following year Meester became the first German producer to make a film in English, *The Whistling Bowery Boy*, a seventy-five-meter effort which was shown with a gramaphone recording at the St. Louis World's Fair in 1904. Meester also pioneered the first *Grossfilm* or long film, *Andreas Hofer*, directed by Carl Froelich in 1909.

While much of Meester's *ouvre* no doubt resembled the offerings of other filmmakers, he was sometimes original in his use of the camera. A notable example would be *Excursion*, a bicycle film made about 1898. The film opens with a long shot of bicycles on a road, followed by a closer shot of the bicycles, then faces of the cyclists, a shot of legs pumping up and down and, finally, a full shot of the cyclists. As Maurice Bardècke and Robert Brasillach suggested, "In this simple little film the whole pictorial sense of the Germans, their attention to detail, their propensity for using the camera's eye to show us things our own eyes would never seek out, are already to be detected."

The early German films, short *Varietés*, running 20 to 40 meters in length, were first shown in cabarets as the culmination of the evening's program. The novelty of the new medium insured a rapid growth. Traveling tent show cinemas (*Wanderkinos*) and nickelodeons (*Ladenkinos*), operating in a fairground milieu of steaming sausages and frothy beer, proved to be a popular diversion for the German laboring class which had expanded to 35 million by 1895.

As the popularity of films increased, the setting acquired more permanence, and by 1904 the German movies were usually exhibited in a converted storefront called a *Kintopp* or shop cinema. White canvas was affixed to the wall and audiences were seated in rows of wooden chairs. It was still very crude, but a substantial improvement over the sawdust floor and tent-like enclosure which had typified the *Wanderkinos*. As critic and historian H. H. Wollenberg stated, "While the owner himself tore off the tickets and kept order, his wife sat at the cash-till, their son played the piano, or wound up the gramaphone, which accompanied the film with its music and drowned the noise of the projector. Usually a compère explained the contents of the film, with often involuntarily funny comments, for until 1907 the films had no printed titles."

Although the film had earned a measure of respectability and could count among its audience an increasing number of middle class patrons, filmgoing remained controversial. Some German critics believed that it posed a potential hazard in a physical sense. The nitrate-based film stock was highly flammable, and theater fires were not uncommon with resulting injuries and loss of life.

Berlin and other municipalities were prompted to enact some of the world's most stringent fire codes. The walls of the projection booth were required to be insulated with a double sheet of iron or steel with an intervening air space. Section 14 of the Fire Prevention Code specified that "In the case of productions in the theaters or halls which hold more than 500 persons, if the operation of the apparatus and the lighting of the theater are not done by the same man, a signal device must be placed beside the apparatus in order that the man in charge of the house lighting may be appraised of an existing fire or other trouble and turn on the lights of the theater." But opposition to the motion pictures persisted, and in the summer of 1907 Berlin police attempted, unsuccessfully to close the city's two hundred cinemas after physicians had proved to the satisfaction of authorities that the quivering movements of the *Flimmerkunst* were harmful to the human eye, particularly the eyes of children.

Beginning in 1896, industrial exhibitions contributed to the prestige and acceptance of the new medium. In June, 1908, Hamburg was host to the first International Cinematographic Industry Exhibition with displays of

12

The *Apollo-Cinema*, Berlin, c. 1905.

Entrance to the refurbished *Apollo-Theater*, Berlin, c. 1910.

Messter's studio and office in Berlin.

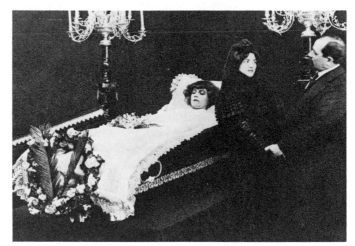

Asta Nielsen in *Zwei Schwestern* (Two Sisters), 1910.

Oskar Messter in his studio.

A Messter film during production, 1912.

apparatus and materials employed in the production of moving pictures. According to *The Scientific American*, the exhibition hall in Hamburg contained "sections devoted to photographs and films, photographic processes, optics and projection, electric motors, illumination, musical accessories (pianos, orchestrions, phonographs, etc.), heating appliances, arrangement of theaters, technical literature, and advertising."

The *Kintopp* soon gave way to the *Lichtspieltheatre*, a structure especially designed for the exhibition of motion pictures. The seven hundred seat Nollendorf Theater, designed in the Greek temple style, was described by a contemporary reviewer to be "architecturally one of the most striking structures in the Kaiser's capital, and does much to beautify the big Nollendorf Platz on which it stands." The Nollendorf boasted a domed roof "built to be removed in summer and during other propitious weather, so that at night spectators have nothing above them but the starlit heavens."

Even the German Kaiser succumbed to the appeal of motion pictures and sanctioned the building of a film theater in the Royal Palace in Potsdam. Dedicated in December, 1912, a distinguished company of military and political guests saw films of recent events including the royal hunt near Hannover and photographs of the Kaiser and the Austrian Archduke Franz Ferdinand. It is not unlikely that the Emperor also saw *Zum 25 zahrigen Regierungs-Jubiläum S. M. Kaiser Wilhelm II im Film*, running 144 meters and produced by the Express-Film Company of Freiburg for public release in December, 1912.

To commemorate the Emperor's Silver Jubilee in 1913, the German film industry issued a book entitled, *The Kaiser on Film*. According to the text, William had become interested in motion pictures during a summer cruise aboard the *Hohenzollern* to North Cape. Films which the court photographer had shot during the day were developed aboard the yacht and shown to William and his guests that evening. The Kaiser was completely won over to the new medium and was thereafter always cooperative when being photographed, posing under all kinds of circumstances. This was perhaps the first indication by a German head of state that the medium of film might serve to publicize and propagandize.

Significant developments also occurred in the construction of movie studios. The little *Drachtstuben-Ateliers* containing a slanted glassed roof on the north side and a glass south wall offered approximately 50 × 80 square meters of studio space. These renovated photography studios were completely inadequate by 1910. They could accommodate two or three players at the most while the building of elaborate settings was impossible. The *Drachtstuben-Ateliers* gave way to one and

two story glass studios which allowed the sun to enter from all sides. Bioskop built one of the largest studios at Neubabelsberg near Berlin in 1911-12 with 300 to 450 square meters of floor space.

The *Glashaus* was firmly established by 1914, the larger structures ranging in size from 300 to 800 square meters with panes of *Rohglas* (fluted glass), *Drahtglas* (wired glass) or *Riffelglas* (rippled glass), but the world war imposed limitations on new construction for about five years. The *Freilicht-Atelier*, an open air studio with an elevated stage supported by scaffolding, was yet another alternative, but the inconstancy of light argued against the expansion of such facilities or the building of new glass studios.

After 1918 German filmmakers adapted other structures for the production of motion pictures, notably the airport hangars in Johannesthal and the Tattersall im Grunewaldt and the immense Zeppelin hangars in Staaken. These cavernous studios offered unparalleled artistic opportunities for the film. The director was able to control every nuance of the filmic environment. While the new lighting equipment was expensive, the *Kunstlicht-Atelier*, or studio lit by artificial light, reduced production costs by eliminating delays due to variable weather. The glass houses were fitted with curtains or painted with an indigo blue and black oil paint, as the *Kunstlicht-Atelier* became the predominant setting for the photographing of motion pictures by the early 1920s.

So great was the demand for motion pictures in the years before 1914, that German firms began to import foreign films from England, Italy and America, but France and Denmark were the largest and most influential suppliers in this period. Before the outbreak of World War I, the French concerns, Pathé, Gaumont, Eclair, and Eclipse, opened branches in Germany while the Nordisk Films Kompagni of Copenhagen, established in 1906 by the enterprising Ole Olsen, proved to be the most competitive. Germany became the principal market for Nordisk which produced several films especially for German audiences, of which *Atlantis* (1913), based on the novel by Gerhart Hauptmann, would be one example. Photographed by Johan Ankerstjerne, it contains dream sequences which anticipate the later expressionistically inspired German films.

The Danish films were made significant by their form and style "which often made them superior to the foreign films of the period." Two Danish productions from 1910, *Die weisse Slavin* (*The White Slave Traffic*), running 700 meters, and *Der Abgrund* (*The Abyss*), directed by Urban Gad, encouraged the Germans, always sensitive to their Danish competition, to produce longer films. Running 775 meters, *Der Abgrund* was almost twice the length of the traditional German offering in 1909-1910. Some German producers were reluctant to lengthen films, fearful perhaps that they would no longer be able to present a variety of programs.

But the transition to longer films, established by 1912, encouraged cinematic artistry and the development of motion picture stars of which the melancholic beauty, Asta Nielsen, must be counted one of the first. Bardècke and Brasillach noted that Nielsen "displayed to the public all the romanticism of the northern countries, full of Ibsen and of the suffering but conscientious character of the Nordic writers and dramatists of the eighteen-eighties." In the wake of *Der Abgrund*, Asta Neilsen and her then husband, Urban Gad, received an offer to appear in German films and made two films for Deutsche Bioscop in 1911. "In 1912 Asta Neilsen returned to Denmark to make two more films, but after these she left for Germany, where the remainder of her career took place," Ib Monty wrote. "Only once, in 1918, did she return to the Danish cinema for a brief guest performance."

Der Abgrund, with its story of a woman who debases herself on account of her passion for a brutal man, broke new ground for the erotic melodrama. "The film caused a sensation in its day," Monty wrote. "People were impressed by the striking representation of an erotic affair (a very sensual gaucho dance caused audiences to open their eyes wide), by the portrayal of a social milieu, but above all by the completely honest and straight-forward acting, devoid of theatrical clichés, of Asta Neilsen." The form and content of the Danish film remained a primary influence on the German industry until the outbreak of war in 1914.

As film production increased, producers turned to the stage for talent. The Association of Berlin Theater-Directors resisted the intrusion of the *Kintopps*, preferring this derisive appellation to the more socially acceptable *Lichtspieltheatre* and at first refused to allow its actors to appear in films. But some *Schauspielers*, such as Albert Bassermann, were attracted to the new medium by the prospect of additional income and boldly violated the restrictions. Bassermann's appearance in *Der Andere (The Other One)*, directed by Max Mack, helped to undermine the power of the theater owners. Exhibited at the Berlin Mozartsall in February, 1913, *Der Andere* became the first German film to be seriously regarded by the press. And the fact that it was based on a play by Paul Lindau gives it the distinction of being the first *Autorenfilm*, or famous author films.

Playwrights like Franz von Schoenthan and Richard Voss and novelists of the caliber of Friedrich Hollaender were commissioned to write for the films while the literature of Hugo von Hofmannsthal, Arthur Schnitzler and Friedrich Schiller was mined for suitable material. Like the French *Film d'Art* (*Assassination of the Duce de Guise*, 1908), these productions were essentially filmed theater and made little attempt to exploit the unique visual properties of the motion picture.

But the theater owners were sufficiently alarmed to take action, and in 1912 the National Association of Managers, Actors and Playwrights, meeting in Berlin, attempted to repress the growth of the new medium. The National Association believed that the motion picture ought to serve science and education but should not be permitted to invade the realm of drama. Members of the Association, reading reports from 120 theaters in Germany, protested that the *Kintopps* had brought the theater business to the brink of ruin. Their litany of complaints contained unintentional humor. One member described how a Berlin leading lady had recently been employed by a film company which had had "no trouble in inducing her to throw herself into a lake to portray the principal role in a piece called *Tired of Life*." The outraged Association adopted resolutions opposing the motion picture and even urged the Reich government to place a prohibitive tariff on all films from abroad.

But these gestures proved of no avail for, as *The New York Times* observed in its report of the conference, " 'Kintopps' continue, in the meantime, to spring up like

Albert Bassermann (Dr. Hallers) in *Der Andere* (The Other), directed by Max Mack, 1913.

15

mushrooms everywhere in Germany." The following year a *New York Times* report described Berlin to be "cinematograph mad."

While some intellectuals scorned the motion picture, other more perceptive academics appreciated its educational potential. The antecedents of the *Lehrfilm*, or instructional film, might be traced to the experiments of Anschütz at the close of the century. But it was not until the founding of the Organization for Cinematographic Study in 1913 that impetus was given to the production of films of an instructive and scientific nature which, it was hoped, would raise the standards of ordinary films. Its organizers included Ludwig Fulda; Professor Brunner, Royal Censor; Dr. Archenhold of the Treptow Observatory; Privy Court Councillor Grimm and other prominent men. The association proposed to underwrite the cost of production in instances where producers felt such films would not be profitable. A museum and archive for the preservation of especially valuable films was also contemplated.

One novel experiment in the genre of the *Lehrfilm* occurred in a Berlin symphony hall in 1914. While a live orchestra played the overture to Bizet's *Carmen*, the audience watched a film of a conductor leading the musicians "as if he were before them in the flesh." Future generations, it was thought, would be able to study the technique of great conductors. Dr. Felix von Weingartner, who witnessed the event, was deeply impressed: "It was amazing, and no doubt it is possible, with the aid of such a film, to give as artistic a performance of orchestra pieces as that rendered by the baton of a living director." Arthur Nikisch was of a similar opinion: "What extraordinary value it would have for us today if we could see and hear how Wagner directed the production of the Ninth Symphony in Beyreuth in 1872! I predict a great development for this invention."

World War I encouraged the development of the *Lehrfilm* for the instruction and training of troops. By 1919 it was seen to have immense possibilities as an adjunct to the classroom and the lecture hall with especially equipped projectors that would permit "freeze framing" *(Standbild)* to allow additional commentary by the speaker or questions from the audience. The *Lehrfilm*, to many, held the promise of revolutionizing the dissemination of knowledge.

Tributaries of the *Lehrfilm* included the *Werkfilm*, or industrial film, designed for management and employees, which visually described the step-by-step creation of a product, the teaching of an industrial skill or methods of improving production. The *Statistische Film* presented statistical data in animated graphs and charts while the *Wissenschaftlichen* or scientific film described new apparatus or depicted the performance of a surgical operation. The possibilities appeared limitless. "There were highly educated old Berliners who declared with a certain emphasis, 'I have acquired all my education from the *Vossischen Zeitung*,' " a reviewer wrote in 1919, "and there will be an increasing number of people who quietly declare, 'I have received all my education from the film.' And this education will be just as good and solid."

"People began discussing the cinema as an art in 1913," Ceram wrote in his book *Archaeology of the Cinema*. "In Germany such discussion arose in connection with the films of Paul Wegener (and we have only to see those films today to realize how absurd that all was)." While the first sentence is correct, Ceram's parenthetical clause in the second sentence is false. *Der Student von Prag (The Student of Prague)* was a seminal work in the history of film. So extraordinary is *The Student of Prague* as a work of cinematic art that one must consider the possibility that the eighteen-year tradition of the German silent film which preceded its release was a great deal richer than has heretofore been thought. While attention has been given to *The Cabinet of Dr. Caligari* (1919-1920) and the cinematic manifestations of expressionism in the years 1920-1924, film historians have, in general, been neglectful of Germany's accomplishments before 1914.

The Student of Prague marks a turning point in the artistic development of the German film. The film was directed by the Dane Stellen Rye in collaboration with Paul Wegener and photographed by Guido Seeber from a script by Hanns Heinz Ewers. Although Rye was officially credited as director, the film bears the imprint of Wegener, who also took the role of the chief character, the student Baldwin. Even though he had been trained in the theater, Wegener, like Melies in France and Porter in America, appreciated the visual properties of the cinema. He believed that the motion picture must strive to achieve something more than mimed theater in the manner of the French *film d'art*. "The real creator of the film must be the camera," Wegener wrote in 1916.

Wegener was inspired to make *The Student of Prague* after viewing a series of comic photos of a man fencing and playing cards with himself. Could similar effects be achieved on film? Wegener sought to explore these possibilities. From the fairy tales and legends of E. T. A. Hoffman, particularly the author's *Das Abenteuer der Sylvester Nacht* and Chamisso's *Peter Schlemihl*, Wegener and Ewers reworked the *Doppelgänger* motive to tell their story of a youth, Baldwin, who sells his soul to the devil, represented by Scapinelli. Although sets for interiors were created at the Bioscop-Atelier in Neubabelsberg, *The Student of Prague* contains an abundance of exterior scenes. Much of the location photography was achieved in Prague, where extensive use was made of the historical castle Beleneder and the Lobbowitz and Fürstenberg palaces.

The film is photographed in keeping with the theme of a fantasy: tree shaded pathways, wrought iron gates, blossoming gardens, stone ballustrades, ornate doorways and a magnificent colonnades. Seeber's camera remains stationary, panning only occasionally on a horizontal axis. Characters are shown primarily in long shot, although in one sequence Seeber creates a dramatic close-up when he photographs the gypsy girl as she flees down a stairway and disappears to the left of the frame.

The Student of Prague also contains a remarkable example of deep focus. We see Baldwin seated at a table in the foreground of the frame while action occurs in the distant background, and later Baldwin is shown leaning despondently against a tree in the foreground as a duel is acted out in the background of the frame. Rye, Wegener and Seeber are no less adroit in their handling of the special effects involving the *Doppelgänger*. When Baldwin has sealed his pact with the devil we see his "shadow self" step from the full-length mirror and follow Scapinelli out of the room.

The acting is naturalistic and restrained; rarely do characters engage in operatic *film d'art* gestures. On occasion, the Countess suggests the grand manner of Bernhardt, but Wegener as Baldwin is consistently naturalistic. John Gottowt as the devilish Scapinelli, bespectacled and bewhiskered, attired in a frock coat and a top hat, has the charm and drollery of a character out of Spitzweg. *The Student of Prague* is a film of great sophistication and a masterpiece of visual storytelling.

Scenes from *Der Student von Prag* (The Student of Prague), directed by Stellan Rye, 1913.

II

The First World War

1914-1918

THE outbreak of the first World War was to have a decided influence on the history of the German film. The events of July and August, 1914, were not entirely unwelcome by the German film industry, which hoped to gain economically from the elimination of a strong competitor, the French, and to a lesser degree, the English. With Italy's entry into the war on the side of the *Entente* in April, 1915, another important film rival was excluded from the Central and Southern Europe market, now effectively dominated by Germany and its ally, Austria-Hungary.

In the months that followed, German entrepreneurs proceeded to consolidate their position. New production companies were created to meet an ever-increasing demand for films for civilian and military showings. In 1913, fewer than thirty companies produced films in Germany, but by 1919 some two hundred and fifty film companies had been licensed to operate in the Reich. German audiences continued to see Scandinavian films, principally Danish offerings produced by Nordisk, but the largest share of the productions was of German manufacture. Dr. Leidig, director of the United Federations of the German Film Industry, recalled in 1919 how the war had suddenly forced the German film to be self reliant: "We had to catch our breath. . . . It was not exactly a smooth path. The industry faced numerous obstacles: securing a halfway sufficient amount of raw material for the production of film stock; struggling on a daily basis with every possible war economic office; experiencing difficulties in the procurement of light, coal and personnel; and battling the opposition of stubborn magistrates. All this had to be overcome and was overcome."

In the initial phase of the four-year struggle, German studios concentrated on patriotic films such as *Die Wacht am Rhien (Watch on the Rhine)* and *Das Vaterland Ruft (The Call of the Fatherland)*. "Sentimental and heroic films about nurses and soldiers were turned out by the score, but with the Iron Cross playing the part that the *Legion d'honneur* played in France," Maurice Bardècke and Robert Brasillach wrote. Quasi-documentary films such as *Cruise of the Moewe* and the more sensational *The Log of the U-35*, based on the exploits of Lieutenant Armand de la Pierre, commander of a German submarine in the Mediterranean, also appeared. The lieutenant is said to have achieved his mission with a definite filmic sense, maneuvering for days "to get an enemy sailing vessel under full canvas and satisfactorily backlighted. Then he sank her against the sun of dawn, ensign flying at the forepeak as it settled into the sea, gilded by the streaming low angle light." But as the war continued, comedies, melodramas and serials unrelated to the world crisis were offered to audiences in search of escapist entertainment.

Morale on the homefront and the ineffectiveness of German propaganda in neutral countries, especially the United States, became a matter of grave concern to the military leadership of Germany as the war dragged on. In Washington, Ambassador von Bernsdorff endeavored to convince propaganda authorities in Berlin to send films to the United States to counteract the more sophisticated efforts of the English and French.

In January, 1917, four months before the United States entered the war, *The New York Times* reviewed *Germany and Its Armies of Today*, observing that it was the first film "to reach this country from Germany in several months." The film contained views of Berlin, "intended to show that things are moving normally in the German capital" and "some of the various kinds of work women are doing. . . ." But of greater interest according to the report were "pictures of the funeral of the German aviator, Boelke—an impressive military ceremony with scarcely a civilian in sight. Interesting, too, are close-up pictures of the Kaiser reviewing troops on the west front." The German exports were for the most part disappointing. "Some few pictures were brought into America and offered for release," Terry Ramsaye wrote in 1925, but "they were clumsily photographed and more clumsily edited. They attained no circulation of importance."

To counteract the emotional "Hun" propaganda of the *Entente* with its unrelenting attack on German *Kultur*, and to more effectively disseminate propaganda at home

A German officer reads the official proclamation of war to Berlin citizens, July 31, 1914.

as well as in the occupied territories and neutral countries, industrialist Alfred Hugenberg established the Deutsche Lichtbild-Gesellschaft (German Photographic Company [Duelig]) in 1916. The films of Duelig, whose management Hugenberg delegated to Ludwig Klitzch, presented the beauty of the German landscape and told of Germany's industrial achievements. As a German reviewer of the period sarcastically observed, foreign audiences who had been subject to *Entente* propaganda were sometimes astonished to see that German people resembled human beings.

These educational (*Lehrerfilm*) and cultural (*Kulturfilm*) films might change the attitudes of some, but as Germany entered the third winter of war, stronger and more direct measures were thought necessary. Erich von Ludendorff, Quartermaster General of the Army, believed that the crisis of morale required the government's intervention in the propaganda sector. "The mind of the German people remained rudderless and uncaptained, the prey of every influence that came," he reflected after the war. "Ignorant and deluded, it sought after phantoms which could never be reached." Criticizing the Reich government for its failure to create an Imperial Ministry of Propaganda, Ludendorff wrote that "Every German, man or woman, should have been told daily what the loss of the war would mean to us. Pictures and the moving pictures should have been forced to preach the same." The general's proposal of a centralized propaganda bureau became a reality fourteen years later with Hitler's establishment of the Reich Ministry of Propaganda and Public Enlightenment under the aegis of Dr. Joseph Goebbels.

To achieve Ludendorff's goal of more direct control over filmmaking, the Army established the *Bild und Film Amt* (Photograph and Film Office [BUFA]) in early 1917. BUFA provided educational, propaganda and entertainment films for Germany's front line and reserve forces, the occupied territories and neutral nations. Central offices were established in the West, the East and the Balkans. The Navy was served by offices at Kiel (Wilhelmshaven) and the auxiliary patrol by a bureau at Swinemünde. In July, a degree of centralization was achieved by Colonel Hans von Haeften, who created a propaganda organization in the military department of the Foreign Office (*Militarische Stelle des Auswartigen Amts*). "By word and picture, and above all, by means of the moving pictures," Ludendorff wrote, "Colonel von Haeften sought to obtain a secure footing in neutral countries."

Haeften established propaganda departments in the embassies of neutral states and in the occupied districts of the East. In a revealing passage from his memoirs, Ludendorff evaluated these efforts and the importance which he attached to film as a medium of persuasion: "Propaganda by pictures and films was encouraged by the formation of a special graphic department, the 'picture and film office,' and later of the Universal Film Company, Limited. The film is a means of popular education, and Colonel von Haeften desired to employ it as such after the war, his war organization being designed to that end." Ludendorff believed that "Pictures and films and illustrations in poster form penetrate farther and have a stronger effect than writing and thus have a greater influence on the great masses of the people."

BUFA grew steadily as Ludendorff's role in the affairs of state increased. By October the BUFA had established its own laboratory, a turn of events which prompted a question in the Reichstag as to whether the government intended to nationalize the film industry.

With the entry of the United States into the war in April, 1917, Ludendorff concluded that more drastic measures should be taken to meet the global thrust of the virulent anti-German propaganda emanating from the well-equipped studios of its powerful new enemy. On December 18, 1917, the German High Command formed UFA (Universum Film A.G.), the successor of BUFA, which brought together prominent financiers and industrialists, and the important Meester-Film, Davidson's Union-Film, Joe May-Film, and in the early twenties, Decla-Bioskop.

The merger with Decla-Bioskop brought Erich Pommer to UFA. Widely respected for his intelligence, good taste, and business acumen, Pommer may have contributed more to the development of the German film in the 1920s than any other individual. The new company was capitalized at 25 million marks, with the German government taking a one-third interest. Established under the auspices of the state, UFA's *raison d'être* was clearly propagandistic. As Dr. Kracauer noted: "The official mission of UFA was to advertise Germany according to government directives. These asked not only for direct screen propaganda, but also for films characteristic of German culture and films serving the purpose of national education."

"The founding of UFA marks the first step in the creation of a young and flourishing film industry," a German journalist of the period noted. "It signals the gathering of forces and the forging of weapons in the struggle for the world market. In one word: the will to power." To achieve its goals, UFA acquired studios at Tempelhof and Babelsberg on the outskirts of Berlin. In the following months, producers, directors, writers and artistic and technical personnel were recruited, as the great combine undertook to produce its first films.

It remained for Ernst Lubitsch, the son of a Berlin

haberdasher, a former Reinhardt actor and comedian turned director, to realize most fully the aims of his UFA sponsors with the production of *Madame Dubarry (Passion)*. Released at the close of 1918, it served the purpose of anti-French propaganda in the guise of "historical" spectacle. With Pola Negri in the title role and Emil Jannings as a decadent King Louis XV, *Madame Dubarry* achieved something of a revolution in the art of film. The *mise en scène* of *Madame Dubarry* suggests the influence of the Italian pre-war costume spectacles, especially *Cabiria*, and the elaborate *Grossschauspielhaus* productions of Max Reinhardt. Lubitsch "humanized" historical personalities in a manner heretofore unseen in continental productions. Although adroit in his handling of mass scenes, Lubitsch, like D. W. Griffith, understood the emotional power of a close-up, the blink of an eyelid, the gesture of a hand.

Upon its release in the United States in 1920, *Madame Dubarry*, retitled *Passion*, was acclaimed the most important European picture since the Italian production of *Cabiria*. Unknown outside Germany, Lubitsch emerged as a director of world stature. And with *Dubarry*, the German film achieved its first major breakthrough in the international market since the Armistice. American critics were nothing less than ecstatic. *Motion Picture News* described the "painstaking direction and acting" and the "seemingly years of rehearsals" that had been spent to make the picture "perfect." The reviewer concluded, "And that is the lesson to be learned from the Germans. If it took fifty years to prepare a perfect war machine, they would take the same length of time in peace to prepare something equally perfect."

In 1921, the Reich government divested itself of its UFA holdings, with the Deutsche Bank acquiring its principal shares together with all government exemptions and protections heretofore enjoyed. Reconstituted as a private company, the primary task of UFA was seen to be the production of commercial films of high artistic quality that would be capable of competing effectively in the world market, especially the American. The propaganda of UFA's original founders, while not entirely lost sight of, was subordinated to the entrepreneurial considerations of profit, an understandable course when one considers the government's imposition of special taxes on film in the midst of a deteriorating German economy. And always present was the specter of foreign competition.

UFA's holdings were impressive. In addition to stages and laboratories at Tempelhof and Neubabelsberg, UFA controlled 100 regional theaters and ten of the largest and best equipped houses in Berlin. On October 1, 1919, UFA formally opened its largest cinema and premiere theater, the UFA-Palast am Zoo, "towering

A German film projectionist.

Photographing a fire sequence on an outdoor stage.

like a beacon in the busy traffic of the Potsdamer Platz." On the continent, UFA acquired cinemas in Spain, Holland, Switzerland and Scandinavia, and its acquisition of the assets of Nordisk Film and Sascha-Film gave it a competitive edge in Denmark and Austria.

The foreign affiliates provided UFA with a vast reservoir of talent: directors, technicians and actors. Austri-

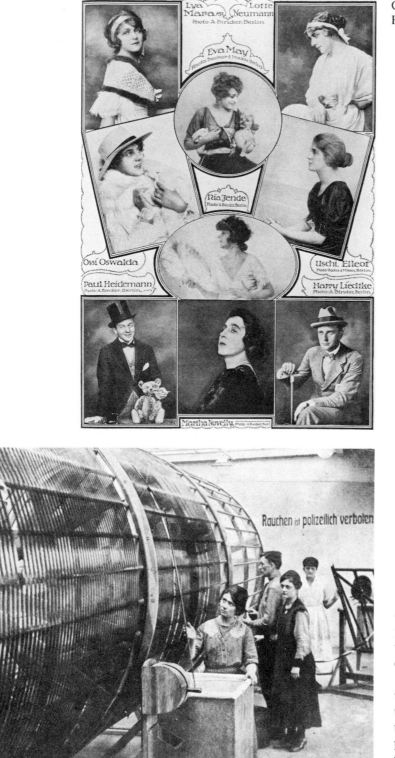

German film players popular during the
First World War.

Women in the German film, 1918-1919.

The "Trockenraum" or drying room, 1918-1919.

ans, Hungarians, Russians, Danes and Swedes must also
be credited for their contribution to the Golden Age of
the German cinema. Dr. F. K. Kallmann, the head of
UFA, reflected with justifiable pride during a visit to the
United States in 1924: "While I might devote hours to a
description of the facilities at Neubabelsberg and Templehof . . . it is the international spirit prevailing there
which I think is its most distinctive feature. One finds
directors, technicians and actors of every nationality."

Although UFA predominated in the German industry, it was by no means a monopoly. At the beginning of
the 1920s Germany's film industry was far less concentrated than that of the United States. Producing companies rose from 131 in 1918 to 230 in 1920, increasing
to 360 in 1922 and to 424 in 1929. And while the
quantity of German films declined from 646 in 1921 to
228 in 1925, the quality of production increased. Of the
small producing companies, some of the more notable
were Terra Film A.G., National Film A.G., the AAFA
Company, Deulig Film Company, Sued-Film A.G.,

Deutsche-Lichtspiel-Syndikat (DLA), Nero Film, Phoebus Film and its successor, Emelka Film of Munich. As film historian H. H. Wollenberg noted: "In the many medium-sized and small companies there was a chance for the development of individuality, many-sidedness, competition and experiment; these psychological factors were most useful to the evolution of the German film."

One of UFA's glass studios at Berlin-Templehof, 1918-1919.

The motion picture camera records the death of a German soldier, victim of a sniper's bullet.

Erich von Lüdendorff appreciated the propaganda potential of motion pictures.

III

The Golden Age of the German Film

1920-1929

The Berlin offices of UFA in the early 1920s.

Germany's situation remained desperate throughout the spring of 1919. The British blockade, which was not lifted until July 12, caused further suffering to the civilian population of the Central Powers. In Germany about three quarters of a million deaths were attributable to malnutrition. In March, 1919, Langwort Summern, the permanent secretary of the Foreign Office, told Frederic Wise, a member of the Reparations Commission, "that 800 people each day were dying of hunger or not being able to get the right food." Maids in hotels gladly received their tips in chocolate and taxi drivers eagerly took bread in lieu of their fare. Potatoes were rationed at four pounds per week and meat at a half pound per week per person. Clothing was almost unobtainable and the purchase of a pair of men's hose required a permit.

The black market provided the affluent with almost any commodity, but the impoverished multitudes were faced with deprivation, unemployment, inflation and the specter of Communist revolution. "What impresses me more than anything, in walking through the crowded streets," Wise noted during his stay in Munich, "is that the German is unable to look one in the face. . . . The people look haggard and strained and the colour of their faces is like parchment. They had obviously suffered, and were suffering."

The anguish of the period was reflected in Fritz Lang's two-part film, *Dr. Mabuse der Spieler (Dr. Mabuse the Gambler)*, released in 1922. Mabuse, the amoral master criminal who gambles with lives and fortunes, seemed the perfect representation of the "chaotic empire" which had come into being after 1918. Lang rightly described *Dr. Mabuse* "as a document of the time." G. W. Pabst's *Die Freudlose Gasse (The Joyless Street)*, released in 1925, was no less grim in its reportage of a society in disarray. But even Pabst's images of hunger, poverty and prostitution fall short of the brutal reality that was Germany in the years 1919-1924.

The proliferation of *Aufklärungsfilme*, "films about the facts of life" or "films of elucidation," but in reality a genre of sex films which flourished during the years 1919 and 1920, were further evidence of the unsettled conditions. During the world war the Society for the Combatting of Venereal Diseases (*Gesellschaft zur Bekämpfung der Geschlechtskrankheiten*) had sponsored a film by Richard Oswald, *Es werde Licht (Let There Be Light)*, on the subject of syphilis. The enterprising Oswald added a second and third part in 1918, and with the abolition of censorship following the Armistice, yet another segment was added.

In the meantime Oswald produced *Prostitution I and II*, which he had co-scripted with Magnus Hirschfeld. The novelty of such films encouraged a host of imitators

A social hour at the *Theater and Film Club*, Berlin, 1919.

whose motive, not unlike Oswald's, was pure exploitation, only thinly veiled as education: *Vom Rande des Sumpes (From the Verge of the Swamp)*, *Frauen, die der Abgrund verschlingt (Women Engulfed by the Abyss)*, *Verlorene Töchter (Lost Daughters)* and *Hyänen der Lust (Hyenas of Lust)* exploited heterosexual depravity, while *Aus Mannes Mädchenjahren (A Man's Girlhood)* and *Anders al die Andern (Different from the Others)* concerned homosexual themes.

Margaret Forman was moved to describe these as films "of the most astounding impossibility." She correctly observed that "Seldom is a great moral pointed as a deterrent to emulation of the ruinous and unholy existences depicted as being led by some of the leading figures in these plays." Forman wrote that "Possibly, to mitigate the implied miasma of its name, one play does end with a moral, or at least with what the producer's mind conceived to be a moral. The woman who errs pays the piper by falling into the hands of a ferocious 'Jack-the-Ripper,' and the spectator is spared few details of the crime." Another reviewer, writing in mid-September, 1919, found these films "really rather revolting when not merely stupid," and more "a sign of decadence in Berlin . . . than of any desire to scare people into cleaner behavior."

Popular demonstrations and legal action against the *Aufklärungsfilme* occurred in Düsseldorf, Baden and Leipzig. The problem was debated in the diets and the National Assembly. The more extreme among the moral censors proposed the socialization of the film industry, an alternative which was rejected in favor of a National. Censorship Law, adopted in May, 1920. A Supreme Examining Board was established. Children under twelve were prohibited from attending films while children between twelve and eighteen could be admitted to films which had been granted a special certificate. No film, however, could be prohibited because of its political viewpoint.

But film was often the subject of political controversy between left and right during the 1920s. *Wilhelm's Good Fortune and Bad Faith*, produced by Ferdinand Bonn in 1919, is a case in point. With a distinctly leftist bent, it portrayed episodes from the life of the former Kaiser: the dismissal of Bismarck, the emperor's speech from the imperial palace at the outbreak of war in 1914, and the Spa Conference which decided his abdication. While Independent Socialists and Communists defended the film, nationalist elements were offended by the bias of the material, particularly the scene in which Wilhelm is shown with his barber, with whose aid he invents his distinctive mustache, known to Germans as *es ist erreicht*. The German Officers League protested, claiming

that the film would lower the prestige of the Reich in the eyes of the world.

The premiere at the Berlin Sport-palast promised to be a confrontation between militants of the left and right. Advocates of the film had allegedly purchased 2,000 tickets which they had distributed "gratuitously among robust-fisted partisans." The nationalists, pan-Germans and anti-Semitic elements printed circulars several days before to advise their supporters to appear at the Sport-palast where the "patriotic weapon," a short rubber club, would be distributed to "reliable persons." Fearful of riots, the government repressed the film "in deference to the feeling of classes and because it is considered advisable to prevent the cinema's becoming a battleground for political fights in times like the present, when party feelings have reached a boiling point."

In the following days the former emperor, from his exile in Holland, instituted a suit against Bonn, charging insult and the misuse of his portrait. The court acceded to Wilhelm's application, and the film was duly confiscated, its domestic showing prohibited, and its export forbidden. The events and personalities of the First World War aroused strong emotions well into the decade, and in 1922 the censors' decision to prohibit a shot of Hindenburg at German headquarters at Colmar in Alsace on the grounds that it might provoke violent demonstrations was characteristic.

Reich Censors showed greater leniency toward nationalist and monarchical films set in a more distant historical past. The premiere of *Fredericus Rex*, directed by Arzèn von Czerèpy, at the UFA-Palast in January 1922, sparked violent clashes between rightist youths and Communists and Socialists. The film was applauded by the nationalistic newspapers while the left accused the German National People's Party of employing professional claquers to shout, "Hoch!" The censors dismissed the disruptions as "passing disturbances" which could be managed by the police. And when the Hessian Ministry of the Interior requested that the film be prohibited, their request was turned down.

Nevertheless, this undeniably propagandistic film had broad appeal and played for many months to enthusiastic audiences in Berlin and the larger German cities. Handsomely mounted against authentic backgrounds and studio interiors, *Fredericus Rex* allowed the German people a momentary respite from the realities of the day, civil strife and a staggering inflation. In the darkness of the theater, audiences could escape into the martial splendor of eighteenth century Prussia to witness events in the life of the Great King, magnified through the magic of the cinema. The film culminates with the death of the old king and the accession of young Fritz to the throne of

The evolution of the motion picture theater from the turn of the century to 1919.

Fern Andra by Emil Herz, 1919.

UFA advertisement in 1919.

A loge in a film theater, 1919.

A sketch by Felix Schwormstädt of a German studio in 1919.

Prussia as some 2,000 extras are seen to proclaim: *"Le roi est mort, vive le roi." Fredericus Rex* no doubt reflected the longing of the German people for a patriarchical leader who would lead them out of the current crisis.

Expressionism was yet another manifestation of the chaotic conditions which prevailed in Germany in the immediate postwar era. The expressionist painters, sculptors and literati rejected the imitation of external reality in order to express the inner self or some essential vision of the world. As an artistic movement, German expressionism antedated the First World War and can be seen to have crested with the collapse of the empire in 1918 and the social revolution which followed. Film, the newest of the arts, was also the last to reflect the expressionist impulse.

Das Kabinett des Dr. Caligari (The Cabinet of Dr. Caligari), directed by Dr. Robert Weine in 1919-20, and *Metropolis*, directed by Fritz Lang in 1926-27, define the parameters of the movement as it was represented in cinema. While some expressionists cherished the darker aspects of man's psyche, the irrational and the primitive, most were at heart optimistic. And, at least initially, many believed that defeat and revolution would lead to a regenerated society founded on peace and social equality.

The Cabinet of Dr. Caligari, based on a story by Carl Mayer and Hans Janowitz, suggests the darker aspect of expressionism with its probing of insanity. According to Siegfried Kracauer, the authors originally intended that their story serve as an allegory against insane authority as represented by the tyranny of Dr. Caligari. But the film ends with Caligari, whom we have perceived to be a mountebank and a madman, transformed into a benign doctor who informs his physician colleagues that he will be able to cure his patient now that he understands the root of his psychosis.

Metropolis, directed by Frizt Lang in 1926 from a scenario by Thea von Harbou, emphasizes the importance of the spiritual as opposed to the material and the possibility that through destruction a new and better world will result. The overthrow of the old order was an essential prerequisite for the coming of the "New Man" and the establishment of the "Kingdom of Love" on earth. It is precisely this attitude which Lang and von Harbou represent at the conclusion of *Metropolis*, when their characters gather on the steps of the cathedral, symbolic of the spiritual force which had been neglected in the machine society of Metropolis. In the closing shot young Freder, the expressionist "New Man," mediates between labor and capital represented by Grot, spokesman for the workers, and Joh Fredersen, the spiritually regenerated master of Metropolis. The final title reads: "There can be no understanding between the hand and the brain unless the heart acts as mediator."

The "pure" expressionism of *Caligari* and *Metropolis* was the exception rather than the rule in the period 1920 to 1927. These two films, seminal in the evolvement of the German cinema, were not, however, characteristic of the several thousand motion pictures produced between 1919 and the close of the silent era. *Caligari* and *Metropolis* represent the extremes of expressionism, recording its beginning and its end as a film genre. While both were artistic, both were uncommercial. Between the poles of *Caligari* and *Metropolis*, a span of seven years, German studios produced a number of films, *Der Golem (The Golem)*, *Von morgen bis Mitternacht (From Morn to Midnight)*, *Hintertreppe (Backstairs)*, *Der müde Tod (Destiny)*, *Raskolnikov*, *Nosferatu*, *Die Nibelungen*, *Orlacs Hände (The Hands of Orlac)*, *Der letze Mann (The Last Laugh)*, *Varieté (Variety)* and *Die Büchse der Pandora (Pandora's Box)* which reflect the influence of expressionism, especially in their use of studio interiors, low-key lighting, stylized décor and bizarre camera angles; but these films bear no distinct resemblance to *Caligarismus*. *Das Kabinett des Dr. Caligari* and *Metropolis* were unique and remain the quintessential documents of cinematic expressionism.

But in spite of the social, political, and economic chaos, film-going remained a popular pastime in the 1920s. The German Ministry of Welfare estimated that 3.5 million persons attended movies every evening. Carlos Mierendorff believed that in Germany the cinema had reached the people, creating a classless audience of "Waiters and laundry maids, porters and models, drivers and housewives, painters and milkmaids, jockeys and schoolgirls, delivery boys and hairdressers, furniture movers and domestic servants, ladies in diamonds and butcher boys and people passing through town." Mierendorff wrote that "The purchasing power of the mark may have declined almost to the vanishing point, and coal, gas, and food may be insufficient, but there are always moving pictures to keep one's spirits up."

While the German film achieved an international renown for the artistry of selected offerings, the industry never rested on a firm financial basis during the "Golden Decade" of the 1920s. In 1925 UFA forced its most serious crisis since the end of the war. Its share plummeted from 69 to 44 marks between October and the end of November, 1925. The firm's indebtedness to Deutsche Bank had increased over a sixteen-month period from six million to twenty-eight million marks. A number of productions were curtailed in an effort to forestall bankruptcy.

Threatened with insolvency and in desperate need of liquid capital, UFA negotiated with Universal Pictures Corporation for a loan of 15 million marks. In return, Universal would "peacefully penetrate" the German

Madame Dubarry (Passion) with Pola Negri.

Emil Jannings as Louis XV in *Madame Dubarry* (Passion).

Madame Dubarry (Passion), directed by Ernst Lubitsch, 1919.

Three famous UFA directors:
Lang, Berger and Murnau, 1924.

Entrance to the UFA lot at Neubabelsberg near Berlin.

market, acquiring sole exhibition rights in 134 first-run UFA theaters and several hundred additional outlets which UFA controlled through lease agreements. A newly constituted Universal sales organization was prepared to handle the distribution of UFA films in countries outside Germany. Universal would additionally be given two of the five votes on UFA's Executive Committee, a step that would have made Universal the principal American distributor of German films. On December 5, 1925, Carl Laemmle, who had quietly presided over these negotiations since the summer of 1924, sailed for Germany on the *Leviathan* to finalize the Universal-UFA agreement.

Universal's principal American competitors, Famous Players-Lasky and Metro-Goldwyn, were aghast. A Universal-UFA alliance would be tantamount to their virtual exclusion from the lucrative German market, an unappealing prospect. Sidney R. Kent, general manager of Famous Players-Lasky and a delegate from Metro-Goldwyn, sailed the same day on the *Majestic*. Laemmle arrived in Cherbourg and boarded the train to Berlin only to discover upon his arrival that the representative of Famous Players-Lasky and Metro-Goldwyn had landed in the German capital ten minutes earlier, flying from London.

A battle of words and money ensued, with Famous Players-Lasky and Metro-Goldwyn threatening to build rival theaters where their films would be exhibited at cut-rate prices, a development that would be certain to bring about UFA's downfall and injury to Universal. Hard

Dance of Death, Flame and *Morphine*, three sensational productions of Gengen-Film, 1919.

Advertisement for Stuart Webb's Film Company, 1919.

bargaining continued until a compromise was reached in the early hours of December 30, 1925.

According to the final agreement, Famous Players-Lasky and Metro-Goldwyn agreed to advance UFA $4 million and share with Universal the right to distribute

German school children attend a film program, 1919.

Hyänen der Lust (Hyenas of Lust).

Opium, directed by Robert Reinert.

Agfa's impressive facility in Berlin.

Advertisement for a home projector, 1919.

its films in UFA theaters. Universal withdrew its fifteen millions marks credit and, while releasing itself of the obligation to place UFA films in America, it agreed to supply UFA with a percentage of its pictures. Famous Players-Lasky and Metro-Goldwyn promised to release ten German productions a year if they were deemed suitable for an American audience.

American intervention proved to be only a temporary solution for the financial ills of UFA. The day of reckoning was at hand. The long and costly production of Fritz Lang's futuristic epic, *Metropolis*, had severely strained the precarious finances of the company. At one point UFA had even considered abandoning the film, but the management proceeded in the belief that it would garner handsome rewards at home and abroad, expectations that proved illusory.

At this juncture industrialist Alfred Hugenberg entered the history of Germany's greatest film concern. Described variously as "Germany's Northcliffe" and the "Nationalist newspaper Croesus," Hugenberg presided over a media empire that encompassed newspapers, magazines, news agencies, publishing corporations, printing plants, paper mills and the Deulig movie concern. An ardent nationalist, monarchist and pan-German, he was firmly opposed to socialism and republicanism. Needless to say, the involvement of this prototypical industrial bourgeoisie in the management of UFA was looked upon with apprehension by the democratic supporters of the Weimar Republic.

The Hugenberg-UFA agreement was consummated in April with the industrialist offering a plan for financial reorganization satisfactory to the creditors of UFA, of which Deutsche Bank was the largest. The agreement allowed Hugenberg to name nineteen members to UFA's twenty-seven-man Executive Committee, including such influential industrialists and financiers as Louis Hagen, Fritz Thyssen, Paul Silberberg, Otto Wolf and others. "The political advantage of controlling such a powerful medium as the film was not lost on heavy industry," John Leopold, Hugenberg's biographer, noted. "Any cinematic presentation could be transformed into propaganda. An innocuous, escapist film could lure troubled minds into a world of material wonders, subtly advertising the products of German industry which could be attained by luck or hard work. Yet the cost of producing a successful film would place definite limitations on propagandizing potential; a major film corporation could hardly become a political tool. Despite this, the corporation presented Hugenberg and his allies with an excellent opportunity to extend their sphere of influence."

The appointment of Dr. Ludwig Klitzsch, formerly managing director of Hugenberg's Scherl publishing concern, as director general of UFA guaranteed a large measure of continuity and moderation in the political arena. Klitzsch was intent on transforming UFA into a profit-making company and the production of high quality entertainment films was considered the best guarantee of success. "No *Metropolis* is looming on the horizon," *The New York Times* wrote in October, 1927. "No mighty super-productions are announced. Thank heaven! Germany is down to the bedrock of having to produce films which will pay for themselves out of Central Europe. This is a normal and healthy condition."

Klitzsch consolidated the debt of the floundering company while reducing UFA's obligations. The Hugenberg-Klitzsch management, however, was determined to make UFA Europe's greatest film concern, an objective which was in large measure realized at the close of the silent era. By 1930-1931, UFA controlled seventy-one companies, six production firms, thirty-seven theater companies, and nineteen foreign branches with primary outlets in Holland, France, Belgium, Austria, Hungary, Poland and the United States. Contractural arrangements secured UFA access to additional theaters in Yugoslavia, Bulgaria, Greece, Rumania, Turkey, Egypt, Syria, Palestine, Spain and English markets, including the dominions and South America. The UFA logo could be seen in "all parts of the world, wherever letter post, air mail, cable or wireless telegraphy extend," a journalist of the period observed. By the dawn of sound, UFA was making 8,000 deliveries each month to German theaters, providing 4,500 outlets with silent films and an additional 2,000 with sound films.

A vigorous policy of expansion characterized UFA's effort in Germany as well. A theater work force of 2000 managed the day-to-day activities of 115 UFA theaters. Older theaters in Berlin, Breslau, Leipzig, Stuttgart, Hamburg, Stettin and Danzig were refurbished while new constructions were undertaken in Hamm, Koblenz, Offenbach, Plauen, Chemnitz and Aachen. UFA's building department employed architects and specialists for stage construction, ventilation, lighting, and, with the coming sound in 1928-1929, acousticians. "The arrangement of the entire hall, as for example the relationship between stage, orchestra and balcony, is the subject of continuous theatrical and practical investigations." The *UFA-handelschaft*, or commerical branch, oversaw interior decoration and the installation of apparatus in suitably designed projection rooms.

The new UFA leadership adopted a more vigorous policy of opposition to its chief competitor, the United States, which was looked upon as the prime source of its troubles and of the German film industry in general. German producers found it increasingly difficult to com-

Advertisement for Stern-Film, 1919-1920.

Producer Erich Pommer presided over "The Golden Age" of the German film.

Conrad Veidt and Mia May in *Das indische Grabmal* (The Indian Tomb), directed by Joe May, 1921.

Lupu Pick directing for Rex-Film, 1919.

Director Joe May

A poster by Otto Stahl-Arpke for *Das Cabinet des Dr. Caligari* (The Cabinet of Dr. Caligari), 1920. Collection, The Museum of Modern Art, New York.

F. W. Murnau: "The film director must divorce himself from every tradition, theatrical or literary, to make the best possible use of the new medium."

Der müde Tod (Destiny) with Bernhard Goetzke and Lil Dagover established Fritz Lang as a major German director (1921).

E. A. Dupont and cameraman Theodore Sparkul during the filming of *Das alte Gesetz* (The Ancient Law).

Schatten (Warning Shadows), directed by Arthur Robison, 1923.

Advertisement for *Der letzte Mann* (The Last Laugh) with Emil Jannings. Directed by F. W. Murnau, 1924.

Zur Chronik von Grieshuus (The Chronicle of Grieshus), directed by Arthur von Gerlach, 1925.

Emil Jannings is greeted by Jesse Lasky upon his arrival in New York aboard the *Albert Ballin*, October, 1926.

Wege zur Kraft und Schönheit (Ways to Strength and Beauty), directed by Dr. Nicholas Kaufmann, 1925.

Emil Jannings in *Der Weg allen Fleisches* (The Way of All Flesh), directed by Victor Fleming, 1927.

pete in the international market with films budgeted at about $100,000, approximately half the amount of a comparable American film. A Hollywood production at $200,000 was certain to make a profit in the United States alone, and its makers could count on additional revenues from Germany, Britain and France. Should the German producer be fortunate enough to capture the home market, financial success in the American, increasingly dominated by major studios and their circuits, remained problematical.

The enactment of the German Contingent Law seemed to afford some protection in the home market. The law forbade the importation of foreign films by anyone save a producer of German films. For each domestic production, one foreign picture might be imported. But the Contingent Law was circumvented by American companies which established production units in Germany. The William Fox Company (Fox Europa), for example, made six films in Germany in 1925 and was therefore able to legally import six Fox films from the United States.

The problems seemed multiple. Germany's prestige productions, *Die Nibelungen*, *Varieté* and *Faust*, for example, offered the possibility of attracting a mass audience and a substantial return, but the "little movies" as *The New York Times* described them, films which were often of high artistic value but considered by Hollywood to have no mass appeal, found the American market virtually closed to their exhibition. The *Times* noted in a sympathetic editorial: "The 'little movies' are eager to obtain for their intellectual audiences those extraordinary examples of lighting and photography in which German companies have specialized. While Hollywood is devoted chiefly to picturizing a story for the romantic-minded, Germany has experimented with odd perspectives, exaggerated action, pure pantomime, whirligig roads and cities out of drawings. There are, of course, pessimists who think that nothing good can come of all this freakishness, but one never knows. But it has possibilities beyond the stereotyped pattern of Hollywood's wholesale sentimentality."

The establishment of a European film union or cartel, under German auspices, was seen as a possible means of meeting the American challenge. In June, 1928, Klitzsch journeyed to Rome and negotiated with the semi-official Institute Nazionale Luce. Mussolini received the general director before the formal signing of the agreement which provided for joint productions and the cooperation of UFA in the rehabilitation of Italian studios, assisted by a German technical staff. At the conclusion of the Italian negotiations, Klitzsch proclaimed the establishment of a European film cartel. "The German-Italian agreement was only an incidental

step to a whole series of general European agreements," Klitzsch informed the press. "A number of leading film enterprises in important European film countries have joined to form a solid front against America in order to be able to negotiate on terms of equality with the greatest film factor in the world."

The French were also sympathetic to the German proposals of a European film *entente*. United, Europe could stem the tide of American pictures and force the United States to apply the principle of reciprocity. "Without this collaboration, 'film Europe' is only an empty sound," Charles Delac, Vice President of the Film Board of Trade of France wrote. "In my opinion there are but two possibilities for Europe—either we must form a European bloc working jointly and regularly among ourselves, or we will gradually but surely be colonized by America." Delac pointed out that "Of the 366 films to be released in Germany next season [1928-1929], 181 are German, against 147 American, whereas only thirty-eight are of European origin." Delac "noticed further that the German-American firms distributing films in Germany will only release thirty-two German films [in the United States] as compared with 105 American."

A Franco-German agreement was signed in October, 1928. Germany agreed to buy thirty-three French productions, an increase of eighteen pictures over 1927, while France would purchase 100 German films, an increase of nine from the previous year. Meanwhile, UFA made a concerted effort to negotiate advantageous reciprocal arrangements with the chief central European film producing states: Austria, Hungary and Czechoslovakia.

In the wake of these negotiations, *The New York Times* editorialized on October 22, 1928, that "American film stars would do well to learn German as well as English." But within a year Germany would stand once again on the abyss of economic crisis in the midst of a deepening world depression. It remained for the National Socialist dictatorship, established in 1933, to "resolve" the problem facing the German film through the implementation of authoritarian controls and, ultimately, the nationalization of the industry. Some of the same dilemmas which faced the German industry in the period 1919-1933, the most notable being the American factor, were to surface after 1945, to challenge once again the economic and artistic viability of the German film.

Although the German silent cinema failed to conquer the American market in a commercial sense, its influence on American production after World War I was decisive. The German conquest was achieved through

Victor Fleming and Emil Jannings during the production of
The Way of All Flesh, 1927.

Director Josef
von Sternberg
characterized
the
temperamental
Jannings as "A
thespian who
was the
equivalent of a
dozen wildcats."

George O'Brien and Janet Gaynor in *Sunrise*, directed by F.
W. Murnau, 1927.

Emil Jannings was the most famous German actor to appear
in American films during the silent era. In 1928 he received
an Academy Award for his portrayals in *The Way of All Flesh*
and *The Last Command*.

Alfred Abel and Rudolf Klein-Rogge in a scene from
Metropolis, directed by Fritz Lang and released in 1927.

Lang directing the flood sequence in *Metropolis*.
Cinematographer Karl Freund stands behind the camera.

Fritz Lang in 1929.

Alfred Hugenberg

the artistry of its films and the creative talent of directors, actors, cinematographers, writers and technicians who emigrated to the world film capital, Hollywood, from the early 1920s. So pronounced was their approach in terms of style and technique, especially in the genre of what has come to be called *film noir*, that one may speak of the Germanification of the American film well into mid-century.

Beginning in late 1920, the first German films since the Armistice began to arrive in the United States. Their origin was at first disguised, so great was the hostility of the public toward any cultural manifestation of the late enemy.

Labor opposed the German imports on the grounds that they encouraged low wages on the continent by showing a preference for productions of major motion pictures on a small budget. The Actor's Equity Association believed that the importation of German films would have an adverse effect on American production and the unemployment of players. And finally, the American Legion opposed the films on patriotic grounds.

American producers and distributors took a more tolerant view, recognizing that the importation of German films might be a profitable business. "This 'German invasion' fright is the oldest and silliest of alarms," Adolf Zukor noted on the eve of his departure for Europe in the summer of 1921. "One would think that the Germans had some magical recipe for making great pictures. As a matter of fact, among all the German pictures there are no more great ones than there are in any given number of American films." Zukor believed that "A European might just as sensibly, after seeing *The Birth of a Nation*, *The Miracle Man* and *The Four Horsemen* fall into a panic of belief that every American film was of equal calibre."

"Mme DuBarry was picturized in Germany, under the direction of the apparently Teutonic Ernst Lubitsch," commented *The New York Times*, "but the writer makes the guess that an examination of Mr. Lubitsch's antecedents would lead to Paris, for the photoplay seems French in treatment as well as subject." The "apparently Teutonic Lubitsch" was transformed into the "Griffith of Europe" as more of the director's historical "super" productions arrived in the United States. In the wake of *Passion* came the films of Joe May (*Die Herrin der Welt*), Paul Wegener (*Der Golem*), Dr. Robert Weine (*Das Kabinett des Dr. Caligari*) and Fritz Lang, whose *Der müde Tod (Destiny)* was studied by Douglas Fairbanks in preparation for his *Thief of Bagdad*.

Not all of the German films were a commercial success. *The Cabinet of Dr. Caligari*, released by Adolf Zukor, appealed to the *aficionado* rather than the general public, but thoughtful persons recognized that something of a cinematic revolution had occurred in Germany which warranted study. The low-key lighting, soft contrasts and diffused illumination of the German films were especially admired. "Directors coming here from Europe are bringing ideas of lighting with them that have never been tried in America," Douglas Hodges wrote in early 1927. "American audiences have become accustomed to the domestic style of lighting and accept it in the absence of any other. The sharp contrasts in blacks and whites will prove inadequate when the European methods of shading have received a fair trial."

Hodges noted further that "Experts in photography in America are already assimilating a wealth of information from close scrutiny of the lighting in *Variety*. The general idea of Europeans in lighting seems to be that there must be only the light that is needed while the American tendency is to flood the set with strong lights that make evening interiors as bright as day." In a few short years the cinematographer of *Variety*, Karl Freund, would himself come to America and have a decided influence on the development of the Hollywood film in the early sound period.

A more critical view of the German cinema was taken by Robert Kane, general production manager of Famous Players-Lasky, who supervised the editing and titling of the German imports. "The German mind cannot condense," Kane stated in 1922. "It is prolix. It must put every detail of the story as originally written in novel form on the screen." Kane had worked nearly four months on the editing of Joe May's 1920 film *Die Herrin der Welt (Mistress of the World)*, cutting 94,000 feet from the original fifty-four-reel film to achieve a twenty-reel feature that would be deemed suitable for American audiences. "Our task is to boil these stories down to from five to nine reels without losing the 'guts' of the story and keeping the beautiful 'shots' intact. It is often a herculean task."

In appraising the German industry's capabilities, Kane believed that German filmmakers were in a more advantageous position than their American counterparts in the production of historical pictures. Kane noted, "They can produce a great historical picture in German for $200,000. The same picture could not be produced here for anything near that figure."

The German influx proved to be the repetition of an earlier pattern but on a greater scale. Before 1918 Hollywood had experienced a French "invasion" in the persons of Maurice Tourneur (Maurice Thomas), Léon Perret, Henri d'Abbadie d'Arrast, Louis Gasnier, Count Jean de Limur and Albert Capellini. The Gallic contingent had made a distinguished contribution, but by the early 1920s, their fortunes were in eclipse, ground down

by a cinematic Moloch which fed on the "new" and the "sensational." The hour of the Germans was at hand.

Ernst Lubitsch was the first of the major German directors to accept an American assignment, arriving in the United States in December, 1921, where he was engaged by Mary Pickford to direct, after prolonged negotiation, *Rosita*. Other German directors followed in the next decade: F. W. Murnau, Ludwig Berger, Paul Leni, Demetri Buchowetski and Ewald A. Dupont, whose *Variety*, photographed by Karl Freund, pricked the imagination of Hollywood as had no German film since *Passion* and *Caligari*. Hollywood, in the person of Universal's Carl Laemmle, appropriated not only the director of *Variety*, but its two principal players, Emil Jannings and Lya du Putti. Karl Freund hesitated but was eventually engaged by Laemmle to photograph *All Quiet on the Western Front*, released in 1930.

Of the German contingent, Lubitsch proved to be the most adaptable to the production procedures of Hollywood. Directing until his death in 1947, he achieved a consistently high standard of artistry. But Lubitsch was not always comfortable with American methods. In 1929 he criticized the "present craze for covering a set with directors of dialogue, directors of dancing, directors of music, and all the other would-be directors who are interfering with the Director's work. I would not make a picture that way, for it could not be a satisfactory picture with so many minds trying to govern it. . . ." By comparison Lubitsch noted that ". . . art directors [in Germany] are a much more intimate part of the production than they are here; they stay right with the picture from start to finish, even being on the set with us while we are shooting, ready to make any repairs or alterations that may be needed. Over here, there is a separate man for all these duties—a separate mind to interpret the original design in its own way. Only once over here have I been able to have my art director work through the picture with me as we did in Europe: that was in *Lady Windermere's Fan* [1925], a picture which I think had the most perfect set of any I have made. . . ." We can never be certain what Lubitsch would have achieved had he remained in Germany during the twenties and early thirties, but it is certain that his decision to emigrate deprived the German industry of one of its greatest talents.

The Hollywood films of Ernst Lubitsch were significantly indebted to the artistry of Hans Drier, who arrived in Hollywood in 1923, a few months after the German director. Drier had studied architecture in Munich and had been supervising architect of the German Imperial Government in the Cameroons. He joined UFA in 1919 where he worked with Lubitsch (*Der Reige/The Dance*, 1920), Dimitri Buchowetzky (*Danton*, 1920) and others.

Opus 1924, directed by Walter Ruttmann.

Überfall (Accident), directed and photographed by Ernö Metzner, 1928.

In *Berlin, Symphony of the Great City*, Ruttmann applied the lessons of the *avant garde* to a film subject intended for mass appeal.

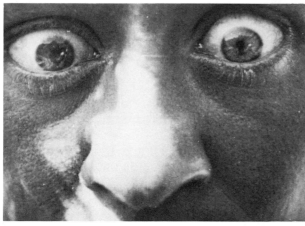

A photo montage advertising *Berlin, die Sinfonie der Grosstadt* (Berlin, Symphony of the Great City), directed by Walter Ruttmann, 1927.

Rennsymphonie, Hans Richter's impressionistic study of people going to a horse race, 1929.

As art director at Paramount until his retirement in 1920, Drier's influence on cinematic design was profound. "Under the control of Hans Drier," John Baxter wrote, "the studio's product achieved an opulence of surface never equalled by others."

The success of *Der letze Mann (The Last Laugh)*, confirmed William Fox in his decision to bring Friedrich Wilhelm Murnau to the United States. Unfortunately, a dark fate awaited the sensitive young director whom Fox, in a moment of not inaccurate hyperbole, described as "the German genius." Murnau's American *ouvre* consists of only four films: *Sunrise* (1927), *The Four Devils* (1928), *City Girl* (1930) and *Tabu* (1931), made in collaboration with Robert F. Flaherty. Although cameraman Karl Struss and the principal players, Janet Gaynor and George O'Brien, were American, *Sunrise* approximated the condition of a German film made in Hollywood. Based on Südermann's *Rise nach Tilsit (Journey to Tilsit)*, Murnau had made extensive preparations for the filming in Germany, working closely with scenarist Karl Mayer and art director Rochus Gliese. "In some ways this American film was the apogee of the German Expressionist cinema," historian David Robinson noted. "The designs of Rochus Gliese . . . evoke an atmosphere no less distinct and haunting than Murnau's *Nosferatu* [1922] had done." Spoiled only by a melodramatic denouement insisted upon by the studio, *Sunrise* remains the most enduring of Murnau's American works.

Upon completion of *Tabu*, photographed in the South Seas in collaboration with Robert Flaherty, Murnau negotiated a new contract with Paramount Pictures, but a short time later he died in an automobile accident near

Mutter Krausens Fahrt ins Glück (Mother Krause's Journey to Happiness), directed by Piel Jutzi, 1929.

The *Roxy-Palast* in Berlin-Schöneberg, 1929. Architect: Martin Punitzer.

Santa Barbara, California, a circumstance, Andrew Sarris noted, which "removed for all time the staggering possibilities of a Murnau-Sternberg-Lubitsch triumvirate at one studio." When his body was returned to Germany, its transport funded by Emil Jannings, some of the most distinguished luminaries of the German *Filmwelt*, Carl Mayer, Robert Herlth, Röhrig, Jannings, Érich Pommer, Carl Hoffmann, Arno Wagner, Rochus Gliese, Fritz Lang, Ludwig Berger and Hans Rameau, convened at Babelsberg to pay their last respects. Robert Flaherty, who happened to be in Berlin, also attended.

Lang delivered Murnau's eulogy, which Robert Herlth recalled: "Lang said he was Murnau's old adversary, but he now spoke in sincere praise. He described Murnau striding into the studio, always good tempered, smiling affably, able by his mere presence to kindle enthusiasm. He seemed like some great aristocrat interesting himself in the cinema partly out of curiosity and partly by way of amusement—which was in fact what a lot of people believed. In reality he was a tireless and thorough worker; behind his gaiety was an indefatigable energy that was none the less there because he liked to hide it."

But the tribute of Emil Jannings, written later, is perhaps the most poignant: "Of all the great personalities of the cinema, Murnau was the most German. He was a Westphalian, reserved, severe on himself, severe on others, severe for the cause. He could show himself outwardly grim, but inside he was like a boy, profoundly kind. Of all the great directors, he was the one who had the strongest character, rejecting any form of compromise, incorruptible. He was a pioneer, an explorer, he fertilized everything he touched and was always years in advance. Never envious, always modest. And always alone."

Besides Lubitsch and Murnau, other German directors entered the American industry during the 1920s. Dr. Ludwig Berger, arriving in 1927, directed his countryman, Emil Jannings, in *Sins of the Father* (1927). His American *ouvre* included a vehicle for Pola Negri, *The Woman from Moscow* (1928) and *The Vagabond King* (1930) with Dennis King.

Ewald Dupont, the director of *Varieté*, and of whom much had been expected, did not make his American directorial debut until 1935 (*Ladies Must Love*). During the interim, he achieved some success in England where he directed *Love Me and the World Is Mine* (1927) and *Moulin Rouge* (1928). The following year Dupont applied his considerable talents to the direction of the first European talking picture, *Atlantic*, based on the tragedy of the Titanic, with Fritz Kortner, Elsa Wagner and Franz Lederer. Dupont returned to the United States in 1933, but retired from direction in 1939 to become an agent and talent scout. His German achievements of the early 1930s, most notably *Peter Voss, der Millionendieb* (*Peter Voss, The Million Dollar Thief*) and *Der Läufer von Marathon* (*The Marathon Runner*), have remained unseen for more than half a century.

Wilhelm Dieterle, an actor by training, had directed in Germany from at least 1923 (*Menschen am Wege/People Along the Way*). In 1929 he was invited to Hollywood to direct German-language sound versions of American films. *Jewel Robbery*, released in 1931, marked the inception of a career that would last for more than thirty years. Although Dieterle remained the quintessential German in manner and perspective, he readily adapted to the procedures of the American industry as Dupont had not. Some of his later successes included *The Story of Louis Pasteur* (1935), *The Life of Emile Zola* (1937), *Blockade* (1938) and *The Hunchback of Notre Dame* (1939). A *Midsummer Night's Dream*, directed in collaboration with the Viennese impresario, Max Reinhardt, was a brave and costly experiment which bore the stylistic imprint of Germanic models, but proved a commercial failure at the time of its release in 1935. Dieterle returned to Germany in 1958, where he became involved in theater and film.

Paul Leni, who had directed Dieterle in *Wachsfigurenkabinett* (*Waxworks*), specialized in the grotesque and the macabre. His four Hollywood films, *The Cat and the Canary* (1927), *The Chinese Parrot* (1927), *The Man Who Laughs* (1928) and *The Last Warning* (1929), testify to his great skill as a designer and director. A career of unusual promise was cut short by his untimely death in 1929.

Lothar Mendes joined his fellow Berliner, Ernst Lubitsch, at Paramount where he directed *A Night of Mystery* (1927). From the early 1930s, Mendes worked in Britain and America, where he found commercial success.

Fritz Lang, director of *Der müde Tod* (*Destiny*), *Dr. Mabuse, der Spieler* (*Dr. Mabuse, the Gambler*) and *Die Nibelungen*, was the principal German director to remain outside the American industry during this first wave of immigration. In October, 1924, Lang visited the United States, accompanied by Erich Pommer. His first glimpse of the shimmering New York skyline provided him with the inspiration for *Metropolis*. He studied American film production, especially the American methods of printing and developing, and the "steady cameras that are used to make your trick effects." He renewed his acquaintance with Lubitsch, conferred with Douglas Fairbanks and D. W. Griffith, whose film, *Isn't Life Wonderful?*, photographed in Germany during the catastrophic inflation, impressed him deeply.

Preeminent in the industry of his homeland, Lang

The *Capitol*, Leipzig, c. 1929.

had no desire to move to Hollywood. During his visit, Lang told an interviewer that his professional success in America would require that he become acquainted with every facet of the society and the film industry. And while he admired the technical resources of the American industry, he found American directors too commercial and less devoted to art than their German counterparts.

American directors of the late 1920s and early 1930s showed themselves to be avid, if not on occasion slavish, pupils of their German masters. Guided by studio moguls whose first consideration was profit, they borrowed without constraint. After B. P. Schulberg saw *Der letze Mann (The Last Laugh)*, he persuaded Adolph Zukor of Paramount to secure the services of the principal player, Emil Jannings. "The film had a profound impact on the Schulbergs," Bud Schulberg wrote in his family memoir. "The result was *The Way of All Flesh*, for which Paramount writers, Jules Furtham and Lajos Biro were advised to study the dramatic elements of *The Last Laugh* (and another Jannings tragedy, *Variety*) and adapt them to an American setting."

Because the formula of *The Last Laugh* and *Variety* was perceived to be the degradation of a respected man, Jannings was called upon to play this role in various guises through four Hollywood productions. But by 1928, the theme had run its course, and with the dawn of sound, Jannings returned to Europe, having served his purpose to an industry which had no further use for

his talents. As a consolation, perhaps, the newly established Academy of Motion Picture Arts and Sciences chose to confer upon him the award of Best Actor for his appearances in *The Way of All Flesh* and *The Last Command*.

The German influence can be seen in lighting, camera angles, the plotting of scenarios and the economical use of subtitles. Such films as King Vidor's *La Bohème* (1926), Victor Flemming's *Flesh and the Devil* (1927), Frank Borzage's *Seventh Heaven* (1927), Victor Schertzinger's *Forgotten Faces* (1927) and the work of Josef von Sternberg, *Underworld* (1927), *The Last Command* (1928) and *The Docks of New York* (1929), bear the distinctive imprint of the German school. The extent of their derivativeness is very nearly embarrassing when comparisons are made with selected German productions of the period. By the early sound period, however, the artistry of the German film had very nearly been absorbed by the American industry as a second wave of German and Central European filmmakers began to arrive in flight from Hitlerism.

Unlike the United States, whose motivation for entering the German market was overwhelmingly commercial, the Soviet Union sought to establish a cinematic connection with Germany for the purpose of propaganda. The first Soviet films were shown in Germany on March 26, 1922, a few weeks before the normalization of German-Soviet relations at Rapallo. During the silent period, Germany became the largest importer of Soviet films. In late 1927, the *Vossische-Zeitung* wrote that it would behoove the German *Filmwelt* to seek an even broader relationship with the Soviet film industry: "We are acquainted with samples of specific Russian film art, such as *Potemkin*, which made the world sit up and take notice," the correspondent wrote. "But, in general, we don't know that the Soviet films that have reached us are but a few of the best results of a huge production of Russian films." Most of the 250 films produced by the Soviets in 1927 had been for home consumption and appear to have been "comparatively primitive" in terms of quality. "In the case of really big Russian films we have to make a distinction between the pictures that serve the Soviet propaganda and the purely artistic pictures that are coming to the front in ever greater numbers in line with the latest policy of Soviet film concerns."

Closer collaboration between the Russian and German film industries with the possibility of joint productions was thought desirable. Recent negotiations to this effect were described as a praiseworthy step along the road to more intimate relations in the realm of movie art. The *Vossische-Zeitung* wrote that ". . . it would still be more important if the German film industry, as such,

43

instead of a single group, could enter into close relations with the Soviet film business. Not only from the commercial point of view, as reflected in a greater distribution of the German product in the Russian market, but above all out of artistic considerations. The artistic forces existing in the German and Russian film industries supplement each other admirably, and it would be deplorable if the two most important film cultures could not find a large-scale basis for joint operations and were not to deliver themselves into the hands of American movie capital."

A restructuring of Sovkino, the Soviet cinema trust, in 1927-1928, worked to the advantage of German producers who had sought to increase profits, receiving an amount closer to $7,000 per film instead of the previous $2,000 to $3,000 per film, and to engage in potentially lucrative co-production activities with Russia.

The first Soviet-German co-production was undertaken with UFA in 1928. *Salamander* and *The Living Corpse* were the results. *Salamander*, directed by Serafima Roshal from a screenplay by Georg Grebner, dealt with the struggle of science with religion and fascism and was the first Soviet film produced in Germany with German stars. The results were not entirely satisfying. Anatoli Lunacharski, who also acted in the film, appears to have been one of the few to praise it in the Soviet media, the party having denounced it as a "false bourgeoisie melodrama." *The Living Corpse*, adapted from a Tolstoi play, was no less disappointing in the judgment of party officialdom.

Prometheus-Film became the principal distributor of Soviet pictures in Germany, and in 1928 Weltfilm was established to lease 16 mm copies to working class organizations. "Whenever we could, we went to see those Russian films which were shown often in Berlin at this period: *Earth, The General Line, The Mother, Potemkin, Ten Days that Shook the World, The Way into Life,* etc.," Stephen Spender recalled in his memoir, *World Within World.* The poet and his left-oriented German and British friends were drawn to the Soviet films ". . . because they had the modernism, the poetic sensibility, the satire, the visual beauty, all those qualities we found most exciting in other forms of modern art, but they also conveyed a message of hope like an answer to *The Waste Land.*"

And Germany in turn exercised its influence on the embryonic Soviet industry. There were few commercial cinemas in Russia; films were often shown to clubs and on traveling stages. But Sergei Eisenstein and his film compatriots appear to have had access to the major German productions which could be reshaped for propagandistic purposes in the U.S.S.R. Jay Leyda, translator and editor of Eisenstein's treatise, *Film Form,* notes:

"The first time Eisenstein ever joined together two pieces of 'real film' was while assisting Esther Schub in the re-editing of Lang's *Dr. Mabuse* [which the Soviets retitled *Gilded Putrefaction*]."

The most controversial of the Soviet films to be shown in Germany during the decade was Eisenstein's *Potemkin,* based on an episode from the 1905 revolution. Edited by Piel Jutzi with dramatic musical score by Edmund Meisel, the German version premiered in Berlin on April 29, 1926. Demonstrations and debate ensued and the showing of the film was cancelled in July on the grounds that it was dangerous to the republic. The Ministries of Interior and Defense criticized it as historically incorrect and misleading, strenuously objecting to the sequence of the Odessa revolution while earlier scenes of officers ill-treating sailors were regarded as an affront to the authority of the military. After a five-hour debate, the German censors approved an abridged version which was released in October and ran for over a year in one Berlin cinema.

Potemkin again became the subject of controversy when it was revived in the summer of 1928. Members of the *Reichswehr* were ordered not to see the film while *Reichswehr* guards dressed in civilian clothes were stationed outside the theater to prevent soldiers from entering, a decision upheld by General Groener, the Minister of Defense, as a legitimate exercise of military authority. The left parties predictably criticized the order as a restriction of political liberty.

To a large extent, the reputation of *Potemkin* was achieved in Germany. Afterwards, cinemas in Moscow advertised it as "the great success in Berlin." Soviet People's Commissar A. V. Lunatsharsky recalled in 1929: "In Russia the great force and the new technique of this splendid film fragment were not immediately understood. Only the German echo made us realize the progress we had made in the art of the film."

In March and April, 1926, Eisenstein visited Berlin to become acquainted with Western cinematographic techniques and to confer with Meisel concerning the music for *Potemkin.* When Meisel had reached the last reel, Eisenstein told the composer, "The music for this reel should be rhythm, rhythm, and before all else, rhythm." The completed score proved to be as controversial and provocative as the startling visual montage. During his stay in Berlin Eisenstein met Murnau and Jannings on the set of *Faust* and visited Lang and von Harbou during the making of *Metropolis.*

The extent of Eisenstein's influence on Lang is debatable, but the German director's film *Spione (Spies),* an espionage melodrama released in 1928, based on the incident of the Zinoviev letter and the sensational reports of Soviet spy activity in London, bears a strong resemblance to the work of Eisenstein and the dynamic editing of the Soviet filmmakers. Lang's compositions in *Spione* contain strong diagonals, and the swift, tightly controlled montage suggests the technique of *Strike, Potemkin* and *October*. Even the goateed Rudolf-Klein Rogge in the role of sinister master criminal, Haghai, enthroned in a wheelchair, bears a curious resemblance to Lenin.

The inventive cutting, creative montage and social comment of the Soviets found expression in experimental shorts of German avant-garde filmmakers, most notably Hans Richter, Walter Ruttmann, Wilfred Basse and Ernö Metzner. Richter's first experimental camera films, *Rhythm 21, 23* and *25*, unified painting and film. "In these years I considered my films purely as experiments," Richter recalled. "They had the task of testing and realizing problems I met in painting." Richter's inflation prologue for Wilhelm Thiele's 1928 film, *Die Dame mit der Maske (The Lady with the Mask)* offered a montage of worthless banknotes fluttering over destitute faces and the slow motion collapse of a building to suggest the failure of the German economy. *Vormittagspuk (Ghosts Before Breakfast)* was perhaps the most memorable of Richter's "film essays." In this quintessential Richterian work, objects (hats, neckties, coffee cups, etc.) rebel against their daily routine.

Walter Ruttmann applied the theories of avant-garde to various "studies," *Opus I, II, III and IV*, made between 1921 and 1924, while his feature-length documentary, *Berlin, Symphony of a City* (1926), which will be discussed in a separate chapter, and *Die Abenteuer eines Zehnmarkscheins (Adventures of a Ten Mark Note)*, made in collaboration with Bela Balasz, Karl Freund

and Berthold Viertel, capitalized commercially on the achievements of the avant-garde. Ernö Metzner's *Überfall (Accident)*, a short film released in 1929, contained a plethora of avant-garde techniques—dissolves, superimpositions, double exposures—in recounting the disasters which occur to a man who unluckily wins some marks in a gambling hall. The intelligentsia was duly impressed and Dr. Hans Sachs, the Viennese psychoanalyst who was present at its Berlin premiere, was observed to have "expressed his great satisfaction at both the scientific and artistic value of the fragment."

The avant-garde was encouraged by the formation of various associations such as the *Volksverband für Filmkunst* (Popular Association for Film Art) in 1928.

The *Mozartsaal* on the Nollendorfplatz, Berlin.

The *Gloria-Palast am Zoo,*
Berlin, c. 1930.

The *Titania-Palast*, Berlin.

Berlin and Prague and featured Vera Baranovskaia, who had achieved renown in Pudovkin's *Mother*. This grimly realistic portrayal of urban poverty was an exercise in pure cinema and revealed Junghans to be a master of the medium. In the early 1930s the Soviets engaged Junghans to make films in the U.S.S.R. Strongly independent, he declined the Soviet proposals to make film propaganda and returned to Germany. His last significant film was *Jugend der Welt* (*Youth of the World*), a documentary· of the 1936 Winter Olympics at Garmisch-Partinkirchen, superbly edited in the tradition of the avant-garde and the Soviet school.

Jutzi's *Mutter Krausens Fahrt ins Glück* was based on a script partially influenced by Otto Nagel and intended as a memorial to the artist Heinrich Zille, whose sketches of the poor had suggested the idea for the film, achieving the standard of the Junghans work in terms of photography and montage. These two films, much neglected in retrospectives of the German cinema, represent the finest achievements of the proletarian genre at the close of the silent period.

The following year Richter was instrumental in establishing the *Deutsche Liga für unabhängigen Film* (The German League for the Independent Film). The League showed films of social comment followed by discussion. The same year Richter wrote *Filmgegner von Leute— Filmfreunde von Morgen* (Film Enemies Today—Film Friends Tomorrow) for the Deutsche Workbund in Stuttgart, "International Film and Photo Exhibition," with stills from such Soviet classics as *Mother*, *The General Line*, *The Man with the Movie Camera*, Carl Dreyer's *Le Passion de Jeanne d'Arc* and Richter's own "film essays."

The exhibit and book which Richter described as a "formulation of my experiences as an avant-gardist and of my theories of film-poetry" emphasized rhythmic cutting, camera movement, montage and trick lenses. The League and the Stuttgart exhibit suggest the opposition of the independent filmmakers, the *Filmfreunde*, the friends of the cinema, to the commercial cinema of Germany and America, a product of the *Filmgegner*, the opponents of authentic film art.

The achievements of the avant-garde combined with the influence of the Soviet cinema resulted in two of the most notable films of the German silent era: Carl Junghan's *So ist das Leben* (*Such Is Life*) and Piel Jutzi's *Mutter Krausens Fahrt ins Glück* (*Mother Krause's Journey to Happiness*). *Such Is Life* was photographed in

Das Kabinett des Dr. Caligari

THE CABINET OF DR. CALIGARI

1920

CREDITS:

Production: Decla-Film Ges. Holtz and Co., Berlin. *Director:* Dr. Robert Weine. *Producer:* Rudolf Meinert. *Screenplay:* Carl Mayer and Hans Janowitz. *Cinematography:* Willy Hameister. *Art direction:* Hermann Warm, Walter Reimann and Walter Röhrig. Filmed at the Lixie-Atelier, Berlin-Wissensee. *Released:* February 27, 1920 (Marmorhaus, Berlin). Released in the United States by Goldwyn (1921). *Length:* 1703 meters (six reels).

CAST

Werner Krauss *(Dr. Caligari)*; Conrad Veidt *(Cesare)*; Friedrich Fehér *(Francis)*; Lil Dagover *(Jane)*; Hans Heinrich von Twardowski *(Alan)*; Rudolf Lettinger *(Dr. Olsen)*; Rudolf Klein-Rogge *(Criminal)*; Ludwig Rex; Elsa Wagner; Henri Peters-Arnolds; Hans Lanser-Ludolff.

Advertisement for
Das Cabinet des Dr. Caligari.

In the garden of the asylum Francis (Friedrich Fehér) relates
the strange story of Dr. Caligari.

A curious fairground of dwarfs and charlatans establishes the
bizarre milieu of *Das Cabinet des Dr. Caligari.*

Werner Krauss as Dr. Caligari and
Conrad Veidt as the somnambulist
Cesare. (*Das Cabinet des Dr. Caligari*)

47

The screenplay of *The Cabinet of Dr. Caligari* was the creation of Carl Mayer, destined to become one of the most important scenarists in the history of the German silent film, and Hans Janowitz, a young Czech poet. According to Janowitz, as related by Dr. Siegfried Kracauer, the genesis of *Caligari* stemmed from a frightening personal experience.

One night in October, 1913, while strolling through a fair near the Holstenwall by Hamburg harbor, Janowitz believed that he might have witnessed the murder of a girl whose death was reported by the press the next day. Janowitz was certain that he had observed her assailant, an ordinary bourgeois, who disappeared in the shadows. Curiosity prompted Janowitz to attend the girl's funeral, where he recognized the suspect who also seemed to recognize him.

The macabre events of that October night made an indelible impression on the sensitive poet, who related the story to Carl Mayer, an itinerant actor and artist whom he met in Berlin after World War I. Mayer in turn told Janowitz of the suicide of his father and, perhaps most importantly, his unpleasant experiences with an army psychiatrist during the war. Mayer and Janowitz shared a flat in Berlin and often walked through the Charlottenburg suburb of the city. One day they happened to enter a fair on the Kanststrasse which advertised an "electrical" man who appeared to achieve marvels of strength in a hypnotized state. According to Kracauer, the "electrical" man "accompanied his feats with utterances which affected the spellbound spectators as pregnant forebodings." During the next six weeks they collaborated in the writing of a story, Janowitz regarding himself as "the father who planted the seed, and Mayer the mother who conceived and ripened it." The central figure of the demonic doctor was christened Caligari, a name which Janowitz claimed to have read in a book called *The Unknown Letters of Stendahl*.

The film begins in a bleak garden where Francis relates past events to an old man seated beside him on a bench. As Francis proceeds with his story, the scene shifts to the fair at Holstenwall. Meanwhile, Dr. Caligari petitions the city clerk for permission to exhibit his somnambulist, Cesare, at the Holtenwall fair. The officious clerk gives his approval, but his rude remarks about Caligari's exhibit result in his death a short time later.

Francis and his two young friends, Alan and Jane, are drawn to the Holstenwall fair and enter the tent of Dr. Caligari. When Alan breathlessly asks the somnambulist to predict his fate, the figure entones that he will die before the next dawn. The friends part, and that night Alan is murdered in his bed.

Suspecting that Caligari is somehow involved, Francis persuades the police to investigate. But they only dis-

cover Caligari seated beside the sleeping form of the somnambulist, later established to have been a dummy. In the interim, the seemingly innocent Caligari has directed Cesare to abduct Jane. The girl is saved from the somnambulist, but Caligari, recognizing that his apprehension is imminent, escapes.

The search for Caligari takes Francis to a mental asylum where he discovers that Caligari, the murderous mountebank and the director of the asylum, are one and the same. Confronted with the corpse of Cesare, the insane director is forced into a straitjacket.

According to Kracauer, Janowitz and Mayer would have preferred that the film end with this revelation. The authors, having conceived of their work as an allegory, wished to draw a parallel between the insane authority of Dr. Caligari and the German military dictatorship of the First World War. While often repeated in film histories, Kracauer's interpretation is conjectural. It is highly unlikely that German audiences would have seen *Caligari* as a political allegory. To suggest that Weine and Pommer dissipated the revolutionary message of the original work is quite false. The actual denouement of *Dr. Caligari* is no less poignant, a shocking twist which is consistent with all that has transpired. The identification of Caligari the charlatan with "Caligari" the director of the asylum is revealed to be a delusion on the part of Francis, who is led away in a straitjacket.

And thus, as Parker Tyler observed some years ago, ". . . he who was shown as mad, and to be restrained, is now the restrainer of the mad." The film concludes with the benign doctor offering the promise of a cure, having now understood the root of Francis's insanity.

Mayer and Janowitz submitted the completed manuscript to Erich Pommer, head of Decla Bioscop. During their discussions, the authors insisted that the film be executed in the style of the painter Alfred Kubin. "While Mayer and Janowitz talked about art, I was thinking of rather different aspects of the script," Pommer recalled. "The mystery and macabre atmosphere of the Grand Guignol was currently in vogue in German films, and this story fitted perfectly. They saw an 'experiment' in the script—I saw a comparatively inexpensive production."

Fritz Lang was to have directed *Das Kabinett des Dr. Caligari*, but Pommer decided that he should continue with the second part of *Die Spinnen (The Spiders)*, which had proved a commercial success. Dr. Robert Weine was assigned the direction of *Caligari*, while Hermann Warm, Robert Herlth and Walter Röhrig of the Decla designing staff created the expressionist backgrounds. When Lang learned that the settings of *Caligari* were to be expressionistic in order to suggest the mind of a madman, he advised Pommer to add a

Rahmenhandlung, a framing story set in reality. Lang argued that the *Rahmenhandlung* would intensify the terror of the expressionist sequences. Pommer adopted this proposal by adding a scene in the garden of the asylum to open and close *Caligari*.

Warm recalled that Röhrig and Reimann spent the whole day and part of the night studying the script. "We realized that a subject like this needed something out of the ordinary in the way of sets. Reimann, whose paintings in those days had expressionist tendencies, suggested doing the sets expressionistically. We immediately set to work roughing up designs in that style," Warm recalled. When Röhrig proposed that lights and shadows be painted on the sets of *Caligari*, Pommer was at first horrified. The idea seemed reactionary, a return to painted backdrops and the artificiality of the theater. But after Herlth submitted the sketches, Pommer allowed Weine to make a series of trial shots. Pommer recalled that "When the test was screened, both Mayer and Janowitz were present. We were all convinced—and the writers dropped their efforts to engage Kubin."

The pre-production phase of *Caligari*, the construction of sets and the painting of backdrops, was achieved in less than a fortnight. The actual filming consumed about four and a half weeks with three interruptions for additional building and set design. Lil Dagover recalled that when she first saw the expressionistic décor, she shook her head in disbelief. "I didn't understand what the whole thing meant. Only after several talks with Pommer, Weine and the architects did I perceive the effect of the scenery and recognize what an important role the film played in the world of art." She came to the realization ". . . that all things possess a physiognomy: the half-darkened room, the weird expression of the trees in the forest at night, the ghostly pale of moonlight, the melancholy and ceaseless trickling of rain. No poetry is as capable of giving expression to the ghostly and the demonic as is the film."

According to Pommer, ". . . the young writers saw each day's rushes, a habit that Mayer maintained throughout his screenwriting career. His powerful visual imagination was kept constantly stimulated by close contact with the entire production process—and from *Caligari* can be dated Mayer's well-known awareness of the camera and settings as vital dramatic elements."

After seeing the bizarre sets, Krauss and the principal players, Conrad Veidt, Lil Dagover and Friedrich Fehér, decided to add expressionist touches to their makeup and wardrobe. Krauss accented his nose and hair with grease paint while Veidt, in the role of the somnambulist, painted shadows beneath his eyes. Lil Dagover made a slight concession to expressionism in her costuming, but as Hermann Warm noted, "Her loveliness brought a

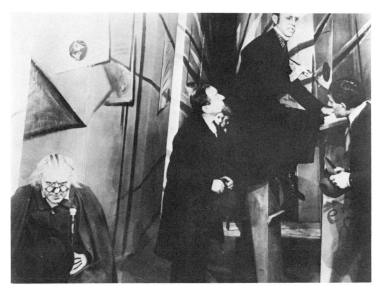

Caligari (Werner Krauss) in the office of the arrogant town clerk. *(Das Cabinet des Dr. Caligari)*

Lil Dagover, Hans Heinrich von Twardowski and Freidrich Fehér. *(Das Cabinet des Dr. Caligari)*

Apprehension of the criminal (Rudolf Klein-Rogge). *(Das Cabinet des Dr. Caligari)*

49

softening note to the hard, absurd and horrible happenings of this film." Meanwhile, an assistant to Weine was dispatched to a second-hand clothier in Berlin to procure appropriate costumes for the character of Caligari: a black cape, a battered top hat, an old-fashioned ivory cane, thick spectacles and a white wig.

Krauss was the consummate actor, and some of the members of the cast and crew preferred to keep a distance from the diabolical Caligari. During a break early in the production, Lil Dagover remembered how Krauss ran past her with distraught motions, oblivious to her salutation, *"Guten Tag, Herr Krauss."* A lighting technician who observed the incident advised her not to worry, "Krauss has identified completely with the madman. You must get used to that." Lil Dagover recalled that "As Caligari, Krauss was in his element. His intelligence and sensibility, and the way in which he empathized with the style of the direction made collaboration with him an educational experience for me. Krauss was convinced from the beginning that a film masterwork of international standard was being created. He carried us all along with his enthusiasm."

For a time, Krauss may have had cause to regret his decision to play in *The Cabinet of Dr. Caligari.* "After a great success everyone wants to make similar films," Krauss reflected in his memoir, *Das Schuspiel meines Lebens.* "That's how it always is. And it didn't take long before they called me 'Caligari' or they said: 'He can only play Caligari. The circus is his *forte!*' I also made a similar film with Alexander Korda and his wife Maria and some others. But after a number of such films, salvation came in the form of *Alt-Hidelberg* [directed by Hans Behrendt, 1923] in which I took the role of Jüttner."

C. Dennis Pegge wrote in his analysis of the structure and editing of *Caligari:*

More than in any previous picture—with the possible exception of *Intolerance*—*Caligari* is split up into separate shots. There are 378 cuts in the completed film. Some shots form continuous scenes, some are logically intercut with others, and some have only a psychic relationship. There is an intricate interweaving both of shots and of sequences. *Caligari* must be recognized as a pioneering effort in editing, but also as a demonstration of that affinity between filmic expression and the thought process that Eisenstein and many others later dwelt upon. The result is an emotional experience that is both intense and at times highly subjective.

As Pegge noted, most of the devices seen in *Caligari*, including parallel action, quick cutting, the iris and the subtitle, had been used previously, but these films had relied on a succession of shots to create continuous action. "What was latent in the approach to film making of directors like Griffith," Pegge writes, "was boldly extended and put into full practice by Robert Weine in *Caligari* and, later, by other German directors in the early 1920's and by the Russians from 1925 onward. *Caligari* was the first major manifestation of a change amounting to a metamorphosis of the silent-film from its primitive to its fully developed form."

Caligari premiered at the Marmorhaus, Berlin, on February 27, 1920, with a musical accompaniment which included selections from Schubert, Rossini and a finale by Paul Lincke. Curiously, neither Weine, Mayer or Janowitz were credited in the titles. A three-reel comedy, *Hoppla, Herr Lehrer,* directed by C. Wolfram-Kiesslich, was included on the program to provide relief from the intense and almost totally humorless feature.

Caligari was not an immediate success, although Berlin kiosks carried posters with expressionist motifs, the image of Cesare and jaggedly written phrases such as *"Wo ist Caligari?"* ("Who is Caligari?") and *"Du Musst Caligari werden"* ("You must become Caligari") in an attempt to familiarize the public with the unusual style

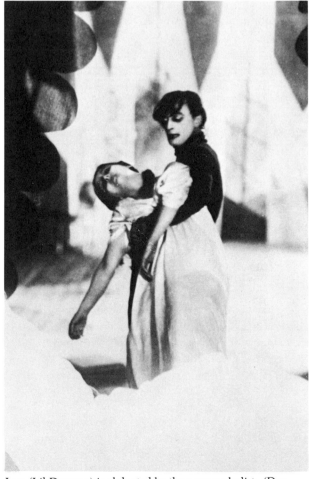

Jane (Lil Dagover) is abducted by the somnambulist. *(Das Cabinet des Dr. Caligari)*

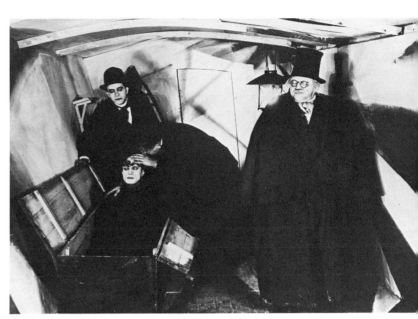

"Like a drop of wine in an ocean of salt water," Paul Rotha observed, *"The Cabinet of Doctor Caligari* appeared in the profusion of films during the year 1920." *(Das Cabinet des Dr. Caligari)*

Inside the showman's wagon: Conrad Veidt and Werner Krauss. *(Das Cabinet des Dr. Caligari)*

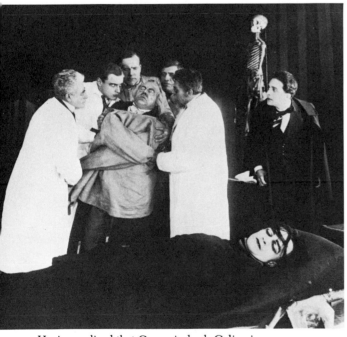

Having realized that Cesare is dead, Caligari goes insane. Werner Krauss (in straitjacket), Friedrich Fehér (far right) and Conrad Veidt (reclining). *(Das Cabinet des Dr. Caligari)*

Friedrich Fehér and Werner Krauss. *(Das Cabinet des Dr. Caligari)*

and theme. It proved more successful with general audiences after its second release at the Mozartsaal. Dr. Giuseppe Becce composed new music for the Mozartsaal performance. Becce's atonal passages no doubt served to intensify the drama of murder and madness.

German critics praised the work. "Not for years, not since the great Wegener films, have I sat so attentively in a movie as at *The Cabinet of Dr. Caligari*," Kurt Tucholsky wrote. Commenting on the audience with whom he had seen the film, Tucholsky found ". . . the public torn between mirth and incomprehension. When he shudders, the Berliner has a laughter which, blown through the nose, is a highly effective preventative. The film is not a business for the provinces, nor I am afraid, a business for Berlin." Tucholsky regarded *Caligari* as "the greatest of rarities: a good film. May there be more."

The film, however, was shown widely in the larger German cities in 1920, returning to its investors a substantial profit on their original $18,000 cost of production.

Even before its distribution abroad, first in France, then later in Britain and the United States, *Caligari* gained the allegiance of critics and intellectuals, many of whom had not seen the film but had either read or heard reports of its artistic achievement. *Caligari* was released in the United States by the Goldwyn Company in the spring of 1921. "It is like a page from Poe," wrote Lawrence Reid in the American trade paper, *Motion Picture News*, ". . . a fantastic, uncanny piece of imaginative fiction . . . a page of diabolical scheming by a distorted, insane mind." Reid surmised that people would be "receptive to it because of the novelty. Its German origin should not stand in the way, since it speaks no propaganda."

But the question of a film's "German origin" remained a sensitive issue, and Goldwyn's advertisers cautiously presented *Caligari* as the "new European film success." In a 1923 article for American readers, Albert Lewin described *Caligari* as a creation "spiritually real and vital in a way peculiar to the screen, as unthinkable in any other form as are the poems of Heine." Lewin concluded that "Charlie Chaplin and *The Cabinet of Doctor Caligari*, in divergent and equally convincing ways, have established beyond cavil the integrity of the motion picture as an art. There is no longer any need for doubt or discouragement."

Caligari must be counted a landmark in the history of film. As Lewin suggested, it enhanced the motion picture as an artistic medium. The makers of *Caligari* had completely integrated décor, costuming and theme. Intellectuals saw the artistic and expressive possibilities of film, not the least of which was the innovative use of psychological subject matter.

Film critic and historian Roger Manvell wrote that "Its contribution was solely that of lighting, the subtle development of visual atmosphere, and the beginning of a conception of screen-acting in the work of Werner Krauss and Conrad Veidt. There is much still to be learnt from it by the competent director, since it was the product of real feeling and devotion to a new and relatively untried medium and was an undoubted success within its own limits."

Der Golem

THE GOLEM

1920

CREDITS

Production: UFA, Projektions-AG "Union," Berlin. *Director:* Paul Wegener. *Screenplay:* Paul Wegener. Based on the novel by Henrik Galeen. *Cinematography:* Karl Freund. *Art direction:* Hans Poelzig. *Costumes:* Rochus Gliese. *Music:* Dr. Hans Landsberger. Conducted by Bruno Schulz. Filmed at the UFA-Unions-Atelier, Berlin Tempelhof. Exteriors filmed at the UFA-Freigelände, Tempelhof. *Released:* October 29, 1920 (UFA-Palast am Zoo) with the subtitle *Wie er in die Welt kam (How He Came into the World)*. Released in the United States by Famous Players (1921). *Length:* 1922 meters (five reels).

CAST

Paul Wegener *(The Golem);* Albert Steinrück *(Rabbi Loew);* Lyda Salmonova *(Miriam);* Ernst Deutsch *(Famulus);* Hanns Sturm *(Rabbi Jehuda);* Max Kronert *(Tempeldiener);* Otto Gebühr *(Emperor Luhois);* Dore Paetzold; Lothar Müthel *(Florian);* Greta Schroder (Rose girl); Loni Nest *(the child)*.

Upon completion of *Der Student von Prag* (1913), Paul Wegener collaborated with Henrik Galeen on a version of *Der Golem*, photographed by Guido Seeber on location in Hildesheim. Wegener and Galeen co-directed with Wegener taking the role of the strange clay figure. Bioscop released the film in 1915, but all prints appear to have been lost, although Donald F. Glut in his book *The Frankenstein Legend: A Tribute to Mary Shelley and Boris Karloff* states that Paul Sauerlaender, a

Hans Poelzig's design of the ghetto remains one of the most astonishing achievements in the history of art direction. *(Der Golem)*

Paul Wegener as the Golem. *(Der Golem)*

The gabeled houses of the ghetto. *(Der Golem)*

Paul Wegener. *(Der Golem)*

Advertisement for *Der Golem.* Collection, the Museum of Modern Art, New York.

Ernst Deutsch and Albert Steinrück. *(Der Golem)*

version, *Der Golem und die Tänzerin (The Golem and the Dancer)*, and in 1919 Nils Chrisander directed *Alraume und der Golem (Alrauem and the Golem)*, based on a novel by Schim von Arnim. Produced by Deutsche Bioscop and photographed again by Seeber, this version, like its predecessors, has remained unseen for many years.

The mystical and the fantastic appealed to Wegener, and in 1920 he attempted a third and more elaborate version of the Golem legend which he co-directed with Carl Boese, *Der Golem, wie er in die Welt kam (The Golem, How He Came into the World)*. Rabbi Loew reads in the stars that a new oppression threatens the Jews of Prague. Through alchemy and magic and secret writing he brings the figure to life. Instructions tell the Rabbi that "If you place the magic word in the amulet on its breast, it will live and breathe as long as it wears it."

The portal of the ghetto. *(Der Golem)*

Paul Wegener in the concluding sequence of *The Golem*.

European film collector, has restored a complete print from a fragment which he purchased in 1958.

The 1915 Gaeleen-Wegener film, often referred to in film histories as the "first" *Golem*, interwove the legend of Rabbi Loew with contemporary events. An antique dealer brings the Golem to life, following the descriptions set down in a cabalistic volume by Rabbi Loew. The creature becomes the antiquarian's servant, but when his amorous entreaties are rejected by his master's frightened daughter, played by Lyda Salmonova, Wegener's wife, the Golem goes on a rampage. In the denouement he falls from a tower and his corpse is shattered.

In 1917 Wegener co-directed and acted in a second

The magic word is AEMAET, the Hebrew word for truth or God. As in the previous versions, he becomes the Rabbi's servant, but eventually turns against him, destroying his laboratory with a burning brand. The Golem disappears and the people give thanks to the Rabbi. Standing outside the gates to the ghetto, the Golem is finally rendered harmless when a child approaches and innocently removes the amulet. The figure collapses, transformed once again into a statue of clay. The Rabbi directs that his remains be returned to the ghetto, and the doors of the portal swing shut.

Architect Hans Poelzig, whom Wegener had known before the First World War, was commissioned to design the sets of a medieval ghetto which his wife Marlene modeled in clay miniatures. From Poelzig's sketches and Marlene's models, designer Kurt Richter supervised the construction of fifty-four houses at Tempelhof. Richter's labyrinthian set of gabeled buildings, portals and fountains ranks as one of the great triumphs of expressionist film design.

Anna Boleyn

DECEPTION

1920

CREDITS

Production: Meester-Film GmbH, Berlin and Projektions-AG "Union," Berlin. *Director:* Ernst Lubitsch. *Screenplay:* Fred Orbing [pseud. Norbert Falk] and Hans Kräly. *Cinematography:* Theodor Sparkuhl. *Art direction:* Kurt Richter. *Costumes:* Ali Hubert. *Released:* December 14, 1920 (UFA-Palast am Zoo, Berlin). *Length:* 2793 meters. Released in the United States as *Deception* by Paramount (April 17, 1921).

CAST

Henny Porten *(Anne Boleyn)*; Emil Jannings *(King Henry the Eighth)*; Paul Hartmann *(Sir Henry Norris)*; Ludwig Hartau *(Duke of Norfolk)*; Aud Egede Nissen *(Jane Seymour)*; Hedwig Pauly *(Queen Catherine)*; Hilde Müller *(Princess Marie)*; Maria Reisenhofer *(Lady Rochford)*; Ferdinand von Alten *(Mark Smeaton)*; Adolf Klein *(Cardinal Wolsey)*; Paul Biensfeldt *(Jester)*; Wilhelm Diegelmann *(Cardinal Campeggio)*; Friedrich Kühne *(Archbishop Cranmer)*; Karl Platen *(Physician)*; Erling Hanson *(Count Percy)*; Sophie Pagay *(Nurse)*; Josef Klein *(Sir William Kingston)*.

The marriage banquet: Henry VIII (Emil Jannings) and Anne Boleyn (Henny Porten).

The considerable reputation of Ernst Lubitsch rests largely on his American period which saw the production of such films as *Trouble in Paradise* and *Ninotchka*. While the American films are deservedly fine, each distinguished by the celebrated "Lubitsch touch," they only partially explain the genius of Lubitsch. It was the *German* Lubitsch who changed the course of motion picture history. The years 1917 to 1922 were a period of enormous productivity, innovation and accomplishment for Lubitsch. As film historian Enno Patalas has written: "These five German years were to the twenty-five American years which followed what a crazy fast-motion shot is to a normal shot."

Lubitsch entered films in 1913 as a Jewish comic and directed his first film, *Fraulein Siefenshaum (Miss Soapsuds)* in 1914. His adroit handling of the material encouraged John Davidson to assign him longer and more serious films with distinguished casts which included Emil Jannings and Pola Negri, formerly Apollina Chalupec, a young Polish actress of Hungarian background. In her autobiography, Pola Negri recalled that

Ernst Lubitsch was everything [Emil] Jannings was not. There was nothing physically commanding about his swarthy humorous Semitic face and his short thickset stature. What was impressive was the agility with which he expressed his often brilliant thoughts and the witty manner in which he indicated that he was two steps ahead of anybody else in any intellectual gambit. A steady stream of eloquence flowed out around the cigar eternally planted between his lips. So irrepressible were his pranks and jokes that those who did not know him well tended to dismiss him as no more than a clown. They could not have been more wrong. One day this same divine sense of the ridiculous would be distilled directorially into something that would be known wherever films were shown as "the Lubitsch touch." It was to be his personal signature on the pictures he made.

Die Augen der Mummie Ma (The Eyes of the Mummy Ma), *Carmen*, *Die Austernprinzessin (The Oyster Princess)*, *Rausch (Intoxication)* and *Madame Dubarry (Passion)* established him as a director of the first rank. *Dubarry* was nothing less than a sensation. Begun in the closing months of the Kaiser's Reich, it premiered in September, 1919, and played for three months at the Berlin UFA-Palast am Zoo. Lubitsch combined the pageantry of the earlier Italian spectacles such as *Cabiria* and *Quo Vadis* with an intimacy of detailing and characterization heretofore unseen in screen epics. Critics acclaimed him the "humanizer of history" and the "German Griffith."

In later years Lubitsch considered *Carmen*, *Madame Dubarry* and *Anna Boleyn* to be his most outstanding achievements of the historical period of his career. "The importance of these pictures, in my opinion, was the fact that they differed completely from the Italian school, then very much in vogue, which had a kind of grand-opera-like quality," Lubitsch wrote in a letter to Herman Weinberg. "I tried to deoperatize my pictures and to humanize my historical characters—I treated the intimate nuances just as important as the mass movements, and tried to blend them both together."

With *Anna Boleyn* released in December, 1920, Lubitsch and his producers sought to capitalize on the success of *Madame Dubarry*, combining spectacle and intimate drama at a cost of over 10 million marks. Replicas of Windsor Castle, Hampton Court, the Tower of London and Westminster Abbey were meticulously recreated by art directors Hans Poelzig and Kurt Richter at Tempelhof. The tournament scene and the coronation in Westminster Abbey were singled out for special consideration: "The coronation with the enthusiastic populace paying homage is more eloquent than any single scene in *Passion*." The same reviewer found the picture long "but time passes unnoticed, so deftly are the scenes arranged, so definite is the action." Jannings played the decadent and fickle Henry VIII in a performance that delighted audiences and pleased most critics: "Emil Jannings as Henry VIII has caught the spirit of the character in an amazingly accurate manner," a reviewer of the period noted. "His shading of the part, his deft touches of humor, his broad conception of the king's bestiality—make it a perfect study in superb panto-mime." Henny Porten appeared as his ill-fated and short-lived consort, Anne Boleyn. She was praised for giving "a consistent performance" which combined "charm, power and a sympathetic appeal."

In 1532 Anne Boleyn, niece of the Duke of Norfolk, returns from France to become lady-in-waiting to Queen Catherine. She loves Henry Norris, a knight, but when he suspects that she has become the mistress of King Henry VIII he breaks off his relationship with her.

The Pope refuses to grant the King a divorce, but Henry, who has secretly married Anne, breaks with the Church of Rome, declares his marriage to Catherine annulled and has Anne crowned Queen in Westminster Abbey.

When Anne gives birth to a daughter, the King is enraged that she did not produce a male heir. Henry begins to pay more attention to Jane Seymour, another lady-in-waiting. Anne tries to dissuade Henry from this course, but to no avail.

At a banquet the court minstrel, Mark Smeaton, sings a song suggesting there is a special relationship between Anne and a certain knight. Sometime afterward the Queen appears at a royal tournament, and when she learns that Henry Norris has been wounded, she is overcome with emotion. The King interprets her behavior as confirmation of the rumors and has her banished to the Tower. Her uncle the Duke of Norfolk takes charge of her case, but turns against her; Henry Norris is prepared to testify in her behalf but dies before he can reach the witness stand, and the uncle obtains a confession from Smeaton that he was the Queen's lover. Anne is sentenced to be beheaded and is led to the place of execution.

Anna Boleyn opened at the UFA-Palast am Zoo in December, 1920, and the following spring it reached America where it was released by Paramount, retitled *Deception*. The studio mounted an impressive promotional campaign. Hugo Risenfeld, managing director of the New York Rivoli, transformed the theater into a Tudor castle, having procured suits of armor, shields, tapestries and other furnishings with which he decorated the lobby, mezzanine and corridors. Risenfeld left no stone unturned in his attempt to provide a suitable environment. When the lights dimmed, four heralds mounted the stage and smartly trumpeted the beginning of the performance. The orchestra, augmented by the addition of several ancient instruments, then played a specially composed overture, followed by a stage prologue titled, "The Hunt Is Up" in which Carl Rollins, baritone, took the role of a minstrel with the Rivoli Male Chorus as huntsmen and courtiers. During the film the orchestra melded selections from Lully, Scarlatti, Couperin, Matteson, Purcell, Corelli, Vivaldi, Gretry,

Emil Jannings as King Henry VIII. (*Anna Boleyn*)

Jane Seymour (Egede Nissen), Henry VIII (Emil Jannings) and the Duke of Norfolk (Ludwig Hartau). (*Anna Boleyn*)

Rameau, Handel and Bach, and as Anne is led to the execution block, Inga Wank, mezzo soprano, sang, "O Death, Rock Me to Sleep," a composition written by Anne Boleyn during her confinement in the Tower a few days before her execution. Organist Firmin Swinnen played Bach's Toccata and Fugue in D Minor for the conclusion.

In general, American critics hailed *Deception* as a masterpiece of the historical genre, "A big, solid, impressive picture, this German-made section of English history," Burns Mantle observed in his *Photoplay* review. "It bulks large . . . in crowds, actors, royal palaces and royal physiques," he wrote, "but it bulks large also, in art, and sets standards in the matter of the historical drama on the screen which native directors will have to consider if ever they become interested in pictures of this type." Critics praised Lubitsch for the authenticity of the production, believing that he had rendered the Tudor period "with all the thoroughness and painstaking detail of his race."

Henry VIII (Emil Jannings) and Cardinal Woolsey (Adolf Klein). (*Anna Boleyn*)

According to *Moving Picture News*, the spectator forgot "time and environment—to become an actual figure of Henry's period." Lubitsch had achieved "this by presenting purely spectacular moments" which he "dramatically balanced with intimate touches." It therefore never occurred to the spectator "that he might be looking at an exposition of dry history or an uninteresting costume production. What is presented is real, moving, dramatic and colorful. And the episodes are constructed in masterly fashion, all building to most effective climaxes, the final one being placed where it should be, at the conclusion, with no sop thrown at the sentimentalist."

Anne Boleyn (Henny Porten) and the Duke of Norfolk (Ludwig Hartau). (*Anna Boleyn*)

Dr. Mabuse, der Spieler

DR. MABUSE, THE GAMBLER

1922

CREDITS:

Director: Fritz Lang. *Production:* Uco-Film, Berlin. *Screenplay:* Thea von Harbou. Based on the novel by Norbert Jacques, serialized in the *Berliner Illustr. Zeitung. Photography:* Carl Hoffmann. *Art direction:* Stahl-Urach (died during the filming of Part I), Otto Hunte. *Associates:* Erich Kettelhut, Karl Vollbrecht. *Costumes:* Vally Reinecke. Filmed at Bioscop-Atelier, Neubabelsberg. *Released:* Part I, April 27, 1922; Part II, May 26, 1922 (UFA-Palast am Zoo). *Length:* 3496 meters.

CAST:

Rudolf Klein-Rogge *(Dr. Mabuse);* Alfred Abel *(Count Told);* Aud Egede Nissen *(Cara Carozza);* Gertrude Welcker *(Countess Lucy Told);* Bernhard Goetzke *(Chief Inspector von Wenck);* Forster Larrinaga *(Secretary Sporri);* Paul Richter *(Edgar Hull);* Hans Adalbert von Schlettow *(Mabuse's chauffeur, Georg);* Georg John *(Pesch);* Grete Berger *(Fine, a servant);* Julius Falkenstein *(Karsten, Wenck's friend);* Lydia Potechina *(Russian woman);* Anita Barber *(dancer);* Paul Biensfeldt *(man with revolver);* Karl Platen *(Told's servant);* Karl Huszar *(Hawasch);* Edgar Pauly *(fat spectator);* Julius Hermann *(Schramm);* Auguste Prasch-Grevenberg; Julie Brandt; Gustave Botz; Leonard Haskel; Erner Hübsch; Gottfried Huppertz; Adolf Klein; Erich Pabst; Hans Sternberg; Olaf Storm; Erich Walter; Heinrich Gotho; Willy Schmidt-Gentner.

Lang's next film, a two-part *Sensationfilm, Dr. Mabuse, Der Spieler (The Gambler)* and *Inferno, Menschen der Zeit (Inferno, People of the Time),* mirrored the social anguish of Germany in the early 1920s, a fact which did not escape German critics of the period who looked upon *Dr. Mabuse* as a document of the time.

The murder of Foreign Minister Walther Rathenau by fanatic nationalists in June, 1922, a month after the release of *Dr. Mabuse,* signaled the beginning of a "witches' sabbath of inflation." All values were destroyed as the exchange rate of the mark soared to infinity and unemployment mounted. Lang remembered a poster in Berlin which summed up the nihilistic state of mind: *Berlin, sein Tänzer is der Tod* (Berlin, your dancing partner is Death). "For Germany the period after the First World War was a time of deepest despair, hysteria, cynicism and unbridled vice," Lang reflected. "Horrible poverty existed alongside swollen new wealth. At that time, Berlin coined the word 'Raffke,' from the raking up of money. 'Raffke' was applied to the *nouveau riche.* Dr. Mabuse is the prototype of this time. He is a gambler. He plays cards. He plays roulette. He plays with people and their fates. Because he does not believe in deep feelings, he tells a woman he loves: 'There is no love; there is only desire.' He plays with the lives of these people, and he plays with death."

Dr. Mabuse was impersonated by Rudolf Klein-Rogge, the former husband of Thea von Harbou, Lang's wife and scenarist. Klein-Rogge described Mabuse as "the exponent of the decaying Europe, armed with the dangerous knowledge of the civilization of his continent. He rises consciously in order to strike a breach into the moral uniformity of his time but less for the sake of material advantage. He wants to be a guiding force, a creator, if only in destruction. In a word, his objective is power, which in our time has been transferred from the individual to the collective."

Mabuse was the creation of Norbert Jacques whose serialized story of a master criminal was adapted for the screen by von Harbou. The film opens with the devious Dr. Mabuse reaping an enormous profit at the stock exchange. Disguised as Hugo Balling, he goes to the Folies Bergères in order to meet Edgar Hull, a wealthy man about town. On stage Cara Carozza, Mabuse's mistress and agent, performs a celebrant dance between two colossal Mardi Gras-like heads decorated with huge phallic noses. Hull observes the performance in his box, unaware that he is being hypnotized by Mabuse. Later that evening Mabuse accompanies Hull, now hypnotized, to a *Spielklub*—a gambling club—where he cheats the young man at cards.

A few days later Hull is visited by Public Prosecutor Wenck who suspects that Mabuse, the Great Unknown, is the man who cheated him. Hull agrees to cooperate with Wenck while occupied with amorous thoughts of the exotic Cara Carozza.

Eventually Wenck, himself disguised, confronts Mabuse in a *Spielklub,* but successfully resists the power of his hypnotic gaze. Mabuse flees from the club but is resolved to destroy the detective and young Hull. Hull is murdered outside *Das Petit Casino* by one of Mabuse's agents. Wenck jails Cara as an accessory, but she refuses

Mabuse: "We must plunge the world into an abyss of terror." *(Dr. Mabuse, der Spieler)*

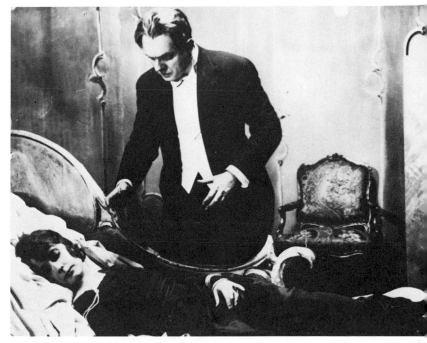

Rudolf Klein-Rogge and Gertrude Welcker. *(Dr. Mabuse, der Spieler)*

Mabuse in the counterfeiters' den. *(Dr. Mabuse, der Spieler)*

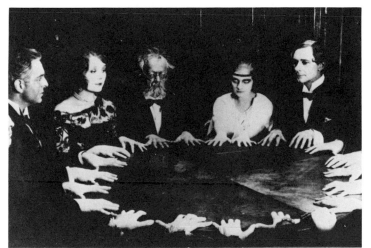

Rudolf Klein-Rogge, Gertrude Welcker and Alfred Abel (far right). *(Dr. Mabuse, der Spieler)*

The disguises of Dr. Mabuse (Rudolf Klein-Rogge). *(Dr. Mabuse, der Spieler)*

Bernhard Goetzke (standing) and Paul Richter (right). *(Dr. Mabuse, der Spieler)*

59

Interior of a *Spielklub*.
(*Dr. Mabuse, der Spieler*)

The stock exchange. (*Dr. Mabuse, der Spieler*)

to reveal the identity of her evil employer and lover. Later, Cara commits suicide in the belief that she has been deserted by Mabuse.

A man of violent passion, Mabuse kidnaps the Countess Told, who has aided Wenck in his investigations. In an effort to destroy the detective, Mabuse, disguised as Professor Weltmann, a psychoanalyst, hypnotizes Wenck at a public lecture and commands him to drive his automobile off an embankment, but Wenck is saved at the last moment by the police. Mabuse has mean-

while removed Countess Told to his lavish headquarters, where a gun battle ensues with the police. Erich Pommer recalled that he "never sensed such a current of excitement in an audience as at the premiere of *Inferno*, the second part of *Dr. Mabuse*, when Mabuse's secret hideout was wiped out by the combined efforts of the police and the army."

Mabuse's accomplices are arrested, but Mabuse escapes to the workshop of his counterfeiter via the sewer tunnels. When Wenck and his officers enter the subterranean hideaway, they find Mabuse squatting on a heap of forged notes, hopelessly insane.

Critics were inclined to favor *Dr. Mabuse* to any of Lang's previous works with the possible exception of *Der müde Tod (Destiny)*, released the previous year. Writing in *Der Kinematograph*, Fritz Olimsky wrote that the artistry of Lang's direction had established "just the right breathtaking tempo." Olimsky remembered especially "the lecture of the hypnotist followed by the frantic car chase through a nocturnal forest (the photographic climax of Part II). Even more memorable is the final struggle against Mabuse, a street battle which is staged with the most modern tactics. In all this there is never the slightest hint of *Kitsch*."

Dr. Mabuse was perhaps the greatest of all Lang's German films in the genre of the master criminal. The popular and critical acclaim accorded *Dr. Mabuse* established Fritz Lang as a major force in the German film.

Das Wachsfigurenkabinett

WAXWORKS

1924

CREDITS:

Production: Neptun-Film AG, Berlin. Released by Hansa-Leih der UFA. Distributed by Wiking-Film AG. *Director:* Paul Leni. Assisted by Leo Birinski. *Screenplay:* Henrik Galeen. *Cinematography:* Helmar Lerski. *Art direction:* Paul Leni. Assisted by Fritz Maurischat. *Costumes:* Ernst Stern. *Released:* November 13, 1924 (UFA-Theatre Kurfürstendamm). *Length:* 2147 meters (seven reels).

CAST:

Emil Jannings, Conrad Veidt, Werner Krauss, Wilhelm Dieterle, Olga Belajeff, John Gottowt, Ernst Legal, Georg John.

Advertisement for *Das Wachsfigurenkabinett.*

Emil Jannings as Haroun-al-Raschid. *(Das Wachsfigurenkabinett)*

What Siegfried Kracauer termed "The cycle of imaginary tyrant films" beginning with *The Cabinet of Dr. Caligari*, achieved its full flowering with *Waxworks*, directed by Paul Leni from a script by Henrik Galeen.

A fairground booth offers a display of wax figures which include "Haroun-al-Raschid," "Ivan the Terrible" and "Jack the Ripper." The showman commissions a young poet (Wilhelm Dieterle) to write stories about these wax figures, and in the film his fantasies come to life. The love story of the young poet and the showman's daughter, Eva, produces a framework for the episodes.

The first story is an improbable satire of despotism set in a surrealistic Baghdad of spiral staircases, plaster minarets and artificial palm trees designed by Leni and art director Fritz Maurischat. As the whimsical Caliph, Haroun-al-Raschid, Emil Jannings must deal with a jealous pastry cook and his coquettish wife. A superbly choreographed chase through the dream-like streets with the pastry cook being pursued by the Caliph's soldiers is the highlight of the sequence and a testimony to the directorial skill of Leni and the artistry of his camerman, Helmar Lerski.

In the second episode Ivan the Terrible is brought to life in the form of Conrad Veidt who inhabits a diabolical milieu of shadowy dungeons, icons and hourglasses.

Paul Leni, assisted by Fritz Maurischat,
designed the sets of *Das Wachsfigurenkabinett*.

Wilhelm Dieterle and Emil Jannings. *(Das Wachsfigurenkabinett)*

Conrad Veidt as Ivan the Terrible. *(Das Wachsfigurenkabinett)*

Expressionistic décor in *Das Wachsfigurenkabinett*.

The fairground booth. *(Das Wachsfigurenkabinett)*

The mad Czar interrupts a wedding party to make the bride his mistress for the night. Having poisoned his victims, he has hourglasses placed before each guest so they may witness the precise moment of their demise. When the Czar discovers an hourglass marked "Ivan," which has been procured by a conspirator, he believes himself poisoned and goes insane.

Galeen's original script contained a sequence about the magician "Rinaldo Rinaldini," whom Dieterle would have also played, but Leni substituted in its stead a short chapter about Jack the Ripper set in a carnival, now deserted of spectators, but replete with specters. The poet dreams that while walking with Eva, Jack the Ripper (Werner Krauss) appears and pursues them down shadowy paths which acquire a momentary reality. Awakened from this dream, against the backdrop of a gigantic Ferris wheel endlessly turning, the poet and Eva are happily reunited.

Rarely screened in retrospectives of the German silent film, *Waxworks* demonstrated, as Paul Rotha was to note, how "Sincerity of purpose and surroundings bring out good work. Transfer the painter from his disordered studio into the luxurious apartment with every new-fangled contrivance to hand and he is at a loss. Thus, for instance, Paul Leni producing *Waxworks* with little money, the goodwill of three fine actors [Emil Jannings, Conrad Veidt and Werner Krauss], handicapped by lack of lights, studio space and time, bound down by limits, was forced to use his ingenuity and to extract the utmost value from a sheet of paper."

Emil Jannings as the doorman of the Atlantic Hotel   *(Der letzte Mann)*

Der letzte Mann

THE LAST LAUGH

1924

CREDITS:

Production: Union-Film der UFA, Berlin. *Director:* Friedrich Wilhelm Murnau. *Screenplay:* Carl Mayer. *Cinematography:* Karl Freund. Assisted by Robert Baberske. *Art direction:* Robert Herlth and Walter Röhrig. *Music:* Giuseppe Becce (original composition). *Released:* December 23, 1924 (UFA-Palast am Zoo). *Length:* 2315 meters (six reels).

CAST:

Emil Jannings *(the Porter);* Maly Delschaft *(his daughter);* Max Hiller *(her fiancé);* Emile Kurz *(his aunt);* Hans Unterkirchen *(hotel manager);* Olaf Storm *(a young guest);* Hermann Vallentin *(a corpulent guest);* Emma Wyda *(a neighbor);* Georg John *(a night watchman);* Erich Schönfelder; Neumann-Schüler; Emmy Wyda.

The Last Laugh is a pivotal work in the history of the German silent film. Perhaps no single German film of the silent period with the exception of *The Cabinet of Dr. Caligari* was to receive as much critical attention as *The Last Laugh,* a film which Robert Sherwood described as "marvelous in its simplicity, its economy of effect, its expressiveness and its dramatic power." As critic Harry Potamkin wrote: "It set down the first form of the cinema: the simple universal theme without complexity of narrative details. *And* it realized, as well as articulated in intention, the principle of constructed, unvacillating environment converging upon the character in relief. It is, to my mind, the only German film I have ever seen that, working upon an inclusive principle and a definite preconception, has realized *itself.*"

Emil Jannings in one of his most memorable screen characterizations. *(Der letzte Mann)*

The proud porter (Emil Jannings) is demoted to lavatory attendant. *(Der letzte Mann)*

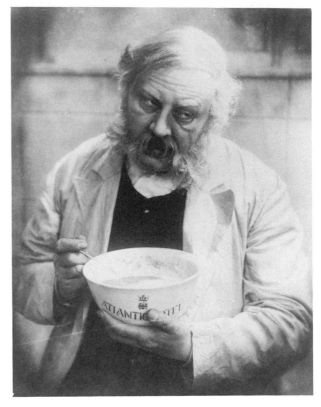

A poster by F. Weber for *Der letzte Mann*.

This inspired offering, produced by UFA in 1924, was the result of a felicitous blending of talent rarely seen in the history of the motion picture: F. W. Murnau directed; Carl Mayer wrote the screenplay; Karl Freund oversaw the photography; Robert Herlth and Walter Röhrig designed the sets; Dr. Guiseppe Becce composed an original musical score; and, not least, Emil Jannings played the role of the hotel porter, giving one of the greatest performances of his screen career.

Lupu Pick very nearly directed *The Last Laugh*, but withdrew after a disagreement with Mayer. As Lotte H. Eisner suggests, "Pick would most likely have deepened this petit-bourgeois tragedy by means of weighty symbolism, as he had done in his film *Sylvester*." But Murnau possessed a very different sensibility. A friend once described him as a "curious mixture of wandering gypsy and cultivated gentleman." Although a disciplined worker, there was a good deal of the poet and dreamer in Murnau which was reflected in the rhythm and imagery of his films. As Eisner notes, "Murnau's films had always possessed a *Kammerspiel-Stimmung* at once more vibrant and more diffused than Pick's, a kind of anxiety floating around the character, as in *Phantom*; as if the ground below their feet was never quite secure, as if Destiny might tear away from every lost feeling of security."

The *UFA Kammer-Lichtspiele*, Berlin, 1924. *(Der letzte Mann)*

The bleak tenements, designed by Walter Röhrig and Robert Herlth. *(Der letzte Mann)*

The film opens in the lobby of the Hotel Atlantis, the camera having traveled continuously from an elevator to the revolving front door, "something between a merry-go-round and a roulette wheel," as Kracauer put it, where the viewer is introduced to a bewhiskered porter, resplendent in his braided uniform and visored cap. The majestic figure is accorded the respect of his family and neighbors. But it is the uniform which they admire, not the man. One day the porter is seen to stagger under the weight of a large trunk. His failure is observed by the manager who summarily demotes him to lavatory attendant. The ornate great coat must be exchanged for a starched white jacket. Towel in hand, he dejectedly performs the demeaning duties of attendant in the marbeled and mirrored confines of the hotel lavatory. Ostracized by family and friends who have discovered his new and unrespectable identity, the old porter returns to the hotel where he is consoled by a solicitous night watchman.

But the porter is spared an unhappy fate by the addition of an epilogue. We learn from a newspaper account that an eccentric American millionaire bequeathed a fortune to the last person who should attend him at the time of his death. The lavatory attendant was this *letze Mann*. After enjoying an enormous meal with his friend the night watchman, he merrily passes

A poster by Kupfer-Sachs for *Der letzte Mann*.

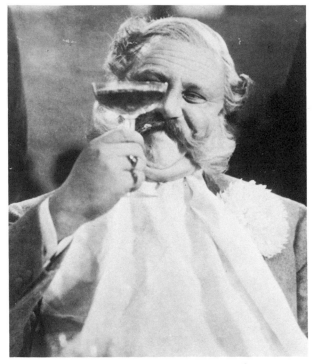

In the humorous epilogue to *Der letzte Mann*, the porter becomes a millionaire.

through the revolving door of the Atlantis, and together with his companion, enters a carriage drawn by four horses.

Murnau was entirely dedicated to the art of making motion pictures. He often worked until 10 p.m. and would meet afterwards with his closest collaborators in his apartment to discuss the next day's shooting or to explore solutions to difficult problems. To give the impression of Jannings hearing the sound of a trumpet in a courtyard, for example, Murnau and his co-workers fitted a camera into a basket mounted on rails. The basket slid down from Jannings' ear to the mouth of the trumpet. And to photograph the dream sequence in which the porter imagines that he can juggle suitcases, Murnau attached valises of various sizes to wires that ran on pulleys. When Jannings touched them, they would appear to fly into the air. The shot was repeated many times because Jannings, who was somewhat apprehensive, held onto the handles a few seconds too long which caused the cables to snap. The actor was on the verge of tears but Murnau remained calm and smiling, seated in his chair. As Robert Herlth recalled, "There was no question, with him, of giving up." The difficult effect was completed at 2 a.m.

Karl Freund, who had photographed Murnau's *Satanes* five years before, worked tirelessly to translate the ideas of Murnau and Mayer into filmic form. Freund's

"unchained camera," as Kracauer noted, "pans, travels, and tilts up and down with a perseverance which not only results in a pictorial narrative of complete fluidity, but also enables the spectator to follow the course of events from various viewpoints." The traveling shot which opens *The Last Laugh* presented Freund with his greatest challenge. "The camera was attached to a bicycle and made to descend, focused on the hotel vestibule," Robert Herlth recounted. "The bicycle went across the hall to the porter, and then, with a cut between shots, continued into the street, which had been built on the lot." Herlth remembered that on other occasions, "the camera was fixed to Freund's stomach, sometimes it flew through the air attached to a scaffolding, or moved forward with Freund on a rubber-wheeled trolley I had built."

The Last Laugh raised the art of the silent film to its highest level of achievement. That it disappeared was a circumstance which Freund lamented in an interview with B. R. Crisler of *The New York Times* in 1937. "The camera is no longer important," he said. "Now we are just a record, like on a gramaphone." Freund believed, as did other artists of the silent screen, that sound had entailed a sacrifice in the visual poetry of motion pictures. But as Crisler observed, "In *The Last Laugh* Mr. Freund's camera was unforgettably not just a gramaphone record, but was a living narrative instrument, as lean and eloquent as the prose of Hemingway at his best."

Varieté

VARIETY

1925

CREDITS:

Production: UFA. *Producer:* Erich Pommer. *Director:* Ewald André Dupont. *Screenplay:* Ewald-André Dupont. Based on the novel *Der Eid des Stephan Huller* by Frederick Hollaender. *Cinematography:* Karl Freund. *Art direction:* O. F. Werndorff. *Music:* Ernö Rapee. *Released:* November 16, 1925 (UFA-Palast am Zoo, Berlin). *Length:* 2844 Meters (7 reels).

CAST:

Emil Jannings *(Boss Huller)*; Maly Delschaft *(Frau Huller)*; Lya de Putti *(Bertha)*; Warwick Ward *(Ar-*

Lya de Putti (dancing on table). *(Varieté)*

tinelli); Alice Hechy; George John; Kurt Gerron; Paul Rehkopf; Charles Lincoln.

The directorial career of Ewald-André Dupont was long and prolific, but his place in the *Ehrenhalle* of German directors rests with a single work, *Varieté (Variety)*, supervised by Erich Pommer and photographed by Karl Freund. In a 1930 appraisal of the German film, Harry Alan Potamkin wrote that *Varieté* "burnt its way through these United States and came near demoralizing the matter-of-fact technique of Hollywood." Perhaps the American public, as Kracauer observed in *From Caligari to Hitler*, "may have been struck by the intensity everyday life assumed in *Variety*. Such accustomed settings as a music hall, a café and a stuffy hotel corridor seemed to glow from within. It was as if one had never before seen these commonplace surroundings." Inevitably Dupont was offered a Hollywood contract as were his two stars, Emil Jannings and his Hungarian leading lady, Lya de Putti. Dupont eventually returned to Europe where he directed in Britain and Germany. After Hitler's assumption to power in 1933, he returned to the United States, but retired from screen direction in 1939.

Varieté opens with a bleak, high-angle shot of prisoners marching in the yard of a penitentiary. The wife and child of Prisoner "28," Boss Huller, have appealed

Emil Jannings as Boss Huller. *(Varieté)*

Warwick Ward as Artinelli. *(Varieté)*

The Wintergarten. *(Varieté)*

The Wintergarten. *(Varieté)*

Emil Jannings (right). *(Varieté)*

for his pardon. Moved by their petition, the warden summons the man to his office where Huller tells him the story of his crime. We learn that the hulking figure was once the proprietor of a provincial carnival, his great days as a trapeze artist having become only a memory. But one night Huller's mundane existence is abruptly transformed when a beautiful Eurasian girl, Bertha-Marie, joins the company as a dancer. Masterful in his use of images, Dupont introduces her symbolically as she climbs the steps of the carnival wagon. As Lotte Eisner notes, she "is seen as a forehead and a pair of immense eyes, then slowly, like a sunrise, her entire face appears, and the mundane fairground seems to be transformed into a metaphysical parable." Huller is enamored by her beauty, and one night they desert the circus for a trapeze act in Berlin. When Artinelli, an internationally famous aerialist sees their act, he proposes that they appear at the Berlin Wintergarten as an acrobatic trio.

The suave and handsome Artinelli seduces the girl, a circumstance which is revealed to Huller by a crude caricature on the marble top of a café table. He plans to murder Artinelli by intentionally missing his grasp during the performance of a triple somersault blindfolded. Huller imagines the death of Artinelli, observed by a sea of eyes from the floor of the Wintergarten, but that night he locks hands with the aerialist, unable to bring himself to commit the murder.

The next morning Artinelli encounters Huller at the boarding house and in the struggle which ensues, Huller kills his rival. Huller returns to his room where Bertha-

Marie reclines on the bed and washes the blood from his arms. His revenge fulfilled, Huller summons a taxi which takes him to the police station. In the final shot, the prison gates open to the sky, leaving the impression, as Paul Rotha observed, "rare in the usual completeness of a German film, that things would still go on."

Varieté is made notable by the virtuoso photography of Karl Freund, whose Vertovian kino-eye-like camera is nothing less than omniscient, giving the viewer a myriad of perspectives in the Wintergarten acrobatic sequences. "In *Variety*, the unaccustomed angle was stressed by necessity," B. R. Crisler observed in an interview with Freund, "owing to cramped quarters in the Berlin Winter Palace where the picture was made, and this film, curiously enough, was an original source-book of the lying-on-the-stomach school of photography." We are at once above and below as the trapezes fly back and forth, observed by the frightened, lustful and expectant eyes of the audience. "Here the camera tells all, both implies and is explicit, strikes at the imagination and spurs it on and sets the text for what must be exactly and immediately understood," the *National Board of Review Magazine* reported. "The trapeze artists begin swinging high over the audience. . . . As they poise and swing and fly through the air from one trapeze to another and are caught and drawn to safety, we follow their movement because the camera, like our gaze, travels with it. But the camera sees more than the eye, and that more completely."

Advertisement for *Faust.*

Faust

1926

CREDITS:

Production: UFA, Berlin. Released by Paraufmet. *Director:* Friedrich Wilhelm Murnau. *Screenplay:* Hans Kyser; based on the works of Johann Wolfgang Goethe, Christopher Marlowe and the old Faust sagas. *Cinematography:* Carl Hoffmann. *Art direction:* Robert Herlth and Walter Röhrig. *Costumes:* Robert Herlth and Walter Röhrig. *Music:* Werner R. Heymann. Filmed at the UFA-Atelier between September, 1925, and May, 1926. *Released:* October 14, 1926 (UFA-Palast am Zoo) with the subtitle *Eine deutsche Volkssage.* *Length:* 2484 meters (seven reels).

CAST:

Gösta Ekman *(Faust);* Camilla Horn *(Gretchen);* Emil Jannings *(Mephistopheles);* Frieda Richard *(Gretchen's mother);* Wilhelm Dieterle *(Valentine);* Yvette Guilbert *(Martha);* Hanna Ralph *(Countess of Parma);* Werner Fuetterer *(Archangel);* Eric Barclay *(Count of Parma);* Hans Rameau *(Bauernbursche);* Lothar Muthel *(monk);* Hertha von Walther; Emmy Wyda.

Upon completion of *The Last Laugh,* F. W. Murnau began preparations for a screen version of *Faust,* adapted by Hans Kyser from the texts of Goethe, principally *Part I,* Christopher Marlowe's *The Tragical History of Doctor Faustus* and the old Faust legends. Kyser's screenplay opens with the prologue in heaven. The Archangel in reply to Mephistopheles' challenge, accedes to the devil's petition to test the integrity of Faust. Mephistopheles appears in Faust's study where a compact is sealed in fire and blood. The community is spared the further effects of a devastating plague, and Faust, having regained his youth, embarks on a search for pleasure, but should Faust find one moment of contentment, Mephistopheles will claim his soul. During the course of his travels through the world with Mephistopheles, Faust has a love affair with Gretchen, for whose downfall he is responsible. When Gretchen is condemned to be burned for infanticide, Faust has an awakening of conscience. He disregards the loss of eternal youth which had been granted by Mephistopheles and rushes toward Gretchen at the place of execution. Faust ascends the funeral pyre and together they go to heaven purified.

In the hope of achieving a large share of the world market, UFA endeavored to bring together an international cast for *Faust*. The studio achieved its goal in

F. W. Murnau: "Real art is simple, but simplicity requires the greatest art." *(Faust)*

The Archangel (Werner Fuetterer) and Mephistopheles (Emil Jannings). *(Faust)*

Mephistopheles (Emil Jannings) in Faust's study. *(Faust)*

part. Emil Jannings was cast as Mephistopheles; Gösta Ekman, a Swede, played Faust; and Yvette Guilbert of France took the comic role of Martha. When the American actress Lillian Gish declined UFA's invitation to play Gretchen, having insisted that Charles Rosher accompany her to Germany to photograph the film, the studio accepted Murnau's choice of Camilla Horn, a German, who had never appeared in films. Finally, Wilhelm Dieterle, another German, was assigned the role of Valentin, making one of his last major screen appearances.

Murnau entrusted the photography to Karl Hoffmann, who worked in close collaboration with art directors Robert Herlth and Walter Röhrig. The unorthodox but imaginative Murnau encouraged Herlth to draw the characters first and allow the sets to grow around them. Murnau believed that simple interiors would allow the actors to dominate the setting. Herlth's design for the room of Gretchen's mother, for example, "became merely a frame for the robust presence of Dieterle, who

Faust (Gösta Ekman) and Gretchen (Camilla Horn). (*Faust*)

Martha (Yvette Guilbert) and Mephistopheles (Emil Jannings). (*Faust*)

was playing Valentin. And Faust's study was not designed as a single room but in accordance with the shots that had been decided on, in four separate parts built one after the other."

Murnau did not hesitate to embrace the ideas of his art director when they accorded with his own thinking

The plague. (*Faust*)

Hoffman then cut the lights, using screens twenty-three cm wide by fifty cm high "to define the space and create shadows on the wall and in the air." *Stimmung*, or atmosphere, was also achieved by smoke. A pile of flammable film stock would be ignited in the doorway of the studio while technicians directed the smoke toward the scene being photographed. The danger was very great, not to mention the discomfort for cast and crew, but the image which resulted contained a marvelous *chiaroscuro* worthy of a Rembrandt etching.

The creation of the prologue in which the Archangel and Mephisto engage in a celestial colloquy and lay a wager on Faust's soul was no less ingenious. Steam was emitted from pipes against a clouded background while arc lights, arranged in a circle, gave the steam the appearance of rays of light. The Archangel was placed in the foreground brandishing a flaming sword. "We did it several times, and each time it was perfectly all right," Herlth recalled, "but Murnau was so caught up in the pleasure of doing it that he forgot all about time. The steam had to keep on billowing through the beams of

Gretchen (Camilla Horn) and Faust (Gösta Ekman). (*Faust*)

He was particularly enthusiastic when Herlth suggested that the marketplace be constructed obliquely in order that the townspeople, panic stricken by the plague, would be forced to move in a confused pattern. Herlth's solution allowed Murnau to achieve the effect in precisely the manner he had sought.

"For Murnau the lighting became part of the actual directing of the film," Herlth recounted. "He would never have shot a scene without first 'seeing' the lighting and adapting it to his intentions." After Hoffmann had lit the first set of *Faust*, Murnau inquired: "Now how are we going to get the effect in the design? This is too much light. Everything must be made much more shadowy."

The aged Faust (Gösta Ekman). (*Faust*)

light, until the Archangel—Werner Fütterer—was so exhausted he could no longer lift his sword. When Murnau realized what had happened, he shook his head and laughed at himself, then gave everyone a break."

The photographing of the demon's flight over the town bearing the curse of the black plague taxed the resources, skill and patience of all concerned. "No other director, not even Lang, ever succeeded in conjuring up the supernatural as masterfully as this," Lotte H. Eisner has written in *The Haunted Screen*. "The entire town seems to be covered by the vast folds of a demon's cloak (or is it a gigantic, lowering cloud?), as the demoniac forces of darkness prepared to devour the powers of light." Jannings was suspended for three hours, his black cape billowing from the force of three electric fans, as soot, ejected from a propeller, enveloped the miniature village beneath him. Jannings finished the shot tired and cursing. The crew was no less exhausted. Murnau remained perfectly calm, however, and when he handed his soiled white jacket to the studio manager, he said simply, "If it's too much for you, don't bother to come." Completely dedicated to his art, Murnau reminded Herlth of "a scientist performing an experiment in a laboratory or a surgeon during a complicated operation."

Arno Richter, assistant to Robert Herlth, remembered that "All those not immediately concerned in the work were refused admission to the studio. This even applied to the great Erich Pommer. . . . Murnau wouldn't even let him come to the daily rushes. So from that point of view everything was peaceful in the studio, but the ardour we put into our work involved us in many arguments and discussions." Herlth often glimpsed Murnau "sunk in an armchair, trying to improve on some unsatisfactory move by an actor, or ticking off the studio manager. But on such occasions he was always good humored; he was never really angry when he sounded angry."

Metropolis

1927

CREDITS:

Director: Fritz Lang. *Production:* UFA. *Screenplay:* Thea von Harbou and Fritz Lang. Based on the novel by Thea von Harbou. *Photography:* Karl Freund, Günther Rittau. *Special photographic effects:* Eugene Schüfftan. *Still photographs:* Horst von Harbou. *Art*

A poster by Schulz-Neudamm for *Metropolis*. Collection, the Museum of Modern Art, New York.

direction: Otto Hunte, Erich Kettelhut, Karl Vollbrecht. *Sculptures:* Walter Schultze-Mittendorf. *Costumes:* Änne Willkom. *Music:* Gottfried Huppertz. Filmed at the UFA, Neubabelsberg and Staaken, May 22, 1925, to October 30, 1926. *Released:* January 10, 1927 (UFA-Palast am Zoo). *Length:* 4189 meters. Released in the United States (Paramount Pictures), August 13, 1927.

CAST:

Brigitte Helm *(Maria);* Alfred Abel *(Joh Fredersen);* Gustave Frölich *(Freder Fredersen);* Rudolf Klein-Rogge *(Rotwang);* Heinrich Georg *(foreman);* Fritz Rasp *(Grot);* Theodor Loos *(Joseph);* Erwin Biswanger *(Georg, No. 11811);* Olaf Storm; Hans Leo Reich; Heinrich Gotho; Margarete Lanner; Max Dietze; Georg John; Walter Kuhle; Arthur Reinhard; Erwin Vater; Grete Berger; Olly Böheim; Ellen Frey; Lisa Gray; Rose Leichtenstein; Helène Weigel; Beatrice Garga; Anny Hintze; Helen von Münchhoten; Hilda Woitsscheff; Fritz Alberti.

According to Lang, the idea for *Metropolis* stemmed from his first impression of the New York skyline viewed from the deck of the S. S. *Deutschland* in October, 1924. "I saw a street lit as if in full daylight by neon lights and topping them oversized luminous advertisements moving, turning, flashing on and off, spiraling . . . something which was completely new and nearly fairy tale-like for a European in those days. . . ." Lang gained the impression that the city "was the crossroads of multiple and confused human forces" irresistibly driven "to exploit each other and thus living in perpetual anxiety." In the days that ensued, Lang explored the city in wonderment. "The buildings seemed to be a vertical veil, shimmering, almost weightless, a luxurious cloth hung from the dark sky to dazzle, distract and hypnotize," he recalled. "At night the city did not give the impression of being alive; it lived as illusions lived. I knew then that I had to make a film about all of these sensations."

After his return to Germany, he collaborated with Thea von Harbou on the screenplay. "We imagined," Lang recalled, "a leisure class living in a big city by virtue of the underground labor of thousands of men on the verge of a revolt led by a daughter of the people." The result was one of the most awesome spectacles in the history of the silent cinema.

Metropolis is a document of German expressionism, more characteristic of the movement, especially as it was reflected in the theater, than its famous predecessor, *The*

The skyscrapers of Metropolis.

The robot is transformed into
the image of Maria.
(*Metropolis*)

Cabinet of Dr. Caligari. The purifying power of sacrifice, the belief that through destruction a new humanity will arise and the prophetic dream of brotherly love, all set forth in Lang's film, bear a strong resemblance to the work of playwright Georg Kaiser, especially his *Gas* trilogy (1917-20): *Die Koralle, Gas I,* and *Gas II.* Kaiser represented a billionaire over three generations, focusing on the social and economic consequences of the industrial age. The decor and staging of *Metropolis* also suggest the influence of Kaiser and the expressionist drama. The expressionist emphasis on the dynamic element, ecstatic gesturing and impulsive movement, is also evident in Lang's portrayal of crowds which move in great geometric patterns to become an integral part of the modernistic architecture.

Lang worked with Karl Freund, the innovative cinematographer of *The Last Laugh* and *Variety. Metropolis* was in part the result of technical *Kniffe,* or photographic trickery, although Freund wrote in an article afterwards that this was not entirely the case. "The giant machines of *Metropolis* really exploded, and a real fire was lighted under the witch Maria, to say nothing of the hundred scenes which were shot naturally without any tricks," Freund noted. Trickery and what a later generation would describe as "special effects" were required, however, to show some of the technical inventions unknown to the period. To achieve the telephonic conversation between the Master of Metropolis and his chief engineer whose image is seen on a television screen, he first shot the engineer and then projected this image backwards through a projection apparatus onto the blank screen of the television. In depicting an automobile drive through the city, Freund photographed the passenger compartment of the car in the studio, mounting the framework on rockers, while assistants dragged futuristic scenery past the window. This sequence, which features Joseph (Theodor Loos) and Slim (Fritz Rasp), survives in stills but is missing from most prints of *Metropolis.*

The Tower of Babel presented the greatest challenge to Freund and Lang. "No technical trick was really supposed to be used for this sequence," according to Freund. They needed six thousand men with shaved

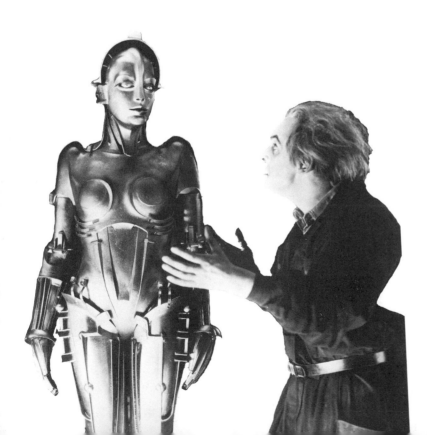

Rotwang the scientist (Rudolf
Klein-Rogge) and the robot (Brigitte
Helm). *(Metropolis)*

heads, but when they could not find enough actors who would shave their heads, the filmmakers recruited a thousand unemployed men who agreed to be shorn. "The hundred barbers who did the shaving could have taken the 'wool' from the Rehbergen, where we did our shooting, to Berlin and sold it to a mattress factory," Freund mused. "Because we still had only a thousand and needed six we shot these thousand men six times and the six pictures, each with a thousand men, became six thousand in the finished negative."

Technical tricks were also the province of Günther Rittau and Eugene Shüfftan. Rittau transformed the robot from a creature of machine parts to a being of flesh and blood; it is unquestionably one of the great moments in the history of the science-fiction film. Rittau devised a series of luminous rings which appear to circumscribe the cubistic machine figure enthroned in Rotwang's laboratory. As the rings travel vertically over the figure, a circulatory system evolves, its tributaries speading throughout the body to create, through a slow photographic dissolve, the human form of the robot Maria.

Cinematographer Eugene Shüfftan, inventor of a mirror process which combined miniatures with full-scale sets, proved an invaluable collaborator. According to the *Aktiengesellschaft für Spiegeltechnik*, Berlin, the "Shüttfan Process" was used for thirteen scenes in *Metropolis*.

The flood sequence presented a special challenge to Freund who accentuated the horror by mounting the camera on a swing to photograph water as it surges through iron doors. A special raft was built to contain the cameraman, his immediate assistants and lighting appa-

```
13. Bild

S t a d i o n   d e s   K l u b s   d e r
S ö h n e  (Sonne)
Leuchten des weissen Steins
Läuferbahn
Mauer
geschmückt mit Figuren im Sinne Archipenkos

d i e  S ö h n e

junge Menschen zwischen 17 und 22
blond,schlank,strahlend,heiter
(von Kopf zu Fuss in weisser Seide)

Gesamtaufnahme: Stadion

     12 Söhne
     mit nacktem Oberkörper
     unter ihnen

     F r e d e r

     Joh Fredersens Sohn
     ...

Einzelaufnahme: Starter hebt die Hand

Ausschnitt:die Startbereiten
          letztes Spannen der Muskel
          Augenblick der Unbeweglichkeit
          ....
          Start

Apparat: vor dem laufenden Felde gleitend

          Freder liegt vorn

Gesamtaufnahme: Stadion gegen Start und Ziel

          schwarzes Band über der Bahn
          Freder
          als erster durchs Ziel.
```

A page from the script of *Metropolis*.

A sketch of the monumental stadium. (*Metropolis*)

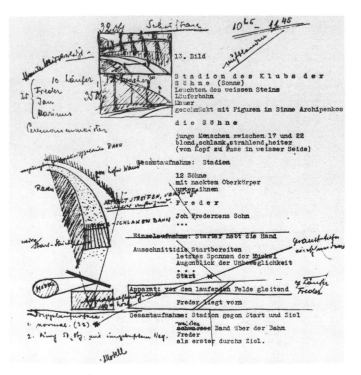

A page from the script of *Metropolis* (stadium sequence) with Lang's notes and diagrams.

ratus. Lang would either accompany Freund or ride in his own raft, maneuvering between hundreds of extras. "With his megaphone he encouraged us, again and again, to be sure and move toward the biggest jets of water," Theodor Loos recalled. The sequence has a documentary quality characteristic of much of Lang's work in Germany and later in the United States.

That Lang worked with the same tenacity in his direction of the principal players is suggested by Gustav Frölich's account of Lang's rehearsal of his love scene with Brigitte Helm in the catacombs. Frölich and Helm watched the director fall to his knees, whispering to and caressing an imaginary person. "Spellbound, Brigitte and I follow[ed] all his movements," Frölich recalled. Finally Lang inquired, looking at Frölich and Helm, "Do you understand?" When they replied in the affirmative, Lang commanded: "Then let's start. Rehearse it." Frölich gestured tenderly as Brigitte Helm stroked his hair, but again the director interrupted, "Not good. . . . You must look at her with deeper feeling." It seemed to Frölich that the rehearsal went "on hour after hour until, fatigued from the effort, [they] continue[d] in a trance, believing in [their] love." Then suddenly, Lang shouted, "Achtung! Lights! Shoot!" According to Frölich Lang shot the scene repeatedly "because the embrace was not deep-felt enough. . . . Then the kiss was too short. . . . I [was] on my knees from morning until midnight. The camera always photograph[ed] our playing from another angle." The love scene was finished two days later.

Metropolis survives in truncated versions, reduced considerably from its original length of 4189 meters. Playwright Channing Pollock, who supervised the editing of *Metropolis* for its American release, excised seven reels from the original seventeen. Missing from the American version is the stadium sequence in which Freder, buoyant and enthusiastic, is shown running a race in a modernistic coliseum. Segments were also deleted which relate to the character Hel, Joh's wife who died giving birth to Freder. Although she is deceased at the beginning of the film, the abridged versions of *Metropolis* make no mention of her existence or the fact that she was also loved by Rotwang. It was thought that the word "Hel" would offend American sensibilities.

Pollock also abridged the scenes between Rotwang and Maria, principally in the scientist's house, which indicate that Maria reminded Rotwang of Hel, the woman he loved but lost to Joh Fredersen. Pollock's abridgement and retitling not only altered the story of *Metropolis*, but its machine-like rhythm as well. "What a captivating symphony of movement!" Luis Buñuel wrote in a 1927 review. "How the engines sing amidst wonderful transparent triumphal arches formed by electric charges! . . . Physics and chemistry are miraculously transformed into rhythm. Not a moment of retardation. Even the titles, already rising and falling, revolving, hazy, melting by and by in light as disintegrating into shadows, unite in the general movement and themselves become images." Such was the dynamism of the original film.

Although portions of *Metropolis* have been irretrievably lost, such as the shot of Joh Frederson and Rotwang at the shrine of Hel, the activities of Slim (Fritz Rasp), Joh Fredersen's agent, and the automobile sequence described by Freund, Dr. Enno Patalas of the Munich Stadtmuseum has achieved a restoration which approximates most closely the original intentions of Fritz Lang.

Released in January, 1927, *Metropolis* proved to be the costliest German film to that time. Budgeted for 1,900,000 marks, its final cost exceeded 5,000,000. Some 37,633 actors and extras participated in the production at UFA-Neubabelsberg which consumed 310 working days and 60 working nights between May 22, 1925, and October 30, 1926. At one point the UFA governing board had considered halting the production because of the enormous expense, but decided to complete the picture in the hope that its distribution abroad, particularly in Britain and the United States, would recoup the huge expenditure. While *Metropolis* proved to be a disappointment in this respect, critics of the period were not entirely opposed to the film. The London *Times* described its "remarkable pictorial power," noting that "When it imitates the stage it often fails; but, when it remains on its own territory, it proves how wide are the boundaries of that territory and how little they have hitherto been explored." Iris Barry wrote in *The Spectator*: "There are moments when it touches real greatness: in its handling of crowds, not for the sake only of the spectacle, but for what emotion the movement of the crowd can express." Writing in *The New Republic*, Gilbert Seldes criticized the story for its "lack of balance" but expressed admiration for the beautiful shots of fantastic buildings, and its terrific use of electrical phenomena as elements in a dynamic compositon which actually becomes the climax of the picture." Seldes believed that "in its correct and complete exploitation of the camera" *Metropolis* "will again do for us what Germany has done twice before," a reference to the innovations of *Caligari* and *The Last Laugh*.

The technological basis of civilization in the twenty-first century is established in the opening sequence: a cubist montage of pistons and machines intercut with a clockface and aerial views of futuristic buildings. In the underground city, battalions of uniformed workers trudge sullenly to their laborious tasks, while in the upper city, Freder, son of the Master of Metropolis, cavorts with young women in a pleasure garden of

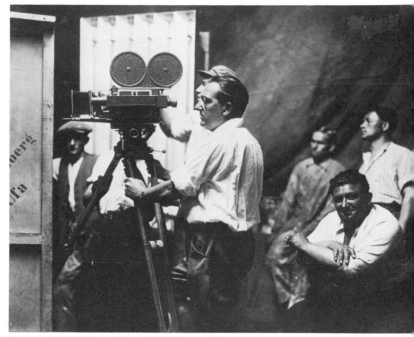

Lang and Karl Freund (seated). *(Metropolis)*

fountains and peacocks. Their frivolity is interrupted when Maria, the daughter of a worker, appears with a delegation of children from the undercity. Freder, the expressionist embodiment of the "New Man," is moved to investigate the conditions of the working people.

In the bowels of Metropolis, a steely labyrinth of dials and catwalks, men labor in exhausting shifts of ten hours. At one point Freder imagines that the machine has been transformed into Moloch, a god of the Phoenicians, to whom human sacrifices were offered. In Freder's vision, Moloch devours columns of workingmen as they march into a fiery mouthlike furnace. Horrified, Freder reports these conditions to his father, Joh Fredersen, Master of Metropolis. Fredersen listens, but is unmoved.

Grot, the chief engineer, brings Fredersen mysterious diagrams scrawled on sheets of paper which have been circulated among the workers. To decipher their meaning, Fredersen calls on Rotwang the scientist, who tells him that the drawings are plans to the ancient catacombs located below the workers' city. Fredersen and Rotwang descend into the darkened catacombs. Hidden from view they spy on a congregation of workers who listen in rapture to the preachings of Maria. In her sermon, she draws an analogy between the exploitation of the workers of Metropolis and the slaves who built the Tower of Babel. She tells the workers to be patient but reminds them that "Between the brain that plans and the hands that build, there must be a mediator."

Fredersen, who no longer considers the workers reliable, confers again with Rotwang who unveils his solution: a robot that will be capable of replacing the human worker. Impressed by Rotwang's achievement, Fredersen commissions the scientist to build a machine in the likeness of Maria. The robot will be sent into the catacombs to preach rebellion amongst the workers. After the destruction of the workers, legions of robots will be created to fill their places at the machines. Fredersen returns to the upper city, leaving Rotwang to kidnap Maria in the catacombs and complete the transformation. Strapped to the laboratory table, her body punctured with electrodes, Rotwang transforms his mechanical figure into the image of Maria.

The robot-Maria, a devilish fanatic, preaches rebellion instead of patience. Inspired by her harangues, the workers of the undercity become a ferocious, club-wielding mob intent on destroying the machines which power the upper city. The workers' quarters are flooded, but through the efforts of Freder and the real Maria, the workers' children are evacuated to safety.

As chaos envelops Metropolis, Grot tells the masses that their irresponsible actions nearly brought about the destruction of their children. Sobered by Grot's words, they set upon the robot-Maria who is lashed to a stake and incinerated. As the flames leap upward, their grimaces of jubilation become expressions of horror as the human face of Maria metamorphoses into the metallic likeness of the robot.

Fearing that the mob will take retribution against him for all that has happened, Rotwang abducts the real Maria and climbs to the roof of the cathedral, pursued by Freder. In the struggle, Rotwang falls to his death.

On the steps of the cathedral, Grot, as the representative of labor, shakes hands with the Master of Metropolis, united by young Freder, who is encouraged to take the role of mediator by Maria. The ceremony is observed by the workers who stand in disciplined ranks before the cathedral. And thus, "There can be no understanding between the hands and the brain unless the heart acts as mediator."

When Lang finished *Metropolis* he had certain misgivings, but in later years he came to see the film differently:

I didn't think in those days a social question could be solved with something as simple as the line: "The mediator between brain (capital) and hand (working class) must be the heart." Yet, today, when you speak with young people about what they miss in the computer-guided establishment, the answer is always: "The heart!" So, probably the scenarist, Mrs. Thea von Harbou, had foresight and therefore was right and I was wrong.

Lang directing Brigitte Helm in the catacombs. *(Metropolis)*

Freder (Gustav Fröhlich) attempts to save the children during
the flooding of the under city. (Metropolis)

under the supervision of Karl Freund. *Art direction:*
Erich Kettelhut. *Music:* Edmund Meisel. *Released:*
September 23, 1927 (Tauentzien-Palast).

Berlin, Sinfonie der Grosstadt

SYMPHONY OF THE GREAT CITY

1927

CREDITS:

Production: Deutsche Vereins-Film AG, Berlin. Released by Deutsche Fox-Defa. *Director:* Walter Ruttmann. *Screenplay:* Walter Ruttmann and Karl Freund. Based on an idea by Carl Mayer. *Cinematography:* Reimar Kuntze, Robert Baberske and Lászlo Schäffer

Walter Ruttmann is chiefly remembered for *Berlin, die Sinfonie der Grosstadt (Berlin, Symphony of a Great City)*, a seminal work in the history of the documentary film. His achievements before and after the celebrated *City Symphony*, while less well known, were no less remarkable, a fact which would seem to make this cinematic painter and *auteur* documentarian an ideal subject for a much-deserved retrospective.

Born in Frankfurt in 1887, Ruttmann entered film after World War I, having studied painting, poster design, photography and architecture in Zurich and Munich. In the early 1920s he created his first films, abstract animated works in the style of the avant-garde called *Opus I, II, III and IV* (1921-1924). He contributed to

Advertisement for *Berlin, die Sinfonie der Grosstadt.*

Arrival in Berlin. (*Berlin, die Sinfonie der Grosstadt*)

Lotte Reiniger's animated feature *The Adventures of Prince Achmed* and composed *Der Falkentraum*, a dream sequence of two black hawks attacking a white dove, for Lang's *Die Nibelungen*. Architecture, abstract painting and the montage of the new Soviet films influenced his evolving cinematic style. *Berlin* would demonstrate his mastery of the medium in all its technical and artistic aspects.

The concept of a city symphony film, however, originated not with Ruttmann but with Carl Mayer while observing the flow of vehicular and pedestrian traffic in front of the UFA Palast am Zoo in 1925. When Mayer told Lupu Pick of his idea, the director and photographer encouraged him, believing that a film might be effectively photographed by concealing a camera in a van. Mayer afterwards presented the concept to Karl Freund who agreed to supervise the photography.

Freund, like Ruttmann, wanted to make a film about Berlin but without a story. As Freund recalled, "I wanted to show everything: men getting up to go to work, eating breakfast, boarding trams or walking. My characters were drawn from all walks of life, from the lowest laborer to the bank president." Mayer disagreed with this approach and disassociated himself from the project. "Carl Mayer wanted the film to be a predominantly social documentary, with the stress on the characters and places within the city," Peter Courie writes. "But Ruttmann at length had his way and concerned himself with creating rhythmical patterns of movement, obsessed as he was with the current mania for montage." Mayer preferred the method of Cavalcanti in *Rien que les heures* (1926). A prostitute and a woman newsvendor provide Cavalcanti's film with a unifying thread, but in *Berlin* Ruttmann emphasizes the collective who are represented impersonally.

Ruttmann was less concerned with the sociological meaning behind the visuals than the visuals themselves. "For Ruttmann, the essence of the city is its rhythm, and nothing else," Jay Chapman notes. "This is felt most deeply by the viewer through the exquisitely controlled rhythm of the editing, as well as the ebb and flow of visual rhythms within individual shots and sequences, which is miraculously sustained for most of the film."

Photographed by Reimar Kuntze, Robert Baberske and László Schäffer under Freund's supervision, *Berlin* consumed eighteen months of production. Freund adopted Pick's suggestion of concealing his camera in a truck with slits in the sides for the unseen lens. For other shots, he mounted his camera in a specially made briefcase which allowed him to shoot surreptitiously. Freund remembered: "I would go into a public house three or four days before I intended to shoot and bribe

An early morning street scene. *(Berlin, die Sinfonie der Grosstadt)*

Silhouette of a worker in the early morning. *(Berlin, die Sinfonie der Grosstadt)*

Geometric patterns in architecture. *(Berlin, die Sinfonie der Grosstadt)*

Dissolving shots of a keyboard establishes the rhythm of work. *(Berlin, die Sinfonie der Grosstadt)*

A moment of life in the great city. *(Berlin, die Sinfonie der Grosstadt)*

85

The poetry of movement: equestrians in the Tiergarten. (*Berlin, die Sinfonie der Grosstadt*)

BZ am Mittag, Berlin's popular afternoon daily. (*Berlin, die Sinfonie der Grosstadt*)

the management to install some powerful lights. After a day or two patrons accepted the lights and ceased to comment. My camera, electrically driven, I would hide in another room while I sat in a chair in the bar myself and pressed an electrical contact. I always contrived that an electric fan should be placed near the camera to drown any faint sound that might reach idle ears. Using hypersensitive stock, I managed to get everything I wanted."

Ruttman opens *Berlin* with a montage in the tradition of the avant-garde: rippling water is transformed into lines and circles which become the wheels and pistons of

The city at night. *(Berlin, die Sinfonie der Grosstadt)*

Director Walter Ruttmann. *(Berlin, die Sinfonie der Grosstadt)*

a locomotive. As the express speeds toward Berlin, Ruttmann intercuts short flashes of wheels, telegraph wires and rails followed by a longer shot of the coupling between two of the coaches. Paul Rotha wrote: Ruttmann "obtained an effect of 'three shorts and a long,' as it were, causing the audience to visualize an emotion that they had experienced themselves in reality." Ensuing shots chronicle the awakening of the city and the rhythm of enterprise: the movement of elevators, the keyboard of a typewriter and the ringing of telephones. Meanwhile, workers build a road, a youth meets a girl and men argue on a street corner.

As the work day draws to a close, the machines halt, the shutters close and the workers leave the factories in pursuit of leisure and sport. But the vigorous rhythm continues after dark, the urban night illuminated by electric signs. Buses and taxis move along glistening, rain-swept streets as fireworks explode in the black sky. A searchlight revolving from a tall building heralds the conclusion of the city symphony.

After *Berlin,* Ruttmann prepared *Wochenende (Weekend),* an imaginative sound montage for German radio in 1928. He unified sound and film in *Die Melodie der Welt (Melody of the World)* in which Oskar Fischinger contributed a brief animated sequence. Ruttmann went on to direct other films in the city symphony tradition, most notably *Kleiner Film einer grossen Statd: Dusseldorf (Small Film of a Great City: Dusseldorf)* and *Stuttgart, Grosstadt zwischen Wald und Reben (Stuttgart, Great City Between Forest and Vine),* both in 1935, and

Hamburg-Weltstrasse, Welthafen (Hamburg—World Street, World Harbor) in 1938. Conscripted for the war effort, he directed *Deutsche Panzer (German Tank)* and *Aberglaube (Superstition)* among others, in 1940. But much of Ruttmann's work since *Berlin*, including a collaborative work with Pudovkin, *Arbeit macht frei (Work Makes You Free)*, and *Acciaio (Steel)*, a feature picture directed in Italy from a screenplay by Luigi Pirandello, have disappeared into archival vaults. Ruttmann died on the Eastern front in July, 1941. His *ouvre* remains to be evaluated by future film historians who will no doubt find further evidence of his mastery of the medium.

Die Büchse der Pandora

PANDORA'S BOX (LULU)

1929

CREDITS:

Production: George C. Horsetzky for Nero Film A.G. *Director:* Georg Wilhelm Pabst. *Assistants:* Mark Sorkin and Paul Falkenberg. *Screenplay:* Ladislaus Vajda. Based on the two plays by Frank Wedekind, *Erdgeist* and *Die Büchse der Pandora. Cinematography:* Günther Krampf. *Editor:* Joseph R. Fliesler. *Art direction:* Andrei Andreiev. *Costumes:* Gottlieb Hesch. *Released:* February, 1929. *Length:* 3254 meters. *Running time:* 131 minutes.

CAST:

Louise Brooks *(Lulu);* Fritz Kortner *(Dr. Peter Schön);* Franz Lederer *(Alwa Schön, his son);* Carl Götz *(Schigolch, Papa Brommer);* Alice Roberts *(Countess Anna Geschwitz);* Daisy d'Ora *(Maria de Zarniko);* Krafft Raschig *(Rodrigo Quast);* Michael von Newlinsky *(Marquis Casti-Piani);* Siegfried Arno *(the stage manager);* and Gustav Diessl *(Jack the Ripper).*

Received with indifference and hostility on the occasion of its initial release in 1929, and for many years unseen and unappreciated, *Die Büsche der Pandora (Pandora's Box/Lulu)* has been rightfully restored to a place of prominence in the pantheon of the German film. Many contemporary critics regard it as one of the finest works of its director, G. W. Pabst. In an attempt to protect public morals, censors did incalculable damage

Siegfried Arno and Louise Brooks. *(Die Büchse der Pandora)*

Louise Brooks and Fritz Kortner. (Die Büchse der Pandora)

Catherine Gaborit has reassembled the nearest to complete print of *Die Büsche der Pandora* which runs about fifteen minutes longer than previous versions. The film is now frequently included in retrospectives of the Wiemar cinema along with the works of Lang, Murnau and others. Much of the credit for the revival of interest

Louise Brooks. (Die Büchse der Pandora)

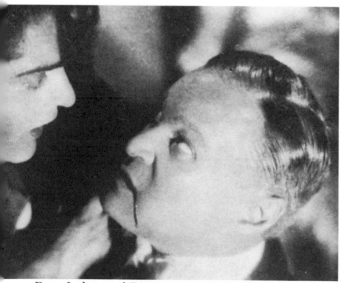

Franz Lederer and Fritz Kortner. (Die Büchse der Pandora)

Louise Brooks and Alice Roberts. (Die Büchse der Pandora)

to the artistic integrity of the work. Title cards were reordered so as to make Schön, Lulu's first lover, appear to be her adoptive father, while the lesbian Countess Geschwitz became a faithful friend. Expurgators also revised the denouement; Lulu was spared the blade of Jack-the-Ripper to be redeemed by the Salvation Army.

in *Die Büsche der Pandora* must go to James Card, curator of the George Eastman House, and Louise Brooks, the star of the film, who was encouraged by Card to write detailed reminiscences of her association with Pabst. Her literate and intelligent articles, together with recollections contained in an interview with the late

Alice Roberts. *(Die Büchse der Pandora)*

Gustav Diessl as Jack the Ripper. *(Die Büchse der Pandora)*

Louise Brooks and Gustav Diessl *(Die Büchse der Pandora)* in settings designed by Andrei Andreiev and photographed by Günther Krampf.

Kenneth Tynan, provide an invaluable source of material for an understanding of the director and his working method.

Pabst based his film on two plays by the anti-bourgeois dramatist, Frank Wedekind: *Erdgeist* (1895) and *Die Büsche der Pandora* (1902). Their heroine is Lulu, "the personification of primitive sexuality who inspires evil unaware." Uncompromising in his antagonism toward all convention, Wedekind possessed a cruelty of observation which approximated Strindberg's. "After depicting a situation that freezes the blood, in language that makes the heart stand still," Felix Bertaux writes, "he bursts forth like Heine with a laugh which seems to say, 'But this is life, as life is lived!' "

Wedekind's drama was adapted for the screen by Ladislaus Vajda. The dancer Lulu persuades the wealthy Dr. Schön to marry her. When he tries to leave her, she shoots him and flees to London with his son Alwa, her foster-father Schigolch and the Countess Geschwitz. Impoverished and a fugitive, Lulu sinks deeper into the sink of erotic iniquity. On Christmas Eve she falls victim to Jack-the-Ripper, whom she has solicited on the streets of Soho.

Pabst had seen Louise Brooks in the Howard Hawks film, *A Girl in Every Port*. Pabst believed that she possessed the qualities of innocence and indifference which defined the amoral character of Lulu. That Lulu should project a passive innocence was especially important to Pabst who had rejected Marlene Dietrich precisely because her allure was tinged with a sophistication that would have contradicted the nature of Lulu as conceived by Wedekind, or as Pabst put it, Dietrich was "too old and too obvious."

Unlike Murnau who made extensive use of the moving camera and long takes, Pabst created a montage of dramatic angles and revealing close-ups. Through the effective use of the close-up, Pabst attempted to reveal the "secrets of the soul." As Lotte Eisner writes, "The amoral, animal-like quality of Lulu is suggested by her luminous white face; the brutish Rodrigo is defined by a single high-angle shot from Lulu's apartment; and Jack-the-Ripper, emerging from the London fog, is studied in the faint glow of a paraffin lamp, his porous skin and taut facial muscles suggesting the depth of the killer's torment. Pabst could indicate all the drama in a single shot."

Die weisse Hölle vom Piz Palü

THE WHITE HELL OF PIZ PALÜ

1929

CREDITS:

Production: H. R. Sokal-Film GmbH, Berlin. *Directors:* Georg Wilhelm Pabst and Dr. Arnold Fanck. *Screenplay:* Dr. Arnold Fanck and Ladislaus Vajada. Based on an idea of Dr. Fanck. *Cinematography:* Sepp Allgeier, Richard Angst and Hans Schneeberger. *Art direction:* Ernö Metzner. *Music:* Willy Schmidt-Gentner. Filmed at the Grunewald-Atelier and in the region of the Bernina Alps. *Released:* November 15, 1929 (UFA-Palast am Zoo). *Length:* 3330 meters.

CAST:

Leni Riefenstahl *(Maria Majoni);* Gustav Diessl *(Dr. Johannes Krafft);* Ernst Petersen *(Hans Brandt);* Mitzi

Dr. Fanck and his crew photographing in the Bernina Alps of Switzerland. *(Die weisse Hölle vom Piz Palü)*

Leni Riefenstahl, Ernst Petersen and Gustav Diessl. *(Die weisse Hölle vom Piz Palü)*

Götzel *(Maria Krafft)*; Otto Spring *(Christian Klucker, a mountain climber)*; Major Ernest Udet *(the flyer)*.

Unlike G. W. Pabst, Dr. Arnold Fanck, the co-director of *Die weisse Hölle von Piz Palü (The White Hell of Piz Palü)*, has been largely forgotten in the history of the German film. Fanck achieved renown in the 1920s and early 1930s as a director of the *Bergfilm*, or mountain film, a genre which he in large measure originated. Working on the fringes of the German industry, Fanck presided over a coterie of dedicated sportsmen, alpinists and cinematographers which included Hans Schneeberger, Sepp Allgeier, Herbert Oettel and Eugen Ham. This group formed the nucleus of Fanck's Freiburg school of filmmaking. Luis Trenker and Leni Riefenstahl, who were later to achieve distinction in their own right, received invaluable lessons from Fanck and his co-workers.

Born in the Reimpfolz in 1889, Fanck was drawn to nature after a youthful excursion to Davos, Switzerland. Naturalist and savant, an expert skier and climber, Fanck studied the natural sciences at Frieburg and Zurich, earning a doctorate in geology. From a young age he demonstrated infinite patience, courage and determination, qualities which were to prove essential in the making of his specialized and often dangerous mountain films.

After service in World War I, Fanck experimented with motion pictures with the intention of producing films that would aid in the instruction of skiing. With

Cameraman Sepp Allgeier and Hans Schneeberger
photographing in the Bernina Alps. *(Die weisse Hölle vom Piz
Palü)*

Ernst Petersen. *(Die weisse Hölle vom Piz Palü)*

few examples among the studio films of the period to guide him in the editing of his unique films, Fanck taught himself the art of montage by trial and error. These early experiments resulted in the production of three short skiing films which he eventually combined into a single feature, *Das Wunder des Schneeschuhs (The Miracle of Skiing)*, released in 1922.

Strongly influenced by the adventure novels of the Swiss Gustav Renker, Fanck made the transition from sports reportage to fiction films with the production in 1924 of *Der Berg des Schicksals (Mountain of Destiny)*, which established him as the foremost figure in the *Bergfilm* genre. *Der Heilige Berg (The Sacred Mountain)*

Gustav Diessl, Leni Riefenstahl and Ernst Petersen *(Die weisse Hölle vom Piz Palü)*

Major Ernst Udet. *(Die weisse Hölle vom Piz Palü)*

and *Der Grosse Sprung (The Great Leap)* followed in 1926 and 1927. In 1928 Fanck and his cameramen traveled to the Upper Engadine where they photographed *Die weisse Stadiom (The White Stadium)*, a short documentary of the Winter Olympics at St. Moritz.

But Fanck's most notable *Bergfilm* was *Die weisse Hölle vom Piz Palü (The White Hell of Piz Palü)* which he co-directed with Pabst from a screenplay written in collaboration with Ladislaus Vajada. As in Fanck's previous films, the scenario pitted man against nature. While climbing Piz Palü, two honeymooners, Maria Majoni and Hans Brandt, meet Dr. Krafft, a noted

Pilot Ernst Udet searches for the stranded party. *(Die weisse Hölle vom Piz Palü)*

Leni Riefenstahl. *(Die weisse Hölle vom Piz Palü)*

alpinist who has been engaged in a hopeless search for his fiancée. During their ascent on the Palu, the party becomes stranded on an icy precipice when Hans injures his leg. Krafft nobly sacrifices himself to save the young couple, whose rescue is effected by the timely arrival of the pilot, Ernst Udet.

Henry Sokal, a young Austrian banker, agreed to produce the film. In our 1974 interview Sokal reminisced: "I met Fanck at a café in Berlin where he told me the story over a glass of wine. I saw the possibility of a commercial success and we roughed out a contract on a paper napkin which we signed the same afternoon."

Under the aegis of Dr. Fanck, Riefenstahl learned the rudiments of climbing, skiing and filmmaking. *(Die weisse Hölle vom Piz Palü)*

Leni Riefenstahl was selected for the feminine lead while Ernst Petersen was cast in the role of Riefenstahl's young husband. Ernst Udet, the famous aviator of World War I, made his film debut as the pilot of the rescue plane. But the choice of a male lead to play Dr. Krafft, the mysterious scientist and mountaineer, proved more difficult. Pabst proposed Gustav Diessl, a Viennese actor who was unknown to either Fanck or Sokal. "I remember the day Diessl appeared for the interview," Sokal stated. "I was convinced that he would be perfect for the stoic figure of Dr. Krafft. But Leni Riefenstahl was of another opinion. During my interview with Diessl she came into the room and stealthily passed a note to me which read: 'If you take this man for the lead, the picture will be ruined.' I do not know why she didn't approve of him, because Diessl was so perfectly suited for the role, a judgment which was vindicated by his fine performance."

The location photography was achieved on the snow-covered slopes of the 12,000 foot high Piz Palü in the Bernina Alps of Switzerland. Dr. Fanck, of course, insisted on realism which required sacrifices from the crew and cast. The director's principal photographers, Sepp Allgeier, Hans Schneeberger and Richard Angst, sometimes worked in hazardous conditions and often in freezing temperatures. "All night long we were drinking hot wine and punch just to keep on breathing," Mare Sorkin, Pabst's assistant, recalled. "That is why the film is so good; you can see all the harshness of the weather on the faces of the people." In one snow scene, Diessl was required to remove his jacket on an icy, windswept ledge. Riefenstahl endured similar discomforts. During the making of one of the night scenes her legs froze and she was forced to stop work for several weeks to allow the tissue to heal and afterward underwent light treatments.

In March of 1928, Dr. Fanck and his crew ascended to Boval and then to the remote Diavolezza hut to make additional shots. The situation here was even more difficult. For one sequence Fanck decreed that Riefenstahl must be lifted twenty meters on a rope over the icy wall of the Morteratsch glacier during an avalanche. She complied, finishing her work black and blue. Sorkin recalled that Leni Riefenstahl drove "herself as hard as anybody, and more. . . . She worked day and night. Even Pabst had to admire her."

Photographing the sequence of the skiers with torches, one of the most beautiful passages in *The White Hell of Piz Palü*, was also achieved at great risk, but Dr. Fanck insisted on authenticity. Holding the camera in his gloved hands, Angst was lowered by rope into an icy fissure some fifty meters deep. And thus literally suspended between "heaven and earth," he achieved the remarkable images of torch bearers peering into the fissure.

The White Hell of Piz Palü was one of Dr. Fanck's most successful films. It opened to critical and popular acclaim in Germany and received favorable reviews by the American press upon its release in the United States by Universal. Mordaunt Hall of *The New York Times* praised the film for its authenticity, noting that it recorded every phase of the mountain's varied life, "the wind-blown summits, the warming of the sun, [and] the avalanches that sweep like torrents down its flank." Hall concluded that "Despite its surface simplicity there is a swift undercurrent of tenseness and anticipation that carries one along through the avalanches, up the precipitous and threatening mountainside and finally to the climax of the rescue."

IV
The Sound Film
1930-1933

Erich Kettelhut designed the casino for *Bomben auf Monte
Carlo* (Monte Carlo Bombardment), directed by Hanns
Schwarz, 1931.

A sound engineer at work during the production of a German film in 1931.

Beginning in the late nineteenth century German filmmakers had attempted to wed sound and image. Numerous experiments involved the gramaphone. On August 29, 1903, Meester demonstrated his *Biophon-Tonbilder der Specht* at the Apollo Theater in Berlin. A 30-centimeter disc provided a "sound track" with a running time of three and a half to four minutes. Between 1903 and 1914 Meester produced over 500 Biophon "sound" films, averaging one film per week and totalling 30,000 meters of negative. When one considers that other firms were also issuing *Tonbild* during this period, the quantity of "sound" films produced in Germany becomes astonishing, a fact which Meester himself noted in an address to the Deutschen Kinotechischen Gesellschaft in Berlin in 1928. Scenes from operas such as *Mein letzter Hauch aus Troubadour* (1907),

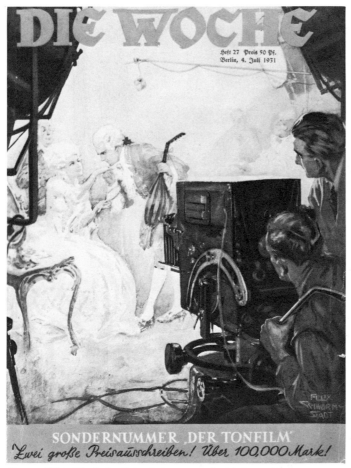

Cover of *Die Woche* by Felix Schwormstädt, 1931.

Otto Gebühr in *Das Flotenkonzert von Sanssouci* (The Flute Concert of Sanssouci), directed by Gustav Ucicky, 1930.

featuring Enrico Caruso, operettas, humorous sketches, cabaret performances, solo instrumentalists and dancers were offered in a filmic format of approximately 60 meters.

The films varied in technical quality and production values. To make their *Tonbilder* more attractive, some filmmakers resorted to trick photographic devices. But by 1914 the public interest in the sound films had waned and theaters gradually discontinued the showing of *Tonbilder*. Exhibitors preferred longer, silent films in imitation of the French, Danish and American offerings. The *Tonbilder* did not die, although disc recording was no longer considered a viable means of synchronizing sound and film. The solution lay in the simultaneous recording of motion pictures and sound. Inventors in Germany, the United States, England, Sweden, France

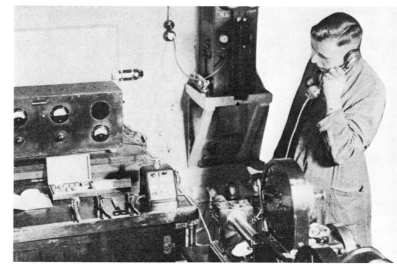

Klangfilm sound apparatus, 1931.

A projection booth showing disc player and sound equipment, 1931.

Advertisement for UFA sound newsreel.

and Japan experimented with the recording of sounds by photographic means.

In the summer of 1918 two young German scientists, Hans Vogt and Josef Engl, achieved a major breakthrough in the development of an improved *Tonbilder*. Vogt had contributed to improving the telephone while Engl, a physicist, had worked for Siemens and Halske on X-ray technology. Joined by Joseph Masolle, a radio engineer, they established a laboratory and offices in Berlin in April, 1919. And when Robert Held, a Berlin banker, proved to be sufficiently impressed with their achievements to finance further researches, the triumvi-

rate moved to a larger laboratory in southeast Berlin in January, 1921, where they produced a sound-on-film recording system which they called Tri-Ergon to signify the contribution of each.

In the spring of 1921 Vogt, Engl and Masolle undertook to market the system, showing short films which included speeches, songs by vaudeville performers and orchestral works. The American Lee DeForest had meanwhile arrived in Germany to exhibit his phonofilm system, which synchronized sound and image with light waves. In August, DeForest projected three short films to a select audience in Berlin. In the first film an assistant played a violin. In the second film a colleague of DeForest "delivered a brief lecture in German on the new invention. Each word was clearly audible as articulated by the moving lips of the moving picture." In the third film, DeForest described his invention in English. "The easily imaginable possibilities of the invention are fascinating," the Berlin correspondent of *The New York Times* reported. "A Presidential candidate can make himself seen and at the same time heard in every smallest town, village and hamlet. So can anybody else worth seeing and listening to." DeForest returned to the United States in September, 1922, where he planned to continue his sales campaign.

The Tri-Ergon system was presented to the public for the first time on September 17, 1922, at the Alhambra Theater in Berlin. The show lasted one hour and included vocal recitations and speeches, variety acts, a scene from grand opera, cello, violin, flute and piano solos, orchestral numbers and excerpts from the play *Der Brandstifer (The Incendiary)*. The sound quality of the Alhambra program was judged to be good although somewhat uneven. Two more public demonstrations of "acoustic film" occurred in the fall, and the next year the Tri-Ergon A.G., a Swiss corporation, was formed with German and Swiss backing.

Tri-Ergon was regarded as the superior system and received twenty-nine orders for the new equipment from German and Swiss exhibitors the first year. UFA, which had equipped some of its theaters with the sound system, was persuaded by Tri-Ergon to acquire recording rights for Germany. UFA produced three hours of sound shorts in 1924, but public response to the new invention disappointed the studio. "In Germany, only the artistically oriented public rejects the color as well as the sound film, at least as entertainment," Guido Seeber wrote in 1927. "Their value is recognized solely for scientific photography, and even then, only when it is a question of improving on older procedures, both practically and economically." Economic and technical factors also impeded the development of sound. The mercurial German economy had contributed to a rise in

Oskar Karlweis and Lilian Harvey in *Die Drei von der Tankstelle* (Three from the Gas Station), directed by Wilhelm Thiele, 1930.

production costs and prices while the Tri-Ergon process, which enlarged the standard thirty-five mm film to forty-two mm, was found to require an adjustment on projection equipment.

Faced with declining revenues, Tri-Ergon decided to secure foreign backing and in 1926 opened negotiations with William Fox, who was experimenting with another sound-on-film system. In July, 1927, Fox, who had purchased Lee DeForest's Phonofilm system, was advised to acquire the American rights to the Tri-Ergon system for $50,000.

The German industry was once again threatened by American domination as Electrical Research Products, Inc. (ERPI), Western Electric's subsidiary for sound motion picture equipment, began to equip European theaters for sound. Would Germany be prepared to hold its own against the expected tide of American sound pictures? The Reich government responded by encouraging the cartelization of all important German sound patents. In 1928, the Tonbild Syndicate A.G. (Tobis) was organized with German, Swiss and Dutch backing.

Having purchased the Tri-Ergon patents, Tobis began to install sound equipment in German theaters in late 1928. At the same time Siemens and Halske A.G. and Allgemeine Elektrizitäts Gesellschaft (AEG), two of the nation's largest electrical concerns which had experimented with the electrical recording of sound, formed Klangfilm. The result was a rapid innovation of the sound system, but outside the laboratory the two companies engaged in a legal battle over patent rights, with Tobis securing an injunction against Klangfilm. The matter was resolved in an out-of-court settlement, and in March, 1929, Tobis and Klangfilm merged, creating a powerful cartel which gave Germany almost complete control of all European recording and reproduction rights for more than a decade.

Germany, however, had lost the initiative in the production of sound feature films to the United States. The legal disputes had proved time consuming, and with capital in short supply, exhibitors found the new sound apparatus offered to them by the Tobis-Klangfilm monopoly, together with the license fees, too costly. And

Advertisement for *M*, directed by Fritz Lang, 1931.
Innovative in its use of sound, *M* is regarded as one of Lang's finest films.

not a few filmmakers, entrepreneurs as well as directors, regarded the *Tonfilm* as a novelty, a passing fad embraced by a fickle public, but one which would never completely usurp the artistry of the silent film. Confronted with these uncertainties, many German producers believed that the most prudent course was to follow the proven path of the Hollywood production.

Tobis proceeded to train technicians *(Tonmeistern)* but was slow to build the requisite concrete reinforced sound stages. Existing stages were hung with heavy draperies to deaden extraneous sound and signs were dutifully posted, *"Ruhe! Tonfilm Aufnahme,"* but these unventilated, makeshift facilities of 1929 left much to be desired. "They [The Germans] have taken over and equipped an old garage on the outskirts of Berlin where musical accompaniments are made and rented a small independent studio in Lichterfelde to accommodate the increasing demand," an observer wrote in 1929. "But all in all, things are still primitive, very primitive."

In January, 1929, Tobis released a program of sound shorts, but it remained for the Deutsches Lichtspiel-Syndikat to release Germany's first sound feature film, *Ich Küsse ihre Hand, Madame (I Kiss Your Hand, Madame)*, a comedy with Harry Liedtke and Marlene Dietrich. Directed by Robert Land, it was essentially a silent film with a song sequence by Liedtke whose voice was substituted by Richard Tauber's for its American release in 1932. "Although a technical and economic basis has been created for the German sound film, the

Mädchen in Uniform (Girls in Uniform), directed by Leontine Sagan, 1931.

decisive question for film production is still unanswered," a correspondent for the Berlin *Vossische Zietung* wrote in March, 1929. "Can the artistic requirements for successful development be created? At present the German sound film is still in the worthy hands of the technicians, to whom artistic creative forces must be allied to give us, not photographed theater, but the new forms of expression of a new art."

It remained for Walter Ruttmann to give at least a partial reply. Ruttmann's *Melodie der Welt (Melody of the World)*, a documentary travelogue commissioned by the Hamburg-Amerika Line, demonstrated the immense possibilities of sound and photographs. Released in March, *Melodie der Welt* combined the music of Wolfgang Zeller and the natural sounds of chains, engines and sirens as the captain issues commands from the bridge of the *Resolute*.

While short subjects of varying quality proliferated, the German newsreel remained silent for all of 1929 and much of 1930. The Fox Corporation introduced the sound newsreel to Germany in September, 1930. The newsreels, which featured reports of riots in Bombay, Captain Coste's landing in New York, and a selection of events taken over the past few years, were shown in sixty German theaters on September 11, having arrived in Hamburg at noon the same day aboard the *Mauretania* for dispatch to Berlin by airplane. German audiences were reported to have been deeply moved by the scenes in Bombay, "as they paint a far more startling picture of events there than newspaper reports had led the Germans to expect."

At London's Elstree Studio, E. A. Dupont directed English and German versions of *Atlantik (Atlantic)*, an "all talking" film of a *Titanic*-like disaster at sea which made a deep impression on German audiences on the occasion of its release in 1929. Although some seventy cities and towns had sound systems by November, 1929, the vast majority of the German productions remained silent through the end of 1929. But the transformation in the next few months was rapid, with Germany's production of sound features rising from three percent in September, 1929, to eighty-four percent in September, 1930.

The greater number of motion pictures produced in the cinema capitals of the world were "talkies" which exploited the novelty of dialogue to the detriment of the visual aspect. "Talkies" should talk, was the American axiom, and the tyranny of dialogue seemed for a time to have destroyed the very basis of motion picture art, movement within the frame and movement through editing or montage. One could easily have agreed with Paul Rotha's statement of 1930 that "The advent of sound and dialogue film marks the opening of the sound cycle in the history of the cinema. Discoveries that have taken twenty-five years to evolve are being thrown aside in the interests of showmanship and commercialism; magnificently the film neglects its proper qualities and returns to the confines of the theater."

But it was precisely the theater, or rather the relationship between theater and film, which facilitated the transition from silence to sound in Germany. As historian Henri Langlois wrote, the Germans were able "to achieve full expressiveness without going through a period of crisis as all the other national cinemas did, some of them taking two years to find a solution whereas the Germans didn't even have to look." That the early German sound films remained a visual experience may be explained in part by a more deeply rooted tradition of pictorial storytelling in the silent films. The explanatory title had never been popular with German filmmakers who had endeavored to communicate visually. This tendency can be seen in Josef von Sternberg's *Der blaue Angel (The Blue Angel)*, produced in 1930, and Fritz Lang's *M*, released in 1931. Both exploited the new sound medium without sacrifice to visual artistry. From the beginning, German directors and their scenarists proved resourceful in their use of music, natural sound and dialogue to achieve a unified artistic work.

The coming of sound offered immense possibilities for the filmed operetta, inspired in part by the success in Germany of René Clair's *Sous les toits de Paris* (1930) with its imaginative blending of sound and images. But previous to Clair, the Germans had broken new terrain with *Melodie des Herzens (Melody of the Heart)* in 1929. *Der Unsterbliche Lump (The Immortal Vagabond)*, 1930, was even more remarkable for its integration of sound and visuals. "Filmed in exteriors," Langlois noted, "*Der Unsterbliche Lump* whisks the microphone through the countryside; and the only difference in conception between Hanns Schwartz's *Melody of the Heart*, a sound film, and the same director's silent *Ungarische Rhapsodie (Hungarian Rhapsody, 1928)* is that there is less artifice and more real feeling in the sound film than in the silent one." American musicals like Warner's *The Singing Fool*, exhibited in Berlin as early as May, 1929, also had their impact on Germany's development of the musical genre

Notable achievements in the musical genre included *Drei von der Tankstelle (Three from the Petrol Pump)*, directed in 1930 by Wilhelm Thiele and featuring Lilian Harvey and Willy Fritsch. This most popular of early sound musicals was accorded a lavish premiere at the UFA-Palast am Zoo in 1930. The festive occasion, as described by a contemporary reviewer, was marked by the "mass arrival of cars. People stand in line by the sold out box office. Wild scalpers demand exorbitant prices.

Police regulate entries and exits. The entire scene is bathed in light and electric advertising. Inside, 2000 people are accommodated in plush seats. Germany's greatest organist plays jazz. America's best animator shows his newest Mickey film. Buds open in slow motion, observed by the scientist. Dance music is heard on the Brühl Terrace. The sound film begins. . . ."

The following year Renate Müller conquered German audiences in *Die Privatsekretarin (The Private Secretary)* while Max Ophuls satirized the film business in *Die verliebte Firma (The Firm in Love)*. But it remained for Lilian Harvey, once again playing opposite Willy Fritsch, to achieve international renown in Eric Charell's *Der Kongress Tanzt (Congress Dances)*. *Ich und die Kaiserin (I and the Empress)* by Friedrich Hollander, *Viktor und Viktoria (Victor and Victoria)* by Reinhold Schuenzel, *Walzerkrieg (War of the Waltzes)* by Dr. Ludwig Berger and *Die Blume von Hawaii (The Hawaiian Flower)* by Richard Oswald, all produced in the period 1932-33, demonstrated Germany's mastery of the operatic style at the beginning of the sound era. "Within the last few years we have been simply flooded with music," C. Hooper Trask reported from Berlin.

Lilian Harvey and Willy Fritsch, 1932.

Käthe von Nagy and Hans Albers in *Der Sieger* (The Victor), directed by Paul Martin and Hans Heinrich, 1932.

104

"The productions ran the scale from farce with music to the full fledged opera. Unless you were melodically inclined, the only thing to do was to stay away from the cinema palaces."

At the close of 1932 Germany presented *Die verkaufte Braut (The Bartered Bride)*, directed by Max Ophuls and featuring Jarmila Novotna and Willis Dongraf-Fassbaender. Advertised as the "first German audible opera," *The Bartered Bride* suggests that sound recording, and especially the amplification of sound, remained a significant problem. Trask wrote in his review that "the reproducing is still as primitive as it was three years ago," noting that "It's really a wonder that the Germans have accepted the talker so whole-heartedly—we would run, not walk, out of a theater where the loud speakers squeak and groan so piteously."

A musical of a very different kind was G. W. Pabst's adaptation of Bertold Brecht's 1928 stage success, *Die Dreigroschenoper (The Threepenny Opera)*, with songs by Kurt Weill. This Nero production was superbly photographed by Fritz Arno Wagner in settings created by Andre Andreiev. Rudolf Forester played Macheath while Carola Neher and Lotte Lenya repeated their stage roles as Polly Peachum and Jenny respectively. Although the film enjoyed a wide popularity with German audiences, Brecht was unhappy with Pabst's treatment, believing that the director had blunted his social criticism in his "prettification" of the work. But Pabst was not entirely at fault. Brecht could be a difficult collaborator and as Martin Esslin, Brecht's biographer, noted: "Since he had written the stage version, Brecht had become much more radically Marxist in his views, and he insisted on giving the story a far more openly anti-capitalist twist, with Macheath ending up as the president of a bank."

Brecht and Weill sued the Nero Company for breach of contract in 1930. The court refused Brecht's demand for an injunction but ruled in favor of Weill. The film company could not alter his score and must allow him to supervise the music. Fearful that Brecht would appeal his decision, Nero offered him a generous out-of-court settlement which he accepted, emerging from the process "both in a martyr's pose and considerably richer than before."

Foreign distribution was a financial necessity and the new *Tonfilmen* were often produced simultaneously in two or three language versions, German, English and French. And some early productions such as *Spieleran einer Kaiserin (The Ring of the Empress)*, with Ivan Petrovich and Lil Dagover, and *Das Land ohne Frauen (The Land Without Women)*, with Conrad Veidt and Clifford McLaglen, also included a silent version. UFA created the position of "Dialect Doctor" and employed Floyd Gibson Young, a Harvard and Cambridge educated American whom the studio considered a specialist in accents, to supervise the English language versions of its films. The studio recognized that a new language was evolving in the United States, and "it is fitting in the highest degree that such an objective entertainment medium as the screen should properly recognize it."

The transition was inevitably painful for some, especially actors and musicians. Among the former were those whose voices were deemed unsuitable for the talking screen while the latter were no longer needed for live orchestra performances. The problem was worldwide. A Berlin writer drew a droll picture of the consternation created in Hollywood by the advent of sound films. He depicted Max Reinhardt and Lillian Gish gazing sadly into each other's eyes and wondering what a "big silent film" will amount to now, but on the other hand, he saw a "wise Mary Pickford" devoting her time to learning a "thousand words of German" so as to surprise "her dear Berliners" by giving them a speech in German in her new sound film.

In an effort to retain a foothold in the German market, Hollywood produced German-language versions of many films, having had little success with the release of silent versions of talking pictures synchronized with music. These efforts were little more than "ponderous slow moving pantomimes with annoyingly elaborate mouth positions," while attempts at dubbing German dialogue proved to be expensive and the results less than satisfactory, as *Wings* and *The Great Gabbo* had demonstrated.

By the winter of 1930 the first German-language versions began to arrive from Hollywood: *Mary Dugan*, *The Big Trail*, *Command to Love*, *Moby Dick* and *On With the Dance*. Paramount's Paris affiliate produced a German version of W. S. Maugham's "The Letter," directed by the versatile Demitri Buchowetzky and released as *Weib im Dschungel (Woman in the Jungle)* in 1931. But the sound quality was poor and Charlotte Ander, who replaced Jeanne Eagles as the murderess in this German version of W. S. Maugham's short story, was miscast, bringing "sweetness and light" to a role that needed "the bitter of almonds and the impenetrability of midnight." More fortunate was Greta Garbo, who surmounted the talkie hurdle with a German version of *Anna Christie*, directed by Jacques Feyder from an adaptation of the Eugene O'Neill play by Walter Hasenclever. In America, MGM's advertising had proclaimed, "Garbo Talks!" while in Germany, posters announced that *"Greta Garbo sprecht Deutsch!"* The Swedish-born actress, always a favorite with Germans, was well received in *Anna Christie*, although Feyder's sentimentalizing of O'Neill's play irritated German critics.

Alfred Döblin during the filming of his novel,
Berlin-Alexanderplatz, directed by Piel Jutzi, 1932.

The arrival in December, 1930, of *All Quiet on the Western Front (In Westen Nichts Neues)*, adapted from Erich Maria Remarque's sensational war novel, proved to be the most controversial of the American imports. The book had been an overwhelming success in Germany, but the extreme right, especially Hitler's National Socialist Party, had taken offense to the pacifistic tendencies of the novel and its criticism of the German army. Remarque had meanwhile removed himself to Switzerland, disturbed by the atmosphere of social hate now dominant in Germany.

The "social hate" alluded to by Remarque manifested itself on the evening of December 5, 1930, at the premiere of *All Quiet on the Western Front*. Dr. Joseph Goebbels was intent on stopping the performance and had masterminded a plan of disruption. Earlier in the evening ten thousand storm troopers had marched through the streets of the West End chanting, "Hitler is at the gates." As the hour of the performance approached, the Nollendorfer Platz in front of the Mozart Hall swelled with storm troopers, police and a bewildered citizenry.

During the showing of the film Goebbels' operatives "spontaneously" interrupted it with catcalls and released white mice, snakes and stink bombs. These tactics were repeated for the next five days while Goebbels' newspaper *Der Angriff* and the Scherl papers, controlled by Hugenberg, campaigned for the exclusion of the film. When Goebbels achieved his goal on December 11, the Chief Censor prohibited further showings of *All Quiet on the Western Front* as a "menace to public safety." The

decision was regarded as a victory for the Nazis in a crucial test of strength with the Republic. Years later, in 1939, Goebbels saw the film again and wrote in his diary afterwards, "A very clever propaganda vehicle. At the time we had to sabotage it."

In the months that followed, *All Quiet on the Western Front*, while prohibited in Germany, was shown in towns across the border on all the frontiers of the Reich. These theaters reportedly did a brisk business, with municipalities offering special bus service from Germany each night as the Reichstag debated the still unresolved issue during March, 1931. Communist delegates demanded the immediate repeal of the censorship edict. The Reichstag at last adopted a Social Democratic motion to the effect that the prohibition of the film had been wrong, but its censorship continued. During the winter UFA reedited the film. The new version was shown to the former German Crown Prince on March 13, 1931, in the belief that his approval would win the support of the nationalist right. But Prince Wilhelm remained steadfast in his opposition to the film, believing "that no matter how much additional cutting and editing of ugly passages were undertaken, the film would never be screened today without running into trouble what with the, God be praised, current attitude of the court. The most one can expect is that the film might become acceptable if it were augmented by a number of beautiful and edifying sequences."

Prince Wilhelm suggested that those concerned with the exhibition of the film might seek the advice of officers who were members of the National Socialist Party. In June the film was at last approved by the Film Censor, but with the stipulation that its showing be restricted to veterans'organizations, pacifist associations, trade unions and professional and educational organizations. The previous winter artist Käthe Kollwitz had written in her diary in reference to the government's censorship of *All Quiet on the Western Front*, "A bad time is coming, or is now here."

Der blaue Engel

THE BLUE ANGEL

1930

CREDITS:

Production: An Erich Pommer Production for UFA.
Director: Josef von Sternberg. *Screenplay:* Josef von

Sternberg in collaboration with Robert Liebmann, Carl Zuckmayer and Karl Vollmöller. Adapted from the novel *Professor Unrat* by Heinrich Mann. *Cinematography:* Günter Rittau and Hans Schneeberger. *Editor:* Sam Winston. *Art direction:* Otto Hunte and Emil Hasler. *Sound:* Fritz Thiery. *Music:* Friedrich Hollander. *Songs:* Friedrich Hollander and Robert Liebmann: *"Nimm Dich in Acht vor Blonden Frauen"* ("Beware of Blondes") *"Ich Bin Die Fesche Lola"* ("I'm Naughty Little Lola"); *"Kinder, Heut' Abend Such Ich Mir Was Aus"* ("I'm Going to Find Someone Tonight"); *"Ich Bin Von Kopf Bis Fuss Auf Liebe Eingestellt"* ("Falling in Love Again"); English lyrics by Sam Lerner. *Released:* April 1, 1930 (Berlin premiere). Produced in German and English versions. Distributed in the United States by Paramount, January, 1931. *Length:* 2965 meters.

CAST:

Emil Jannings *(Professor Immanuel Rath);* Marlene Dietrich *(Lola Fröhlich):* Kurt Gerron *(Kiepert, a magician);* Rosa Valetti *(Guste, his wife);* Hans Albers *(Mazeppa);* Reinhold Bernt *(the clown);* Eduard von Winterstein *(director of the school);* Hans Roth *(the beadle);* Students: Rolf Muller *(Angst),* Rolant Varno *(Lohmann),* Karl Balhaus *(Erzum)* and Robert Klein-Lork *(Goldstaub);* Karl Huszar-Puffy *(the publican);* Wilhelm Diegelmann *(the captain);* Gerhard Bienert *(the policeman);* Ilse Fürstenberg *(Rath's housekeeper).*

Emil Jannings returned to Germany at the close of the silent era but hesitated to make his debut in sound pictures. He was persuaded that only Josef von Sternberg, who had directed him in *The Last Command* (1928), possessed the necessary skill and temperament to guide him through the tribulations of the new medium. As Sternberg recalled: "I was touched by this request from a proud and capable actor whom I had told in no uncertain terms that I considered him a horrible affliction and a hazard to any aesthetic purpose, and, this being my nature, I accepted."

Marlene Dietrich, Hans Albers and Emil Jannings. *(Der blaue Engel)*

Marlene Dietrich. *(Der blaue Engel)*

Marlene Dietrich. *(Der blaue Engel)*

When Sternberg reached Berlin in the summer of 1929, no decision had been reached concerning the subject of Jannings' film. A biography about Rasputin was discussed but finally rejected by Sternberg. Jannings then proposed an adaptation of Heinrich Mann's novel, *Professor Unrat*, the story of a schoolmaster who falls in love with a cabaret singer who has a child from a previous lover. The schoolmaster marries the woman but loses his professorship. He avenges himself on society by becoming a politician and a gambler. In the denouement, he and his wife are arrested.

Sternberg was intrigued by the first part of the novel but preferred to create his own ending, which he wrote in collaboration with Robert Liebmann. Mann readily agreed to this change and to the alteration of the title to the more exotic *Der blaue Engel*. Sternberg and Liebmann recount the fall of Immanuel Rath, a professor of English literature in a German boys' high school. When the professor discovers that his students have become enamoured over Lola Fröhlich, a cabaret singer who performs at the Blue Angel, he visits the establishment one evening. The students take refuge in the cellar of her dressing room, but lifting the trap door they observe with amusement the professor's admiration for the beautiful Lola. Later, when it is believed that the police are planning to raid the cabaret, the professor is persuaded to hide in the darkened celler only to be confronted by his pupils, who taunt him with words and fists.

Having spent the night away from his lodging, Rath arrives late for his class, which has become a bedlam and the professor a figure of ridicule. But he loves Lola and accedes to the principal's request for his resignation.

He marries Lola and becomes a member of her itinerant acting group, taking the role of a clown. When the troup returns to his hometown, Rath is forced to go on stage where he is observed by a noisy audience which includes his former students. As the humiliating performance proceeds, with Rath impersonating a rooster, backstage Lola is seen to enjoy the attentions of a new lover, Mazeppa. Enraged, Rath tries to kill the man but is restrained. He staggers back to his old classroom and dies at his desk as the clock tower strikes the hour.

"In converting the novel into a film which would meet my standards of visual poetry," Sternberg recalled, "I introduced the figure of the clown as well as all the episodes and details that led the professor to be confined in a straight-jacket." According to Sternberg the contribution of Carl Zuckmayer was "negligible" although the playwright claimed in his memoir, A *Part of Myself*, that "the scenario and dialogue were entirely my own." Sternberg was no less adamant in denying the contribution of Karl Vollmoeller, also credited as a scenarist. It is possible that Sternberg's UFA producers may have insisted on the German names, fearful that the German press would criticize an American for adapting a German work.

In the weeks that followed, the director "collected," as he was later to recount, "a cast of actors and actresses for this opus the like of which had never before been collected in a film, and in the center of this weird accumulation was a thespian who was the equivalent of a dozen wildcats." The thespian in question was, of course, Jannings, whose mercurial temperament, vanity, childishness and tantrums sorely tried the patience of Sternberg.

The casting of Lola proved more difficult. Against Sternberg's objections, Heinrich Mann proposed Trude Hesterberg, a well-known cabaret artist and a close personal friend. Mann attempted to make her acceptance a condition for the filming of his novel, but Sternberg remained adamant in his refusal to accept her. The impasse was broken when Hesterberg voluntarily removed herself from consideration. Actress Lucie Mannheim, who had the support of the UFA organiza-

tion, was no more acceptable to Sternberg. The director continued his search for the elusive Lola, a feminine type in the mold of Wedekind's Lulu. "Berlin was bursting at the seams with actresses padded with rolling fat, but none seemed to have rolled it where it might have been viewed favorably." Then one evening he saw Marlene Dietrich in a performance of Georg Kaiser's *Zwie Krawatten*. "Never before had I met so beautiful a woman who had been so thoroughly discounted." Her screen tests were a disappointment, but producer Erich Pommer supported Sternberg in his decision to give the role to Dietrich.

The production of a sound film presented special problems in 1929, and the making of *The Blue Angel* tested the ingenuity of the director and his cameramen, Günther Rittau and Hans Schneeberger. To muffle the noise of the camera, the apparatus was concealed in a huge crate and moved to a new enclosure for each set-up. And because post-production looping was impossible in this period, all sound, including Dietrich's songs, was recorded at the time of production.

Recording the voice of Emil Jannings provided Sternberg with a special problem. Sternberg objected to his careful but unnatural enunciation. When the actor reminded the director that they were making a *German* film, Sternberg replied, "Emil, I like your voice when you speak to me, but not when you address the microphone. We are making a German film but with sound." Not uncharacteristically, an argument ensued. Jannings defended himself as a master of *die Deutsche sprache* while Sternberg pleaded for naturalness in delivery. Sternberg recalled that until this time he had "credited him with genius enough to be effective even when called upon to outrage the German language."

As the film neared completion in October, 1929, a new threat appeared in the person of Alfred Hugenberg, UFA's largest shareholder and an ardent nationalist. When Hugenberg discovered that the source of *The Blue Angel* was not Thomas but Heinrich Mann, whose leftist politics he abhorred, he threatened to cancel the production. Then Hugenberg was shown a letter from Heinrich Mann disagreeing with the finished filmscript. The ruse proved to be a success, and Hugenberg allowed the film to be completed.

Mann was entirely satisfied with Sternberg's cinematic treatment of his work. He recognized that a "true novel cannot be filmed integrally" because "it has many sides, only one of which faces the film, which has to be shot in its own terms." Mann wrote that "The decisive split between the film and the novel is due to an idea conceived by Emil Jannings who, from the very beginning, thought of his part in cinematographic terms. Sternberg wanted to enlarge on the scenes set in the harbor drive, a location dear to this director of films about the underworld."

Mann believed that Sternberg had given the action "a new twist . . . but this does not affect the characters, who remain basically the same. They now disport themselves in the film rather than in the novel, which changes their actions but not their nature. The more insight I gained the more I abandoned the literary point of view, and the farther I was from exclaiming: 'How much you have changed!' The plot differs only in the second half from that of my novel. But even if it were totally different, I would still welcome it, [since] these characters, bursting forth with life, have been transplanted just as they are. And even a few of my lines have been salvaged."

In designing the backgrounds of *The Blue Angel*, Sternberg claimed that he did not research the subject,

Marlene Dietrich. *(Der blaue Engel)*

nor was he interested in visiting Lübeck, the port city which had served as the location of Mann's novel. He also declined invitations to inspect German schools. The director sought a stylized milieu pregnant with meaning but divorced from the real world. In collaboration with two gifted designers, Otto Hunte and Emil Hasler, he achieved an atmosphere which appears to have been in complete harmony with the intentions of Heinrich Mann.

The Blue Angel premiered in Berlin at the Gloria Palast on the evening of April 1, 1930. Dietrich appeared on stage at the end of the performance to receive an ovation and floral bouquets. That same evening she boarded the boat train for Bremen, where she embarked on a liner for America, destined to become a celebrated star. "In a way," Sternberg reflected in his memoirs, "by having made *The Blue Angel*, the most widely circulated German film, I had made a German woman the toast of many lands, and, if nothing else, had spread good will for the Germans at a time when they were not very popular."

A short time later Heinrich Mann saw the film in Nice with Erich Pommer. Mann could not help but be astonished at the journey which his novel and characters had taken. "There were only three spectators in the large French theater; and we saw the admirable Jannings smile—the gentle, childlike smile of a late and dangerous happiness breaking forth and shining through an unhappy face." The novelist was satisfied that Sternberg's "gaudy pictures" had captured "the terror of a fate lived to its bitter end."

Der Kongress tanzt

THE CONGRESS DANCES

1931

CREDITS:

Production: An Erich Pommer Production for UFA. *Director:* Erich Charell. *Screenplay:* Norbert Falk and Robert Liebmann. *Cinematography:* Karl Hoffmann. *Art direction:* Robert Herlth and Walter Röhrig. *Costumes:* Ernst Stern. *Sound:* Fritz Thiery. *Music:* Werner R. Heymann. *Dialogue and lyrics:* Rowland Leigh. *Released:* October 20, 1931. *Running time:* 95 minutes. Distributed in the United States by United Artists Corp.

Lilian Harvey *(Christel)*; Willy Fritsch *(Czar Alexander)*; Conrad Veidt *(Prince Metternich)*; Lil Dagover *(The Countess)*; Henry Garat *(Czar Alexander/Uralsky)*; Gib McLaughlin *(Bibikoff, the Czar's Adjutant)*; Reginald Purdell *(Pepi, his secretary)*.

The revolution of the sound film and the deepening economic depression encouraged the production of German musicals, the quintessential example of escapist entertainment. *Drei von der Tankstelle (Three from the Petrol Pump)*, *Zwei Herzen und ein Schlag (Two Hearts in Three Quarter Time)*, *Bomben auf Monte Carlo (Monte Carlo Madness)*, *Viktor und Viktoria (Victor and Victoria)* and *Walzerkrieg (War of the Waltzes)* were but a few of the outstanding musicals to reach the German screen in the period 1930-1933.

But the most memorable achievement of the genre was Erich Charell's 1931 production for Erich Pommer, *Der Kongress tanzt (The Congress Dances)*, a glittering pastiche of sweeping staircases, open air cafés, costumed balls and military parades set in the period of the Vienna Congress. "It is rather like a group of Dresden china figures that have come to life and are beguiling one with a dream—like a happy little love story," Mordaunt Hall wrote in *The New York Times*. "It frolics along at a leisurely pace, skipping from one scene to another in nonchalant fashion, revealing the discomfort of some persons and the gayety of others."

Leading members of the cast included Lilian Harvey as Christel, Willy Fritsch as Czar Alexander and Conrad Veidt as Prince Metternich. Lil Dagover appeared in a supporting role as the Countess. "I and other players were a little in the background behind the enchanting trio of Harvey, Fritsch and Veidt," Lil Dagover recounted in her memoirs. "There was also our magnificent Adele Sandrock, whom I found simply delightful in her Biedermier costume."

Sometimes described as "the Ziegfeld of the German musical comedy," Charell had directed lavish musical entertainments at the Gross Schauspielhaus of which *Zum weissen Rössel (At the Sign of the White Horse)* had been his most recent success. "He was the ideal showman, having the sure sense for the fine point of a joke," Lil Dagover recalled. "And he had choreographic talents and the know-how to manage mass scenes. The only thing which he did not understand was camera technique. That Erich Pommer nevertheless employed him for *Congress Dances* spoke for the knack of our production chief. There were sufficient experts available in the studio but to present a film in the manner of a theatre revue, only Charell could achieve."

Lilian Harvey. *(Der Kongress tanzt)*

Congress Dances was reportedly the most costly German musical to that date. "Huge sums go whirling through the air, some mention four million marks as the film's cost, and the most conservative estimate is two millions," C. Hooper Trask wrote from Berlin. "This is an overwhelming figure to have spent on a film in post-war Germany which is balancing so precipitously on the sharp edge of bankruptcy. All the more credit to the courage and enterprise of UFA in these dark and uncertain times. *The Congress Dances* will bear the German banner around the world."

The time is 1814 and Czar Alexander arrives in Vienna to discuss the permanent exile of Napoleon, whom the victorious powers have banished to Elba. As his carriage passes through the streets, he is hit by a bouquet bearing the name of a firm for whom the beautiful Christel Weinzinger sells gloves. As punishment for having thrown the bouquet, which is at first thought to be a bomb, Christel is to receive twenty-five lashes. But Pepi, private secretary to Bibikoff, the Czar's adjutant and Christel's beloved, intervenes on her behalf and Prince Metternich pardons her.

Metternich endeavors to keep the Czar away from the meetings of the Congress by having pretty women enter-

The Czar of Russia arrives in Vienna. *(Der Kongress tanzt)*

Lilian Harvey. *(Der Kongress tanzt)*

Lilian Harvey and Willy Fritsch. *(Der Kongress tanzt)*

tain him, but the Czar is not to be deceived. He employs a double, Uralsky, who officiates when the occasion rises. Uralsky's lot is an unhappy one. Instructed to go the opera in the Czar's stead, he is reminded not to yawn. And while he is kissing the hands of women in a long line, the Czar is cloistered with Christel in a café and being entertained by a singer.

The Czar is enamored of Christel and decides to move her to a villa. She receives the invitation at the moment when the other salesgirls are expressing doubt that she has met the ruler of Russia. "Here there is a joyous series of scenes wherein Christel bows and bows to everybody as she rides in the satin-covered open coach. When she reaches her lovely villa, she skips and leaps around, so frightfully glad to have a Czar for a sweetheart." Christel finds the Czar's behavior mercurial: one day his kisses are full of passion, the next he is sullen. Christel does not know that the Czar has a double with whose help the all-powerful Metternich is being guided diplomatically. When word reaches Vienna that Napoleon has landed in France, the Congress adjourns. Christel bids the Czar a tearful farewell, but for Pepi there is new hope.

The film contains an abundance of humor, as when the dance music causes "the eminent statesmen and monarchs to rock back and forth in perfect rhythm on their chairs, and then they all leave the serious subject of Napoleon's exile for the waxed floor. Only Metternich is left, with empty chairs swaying to the music before him." Critics were justifiably impressed, particularly with the "very lovely sequence in which the heroine rides in an open carriage through Vienna and out into the country. This journey is accompanied by a Viennese folk song which the heroine is singing and which is taken up by various groups of people she passes: the market women, the soldiers, the workers, the washer-women, and finally a group of children dancing on a lawn."

The charming and vivacious Lilian Harvey was the daughter of an English mother and a German father. Fluent in German, French and English, she started her career as a dancer and entered films under the direction of Richard Eichberg, who cast her in *Liebe und Trompetten (Love and Trumpets)* and then *Die Keusche Susanne (The Innocent Susanne)* opposite Willy Fritsch, who became her co-star in eleven sound films, including *The Congress Dances.* Produced in German, French and English versions, *The Congress Dances* brought her international fame and a Hollywood contract. Lilian Harvey remained in America only briefly. Returning to Berlin, she appeared in *Schwarze Rosen (Black Roses)* directed by Paul Martin, but the outbreak of war in 1939 terminated her German career. She spent the war years in England but moved back to Europe after 1945, living

Lil Dagover and Conrad Veidt.
(Der Kongress tanzt)

first in Denmark and then at Antibes on the French Riviera where she died in 1968. *The Congress Dances* remains a fitting memorial to the diminutive, wide-eyed and supremely talented Anglo-German actress.

M

1931

CREDITS:

Production: Seymour Nebenzahl for Nero-Film A.G. Released by Vereinigte Star-Film GmbH. *Director:* Fritz Lang. *Screenplay:* Thea von Harbou and Fritz Lang. *Cinematography:* Fritz Arno Wagner and Gustav Rathje. *Art direction:* Karl Vollbrecht and Emil Hasler. *Backdrop photographs:* Horst von Harbou. *Sound:* Adolf Jansen. *Sound editor:* Paul Falkenberg. *Music:* from *Peer Gynt* by Edvard Grieg. *Production manager:* Karl Vash. *Released:* May 11, 1931, with the subtitle *Dein Mörder Sieht Dich an (The Murderer Within Us)* Released in the United States by Paramount Pictures, 1933. *Length:* 3208 meters.

CAST:

Peter Lorre *(Hans Becker, the murderer);* Otto Wernicke *(Inspector Lohmann);* Gustaf Gründgens *(Schränker);* Ellen Widmann *(Mrs. Beckmann);* Inge Landgut *(Elsie Beckmann);* Ernst Stahl-Nachbaur *(Chief of Police);* Franz Stein *(The Minister);* Theodor Loos *(Inspector Groeber);* Fritz Gnass *(the burglar);* Fritz Odemar *(the safe-breaker);* Paul Kemp *(the pick-pocket);* Theo Lingen *(the con-man);* Georg John *(the blind beggar);* Karl Platen *(the night watchman);* Gerhard Bienert *(the Inspector's secretary);* Rosa Valetti *(the landlady of the "Crocodile Club");* Hertha von Walther *(a prostitute);* Rudolf Blumner *(the lawyer).* With Almas, Balhaus, Behal Carell, Dahmen, Doblin, Eckof, Else Ehser, Elzer, Faber,

Franz Becker (Peter Lorre), the child murderer, sees the reflection of his evil self. *(M)*

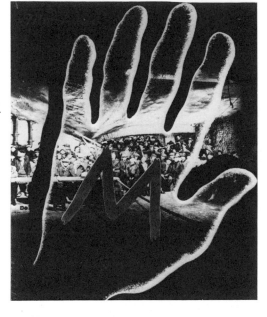

Advertisement for *M*.

Schraencker (Gustav Gründgens) and his gang. The underworld organizes to find the child murderer. *(M)*

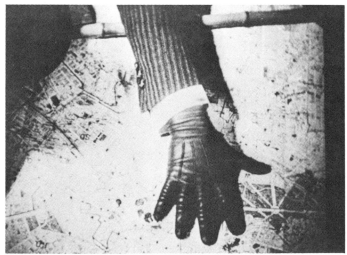

Schraencker's gloved hand. *(M)*

116

Ilse Fürstenberg, Gelingki, Goldstein, Goltz, Heinrich Gotho, Gretler, Hadank, Hartberg, Hempel, Hocker, Hoermann, Isenta, Harchow, Kepich, Hermann Krehan, Kurth Leeser, Rose Lichtenstein, Lotte Löbinger, Lohde, Loretto, Maschek, Matthis, Méderow, Margarete Melzer, Trude Moos, Netto, Neumann, Nied, Maja Norden, Edgar Pauly, Klaus Pohl, Polland, Rebane, Paul Rehkopf, Reihsig, Rhaden, Ritter, Sablotzky, Sascha, Agnes Schulz-Lichterfeld, Leonard Steckel, Stroux, Swinborne, Trutz, Otto Waldis, Walth, Wanka, Wannemann, Wulf, Ziener and members of the underworld, police and people of Berlin.

". . . When the screen became equipped to speak," Lang recollected in a 1953 interview, "I gave up using casts of thousands of players, to concentrate on works which focused on small groups of individuals." The result was *M*, Lang's masterpiece, produced in 1931.

The screenplay for *M* was written in close collaboration with his wife, Thea von Harbou. "Originally, it was not the story of a child-murder," Lang recalled. ". . . We discussed the most heinous crime, and we came [upon] the writing of anonymous poison letters. . . . We started to work on it and one day . . . I don't know what made me do it, [but] I said wait a moment, I think I have another thing: a child-murderer, a man who is forced by some urge, by some perverted urge . . . a sick man . . . to kill."

Lang and von Harbou may have studied the career of Peter Kürten, arrested in May, 1930, for a series of murders in and around Düsseldorf. Unlike the fictional Franz Becker of *M*, however, Kürten was a mass murderer who killed both adults and children. One of his last victims had been an eight-year-old girl murdered in the city's zoological gardens in November, 1929. According to a press account of the period, the underworld of Düsseldorf had pursued the killer because he had disrupted their "legitimate" criminal activity, a situation which parallels the fiction of Lang's *M*. Always loath to admit the source of his films, Lang denied that the Kürten case had any bearing on *M*. Historian Otto Friedrich may be correct in suggesting that *M* was but another manifestation of the crime and violence which gripped the Weimar Republic in the last years before Hitler.

Because the completed screenplay of *M* represents a synthesis of two creative talents, Lang and von Harbou, it is difficult to separate the work of each. Von Harbou apparently wrote much of the dialogue, including the superb speech which Peter Lorre delivers before the kangaroo court. This was Lang's recollection at the time of our interview in March, 1973. He told me further that

Schraencker (Gustav Gründgens) disguised as a policeman. *(M)*

An arresting silhouette of Schraencker and his underworld cohorts. *(M)*

although he could not remember his precise contribution to the writing of *M*, he believed that he wrote most of Lohmann's dialogue and the speeches of his police colleagues.

"In these days I was working with the Scotland Yard of Berlin, which was Alexanderplatz," Lang related in 1971, "and I [saw] many, many cases of murder, almost immediately." The experiences with the police convinced Lang of the injustice of capital punishment. He believed that through application of the supreme penalty "we force the one who throws the switch or pours the poison into the room . . . to commit the same crime for which we kill another. . . . I don't think anybody has the right to kill anybody."

In casting the role of Franz Becker, the murderer, Lang sought to avoid the stereotype criminal, a brutish type with bushy eyebrows. Lang knew that he had found the ideal type when he saw Peter Lorre, a young Hungarian, in a stage production of *Die Pioniere von Ingolstadt* by Marie Louise Fleissner. Later, during Lorre's performance in Frank Wedekind's *Fruelings Erwachen*, Lang offered him the role of Becker in *M*. In appearance, voice and expression, Lorre captured the inner torment of the perverted killer.

M was moreover enhanced by the performance of Otto Wernicke who achieved renown as the persevering Inspector Lohmann. Gustav Grüdgens, later General Director of the *Preussische Staatstheater*, gave a distinguished performance as Schraenker, suave leader of the underworld organization. The part was originally con-

Peter Lorre. *(M)*

117

ceived for Hans Peppler, who would have acted like a typical figure of the Berlin underworld, but he died prior to the production. The choice of Gründgens required that Lang alter his concept of the character. Lang and von Harbou rewrote the part, making Schraenker an "international type" in marked contrast to his associates, a host of thieves, pickpockets and con men. Lang remembered: "Apart from his dominating presence and his elegant appearance, his black gloves immediately awakened in the spectator a thought association that this man would never leave a fingerprint behind. Only one sentence was necessary to distinguish him from the other criminal types. The sentence that came to me and which I added to the original dialogue was 'The best man between Berlin and Frisco.' " Rosa Valetti as the keeper of the Crocodile Club and Fritz Gnass as the burglar were memorable in supporting roles.

But the cast of *M* was not entirely professional, however. During the filming of the kangaroo court sequence, Lang employed underworld figures. Those who agreed to be photographed were seated in the front row of the "jury" to the left of the frame. According to Lang, shooting was interrupted one day when a member of the group informed the director that the police would arrive within the hour to make arrests. Lang persuaded the "jurors" to stay fifteen minutes longer; this additional time allowed him to finish two short scenes and disperse the "jurors" before the arrival of the police.

The film opens with a group of children playing in a tenement courtyard. The children chant, "Just you wait

Schraencker (Gustav Gründgens) at the trial of the child murderer.

a little while/The evil man in black will come/With his little chopper/He will chop you up," as Mrs. Beckmann prepares the noon meal in anticipation of her daughter Elsie's return from school. The children are shown leaving the school, but Elsie Beckmann goes in a different direction, stopping along the way to bounce her ball off a billboard which contains a reward poster for the child-murderer. Suddenly, a man's shadow falls across the poster as the doomed child looks up. Growing anxious, Mrs. Beckmann periodically goes to the stairwell as the other children arrive home.

The murderer buys Elsie a balloon from a blind beggar as he whistles a few bars from Grieg's *Peer Gynt* which becomes the murderer's theme. Meanwhile, Mrs. Beckmann frantically shouts the child's name as we see the table set for a lunch she will never eat. Then Elsie's ball rolls out of some shrubbery, and her balloon floats away, catching on a telegraph wire, as Mrs. Beckmann is heard calling, "Elsie! Elsie!"

While a news vendor proclaims the latest crime, the murderer scrawls a penciled letter to the press: "I haven't finished yet." Succeeding shots explore the psychology of the citizenry, unsettled by the latest murder. People make accusations against one another while others who claim to have seen the murderer deluge the police with false reports.

As police detectives gather evidence at the scene of the crime, Inspector Lohmann interrogates underworld figures at the Crocodile Club, a thieves' hangout.

Schraenker, the underworld boss, becomes disturbed by the interference of the police in the affairs of the "legitimate" crooks. He decides that the underworld must pursue its own investigation, using the "Beggars Union," which will watch for the murderer from assigned locations throughout the city.

Having secured a list of the names and addresses of former mental patients, Lohmann instructs his investigators to watch for a red pencil and an old wooden table on which the murderer might have written the letter to the press. As the investigation continues, a detective goes to the residence of Franz Becker where he discovers incriminating evidence.

Becker, meanwhile, stands on a street corner observing a potential victim, a little girl, whose image is reflected in a mirror. He follows the child at a distance, whistling the *Peer Gynt* tune, but stops when she is joined by her mother. In the background, a sign in the form of a phallic arrow goes up and down against a whirling circle. The police in the meantime link Becker to the murders by the discovery of an Ariston cigarette wrapper found in his room.

Later, Becker encounters another child, purchases a balloon from the blind man, and proceeds to a candy store. But the blind man, remembering the *Peer Gynt* tune, alerts Henry, one of the underworld figures, who follows them. Having chalked the letter *M* on the palm of his hand, Henry passes the murderer, imprinting the mark of Cain on his shoulder. When the murderer sees the letter in a mirror, he flees, taking refuge in an office building.

Disguised as policemen, the gang enter the building, apprehend the murderer in a storage room, and take him to an abandoned warehouse where he is to be judged by a court of the underworld. Schraenker and the jurors, among whom are the mothers of the murdered children, show little sympathy for Becker, who pleads that he cannot help what he does. His "lawyer" tells the court that the murderer is a sick man "and a sick man should be handed over, not to the executioner, but to the doctor."

But the police, who have discovered the location of the trial, interrupt these proceedings and take Becker into custody. In most prints of *M*, the screen then fades to black as we hear the *Peer Gynt* music and the voice of Mrs. Beckmann: "We, too, should keep closer watch on our children." In the original version, however, Lang dissolved to an actual court where judgment is being given. The final shot showed three tearful women in mourning clothes. One says, "We should learn to look after our children more," as the film closes, with the underworld, the law, and the victims' parents each having rendered judgment.

Lang and his producer, Seymour Nebenzahl, were no doubt concerned that *M* would encounter opposition from the conservative *Filmprufstelle*, the Film Examiner's Office. Lang recollected that he and Thea von Harbou waited two hours while the censors deliberated. According to Lang, they felt "like schoolboys who have made some homework and are waiting for a good grade or lousy grade." But when the censors appeared, one of their group announced: "Mr. and Mrs. Lang, this film shows everything which we are opposed to showing in a picture, but it is done with such honesty and integrity that we don't want to make one cut."

Kameradschaft

COMRADESHIP

1931

CREDITS:

Production: Nero-Film AG, Berlin-Paris (Deutsch Französische Geimschaftsproduktion). *Director:* Georg

A sketch by Ernö Metzner for the mine shaft. *(Kameradschaft)*

Wilhelm Pabst. *Screenplay:* Ladislaus Vajda, Karl Otten and Peter Martin. Based on an idea by Karl Otten. *Cinematography:* Fritz Arno Wagner and Robert Baberske. *Art direction:* Ernö Metzner and Karl Vollbrecht. Filmed in studios in Staaken near Berlin and on locations in Lens, Bethune and Gelsenkirchen. *Released:* November 17, 1931. Released in France as *La Tragédie de la Mine. Length:* 2520 meters (nine reels).

CAST:

Alexander Granach, Fritz Kempers, Ernst Busch, Elisabeth Wendt, Gostav Püttjer, Oskar Höcker, Daniel Mendaille, George Charlia, Andréa Ducret, Alex Bernard, Pierre Louis, Heléna Manson.

From the perspective of the 1980s it is difficult to appreciate the enmity that existed between Germany and

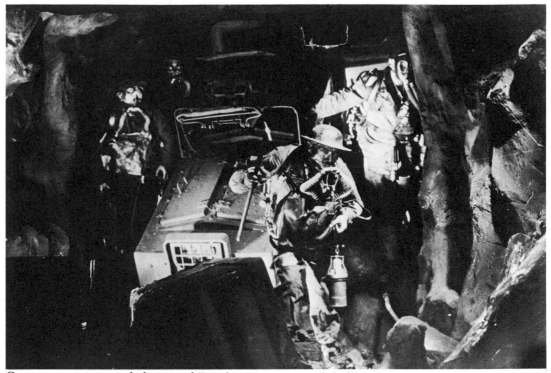

German rescuers approach the trapped French miners. *(Kameradschaft)*

A mine interior. *(Kameradschaft)*

France in the twenty years between the end of World War I and the outbreak of World War II. The human and material destruction suffered by both powers during the Great War, combined with the Treaty of Versailles and the occupation of the Ruhr, created an atmosphere of bitterness, fear and recrimination. While intellectuals of the stature of Thomas Mann and Erich Maria Remarque might advocate reconciliation, many Germans were prepared to see France as the historical enemy. Viewed in this context, G. W. Pabst's 1931 film, *Kameradschaft (Comradeship)*, must be considered a courageous statement on the theme of Franco-German *rapprochement*.

Newspaper accounts of a French mining disaster at Courrièrs in 1906 in which 1200 men lost their lives provided the basis for *Kameradschaft*. Pabst and his scenarist, Ladislaus Vajda, who worked from a story outline by Karl Otten and Peter Martin, transferred the locale to Lorraine on the Franco-German frontier in the period after 1919.

When a fire breaks out in a mine on the Franco-German frontier, German miners volunteer to effect their rescue. Although the German gesture is received with some hostility, the harrowing rescue proceeds as the miners make their descent and crawl through a labyrinth of darkened tunnels and narrow passages.

Meanwhile, the wives and daughters of the entrapped victims clamor at the iron gates. Poignant is the sequence in which a crazed French miner sees his gas-masked German rescuer as an enemy soldier on the battlefield of 1914-18. In the darkness of the cavern, the man relives the horror of trenches and hand-to-hand combat.

The dead and unconscious are at last brought to the surface on stretchers as German officials stamp the protocols that will re-establish the frontier, 1919. When the film premiered in Berlin, the audience received this

final scene "with protests and jeers," a circumstance which may have persuaded Pabst to omit this scene in subsequent showings of *Kameradschaft*, although both versions survive in archival prints.

After making a thorough study of the mines of the Ruhr district and the coal mining regions of northern France, Pabst entrusted the design of a mine shaft and related structures to Ernö Metzner and Karl Vollbrecht. Constructed in the Zeppelin hangar at Staaken, the fabrication of the mine shaft challenged the artistic as well as the engineering skills of Metzner and Vollbrecht.

"There is no echo in a mine," Metzner wrote after the production. "Light and sound stay close to their source in the silent darkness. The noise of rolling coal-piles, shaking troughs and blasting shots dies away without echo." Special precautions were therefore taken to eliminate the sound of machinery and the grating noise of wheels on rails and the explosion. A realistic silence was achieved "by placing old rubber tires, cut up, under the sleepers of the rails, thus making them soundproof for a length of 300 yards. The essential quietness of all the rolling, falling and stamping is perfected to a high degree by covering the whole floor of the tunnels with wet packed mud." The reality of the setting was "augmented by heaping up buckets of coal-dust, fine as flour," while "rocks that had been cast in real mines and copied in plaster of Paris, genuine coal, wood and coal-dust, engines, lorries, windlasses and machines taken from

The shower sequence underscores the theme of the brotherhood of man. *(Kameradschaft)*

mines" reinforced the illusion which the camera caught in a "masterly way." Metzner observed that "Real shaking troughs driven by compressed air convey the dug coals to the electric train which drives through the tunnels of the studio spraying sparks from the aerial line as in a mine." It was, in short, "a mine as it really works."

Metzner's design of the explosion in the mine shaft,

ignited by a narrow flame, was particularly ingenious. While precautionary measures were taken during the filming in the water tanks to protect the cast and crew from the danger of electrocution, a far greater hazard was posed by the tons of rock which had been placed high above the floor. Metzner "hinged" some of the principal boulders and devised a protective covering for the actor who must appear to be crushed by the falling debris. "The pile of stones which rushes down from very high-up with great force is unchecked and natural," Metzner wrote, "yet the security is sufficient in spite of the great masses and the load of many hundredweight."

To achieve the collapse of a tunnel for a length of 25 yards, Metzner devised a timbered "roller-blotter" which weighed more than three tons. Lowered from a vertical position by iron pulleys, it proved effective in pressing in the ceiling of the tunnel in the wake of the explosion. "The scene was satisfactorily photographed without being repeated," Metzner recounted, but "more important, the film was finished without any accident."

Fritz Arno Wagner and Robert Baberske made additional location shots at Lens, Bethune and Gelsenkirchen. As John Grierson suggests, Pabst's treatment of the mining exteriors was no less superb: "The crowd scenes are handled with a skill which I doubt many other directors in cinema can match. . . . There are effects in the film which tear one to shreds."

And one such scene must certainly be that in which a French miner, entrapped by debris, attempts to signal by hammering.

But when at last the sound of far-off voices interrupts his desperate waiting, his hammering turns into rapid drum-beats and suddenly resembles the sound of machine-guns with which the voices of the Germans now also mingle. Now the gas-mask and helmet of the German rescuer who forces his way through the wall completes the war-time vision of attacking Germans in steel helmets and the rescued miner—on the edge of insanity—furiously rushes at his rescuer.

Kameradschaft premiered in Berlin in November, 1931, where, as Kracauer notes, it was "praised by the reviewers and shunned by the public. In Neukolln, one of Berlin's proletarian quarters, it ran before empty seats." A. Krasza-Krauz may have understood the difficulty when he wrote that "People are either of different opinion or they know all these problems too well. This seems to be the chief reason why G. W. Pabst's new film did not gain the success which had been prophesied by the critics." The French-language version, *La Tragédie de la Mine*, proved immensely popular in Paris, however, where it played to audiences of 5,000 per day for five weeks. Lee Atwell, Pabst's biographer, writes:

Kameradschaft is the work of an artist ultimately more involved with people and human feelings than with ideas or class struggle, marking the limitation and strength of his art. The French must have understood this and appreciated it for they immediately acclaimed the film a masterpiece, and shortly after its premiere in Paris, Pabst was awarded the coveted Legion of Honor by the French government for furthering the cause of friendship between peoples and countries.

The influence of Pabst on the British documentary school, represented by such figures as Basil Wright, Humphrey Jennings, Alberto Cavalcanti and Paul Rotha, was considerable. In 1967 Rotha recalled: ". . . I am always proud that I was once closely associated with him and gratefully record how much his films and way of working influenced me when later I came humbly to direct films myself. To have known and talked with Pabst is like saying you knew and talked with Leonardo."

Das blaue Licht

THE BLUE LIGHT

1932

CREDITS:

Production: Leni Riefenstahl-Studio der Sokal-Film GmbH. Released by Aafa-Film AG; after 1938 by Degeto-Kulturfilm GmbH. *Director:* Leni Riefenstahl. *Production director:* Walter Traut. *Screenplay:* Leni Riefenstahl and Béla Balácz. *Photography:* Hans Schneeberger. *Editor:* Dr. Arnold Fanck [uncredited]. *Sound engineer:* Dr. Bittmann. Recorded on Tobis-Klangfilm. *Music:* Guiseppe Becce. *Length:* 2344 meters. *Running time:* 77 minutes. *Released:* March 24, 1932. Distributed in Britain and the United States by Universal Pictures Corp.

CAST:

Leni Riefenstahl *(Junta);* Mathias Wieman *(Vigo);* Beni Fuehrer *(Tonio);* Max Holzboer *(Der Wirt);* Franz Maldacea *(Guzzi, a goatherd);* Martha Mair *(Lucia);* and the people of the Sarn Valley.

Riefenstahl's decision to direct her own film, *Das blaue Licht (The Blue Light),* brought her to a crossroads in her association with Dr. Arnold Fanck, who had

(Opposite page) The fictional village of Santa Maria. *(Das blaue Licht)*

taught her the rudiments of filmmaking. After the completion of the last Fanck films, *Storms Over Mont Blanc* and *The White Flame*, she was resolved to become a filmmaker in her own right. Riefenstahl had become typed as a sportswoman, a designation which she resented. She longed for a serious role, and when none was forthcoming she decided to write one for herself. "Without knowing exactly where I wanted to go, I also found myself expressing the path that would be mine later," she told Michael Delahaye in a 1965 *Cahiers du Cinema* interview. "For, in a certain fashion, it was my destiny that I had had a presentment of and to which I have given form." This is a thought that Leni Riefenstahl has often expressed in interviews since World War II. Like Junta, her witch girl heroine who was misunderstood and persecuted by the villagers of Santa Maria, so Riefenstahl believes that she has suffered a similar fate as a filmmaker. And like Junta, only in death will she at least be accorded understanding if not sympathy.

Completed in 1932, *The Blue Light* represents the capstone of her apprenticeship with Fanck. It was a brilliant artistic success, a *tour de force* which more than demonstrated that the pupil had learned her lessons well. *The Blue Light* marked the rise of Riefenstahl and her coterie of documentarists, many of whom had worked with her on the *Bergfilms*, and the decline of Fanck and the *Frieburgschule*. Fanck's surrender was complete, and within a few short years, unable to sustain himself as an independent filmmaker, he became her employee, fashioning documentaries.

In *The Blue Light* Riefenstahl wanted to give free rein to her "juvenile sense of romanticism and the beautiful image." From her earliest association with Fanck, she had been inspired by the Dolomites and the primitive beauty of the Tirolean landscape. The cathedral-like peaks, coniferous glens and quiet Dolomitian villages seemed to bring out the Rousseauean spirit in Riefenstahl, as East Africa would thirty years later. "I do not like civilization," she told me in 1970. "I like nature, pure and unspoiled."

The story of *The Blue Light* was based on Gustav Renker's 1930 romantic novel, *Bergkristal (Crystal Mountain)*. Reducing Renker's novel to an eighteen-page treatment, she collaborated with the gifted Béla Balácz, a Hungarian Jew and Marxist revolutionary who had achieved eminence in the 1920s as a film theorist, critic and scenarist, in the writing of the final screenplay. They completed this task over a five-week period at St. Anton, Austria, where Dr. Fanck was finishing work on *Die weisse Rausch*.

Like most of Riefenstahl's co-workers, Balácz collaborated on a deferred salary basis. "It was an ideal cooperation, and we had a wonderful and good relationship," she recalled. In addition to the writing of the screenplay, Balácz made a valuable contribution to the dialogue of *The Blue Light* and directed some of the most important scenes in which she acted. Originally, *The Blue Light* was to be an *Autoren Kollektiv* with Riefenstahl, Balácz and Schneeberger receiving collective credit for the making of the film. They were so listed in the March 26, 1932, issue of *Kinematographen*, but after the release of *The Blue Light* in April, 1932, the credits were revised, with Leni Riefenstahl as director, Balácz as a co-scenarist and Hans Schneeberger as cinematographer. Henry Sokal, who produced *The Blue Light*, recalled in 1974: "Riefenstahl, of course, wanted to be designated as director. It was important to her for reasons of prestige, but *The Blue Light* was properly a collaborative effort of the three. But while she owed a great deal to Balácz and Schneeberger, Riefenstahl was the catalyst; *The Blue Light* is inconceivable without her. Despite the passage of time and my opinion of Leni Riefenstahl personally, I still consider *The Blue Light* to be an outstanding film."

In June, 1931, Riefenstahl and Schneeberger selected locations for the filming of *The Blue Light*. The search

Leni Riefenstahl as Junta. *(Das blaue Licht)*

People of the Sarn Valley.
(*Das blaue Licht*)

Vigo (Mathias Wieman) discovers Junta (Leni Riefenstahl) in the crystal cave. *(Das blaue Licht)*

for a suitable village that would serve as Santa Maria proved difficult. Three picturesque villages in the Swiss Canton of Tessin (Ticino), Foroglio, Conlerto and San Carlo, were chosen for the beautiful establishing shots of *The Blue Light* while the Dolomite town of Sarentino, nestled in the verdant valley of the Sarn, as charming today as it appears in the film, provided the principal backgrounds for the action sequences. The peak of Mount Crozzon in the Brenta Dolomites became Junta's mountain, "Monte Cristallo," the source of the mysterious blue light.

Hans Schneeberger proved to be an invaluable collaborator. Fanck regarded him as his most outstanding student while many professionals considered him to be the finest cameraman working in the German industry at that time.

The cinematographic requirements of *The Blue Light* challenged the inventiveness of Schneeberger. To heighten the drama of clouds and sky and the beauty of trees and foliage, Schneeberger photographed with Agfa infrared negative film in *The Blue Light*. And when Riefenstahl saw Schneeberger's tests, she was enthusiastic for the new process. Schneeberger persuaded Riefenstahl to photograph portions of *The Blue Light* with infrared stock. Because Riefenstahl favored an irridescent light that would heighten the romanticism of the story, Schneeberger found that he could obtain this effect by photographing for only a few moments in the early morning hours of the day. For other shots, Schneeberger and Riefenstahl were able to film for no more than two hours a day.

The low blue and high green and red sensitivity of the Agfa stock heightened the romantic aspect which appealed to Riefenstahl. And by using a heavy red filter, a distortion was achieved which excluded all blue. As a result, the blue turned black. This was particularly effective when photographing the moon against a darkened sky. Heinz Jaworsky, Schneeberger's assistant, recalled that Riefenstahl suggested one day that Schneeberger should add a green filter to the red in order to stylize the forest scenes still further. Schneeberger argued that no image would appear on the film. But Riefenstahl's instinct proved to be correct when her idea was demonstrated: the green leaves turned white, creating an optical effect of unusual beauty.

The success of their work was confirmed by Dr. Fanck in Berlin who received some three thousand meters of material forwarded by Riefenstahl from the Dolomites. Sokal, who had also remained in Berlin, remembered that Fanck was initially disappointed after projecting the first rushes and predicted that the film would be her ruination. "I think Dr. Fanck was a little jealous of Riefenstahl," Sokal reflected. "He had never encouraged her to make *The Blue Light* but I was impressed by the material and sent her a telegram: 'Continue as you are doing. I think it's wonderful.' "

After three months of filming in the Dolomites, Leni Riefenstahl and her crew returned to Berlin at the end of September, 1931. Against the advice of Fanck, Riefenstahl proceeded to edit *The Blue Light* herself. Her rough cut disappointed Fanck. Riefenstahl listened tearfully as Fanck, once again her teacher, pointed out her mistakes, especially her tendency to cut on still images. He reminded her that the essence of film is movement which the editor must capture in the montage. Fanck told her that in its present form her film was unusable; it did not, in fact, have a single proper cut.

"We discussed the problems at length," Dr. Fanck recalled. "She was in tears and thought the situation regarding *The Blue Light* was hopeless. I told her that a nature film such as *The Blue Light* was more difficult to assemble than a studio contrived fictional film. Unlike the director of the studio film who is able to pre-edit his material in the script, the creator of a nature film must build from images which have been shot spontaneously, and for this reason the nature film requires a large amount of creativity on the part of the editor. There was no other possibility than to start anew."

Fanck recognized that her future as a director hinged, to a large extent, upon the success or failure of this film, and with characteristic kindness, he offered to re-edit portions as a demonstration of what might be done.

Riefenstahl was at first horrified by Fanck's "destruction" of her *Blue Light*. But as one new sequence followed another, her tears of frustration changed into an expression of happiness. In the weeks that followed, Dr. Fanck completely re-edited *The Blue Light*, forging Schneeberger's magnificent images into a work of art.

From Fanck who had taught her every aspect of the medium, Riefenstahl learned the technique of editing which in time would become her special forte, perhaps her single most important contribution to the art of the motion picture. Sequences in *Triumph of the Will*, but especially *Olympia*, considered by many to be her greatest work, attest to Riefenstahl's mastery of film editing.

The Blue Light opens with a title card and credits followed by the inscription:

We, the people of the Dolomites, far from the strife and turmoil of the outside world, dwell in the rugged, primitive wilderness and magnificence of the Italian Tirol. We are a simple peasant folk and strange legends have come down to us through the centuries casting a shadow on the peace of our lives. Above all do we cherish the legend of *Junta*, the Mountain Girl whose story we have reverently engraved for future generations.

As the inscription fades we see the exterior of a village inn and the arrival of a young couple who have motored to Santa Maria for their honeymoon. In the coming days they plan to climb the Dolomite peak of Monte Cristallo. The couple is engulfed by a group of children who try to sell them crystal rocks for which the village of Santa Maria is famous. Tiny hands reach out with bits and pieces of crystal. One child offers the woman an oval portrait of Junta. Later, when the woman inquires of the innkeeper if such a person lived, she is shown a leather-bound book which carries the inscription: *History of Junta* 1866. In close-up we see Junta's portrait mounted in a piece of quartz. The framing story concludes with a dissolve from the quartz to the hands of Junta in the act of grasping a piece of crystal. Other establishing shots show her standing by a silvery waterfall which spills into a glacial valley. Her attention is distracted by the approach of a *diligence* which winds its way along a dusty mountain road toward Santa Maria. Her curiosity aroused, Junta climbs over the rocks to gain a better perspective of the coach and its occupant, Vigo, a young artist who has come to paint and holiday in Santa Maria. When the coach comes to a halt, Vigo climbs down and is escorted to the village by the innkeeper. On route they come upon a group of crucifixes which honor the young men of the village who have met death on the slopes of Monte Cristallo.

At the inn Vigo is impressed by the somber nature of the villagers who sit at tables, mute, unsmiling and

Tonio (Beni Fuehrer) and Lucia (Martha Mair). *(Das blaue Licht)*

Leni Riefenstahl. *(Das blaue Licht)*

despondent. The innkeeper tells Vigo that a curse has fallen over Santa Maria. On the night of the full moon a strange hallucinatory blue light radiates from the craggy summit of Monte Cristallo. The young men from the village, mesmerized by the light, have fallen to their deaths while searching for its source.

Later, Junta stealthily enters Santa Maria. When she appears, the villagers observe her scornfully. Junta tim-idly makes her way to the center of the village carrying a basket of crystal. She appears before a corpulent merchant who examines one of her crystals. When the man refuses to return the quartz she bites his hand, seizes the crystal and flees. A hostile crowd pursues her through narrow streets until Vigo, who has witnessed the disturbance from his window, blocks their path, giving Junta an opportunity to escape.

When Junta reaches the safety of her hut in the mountains, exhausted and angry, she explains to her little brother Guzzi, a goatherd, all that has transpired. Her feverish gestures are juxtaposed with shots of a cooking pot bubbling and frothing on an open fire.

Vigo, winded and perspiring, makes his way up the valley in pursuit of Junta. Munching an apple, she coyly observes him from a distance as he calls her name. When Junta playfully throws the core in his direction, he sees her reflection in a pond and makes his way to her hut on the summit. Junta extends a cordial greeting, grateful for the protection that he accorded her from the angry villagers.

Vigo returns to the village, very much in love with Junta. We see a smiling Vigo drinking in the village tavern. At another table a young plowman who also loves Junta watches the artist with a jealous glare.

As darkness envelops the valley, an ominous shadow falls across the cathedral-like spire of Monte Cristallo. The superstitious villagers shutter their windows and bolt their doors as the moon rises in the sky. Vigo watches the strange light from Monte Cristallo.

A script page from *Das blaue Licht* with Riefenstahl's penciled notations for the filming of the waterfall sequence.

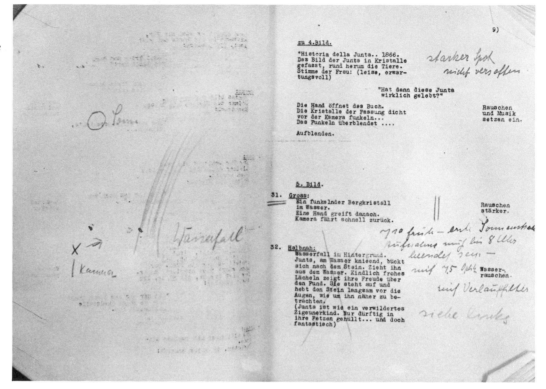

Mesmerized by the light, Junta makes her way to the top of the mountain. She is shown in silhouette, climbing over rocks and leaping across a great fissure. Reaching the summit, she enters a wondrous cavern of sparkling stalactites, the source of the blue light.

On this same night the young plowman attempts to scale Monte Cristallo, but when the moon disappears behind a cloud he loses his footing and falls to his death. His demise is represented by close-up shots of shrines with religious figures. Vigo, however, succeeds in reaching the crystal cave where he discovers Junta and the secret of the blue light.

The next sequence, the funeral cortège of the plowman, is exciting for its photographic excellence and suggests the high angle shots of parades in *Triumph of the Will*. In *The Blue Light* we are shown a high angle shot of mourners walking in a long formation. The shot is made extraordinary by small touches such as the solitary figure of an old man who walks with a cane after the procession has passed. The gaunt figure casts a long shadow across the road before moving out of the frame and concluding the sequence.

Motivated by his love for Junta, Vigo seeks to dispel the myth of her witchery. When he tries to explain his good intentions, she smiles but has no understanding of his words. Vigo returns to Santa Maria and sketches a map to the crystal cave. The villagers gather baskets, hammers, picks and ladders and make their way to Monte Cristallo. They destroy the crystal cavern with ruthless insensitivity, heaping their baskets with chunks of quartz. Returning to Santa Maria, they celebrate their exploit as we dissolve from fragments of sparkling crystal to a closeup of two wine glasses clinking in the tavern.

Later, Junta discovers the destruction wrought by the villagers. In a subjective shot we see the interior of the gutted cave littered with crystal fragments, hammers, ladders and baskets, a triumph of the material world over the spiritual. In their pillage, the villagers destroy Junta's secret and her reason for living. In a closeup we see her hands clinging to the steep cliff, but her will to live expires and she falls from the precipice.

Vigo discovers her lifeless body in a bed of grass and wild flowers at the base of Monte Cristallo as the screen dissolves from a crystal rock, still clutched in her hand, to the oval portrait on the cover on the book, *History of Junta*. Deeply affected by what they have read, the honeymooners stand by the window and contemplate the luminous waterfall, a living symbol of the mysterious Junta.

The Blue Light premiered at the UFA-Palast am Zoo on the evening of March 24, 1932. *It* enjoyed a moderate success in Germany, Austria and Switzerland, the countries which had been most receptive to the mountain films of Dr. Fanck. But in general, the *Bergfilm* audience found it too *kunstlerisch*, or artistic. It did well in London as an art house exhibit and encouraged a spate of travel to the Dolomites by young Cambridge students who searched in vain for the fictional village of Santa Maria.

The Blue Light received the serious although not uncritical attention of British film critics, who were more favorably disposed toward films which dealt with social themes. Trude Weiss in *Close-Up* found that the story of Junta offered ". . . A very fascinating plot for a film, but at the same time so tremendously delicate and difficult to do that only the most experienced director would have been capable of handling it." She believed, however, that Leni Riefenstahl had shown courage in making "herself not only the leading actress, but also the scenario-writer and directress of the film."

The Blue Light found an even less appreciative audience in the United States on the occasion of its release in 1934. Its subtle, romantic style was too much at variance with Hollywood's fast-paced, star-studded, all talking features. As *Variety* noted in its review, the story simply did not "grip." Harry T. Smith, however, wrote an appreciative piece in *The New York Times*, noting that "A summary of the story gives no adequate idea of the beauty of the action and the remarkable camera work, especially in connection with the light effects."

Since the mid-1930s *The Blue Light* has been shown only occasionally in the United States. The prints that circulate are usually silent versions and of poor quality. They provide only a shadow of the original film and do not suggest the superb monochromy of Schneeberger's photography. In the early 1950s, Riefenstahl re-edited the film, eliminated the modern-day framing story, photographed new titles, re-recorded the voice track and added new music composed by Guiseppe Becce. This version conveys the full dimension of the original work.

Kuhle Wampe

1932

CREDITS:

Production: Prometheus-Filmverleih und Vertriebs GmbH in Gemeinschaft mit Praesens-Filmverleih GmbH. *Director:* Slaten Dodow. *Screenplay:* Bertold Brecht and Ernst Ottwald. *Cinematography:* Günther Krampf. *Music:* Hanns Eisler and Josef Schmid. *Released:* May 30, 1932. Released in the United States as *Whither Germany? Length:* 2017 meters.

CAST:

Hertha Thiele, Ernst Busch, Martha Wolter, Adolf Fischer, Lili Schönborn, Max Sablotzki, Alfred Schaefer, Gerhard Bienert, Martha Burchardi, Carl Heinz Charell, Karl Kahmen, Fritz Erpenbeck, Josef Hanoszek, Richard Pilgert, Hugo Werner-Kahle, Hermann Krehan, Paul Kretzburg, Anna Müller-Lincke, Rudolf Pehls, Erich Peters, Olly Rummel. Willy Schur, Martha Seemann, Hans Stern, Karl Wagner.

After his celebrated dispute with director G. W. Pabst over the filming of *Die Dreigroschenoper* (The Threepenny Opera) produced by Nero Film Company in 1931, Bertold Brecht had come to the conclusion that a proper proletarian motion picture could only be achieved by a leftist *Kollectiv* outside the commercial filmmaking establishment. With the help of various communist organizations, notably the Labor Sports Union, Workers Theater Union and the Workers' Chorus of Greater Germany, Brecht and his principal collaborators, Slaton Dudow, Hanns Eisler and Ernst Ottwald, prepared an authentic "workers' film" which they named *Kuhle Wampe*, a district on the outskirts of Berlin inhabited by unemployed. The *Kollectiv* negotiated a contract which made them authors in a legal sense while giving them an "otherwise unattainable freedom."

Brecht and Ottwald wrote the screenplay, Dudow directed and Eisler composed an imaginative musical score. They were ably assisted by cameraman Günther Krampf, the aforementioned communist Sports Union, and theatrical groups and professional players who sym-

Advertisement for *Kuhle Wampe*.

pathized with his philosophy. *Kuhle Wampe* consumed nearly a year of production. Brecht appears to have been completely satisfied with the result. As Klaus Völker noted in his biography of the playwright: "*Kuhle Wampe* was to remain the only film in which Brecht succeeded in carrying out his ideas in every phase of the work."

Completed in the spring of 1932 as Germany veered closer to civil war, *Kuhle Wampe* was initially prohibited on the grounds that a number of scenes preached resistance to state authority. According to the charges: "The film offends against the vital interests of the state. The system of justice as an institution is held up to ridicule. . . . The frequently repeated summons to solidarity and self-help is nothing but a summons to violence and subversion. This summons to solidarity runs like a thread throughout the film, and culminates in a summons to change the world." The suicide of a young worker, linked to a presidential emergency decree, was considered an offense to the president of the republic.

The film describes the plight of the Bönickers, a working class family living in Berlin during the Depression. Evicted from their tenement, they move to Kuhle Wampe, a shanty encampment on the outskirts of the

Herta Thiele and Ernst Busch. (*Kuhle Wampe*)

Kuhle Wampe.

capital. When their daughter Anni becomes pregnant, her fiancé Fritz, a chauffeur, promises to marry her, but they quarrel and Anni goes to Berlin where she has an abortion. Meanwhile, the son of the family commits suicide, having learned that his dole will be terminated by a new emergency decree. "One less unemployed," a woman on the street cynically comments. Anni and Fritz are reconciled during a communist sporting event, symbolic of the new, revolutionary-minded generation. The film concludes with youths singing "Forward, never relax . . . don't be resigned, but determine to alter and better the world."

Some communist critics expressed reservations concerning the "coldness" of Brecht's approach to the subject, but especially irksome was the contrast between the older workers and the younger proletarians. Völker notes that "The argument underlying this contrast was really aimed at the languid acceptance of the 'jungle' by certain classes of workers, at the strange effect ownership has on the poor, who give up all thought of revolution the moment they come into possession of an allotment garden or a small pension."

Rarely screened in retrospectives of the German film, *Kuhle Wampe* is a fascinating document of German life on the eve of Hitler's dictatorship. Of its many beautiful songs, "The Song of the Homeless" was perhaps the most prophetic: "Think hard, but strain every nerve;/For things like these cannot go on forever."

Der Rebell

THE REBEL

1932

CREDITS:

Production: Deutsche Universal-Film AG. *Director:* Luis Trenker and Kurt Bernhardt. *Screenplay:* Robert A. Stemmle and Walter Schmidt-Kunz. Based on a manuscript by Luis Trenker. *Cinematography:* Sepp Allgeier, Albert Benitz, Willy Goldberger and Reimar Kuntze. *Music:* Giuseppe Becce. *Released:* December 22, 1932 (Stuttgart) and January 17, 1933 (Berlin). *Length:* 2542 meters.

CAST:

Luis Trenker, Luise Ullrich, Victor Varconi, Fritz Kampers, Olga Engl, Erika Dannhoff, Ludwig Stoessel, Reinhold Bernt, Albert Schultes, Arthur Grosse, Amanda Lindner, Otto Kronburger, Emmerich Albert,

Hans Jamnig, Luis Gerold, Hugo Lehner, Inge Konradi, Panzl.

Luis Trenker, like Leni Riefenstahl, had also served an apprenticeship with the mountaineer and film director Dr. Arnold Fanck. And like Riefenstahl, with whom he had co-starred in *Der Berg des Schicksals (The Mountain of Density)*, Trenker was to separate himself from Fanck and the Freiburg school to direct his own films. *Berge in Flammen (The Doomed Battalion)*, 1931, based on an episode from World War I, marked the beginning of a directorial career that would span four decades.

For his next film, *Der Rebell (The Rebel)*, Trenker chose an incident from the patriotic history of the Tirol: the revolt of Tirolean peasants against the Napoleonic Army of occupation.

When Trenker had first broached the subject to Carl Laemmle, the president of Universal Pictures, during a visit to Los Angeles in the spring of 1932, Laemmle had replied, "Oh, stop it! Who in the world would be interested in the Tirolean struggle for freedom in 1809—no one in the United States even knows where the Tirol is located." But Trenker convinced Laemmle that his film, produced in German and English versions, would have interest for everyone. Upon his return to Europe in June, Trenker started filming at Malojapass near St. Moritz and Zuoz, working from a screenplay which he had written in collaboration with Robert Stemmle and Kurt Bernhardt. Trenker envisioned *Der Rebell* as a freedom film that would have a universal meaning, transcending time and place. But at the same time he "wanted to recreate the Tirol of 1809 as a warning and example . . . pointing to Germany's fate after the Versailles *Diktat* of 1919."

In addition to directing, Trenker took the role of leading character, Severin Anderian, a Tirolean medical student who returns to his native mountain village only to discover that his mother and sister have been murdered by the French invaders and the village burned. He retaliates by killing two French officers and flees to the mountains where he organizes a resistance.

Anderian is loved by the daughter of a Bavarian magistrate who brings him information about the French plans. Disguised as a Bavarian officer, the student-revolutionist attends a ball given by the French at Innsbruck. Having learned that the French are sending reinforcements, Anderian directs the guerrillas to prepare an ambush. As the French troops pass along the road below, the Tirolese let loose masses of rocks and tree trunks which strike their targets with deadly precision. Anderian and two comrades are captured and shot. In a visionary concluding sequence the ghostly figures of

the three men rise from their prostrate bodies and, valiantly singing a patriotic song, march at the head of the peasant forces, ascending along the rim of a distant cloud, until finally, as the song swells to its conclusion, they disappear into the skies.

Trenker employed most of the crew who had worked on *Berge in Flammen*, assigning the principal photography to Albert Benitz and Sepp Allgeier, two of Dr. Fanck's finest cameramen, who were assisted by Willy Goldberger and Reimar Kuntze. Trenker engaged Luise Ullrich for the feminine lead in the German version while Vilma Banky played her counterpart in the English version. The most exciting scenes were photographed near Finstermünz between the little Tirolean villages of Pfunds and Nauders. The villagers of Pfunds were attired in French and Bavarian uniforms to play the enemy, while the people of Nauders were cast as the rebellious peasants.

The climactic moment of *Der Rebell* called for an avalanche of logs and boulders which must appear to descend with devastating force on the enemy columns as they advance through the valley of Finstermünz. According to Trenker, "Trees were felled and loads of heavy boulders were piled up and secured with ropes so that a few blows of an ax would suffice to set the avalanche in motion against the enemy battalions as they marched through, just as the Tirolean peasants had done in 1809." Three cameramen were placed in strategic locations while several hand-held cameras photographed the scene from other angles. Trenker's intention was to create "a total impression of the upheaval: people, rock walls, the rolling avalanches and the roaring waters in all its savage fury. Heaven and earth were called upon to participate."

A series of three rifle shots signalled the commencement of the action and within moments the mountain slope became a scene of tumult and devastation as the debris swept down the face of the mountain. After the dust had settled, Trenker discovered to his great relief that no one had been seriously injured. The director and cast then traveled to Schloss Kufstein where the final scenes were shot. Interiors were photographed in the studio at Tempelhof.

Der Rebell must be counted one of Trenker's finest works in the genre of the *Bergfilm*. "Action and physical movement, troops defiling down long winding roads, midnight alarums in sleepy mountain towns, the thrill of the manhunt along broken ridges and up past the snow line, the excitement of bodies tumbling into space or rolling over and over down rocky slopes—these are the materials in which it deals," *The New York Times* wrote at the time of its American release in July, 1933.

Der Rebell premiered at the UFA-Palast am Zoo

Luis Trenker. *(Der Rebell)*

Luis Trenker as the Tirolian nationalist Anderian. *(Der Rebell)*

Trenker directing a scene from *Der Rebell*.

Luis Trenker. *(Der Rebell)*

Luis Trenker. *(Der Rebell)*.

before an audience of 2,000 on January 17, 1933, fourteen days before Hitler's assumption to power. Seated in his loge, Trenker detected "a tension in the air the like of which I had not experienced at any previous performance of my films." His apprehension was confirmed during the showing of the film: "The public became wilder with each new stone avalanche, clapping and stomping without inhibitions. I sat rigidly and helplessly next to [Paul] Kohner and could not understand, and yet I understood." The filmmaker, while admittedly patriotic, claimed to have "neither expected nor intended this kind of effect." Seated in the darkness of the UFA-Palast, Trenker suddenly "recognized how clearly Hitler had fanaticized the masses."

Goebbels and Hitler saw the film on January 18, 1933, a day after its Berlin premiere. Hitler was enthusiastic in his praise of *Der Rebell*. When Trenker visited Berchtesgaden in the summer of 1933, the Führer told him that he had seen the film four times "and each time with new enthusiasm." The future Minister of Propaganda described it as "a first-class production of an artistic film. Thus I could imagine the film of the future, revolutionary in character, with grand mass-scenes, composed with enormous vital energy." He noted that the audience was "deeply moved" by "one scene in which a gigantic crucifix is carried out of a small church by the revolutionaries. . . . Here you really see what can be done with the film as an artistic medium when it is really understood. We are all much impressed." And in

his celebrated *Kaiserhof* speech to the German *Filmwelt* in May, 1933, Goebbels praised *Der Rebell* for its artistic rendering of the national epic.

Shortly after the Nazi seizure of power, Trenker was invited to the Propaganda Ministry. After Goebbels had expressed his appreciation of *Der Rebell*, Trenker boldly advised the minister that he should not interfere with Deutsche-Universal, nor should he restrict film artists for racial reasons. Goebbels replied, "Many things will change. Everything will have to change." Change was to occur more rapidly than Trenker imagined. Shortly after Trenker's conversation with Goebbels, Joseph Herzberg wrote an objective account of the interview in *Filmkurier*, an indiscretion which resulted in the journalist's dismissal.

While Goebbels and Hitler admired *Der Rebell* for its nationalistic sentiments, one must be cautious to infer, as did Siegfried Kracauer, that it is "a thinly masked pro-Nazi film." Trenker had no intention of promoting Nazi ideology, the film having been undertaken in 1932 when Hitler's future was still in doubt. As previously noted, the cost of its production had been borne by Deutsche-Universal, the German subsidiary of Universal Pictures, a predominantly Jewish-directed firm. Kurt Bernhardt (Curtis Bernhardt), a prominent German-Jew, had been a close collaborator on the screenplay and direction. It never occurred to Bernhardt or Trenker that *Der Rebell*, conceived as a "freedom film," would appeal to the Nazis.

Luise Ullrich and Luis Trenker. *(Der Rebell)*

Luis Trenker. *(Der Rebell)*

Luis Trenker (center).
(Der Rebell)

137

Film in the Third Reich

1933-1938

Hitler's assumption to power on January 30, 1933, would have a profound effect on the course of the German film. On March 11 Hitler named Dr. Joseph Goebbels *Reichminister für Volksaufklärung und Propaganda* (Minister for Public Enlightenment and Propaganda), establishing his offices in the palace of the former Prince Leopold in the Wilhelmplatz exactly opposite the Reich Chancellory. To centralize his authority, Goebbels established the *Reichskulturkammer* (State Chambers of Culture) for art, music, theater, authorship, press, radio and film, with the propaganda minister serving as president. The *Filmkammer* was established in July and on September 22 became an official section of the *Kulturkammer*.

Emil Lohkamp in the title role of *Hans Westmar*, directed by Franz Wenzler, 1933.

Rudolf Forester in *Morgenrot* (Dawn), directed by Gustav Ucicky, 1933.

(*Opposite page*) Storm Troop Chief Victor Lutze, Hitler and Leni Riefenstahl at Nuremberg on the eve of the 1934 *Reichsparteitag*.

Paul Wegener as a communist leader and Emil Lohkamp in the title role of *Hans Westmar*, 1933.

All German citizens who participated in the production of motion pictures were required to be members of the *Kulturkammer*. Every aspect of the German industry was supervised by departments within the Chamber. A Finance section which acted as an agency for the *Filmkreditbank* (Film Credit Bank) subsidized the companies for the production of "worthy projects"; the Reich Film Dramaturge censored scripts; the Reichs Film Impresario saw to "the aesthetic and intellectual integrity of the entire production"; and the Film Evaluation Office decided whether a film was entitled to reduced taxation or no tax at all. During the next few years the *Filmkammer* extended its jurisdiction over every aspect of the German film.

Goebbels was deeply interested in the motion picture and took an active role in its development during the twelve years of the Third Reich. According to Rudolf Semler, Press Officer to the Propaganda Ministry, Goebbels once described his plan to write "a treatise on films, a standard work which would have the same importance for the film as [Friedrich] Lessing's book [*Hamburgische Dramaturgie*] has for the theater."

On March 28 Goebbels addressed members of the German film community at the Hotel Kaiserhof. Goebbels described himself as an "impassioned devotee of cinematic art" and elaborated at length on the new cultural and artistic mission of the film in the National Socialist State. "I gain the impression that all present are honestly willing to cooperate," Goebbels afterwards wrote in his diary.

But not all were persuaded by the pronouncements of the Propaganda Minister. Not long after Goebbels' speech at the Kaiserhof, Fritz Lang received a summons to appear at the Propaganda Ministry. Lang arrived at the appointed hour. After waiting in an anteroom where brown-shirted storm troopers observed him, he was ushered into the office of the Reichminister. "It was a big room with four or five big windows," Lang later recalled. "At the far end was a big desk, and Goebbels came forward dressed in the party uniform." Goebbels effused cordiality and told Lang that he and the Führer had seen *Metropolis* in a German town, and at the time had said that Lang was most suited to direct National Socialist pictures. When Goebbels offered Lang a key position in the "new" German film industry, Lang reminded the minister that he had Jewish ancestry on his mother's side. Goebbels replied that this would be overlooked in light of his service during the Great War.

Lang had no desire to assume a position in National Socialist film production. Strong-willed and independent, a firm believer in freedom, he could never bring himself to conform to the *Gleichschaltung* of the New Order. Shortly after the Goebbels interview, he left

Flüchtlinge (Refugees), directed by Gustav Ucicky, 1933.

Paul Hartmann in *Der Tunnel* (The Tunnel), directed by Kurt Bernhardt, 1933.

Olga Tschechowa, Paula Wessely and Adolf Wohlbrük in *Maskerade* (Masquerade), directed by Willi Forst, 1934.

Germany for France where he embarked on a new career, first in Paris and later in Hollywood. He never regretted this decision. In a 1945 interview, speaking in the present tense, he reflected: "I give up my fortune, my fine collection of books and paintings. I must begin over again. It is not easy. But, yes, it was good. I was *arrivé*—fat in my soul, fat around my heart. Darling, too much success . . . oh, it is not good for the man."

Lang trod the path of exile with a host of other German film notables: producers, directors, cameramen, art directors, technicians, writers and actors. During the fifteen-year life span of the Weimar Republic their craftsmanship, artistry and business acumen had

Paula Wessely and Willi Forst in *So endete eine Liebe* (End of an Affair), directed by Karl Hartl, 1934.

Entrance to a cinema advertising *Vorstadtvarieté* (Suburban Cabaret) with Luise Ullrich, 1934.

Hitler and General Werner von Blomberg attend the premiere of *Der Sieg des Glaubens* (Victory of the Faith), December, 1933.

made the German film an international success. The Golden Age of the German cinema passed into history. In the weeks, months and years that followed Hitler's accession to power, the roster of film *émigrés* swelled in numbers to include producers Erich Pommer and Seymour Nebenzal and Henry R. Sokal, followed by a host of directors: E. A. Dupont, Dr. Robert Weine, Leopold Jessner, Richard Oswald, Berthold Viertel, Robert Siodmak, Detlef Sierck (Douglas Sirk), Hans (John) Brahn, Leontine Sagan, Frank Wysbar, Carl Junghans, Joe May, Paul Czinner, Hermann Kosterlitz, William Thiele, Billy Wilder, Fred Zinnemann, Andrew Marton, Edgar G. Ulmer and Reinhold Schünzel. Of the actors who chose exile, some of the most prominent included: Albert Bassermann, Fritz Kortner, Hans H. von Twardowsky, Conrad Veidt, Oskar Homolka, Peter Lorre, Alexander Granach, Franz (Francis) Lederer, Helene Thimig, Felix Bressart and Ernst Deutsch. And to this exodus must be added the camerman Curt Courant, writers such as Walter Reisch and composers of the stature of Hanns Eisler, Friedrich Holländer, Werner Heymann and Walter Jurmann. The Berlin correspondent of *The New York Times* noted in May, 1933: "So much turbulent political water has flowed by in recent

Labor Corps (Arbeitsdienst) commemorate the dead of World War I in *Triumph of the Will*, 1935.

Hitler and his entourage at premiere of *Der Sieg des Glaubens*, December, 1933. Leni Riefenstahl and Magda Goebbels are seated on the far right.

142

Advertisement for *Das Mädchen Johanna*
(Joan of Arc), 1935.

Triumph of the Will opens with the fuselage of Hitler's
airplane as it approaches Nuremberg.

Aerial perspective of Nuremberg as the Führer's airplane
makes its descent.

Hitler saluting during the
march past in Nuremberg
from *Triumph of the Will*,
1935.

Premiere of *Triumph des Willens* (Triumph of the Will), 1935.

Leni Riefenstahl on the evening of the premiere of *Triumph of the Will*, March 30, 1935.

Dr. Hans Pfitzner, Goebbels, Lilian Harvey and Leni Riefenstahl, 1936.

Goebbels and Reich Press Chief Dr. Dietrich attend the premiere of Karl Ritter's *Urlaub auf Ehrenwort* (Furlough on Word of Honor) at the UFA-Palast am Zoo, 1937.

weeks, that a flood is about the only word to describe it. And it has washed up the German film industry very efficiently."

The exodus of such creative persons was not without significance on the development of the German film, but the loss should not be exaggerated. Many talented filmmakers, directors, cameramen, actors, writers and musicians remained, either by choice or necessity. A few were hostile, some were neutral, and others were supportive, motivated by opportunism or by a sincere but misguided belief that National Socialism represented Germany's salvation in a cultural as well as a political sense.

Directors working in the German industry after 1933 included Carl Froelich, Willi Forst, Reinhold Schünzel, Gustav Ucicky, Luis Trenker, Arthur Robison, Curt Oertel, Walter Ruttmann, Hans Steinhoff, Karl Ritter, Josef von Baky, Leni Riefenstahl, Arthur Rabenalt, Helmut Käutner, Wolfgang Liebeneiner, Carl Boese and Veit Harlan. Some of Germany's preeminent cameramen, Bruno Mondi, Friedl Behn-Grund, Carl Hoffman, Fritz Arno Wagner, Günther Rittau, Eugen Klagermann, Albert Benitz and Hans Schneeberger, also remained as did art directors Hermann Warm, Robert Herlth, Otto Hunte, Hans Sohnle and Walter Röhrig. And the industry could still draw from a reservoir of talented thespians: the triumvirate of Emil Jannings, Heinrich George and Werner Krauss would have lent distinction to any industry. Other eminent players included Willy Birgel, Ewald Balser, Willy Fritsch, Aribert Wäscher, Lil Dagover, Hans Albers, Paul Richter, Henny Porten, Zarah Leander, Gustav Diessl, Viktor de Kowa, Leo Slezak and Eugen Klopfer. Musicians as diverse as Peter Kreuder, Dr. Giuseppe Becce, Franz Grothe and Herbert Windt lent their considerable talents to the composition of film music.

Goebbels returned to the Kaiserhof in May, 1933, to address representatives of SPIO (Film Producers' Organization) and DACHO (German Actors' and Directors' Association). He sought to reassure the industry that its nervousness and uncertainty were unwarranted. Film producers who did their duty were not to be concerned about the prohibition of their films. And while the minister admitted that entertainment films were necessary, they must stay within the moral and political parameters set by the regime.

Goebbels then singled out four films for commendation: *Potemkin*, *Die Nibelungen*, *Anna Karenina* and *Der Rebell*. He described *Potemkin* as an example of cinematic propaganda; Lang's *Die Nibelungen* as "an epic film that is not of our time, and yet it is so modern, so contemporary, so topical, that even the stalwarts of the National Socialist movement were deeply moved"; the silent version of *Anne Karenina* (*Love*) with Greta Garbo as representative of the purely artistic film, and Luis Trenker's *Der Rebell* as a film that treats a nationalistic theme while achieving the highest critical standards. Adolf Engls, newly appointed commissioner of the reorganized *Reichsverband*, the German theatrical association, and Arnold Raether of the Ministry of Fine Arts spoke more bluntly at the conclusion of Goebbels' address. Engls announced that the "Friedrichstrasse crowd," a reference to Jewish film producers whose offices were located on that street, "was finished." German films must be made by Germans; only the Aryan could understand the spirit of the German *Volk*. And finally, Raether, bluntness incarnate, told the producers that their purpose was to educate the people and to propagandize.

The words of Goebbels, Engls and Raether, a studied mixture of subtlety and bombast culled from the lexicon of the intellectual and the workingman, suggest the "revolutionary" direction of Nazi film policy in its initial phase. Goebbels encouraged the production of nationalistic and patriotic films: *Blutendes Deutschland* (Bleeding Germany), a quasi-documentary on the subject of "national resurgence dedicated to the German people" which opened at the UFA-Palast am Zoo in March, replacing Lang's crime thriller, *Das Testament des Dr. Mabuse (The Testament of Dr. Mabuse)*, prohibited by the *Filmprüfstelle* "as a danger to public order and safety"; *Hitler-Junge Quex (Hitler Youth Quex)*, directed by Hans Steinhoff and by far the most successful and entertaining of the politically oriented films made in 1933; *S. A. Mann Brandt (Stormtrooper Brandt)*, a tedious polemic directed by Franz Seitz; and *Hans Westmar*, based on a biography of Horst Wessel by Hanns Heinz Ewers and directed by Dr. Franz Wenzler.

Goebbels had intended to release the film as *Horst Wessel*, but objections were raised concerning its portrayal of the "martyred" storm trooper whose biography it was thought to have denigrated. The film was reedited after a preview attended by Goering and other party notables in October. Released in December, Horst Wessel was transformed into a fictional character, Hans Westmar, with the subtitle, "A German Life Tragedy of the Year 1929."

The failure of *S.A. Mann Brandt* and *Hans Westmar* changed the attitude of Goebbels toward the motion picture as a vehicle for the dissemination of National Socialist ideas. Hitler appears to have come to similar conclusions. Shortly after assuming power, he had seen a nationalistic film at the Reich Chancellory in the company of Magda Goebbels and Nazi intimates. According to Hermann Rauschning, he later "expressed himself on the new movie [unidentified] and on nationalistic movies in general. Even the so-called experts, Hitler said, imagined that all was well as long as they chose a nationalistic and patriotic subject. He sneered at the wrong speculations on enthusiasm and patriotic fanaticism which would bring from the audiences merely negative reactions, and he developed a few basic principles as to the usage of movies as a political weapon." Unfortunately, Rauschning makes no mention of the "basic principles." But Goebbels recognized that the didactic "political film" had failed artistically and commercially. Audiences were receptive to entertainment but hostile to preachments. The political message, he reasoned, might be effectively presented in the context of the entertainment film.

The historical film was most suited to this purpose. *Das Mädchen Johanna (Joan the Girl)*, directed by Gustav Ucicky and shown at the International Film Congress in Berlin in April, 1935, presented Joan of Arc as a Hitler prototype, "a leader who saved her people from despair," and, like Hitler, "was driven forward by a deep belief that it was her duty to defend her country against a foreign enemy and to crush enemies within her nation." In like manner, *Der alte und der junge König (The Old and the Young King)*, also released in 1935, created a Führer prototype in the guise of Frederick the Great. Afterward, Goering conferred with Emil Jannings and director Hans Steinhoff and "stressed the similarity of the statesmanlike tasks which the great soldier-king

Hitler (right) in conversation with Willy Fritsch and Leni Riefenstahl, 1937.

(Frederick the Great) and he himself had undertaken, wherein lie the foundations for the artistic greatness of the Fatherland."

The Reich Film Law, enacted on February 16, 1934, established a Censorship Committee which allowed German films to be judged in six categories: (1) Particularly valuable politically and artistically; (2) Valuable politically and artistically; (3) Valuable politically; (4) Valuable artistically; (5) Culturally valuable; (6) Of educational value. In addition, the Film Law of 1934 established a strict form of censorship. A *Reichsfilmdramaturg* (Reich Film Supervisor) was designated to examine film scripts and accorded full authority to reject scripts and "to advise the film industry on the selection and adaptation of film stories." After a screenplay passed the *Reichsfilmdramaturg*, the completed film was shown to the Censorship Committee consisting of permanent members and four judges nominated by the Propaganda Minister. This body was empowered to withhold permits for films if they were "likely to endanger the vital interests of the state or public order or safety, to offend National Socialist, religious, moral and artistic feelings, to have a corrupting influence, or to prejudice German prestige or German relations with foreign countries."

The censorship provisions were extended to German versions of foreign films and, previous to the outbreak of World War II, to British and American films entering Germany. Among the American films forbidden exhibition in 1935 were: *Nana, Flying Down to Rio, The Thin Man* and *The Iron Duke*. The censorship of the French version of *Les Misérables* suggests the attitudes and decision-making procedures of the censors. On December 13, 1935, Hans Weidermann, vice-president of the

The 1938 Berlin Film Ball: Robert Stemmle, Willy Birgel and Goebbels.

Reich Film Chamber, told members of the *Reichfachtschaft Film*, the employees' group of the Reich Film Chamber, that "While we must reject the material of this film and the manner in which it is presented, let it not be denied that we know and recognize its artistic achievement. It is essential for the German artist to see such foreign art; the public on the other hand must have quiet, until it is once more healthy and strong." At this same meeting other speakers attacked *Les Misérables* on the grounds that it "portrays the criminal as innocent, as morally justified, while the state and its institutions . . .

147

are portrayed as guilty of the misfortunes of the criminal. This whole theme is carried out in a very reprehensible manner which taints every spectator. On these grounds the film had to be rejected for German exhibition."

In 1936 the regime outlawed the criticism of motion pictures. In place of criticism, Goebbels substituted description. The basic task of the writer was to describe content, although he might comment positively on the artistry of the film. "The reporting of art should not be concerned with values," Goebbels stated, "but should confine itself to description. Such reporting should give the public a chance to make its own judgments; it should stimulate it to form an opinion about artistic achievements through its own attitudes and feelings." Goebbels further decreed that reviews could not be carried in the press on the morning *after* the premiere, but in the afternoon edition at the earliest, believing that a journalist could not otherwise "collect and digest his impressions" and make a responsible judgment.

Of even greater significance was the Reich Government's decision to achieve economic control of the German film industry, a process which began surreptitiously at the end of 1936 and continued until the early war years. Through stock purchases the regime anonymously acquired UFA on March 19, 1937, with its vast studio complexes at Neubabelsberg in southwest Berlin and at Templehof south of the Berlin airport. Tobis was

Model of the Reich Film Academy at Babelsberg, 1938.

Dr. Goebbels lays the cornerstone of the Reich Film Academy, 1938.

acquired on December 1, 1937, and a new board of directors composed of many people from the *filmwelt* such as Eugen Klöpfer, Paul Hartmann, Mathias Wiemann, Karl Ritter and Carl Froelich was established. Bavaria, Terra and the Froelich Company

Dr. Leonh. Furst, Alfred Weidenmann and Dr. Hans Traub at the UFA-Lehrshau (Film Institute).

148

Dr. Goebbels and Vittorio Mussolini visit the set of
Preussische Liebegeschichte (Prussian Love Story). Willy
Fritsch (in uniform) and State Secretary Hanke, 1938.

shared a similar fate, passing from private ownership to
government control. By 1942 all the remaining studios
had become subordinate to the State. It was a decision
which Goebbels, the inveterate empire builder, did not
regret, as his diary entry for January 22, 1942, suggests:
"Movie production is flourishing almost unbelievably
despite the war. What a good idea of mine it was to have
taken possession of films on behalf of the Reich several
years ago! It would be terrible if the high profits now
being earned by the motion-picture industry were to flow
into private hands."

That the State was intent on assuming a permanent
role in the German film industry was symbolized by the
creation of the Reich Film Academy at Babelsberg in
March, 1938. A document, ceremoniously sealed in the
foundation stone, proclaimed that "On this site, after a
period of political disunity and moral decay, the art of
the German film will find its spiritual center." In his
dedication speech, Goebbels expressed the hope that the
Academy would be guided by three mottoes: that art is
more concerned with knowing than wishing; that business and technique are always subordinate to art; and
that service to the people is the highest honor and the
highest duty of art. The future academy was intended to
serve as the cultural and technical headquarters of the
German film industry, offering instruction in acting,
directing, cinematography and sound. The classically
designed Academy buildings were to be located on the
grounds of UFA's Babelsberg lot which would allow
students to observe and work in the studio while having
access to the UFA-Lehrschau, a library and museum
under the directorship of Dr. Hans Traub. For filmmakers of the future, Goebbels no doubt intended that the
Academy would serve as the sole avenue of entry into the
German industry.

Goebbels made an intense effort to cultivate good
relations with the German *filmwelt*. He accorded the
community an official recognition which it had never
known. And while some made him the butt of innu-
merable jokes, many appreciated his patronage in the
form of directorial or acting assignments, public recognition for achievement or invitations to his residence on
the *Reichkanzlerplatz*, or country estate, at Schwaen-
werden. As director Wolfgang Liebeneiner, whom
Goebbels elevated to professor in 1943, notes: "The great
change has come. The art of the film has established
itself. Just as during the Renaissance the Medici and
other prominent persons in the Italian states gave con-
tracts to artists and let them go to work with their road
already planned out for them, orders for films are given
us in Germany today. I have been in Rome and Florence and everybody will agree with me that those artists
who worked there carrying out orders for the state or for

some Maecenas or other did not produce the worst works of art. In their works they have lived until long after their own age. That is why we film people are happy today to have been given a clear and precise task, and we are proud that in fulfilling that task we have been given a free hand."

Goebbels, of course, liked to think that he belonged to this community of artists, as a diary entry for March 5, 1942, during the celebration of UFA's twenty-fifth anniversary indicates: "Late at night I went for a short visit to Professor Froelich [president of the Reich Film Chamber]. All the big shots of the UFA were assembled there. They were very happy that I sat down with them for an hour. . . ."

During his tenure as Minister of Propaganda, film balls, congresses, festivals and specially designated film weeks proliferated. Goebbels always seemed to find time from other duties to appear personally as the representative of the German film. In August, 1939, during the mounting crisis over Poland, inspired in part by his own propaganda, he attended the Venice Film Festival to be ceremoniously received by his Italian fascist counterpart, Dino Alfieri. His speeches and diaries suggest that he gained an enormous sense of power as the principal overseer and official "protector" of the German film.

Leni Riefenstahl was destined to become the most preeminent documentarist of the Third Reich. Hitler had admired Riefenstahl's *Das blaue Licht (The Blue Light)*, and after his assumption to power commissioned her to make a documentary of the September 1933, Nuremberg Party Congress. Hitler, the *Kunstler-politiker* and master propagandist, no doubt recognized that the motion picture with its myth-making capabilities might do more than report, in the manner of a *Wochenschau* (newsreel), the activities of the Party. He believed that Riefenstahl would capture the inherent romanticism and theatricality of the Nazi movement. "He wanted a film showing the Congress through a non-expert eye, selecting just what was most artistically satisfying in terms of spectacle," Riefenstahl recalled. "He wanted a film which would move, appeal to, impress an audience which was not necessarily interested in politics."

Her task was not accomplished without difficulty. As Albert Speer noted: "Nazis were by tradition antifeminist and could hardly brook this self-assured woman, the more so since she knew how to bend this men's world to her purposes. Intrigues were launched against her and slanderous stories carried to [Rudolf] Hess, in order to have her ousted." Goebbels, who was to be her perennial antagonist, was no doubt jealous of her privileged position vis-à-vis Hitler and may have expressed irritation

that his ministry had not been assigned the task of producing the Nuremberg film.

The result was *Der Sieg des Glaubens (Victory of the Faith)* which premiered on December 2, 1933, at the UFA-Palast am Zoo. Hitler's promotion of Ernst Roehm to the post of Reichminister on the same day suggests the importance of the film as a National Socialist event. *Film-Kurier* described the film as "a great beginning for a new German unity which will go forward with the cry, 'Peace, Bread and Equality.' "

The Berlin correspondent of the London *Observer* wrote that while "Leni Riefenstahl has made an excellent job of arranging her material, she has not produced a work comparable, shall we say, with Eisenstein or Pudovkin." Hitler was sufficiently impressed, however, to commission Riefenstahl to direct a second and far more important documentary, *Triumph des Willens (Triumph of the Will)*, a cinematic record of the ceremonious 1934 Nuremberg *Reichsparteitag*. Riefenstahl has steadfastly defended the film as a documentary, an artistic reportage of events seen and heard at the *Reichsparteitag*, and has disclaimed any propagandistic intent. Critics such as Erwin Leiser view *Triumph of the Will* in a very different light and have waged a largely successful campaign against the film and its creator. After nearly fifty years, it remains an essential work for those who seek to understand the psychology of Hitlerism.

Triumph of the Will was accorded a lavish premiere at the UFA-Palast am Zoo on the evening of March 30, 1935. Five days earlier the British Foreign Secretary, Sir John Simon, and Anthony Eden, Lord Privy Seal, had conferred with Hitler in Berlin. Simon and Eden reportedly declined Hitler's invitation to see the film. The Berlin correspondent of the London *Observer* regretted this decision, believing that the statesmen "would have received from the film document convincing proof that the passionate, dynamic explosive energy displayed by Chancellor Hitler this week in the diplomatic talks is the concentrated personal expression of a national energy, equally passionate and dynamic." *Triumph of the Will* remained the definitive, celluloid statement on the subject of the Nürnberg *Reichsparteitag*. Although special newsreels *(Wochenschauen)* documented succeeding rallies, the Party never again produced a rally film of equivalent scope.

Riefenstahl completed her political trilogy with *Tag der Freiheit, unsere Wehrmacht, 1935 (Day of Freedom, Our Army, 1935)*, a documentary short produced at the request of the German Army which had been practically excluded from *Triumph of the Will. Tag der Freiheit* is stylistically akin to her other films with mythic images of earth and sky, fire and water, but its diagonal compositions of artillery pieces being cranked into readiness and

Goebbels' "Liduschka," Lida Baarova.

Goebbels' "Liduschka," Lida Baarova.

Leni Riefenstahl receives Hitler's congratulations at the premiere of *Olympia*, April 20, 1938.

Peter Ostermayr (second from left), Paul Richter (back to camera) and Eva Braun during the production of *Der laufende Berg*, directed by Hans Deppe, 1941.

the vitality of the montage suggest the technique of the Soviet school and Eisenstein's *Potemkin*.

By the time *Tag der Freiheit* was released in December, 1935, Riefenstahl was already occupied with preparations for filming the 1936 Summer Olympiad in Berlin. Honed from 400,000 meters (1,300,000 feet) of film with an elaborate prologue by Willy Zielke, Riefen-

Hitler had a special fondness for Olga Tschechowa, the niece of Chekhov, who appeared in various productions including *Rote Orchideen* (Red Orchids), directed by Nunzio Malasomma, 1938.

stahl's *Olympia* did not receive its premiere until the spring of 1938. Her critics doubted that the public would be interested in seeing an Olympic games film two years after the event which it portrayed, but Riefenstahl was confident that her *Olympia* would transcend time and place, a judgment which has in large measure been vindicated, although its images of antiquity and heroic athletes reflect a National Socialist *geist*.

Olympia was Riefenstahl's last significant documentary. Afterwards she planned a cinematic version of *Penthesilea* from the play by Heinrich von Kleist. "All the artistic tasks which I had had to solve thus far I contemplated as steps for *Penthesilea*," she wrote in 1939. "Ever since *The Blue Light* I had dreamed of filming Klesit's tragedy, partly as an actress—it was a part I desperately wanted to play—but mainly as a director." Her pre-production notes composed in 1939 suggest a stylized film of incomparable grandeur and potentially of great cost. Plans to produce *Penthesilea* were cancelled following the outbreak of World War II. *Tiefland*, based on the opera by Eugen d'Albert, promised to be a more economical work. Begun in the latter part of 1939, it proved to be her final effort as a director and actress. Tainted by her association with Hitler and the National Socialist regime, Leni Riefenstahl was unable to reestablish her position in the German film after 1945.

Between 1933 and 1935 Goebbels and his Ministry of Propaganda attempted to purge the German film industry of *Volksfremde*, non-Aryan elements. On October 1, 1935, one month after the promulgation of the infamous Nuremberg Racial Laws, the industry was declared to be officially *judenrein*, "cleansed of Jews." In December, Jewish movie and theater owners were ordered to liquidate their assets. While *die juden frage*, the Jewish question, remained a basic tenet of Nazi ideology and propaganda, feature films were surprisingly free of anti-Semitic propaganda in the years between 1933 and 1939. In July, 1935, however, Goebbels sanctioned the release of a 1933 Swedish comedy, *Petterson and Bendel*, which depicted "the rise of Bendel, a penniless East European Jew who through a series of swindles becomes a power in business. Among those whose trust he betrays is the young, frank, honest Nordic Swede Petterson."

The showing of *Petterson and Bendel* triggered the most violent outbreak of anti-Semitic rioting in Berlin since Hitler's accession to power. The disturbance stemmed from a report in the *Völkischer Beobachter* that Jewish patrons had booed the film. "Such insolence is not to be endured," the report concluded. On Monday evening, July 15, storm troopers dressed in civilian clothes proceeded to bully and assault Semitic-appearing patrons as they left the theater and within a short while the melee spread to the open-air cafés along the Kurfeur-

stendamm. "Far into the night the crowd grew," *The New York Times* reported. "The Kurfeurstendamm district, in which many Jews live, continued to echo the anti-Semitic war cry, 'destruction to the Jews.' " The *Zwoelf Uhr Blatt* expressed editorially the official view that the Jews "feel themselves again at home and assume the right to reject by whistling and whispering mocking remarks in a German photoplay house a film that had been declared 'valuable for the interests of the state.' "

The possibility that storm troopers had instigated the riot by hissing was suggested by Varian Fry, editor of *The Living Age*, who witnessed the events on the Kurfuerstendamm and afterwards conferred with Dr. Ernst Hanfstaengl who had told him, unofficially, that this was in fact the case. Hanfstaengl later denied that he had made this statement which was reported in the *Times* shortly after Varian's return to the United States. The extent of official involvement is conjectural, but the disturbances occasioned by the showing of *Petterson and Bendel*, coupled with anti-Jewish policies, can be seen in retrospect as a portent of the darkness to come.

The assassination of the German attaché Ernst von Rath in Paris by a young Polish Jew and the ensuing pogrom, *Kristalnacht*, of November 9-10, 1938, marked a watershed in the relations between the Reich government and its Jewish population. Violence to Jews and the destruction of Jewish religious and private property, carried out chiefly by the S.A., characterized the days of wrath following the death of von Rath.

The events of *Kristalnacht* no doubt confirmed Warner Bros. in its decision to produce the first anti-Nazi feature film, *Confessions of a Nazi Spy*, based on investigations of the F.B.I. concerning German espionage in the United States. Directed by Anatole Litvak in a semi-documentary, *March of Time* style, "*Confessions of a Nazi Spy* was made in an atmosphere close to that which it creates in the audience," Adam Garbicz and Jacek Klinowski note in *Cinema: The Magic Vehicle*, with "official and semi-official demands and protests from the Nazi government, threats to U.S. exports and the relatives of the participants in the film living in Germany." Hitler alluded to the case on January 30, 1939, in his anniversary address to the Reichstag. "Announcements by American film companies that they intend to produce anti-Nazi—that is, anti-German—films, can but induce us to produce anti-Semitic films in Germany," the Führer warned. "Here, too, our opponents should not permit themselves any delusions as to the effectiveness of what we can do. There will be very many states and peoples who will show great understanding for supplementary instruction of this kind on such an important subject."

In accordance with this policy, *Robert und Bertran*

was released in July, 1939. *Die Rothschild Artien von Waterloo (The Rothschilds' Shares in Waterloo)*, *Jud Süss (Jew Suss)*, *Der ewige Jude (The Eternal Jew)* followed in 1940, the year of Hitler's spectacular military victories. And with characteristic arrogance, the Nazis intensified their anti-Semitic campaign at home and abroad. *Robert und Bertran*, directed by Hans Heinz Zerlett, contained broad caricatures set against an eighteenth century background. Erich Waschneck's *Die Rothschild Artien von Waterloo* served the cause of anti-Semitism and Anglophobia through its misrepresentation of the Rothschilds' financial dealings in the aftermath of the Battle of Waterloo.

Jud Süss was derived in part from the novel by Lion Feuchtwanger and historical incidents concerning Süss Oppenheimer, advisor to Duke Karl Alexander of Württemberg. Directed by Veit Harlan on orders from Goebbels, it was the most prestigious of the group. Werner Krauss, Germany's most renowned actor, was recruited for the role of Rabbi Loew, while Ferdinand Marian was cast as the ill-fated Süss Oppenheimer of Frankfurt. Kristina Söderbaum, Harlan's Swedish wife, took the role of Dorothea Sturm, a fictional heroine whom Süss abducts and rapes. Before his death in 1964, Harlan claimed that he endeavored to present a more balanced view of Süss Oppenheimer, but that Goebbels objected.

In his original treatment, Harlan had Süss, incarcerated in an iron cage, curse his judges: "No sleep shall soothe your eyes; wicked neighbors shall destroy your peace. May your first-born son bring you shame, may your memory be cursed, and may your cities be destroyed by fire from heaven. . . ." But Goebbels vetoed this finale and instructed Harlan that Oppenheimer must be humbled rather than martyred. After extensive reediting to eliminate ambiguities, *Jud Süss* was premiered in September, 1940, and received a wide distribution in Germany, the occupied East and France. The fact that Heinrich Himmler required his S.S. to view the film suggests that it must be accorded a role, however small, in the lamentable history of Jewish persecution.

Der ewige Jude (The Eternal Jew), a "documentary" produced under the supervision of the Reich Film Intendant, Dr. Fritz Hippler, and released in November, 1940, was the most inflammatory of the anti-Semitic films. Pathetic scenes of Jews in the impoverished Lodz ghetto, images of the ritual slaughter of cattle, an excerpt from the American version of *The House of Rothschild* and the confession of the child murderer (Peter Lorre) from Lang's *M* were juxtaposed to create a gross misrepresentation of Jewish life and culture. In an excerpt of Hitler before the Reichstag on January 30, 1939, audiences once again listened to the Führer's dire prediction: "Today I will once more be a prophet. If the interna-

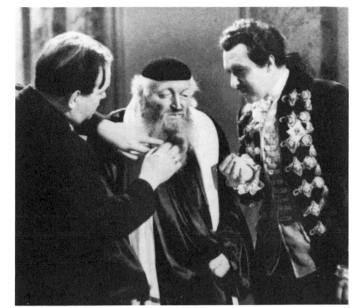

Veit Harlan, Werner Krauss and Ferdinand Marian during the production of *Jud Süss* (The Jew Süss), 1940.

Advertisement for *Der ewige Jude* (The Eternal Jew), created under the supervision of Dr. Fritz Hippler, 1940.

tional Jewish financiers in and outside of Europe should succeed in plunging the nations once more into a world war, then the result will not be the bolshevization of the earth, and thus the victory of Jewry, but the annihilation of the Jewish race in Europe!" Lacking in subtlety or artistic merit, *Der ewige Jude* appealed to the basest instincts.

As night descended on German Jewry during the winter of 1940-1941, Joachim Gottschalk, one of Germany's most esteemed film players, became the tragic victim of Nazi Aryanization policies. Gottschalk was married to a German Jew who had borne him a child. Despite the official pressure, Gottschalk refused to divorce her. Goebbels tolerated their "mixed marriage" until 1941 when the order was issued for the deportation of Jews to the East. Gottschalk would not be able to join her and separation was unthinkable. With her arrest imminent, the Gottschalks, together with their child, committed suicide. In 1947 director Kurt Maetzig told their story in a poignant film, *Ehe im Schatten (Marriage in the Shadows)*.

Needless to say, the Aryanization policies were not consistently enforced with respect to the *filmwelt*. When on orders from Goebbels the Viennese stage and film actor Hans Moser was prohibited from further employment because of the non-Aryan ancestry of his wife, Heinrich Hoffmann, Hitler's photographer, intervened on his behalf. "The opportunity occurred after the showing of one of Moser's films in the Chancellory, with which Hitler was obviously delighted," Hoffmann remembered. " ' Moser is very popular with the public,' I said. 'The people won't like it at all if he's forbidden to play simply on account of his wife. Why, you yourself always enjoy his films!' I had struck while the iron was hot; Hitler was still in good spirits after the film, and he agreed cordially with me; and the ban on Moser was forthwith removed."

Mazurka

1935

CREDITS:

Production: Cine-Allianz-Tonfilmprod. GmbH. Distributed by Rota-Filmverleih AG (Tobis-Konzern). *Director:* Willi Forst. *Screenplay:* Hans Rameau. *Cinematography:* Konstantin Irmen-Tschet. *Music;* Peter Kreuder. *Released:* November 14, 1935. *Length:* 2602 meters.

CAST:

Pola Negri, Albrecht Schoenhals, Ingeborg Theek, Faanziska Kinz, Paul Hartmann, Inge List, Friedrich Kayssler, Edwin Jürgensen, Hans Hermann Schaufuss, Ernst Karchow, Erich Dunskus, Ruth Eweler, Margarete Schön, Margot Erbst, Aribert Grimmer.

Pola Negri, who had achieved international stardom in the silent film, suffered a severe setback after the failure of her first talking film, *A Woman Commands*, released in 1931. Still very beautiful and undeniably talented, she remained in the United States, hopeful that Hollywood would give her another opportunity to act in sound films. But after two years of waiting, she could only conclude that the Hollywood film establishment was no longer interested in the woman who had electrified audiences in *Madame DuBarry (Passion)*, *Forbidden Paradise*, *Hotel Imperial* and *Three Sinners*.

Redemption came in the person of Carl Laemmle who offered her the principal role in *Mazurka*, from a screenplay by Hans Rameau, to be produced in Berlin by Universal's German affiliate and directed by Willi Forst. Negri was at first hesitant. The prospect of returning to Europe did not appeal to her, but after reading Rameau's script, Negri was convinced that she "had to play the leading role, which offered not only a strong dramatic potential but a natural opportunity for interpolated song." As she later remembered, "The part ranged through a montage of emotions from youthful naîveté to physical passion to despair to mother love." And no less intriguing was the opportunity it would afford her "to depict a woman aging from early marriage through the time when she had a grown daughter."

In *Mazurka* Rameau reworked the venerable theme of "Madame X" in which the marriage of an opera singer is ruined by an adulterous affair. Fifteen years elapse, but the woman's redemption is made possible when her daughter, who has never known her, is faced with a similar situation with the same man. To protect her daughter, she shoots the man but refuses to speak at the trial. Only when the public and witnesses, among them her daughter, are excluded from the proceedings, does she divulge her motives: she remained silent to protect her daughter from finding out that she is her mother. Moved by her courage, the court decrees the minimum punishment with the hope of a complete pardon at a later date.

Pola Negri arrived in Bremerhaven where she was met by Willi Forst who accompanied her by train to Berlin. During the train journey to Berlin, Forst described the production, "giving all his revolutionary ideas on flashback techniques to be employed." Negri forgot her ap-

Albrecht Schoenhals and Ingeborg Theek. *(Mazurka)*

Director Willi Först. *(Mazurka)*

Albrecht Schoenhals and Pola Negri. *(Mazurka)*

Pola Negri. *(Mazurka)*

Ingeborg Theek. (*Mazurka*)

Pola Negri. (*Mazurka*)

prehensions as she listened to Forst's "innovational concepts." An earlier reading of the manuscript had confirmed her opinion that "the picture could be a powerful psychological drama with a wonderful part for me," but after "hearing Willi expound on it, I knew that it was going to be far more than that, and all of my professional regrets over leaving Hollywood completely evaporated."

Mazurka was to be produced at Tempelhof where Negri had made *Passion*, *Carmen* and many of her other early successes. "I even had my old dressing room," she recounted, and "after a few days, it was hard to believe that I had ever been away."

But Negri had been away from Germany longer than she realized. In January, 1935, the production was abruptly cancelled. The Ministry of Propaganda informed her that she would not be able to act in Germany. When Goebbels received her at the Wilhelmplatz on the 26th, he raised the question of her ethnicity, insisting that she had a Jewish heritage on her father's side. She was further accused of having worked against Germany during the Silesian plebiscite and of having otherwise shown hostility toward the Reich. Goebbels informed her further that his Ministry had received numerous anonymous letters accusing her of anti-German activities abroad.

The actress emphatically denied these charges and requested the intervention of the Polish ambassador, Josef Lipski, who promised to do all he could to resolve

the matter. Ancestral records were researched in Poland and Czechoslovakia, but it appears to have been the intervention of Lipski at the highest echelons of Nazi power that secured a reversal of the minister's order. A few days later she was officially certified a "Polish Aryan." On January 31, 1935, the Ministry of Propaganda announced that "Grave accusations were leveled recently against the actress Pola Negri. On orders of the Führer and the Reich Chancellor these accusations have been investigated, and it has been ascertained that no proof in support of them could be produced. There is, therefore, no reason to oppose Negri's artistic activity in Germany, all the more so because the additional assertion that she is of Jewish descent has been proved untrue. She is Polish and therefore Aryan."

Pola Negri would have preferred to leave Germany but her studio contract obligated her to complete the production which was delayed still further by the long illness of Ingeborg Theek, a young actress of Garboesque beauty who took the role of Negri's daughter. But the talented and resourceful Forst guided the picture to a successful completion by the summer. "This man can create atmosphere with the subtlest of means," observed a German critic: "the alcoholic mood of the small tavern, the lovely photography of a child's crib, the weighty mercilessness of a jury courtroom, the small gestures of people—the many enchanting details. All this is proof of a great director."

After the premiere in November, 1935, Pola Negri

156

Ingeborg Theek. *(Mazurka)*

entrained for the south of France to visit her mother, confident that *Mazurka* would mark her return to the American screen. German critics wrote approvingly of her performance. Describing her emotional performance in the courtoom sequence, the *8-Uhr-Abendblatt* described Negri's "mastery of expression when her rigid face dissolves into liberation from guilt atoned. As always, her face changes abruptly and impressively. She conveys entire ranges of psychological development in one quiver of the mouth: the ravaged face of the cabaret dancer, the distraught countenance of the pale defendant and the relieved expression of the repentent sinner. She adapts to the more discreet medium of film with the discipline of the great actress, surmounting even her linguistic insecurity with her powerful facial expression."

The *Berliner Volks-Zeitung* wrote that "her gestures are composed, poignant; one quiver of the corner of her mouth reveals an inner world, one glance runs the entire gamut from scepticism to understanding. To this add her voice, colored by a foreign accent. Pola Negri has indeed returned." *Variety*'s Berlin correspondent was equally enthusiastic in its description of Pola Negri's "victorious re-entry" into films, noting that "sound only rounds out her success" while "her Polish accent augments her exotic quality and, speaking or singing, she uses her mature voice with infinite variance." And when the film reached London in February, 1937, the *Times* wrote that "On the whole, with the aid of excellent acting and carefully constructed settings—the dresses of some 20

years ago are accurately reproduced—the film avoids monotony and obvious crudity. . . ." But the distribution of *Mazurka* in the United States was precluded by the decision of Warner Brothers to acquire the rights for an American version with Kay Francis. In the wake of this bitter disappointment, Pola Negri saw no alternative but to continue in German films, and when UFA offered her a generous contract and the feminine lead in *Moscow-Shanghai* under the direction of Paul Wegener, she decided to remain.

While Goebbels remained cool to Negri, Hitler enjoyed her performance in *Mazurka*, as did Hermann Goering whom she met at a reception in the Polish embassy. He congratulated her on the success of *Mazurka* and, according to her recollections, "brought up the subject of one of the first films that I had ever made. Almost twenty years had passed, and I had almost completely forgotten this Polish two-reeler. 'I recall you so vividly in *The Yellow Pass*,' he said suavely. 'You were little more than a child—but what a convincing performance—almost as if you were acting out your own experiences.'" Negri let him continue, uncertain of where he was leading. "'Don't you remember? You played a young Jewish student. I shall never forget the effect of that film on me. It was so moving.'" The Marshall "slithered over the words" and she "wondered what was really going on in the sinister mind so artfully concealed behind his jovial cherubic face. Watching for storm signals and fearful that I might say too much on the wrong subject, Ambassador Lipski interrupted and whisked me away."

Fährmann Maria

FERRYBOAT PILOT MARIA

1936

CREDITS:

Production: Pallas-Film GmbH. Released by Terra-Filmverleih GmbH. *Director:* Frank Wysbar. *Screenplay:* Hans Jurgen Nierentz and Frank Wysbar. *Cinematography:* Franz Weihmayr. *Music:* Herbert Windt. *Released:* January 7, 1936 (Hildesheim) and February 7, 1936 (Berlin). *Length:* 2285 meters.

CAST:

Sybille Schmitz, Aribert Mog, Peter Voss, Carl de Vogt, Karl Platen, Eduard Wenck, Gerhard Bienert.

Born in Tilsit in 1899, Frank Wysbar directed his first film in 1932, *Im Banne des Eulenspiegels*, having acquired technical training from his association with directors Carl Boese and Carl Froelich. Wysbar's most distinguished work before the celebrated *Fährmann Maria (Ferryboat Pilot Maria)* was *Anna und Elisabeth (Anna and Elizabeth)*, released in 1934, a film which National Socialist critics, in light of the official *gleichshaltung*, viewed with misgivings. Oskar Kalbus, for example, accused Wysbar of "indulging in liberalism and morbidity" and scolded the director for having failed to "liberate the characters from the liberal and spiritual decadence." *Fährmann Maria*, his greatest work, was no less controversial for its use of symbolism and mysticism.

"Frank Wysbar was interested in the psychological, and his directorial style reflected the atmosphere and rhythm of the ballad," historian Jerzy Toeplitz recently wrote in *Geschichte des films*. "He intentionally smoothed out contours which were too sharp and realistic and endowed his stories with the coloring of a legend, a dream or a poetical fiction."

Based on a script which Wysbar co-wrote with Hans Jürgen Nierentz, *Fährmann Maria* is set in a small village surrounded by marshes. The ferryboat, operated by an old pilot, is the only connection between the village and the outside world. One night a man dressed in black, Death, summons the old man from the opposite bank. No one wants to assume the job of the

Sybille Schmitz and Aribert Mog. (*Fährmann Maria*)

deceased pilot, but one day a humble young woman appears in the village and accepts the job.

Shortly after beginning her job, Maria hears a cry for help deep in the marshes. She finds and shelters a man from pursuing horsemen. The riders, clad in black and riding white steeds, call the ferry but eventually give up when Maria refuses to answer their call. Having regained his health under Maria's care, the stranger tells her that he must leave in order to fight the enemy which threatens his country. He promises to return and entreats her to wait for him.

But Death is not far away and during a village dance he once again makes his appearance, summoning the pilot to convey him across the marsh. While the stranger passes a feverish sleep in the hut, Maria leads Death to the dance in an effort to hide the whereabouts of her beloved. She escapes Death's clutches, taking refuge in the church, but the black figure will not be deterred. Resolved to die in the place of her beloved, Maria leads Death deeper into the marshes, following an uncertain path. Death loses his footing and sinks into the swamp. Maria crosses to dry land having proved that sacrificing love can conquer death and darkness. She returns to the hut and the embrace of her beloved. Together, they cross to the opposite shore for the last time and journey to the stranger's homeland which now belongs to both of them.

The release of *Fährmann Maria* in February, 1936, was attended by some controversy. "It is astonishing that this film with its blending of dream and reality and with its unknown persecutors, arriving by night in black uniforms, should have been spared the censorship and the thunderous attack of the official press," Toeplitz writes. "Perhaps the co-author of the script, Hans Jurgen Nierentz, the future *Reichsfilmdramaturg* and a *persona grata* in the National Socialist Party, provided a shield." Adverse comments, however, appeared in the wake of its release. Writing in the periodical *Volk und Rasse (People and Race)*, a certain Dr. Lemme believed that the film did not meet "the standards of racial hygiene." Lemme found Maria, a brunette, played by Sybille Schmitz, particularly objectionable, arriving in the village dressed in "rags and tatters." Because the character's national and ethnic origins were unclear, Lemme doubted that her Germanic lover, played by Aribert Mog, could accept her statement, "I, too, now have a homeland because I love you." According to Lemme, the film erroneously implied that one might acquire nationality through love rather than race.

But not all German reviewers were so short-sighted and unappreciative. The widely read *Berliner Volks-Zeitung* wrote that cinematographer Franz Weihmayr had "created wonderful chiaroscuro pictures pregnant with atmosphere. The film is a triumph of photography which is so artistic and so powerful that the actors appear like phantoms." The reviewer believed that the principal weakness of *Fährmann Maria* concerned the use of sound. While the reviewer praised Wysbar's minimalist approach in the use of sound, he believed that at times "words and sound effects receive excessive emphasis which places a burden on the players linguistically." He reflected further that "reality and logic tended to interfere with the unreal action," noting that "when Maria storms into the tower and pulls the bell-cord in despair, the clapper resounds at first, but soon the bell becomes silent (a beautiful episode for a sound film). But afterwards the Stranger says, logically, but superfluously, 'Tonight no bells are ringing in the village.' Perhaps the 'Stranger,' namely Death, did not 'really' drown in the swamp." In spite of these objections, the *Berliner Volks-Zeitung* concluded that Wysbar had created a work of artistic distinction, and indeed it was and so remains. *FilmKurier* was no less enthusiastic, believing that this "pioneering work will be of particular interest to those Berliners who are interested in film. It is a courageous effort which certainly merits this interest."

At the close of the decade Frank Wysbar quietly emigrated to the United States. In the early 1950s he directed over 300 films for television but never established himself as a major force in the Hollywood industry. Wysbar returned to Europe in 1956, directing in Germany and Italy, and died in Mainz in 1967.

Der zerbrochne Krug

THE BROKEN JUG

1937

CREDITS:

Production: Tobis-Magna-Filmproduktion GmbH. *Director:* Gustav Ucicky. *Screenplay:* Thea von Harbou. Based on the play by Heinrich von Kleist. *Cinematography:* Fritz Arno Wagner. *Music:* Wolfgang Zeller. *Released:* October 19, 1937. *Length:* 2348 meters.

CAST:

Emil Jannings, Angela Salloker, Paul Dahlke, Elisabeth Flickenschildt, Friedrich Kayssler, Max Gülstorff, Lina Carstens, Bruno Hübner, Walter Werner, Erich Dunskus, Gisela von Collande, Lotte Rausch.

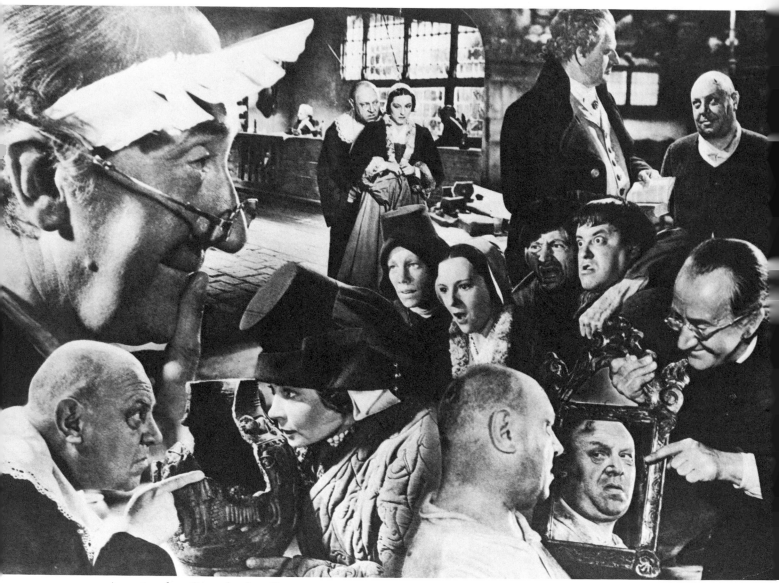

A montage from *Der zerbrochene Krug.*

Der zerbrochene Krug (The Broken Jug) was brought to the screen in 1937, adapted by Thea von Harbou, the former wife of Fritz Lang, from the play by Heinrich von Kleist. Gustav Ucicky directed while Fritz Arno Wagner, one of Germany's most accomplished cameramen, created "an exciting tension of visuals with a variety of angles, close-ups and wonderfully captured facial expressions." An excellent cast included Emil Jannings as the half-villainous, half-naïve judge, Adam; Angela Salloker as Eve, the object of the magistrate's affection; Lina Carstens as her mother and the owner of the jug; Friedrich Kayssler as the inspecting judge; and Max Guelstorff as a clerk of the court.

When Adam, the magistrate of a little Dutch village, breaks into Eve's bedroom more than a little drunk, he is surprised by her lover, who severely beats him and makes his escape in the darkness. During the scuffle, Adam loses his wig and smashes a famous antique jug belonging to Eve's mother. The next morning Adam is nursing a hangover when the visiting magistrate appears. Adam must hold court sans wig. The first case is brought by Eve's mother, who has come to have justice rendered in the matter of her broken jug. Adam tries to incriminate Eve's lover, but the visiting magistrate is suspicious. And when a witness arrives with the wig found under Eve's window, Adam, realizing that his guilt is established, leaps through the courtroom window into the river.

Jannings once again revealed his enormous talent for characterization. "[Friedrich] Hebbel has said that since Falstaff no comic character has been created who could

Emil Jannings and Angela Salloker. *(Der zerbrochene Krug)*

Lina Carstens. *(Der zerbrochene Krug)*

review: "If the uneasy shade of Heinrich von Kleist could visit the Eighty-sixth Street Garden these days and see the joyous enthusiasm with which the German-speaking spectators are welcoming the Tobis version of his *Der zerbrochene Krug*, it probably would join in applauding the excellent work of Emil Jannings as the central character of his nineteenth-century satire on the functioning of some rural courts of Holland."

Although *The Broken Jug* was designated *Staatspolitisch und kunstlerisch wertvoll*, politically and artistically valuable, Goebbels had opposed the production and shortly after its release in October, 1937, sought to restrict its showing. The minister may have considered Jannings's portrayal of the lame Dutch magistrate to be a caricature of himself. When Martin Bormann, Hitler's private secretary and Goebbels's enemy, informed the Führer of the case, Hitler judged that Goebbels had misused his authority. According to Albert Speer, "Hitler gleefully watched the film, which had been withdrawn from circulation, and gave orders that it be shown again in the largest Berlin movie theater. But—and this was typical of Hitler's sometimes amazing lack of authority—for a long time this simply was not done. Bormann, however, kept bringing up the matter until

Angela Salloker. *(Der zerbrochene Krug)*

hold a candle to the village magistrate, Adam," a writer in the German press observed. "Jannings becomes this archetypal character to the fullest degree. He is true to form: bold, gluttonous, alcoholic, lecherous, lying and vulgar even to the extent of belching but despite all of this, lovable." Writing in *Sight and Sound*, Arthur Vesselo wrote that "Jannings takes his role with stout and unmistakable gusto. This is a part which he does well, and which his countrymen presumably greet with ringing cries of '*da capo*.' " Harrison T. Smith of *The New York Times* was no less praising in his January, 1938,

Director Gustav Ucicky and Emil Jannings during the production of *Der zerbrochene Krug*.

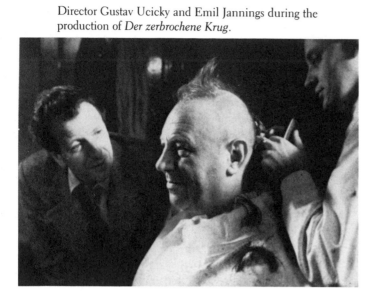

Emil Jannings. (*Der zerbrochene Krug*)

The village. (*Der zerbrochene Krug*)

Hitler showed serious irritation and let Goebbels know that his orders had better be obeyed."

The Broken Jug was revived five years later for a showing at the UFA-Palast am Zoo. Wilhelm Hackbarth described it as "a milestone in the recent history of the art of the film, a work that has maintained its validity, and by the boldness of its idea and its superlative realization points the way for advances into new filmic territory." Hackbarth considered it "a film of lasting value, a judgment confirmed by the expressions of gratitude shown by the guests at this festival revival, namely, wounded soldiers and workers from armament factories. Afterwards Emil Jannings, the real creator, appeared and bowed to a prolonged ovation."

Olympia

I. Teil: Fest der Völker

PART I FESTIVAL OF THE PEOPLE

II. Teil: Fest der Schönheit

PART II FESTIVAL OF BEAUTY

1938

CREDITS:

Production: Tobis Filmkunst GmbH./Olympia-Film GmbH. *Director:* Leni Riefenstahl. *Production supervisor:* Walter Traut. Direction and photography for the prologue of Part I: Willy Otto Zielke. *Cinematography:* Hans Ertl, Walter Frentz, Guzzi Lantschner, Kurt Neubert, Hans Scheib and thirty-nine additional cameramen. *Newsreel:* Fox, Paramount, Tobis Melo, UFA. *Editor:* Leni Riefenstahl. *Art direction:* Robert Herlth. *Sound engineers:* Siegfried Schulze and Hermann Storr. *Sound mixing:* Max Michel, Johannes Lüdke, Arnfried Heyne and Guzzi Lantschner. *Sound assistants:* Wolfgang Brüning and Otto Lantschner. *Speakers:* Dr. Paul Laven and Rolf Wernicke (for the German version). *Music:* Herbert Windt and Walter Gronostay (for the polo sequence and the Reiten-Fünfkampf, Part II); the Kittel Choir under the direction of Professor Kittel; the Philharmonic Orchestra under the direction of Müller-John; and the UFA-Symphony Orchestra and the Tofi-Orchestra. *Technical advisor:* Rudolph Schaad. *Publicity and Still Pho-*

The lighting of the Olympic torch. *(Olympia)*

tography: Rolf Lantin. *Released:* April 20, 1938, in German, English, French and Italian versions. *Length:* Part I, Festival of the People: 3429 meters. Part II, Festival of Beauty: 2722 meters.

Olympia represents Leni Riefenstahl's crowning achievement as a filmmaker. Had she directed no other film, *Olympia I and II, Fest der Völker (Festival of the People)* and *Fest der Schönheit (Festival of Beauty)* would have secured her a place as one of the century's most important documentary filmmakers. *Olympia* ranks as one of the most artistic documentaries ever created. Any serious study of the film medium is incomplete without knowledge of its construction. Like Griffith's *Intolerance*, Eisenstein's *Potemkin*, and Welles's *Citizen Kane*, Riefenstahl's *Olympia* is nothing less than an education in the art of the motion picture. For the editor it provides rare and unusual examples of the art of montage; for the cameraman, an infinite variety of angles and perspectives; and for the sound specialist, invaluable lessons in the creative use of music, narration, natural sound and silence.

Riefenstahl was at first reluctant to direct the official film of the XI Olympiad in Berlin. She opposed the idea of a feature-length sports newsreel that would appeal

Dawn on the Acropolis. *(Olympia)*

only to sports enthusiasts. In like manner, she expressed disdain for a fiction film with sporting sequences in the manner of E. A. Dupont's *Der Laufer von Marathon (The Runner from Marathon)*, based on the Los Angeles Olympics of 1932. "I recognized from the outset that a fictional story would only appear trivial when placed alongside the dramatic conflict of the Olympiad," she reflected in later years. "But my opposition did not have the foresight to believe that it was possible to make a good Olympic film without a story." She conceived a film that would transcend time and place while preserving the integrity of the events. "I thought about it for a long time, and in the beginning I did not realize what a difficult adventure I had embarked on," Riefenstahl remembered. "I knew that I was the only one who could do [it] because I was the only one who had experience with making such a documentary. I felt it almost a duty to make that film."

Professor Diem, Secretary General of the German Olympic Committee, admired the artistry of her previous films, especially *The Blue Light*, and esteemed the organizational capacity which she had shown during the making of *Triumph of the Will*. Diem recognized, of course, that the task of producing a motion picture of the Olympic Games would require the filmmaker to draw upon enormous resources. The cooperation of the Reich government would be essential to the success of the film. Diem therefore looked upon her contact with Hitler not as a liability but as an asset that would allow her to complete a monumental task.

Dr. Goebbels may have opposed Riefenstahl's nomination to direct the Olympic Games film. He informed her that his Propaganda Ministry was capable of making a film of the summer Olympiad, a fact which she did not dispute. Goebbels looked down on Riefenstahl as an *ehrgeizige Frau*, a female upstart. He envied her independence and the privileged position which she enjoyed with Hitler. On a more practical level, Goebbels may have been concerned about the length of her proposed *Olympia* and the year and a half of post-production work that would be required before its premiere.

Riefenstahl was firm on both points. A film reflecting the epic nature of the games could not be achieved in the format of a single film. She conceived of a two-part work, *Festival of Beauty* and *Festival of the People*, which could be screened on separate evenings. Having estimated that it might take up to two years to edit her Olympic documentary, there remained the question of whether the public would in 1938 be interested in a sports film about events in 1936. Riefenstahl replied that her film would represent the *idea* of the Olympiad. It would be a film for all time, a judgment which has been vindicated by history.

During the second half of 1935 Leni Riefenstahl selected her camera crew for *Olympia*. Because some of the key cameramen from the Fanck school, most notably Hans Schneeberger, Richard Angst and Sepp Allgeier, were occupied with other film projects, Riefenstahl was obliged to choose from the "second generation" of Fanck cameramen, young photographers who had served an apprenticeship with Dr. Fanck's "first generation" graduates. Most of her principal photographers were accomplished sportsmen and dedicated filmmakers—youthful, ambitious and enthusiastic—and suited by temperament and experience for the task that lay ahead.

Aside from Walter Traut, her director of production, Riefenstahl's closest co-workers on *Olymia* were Walter Frentz and Hans Ertl. Frentz had collaborated with Riefenstahl on *Victory of the Faith* and *Triumph of the Will*. Quiet and intense, Frentz combined a knowledge of electricity and physics with a painter's eye for composition. Ertl had been associated with Dr. Fanck. Riefenstahl considered him to be her finest cameraman and assigned him to photograph the rowing at Grünau and the swimming competition. In the swim stadium he achieved superb underwater effects with a specially built apparatus.

Riefenstahl and her cameramen worked long and hard in the months preceding the contest, studying every kind of sport and its possibilities for filming. "The activity of the staff and the requirements placed upon the technical material required hard, untiring, continuous training on all the sites during the last weeks before the opening of the Games," she wrote afterwards. "The film group was soon in excellent form. All technical details had been prepared in the very best way; the focal distance and the slow motion camera had been carefully studied so that photographs could be seen in the greatest detail. The most suitable film material had been found as well as the best filters."

Riefenstahl's preparations were elaborate and painstaking. She made a careful study of the characteristics of various kinds of black-and-white film, Agfa, Kodak, and Perutz and Gevaert. Ernst Jaeger, Riefenstahl's publicist in this period, recalled the thoroughness of her preparations: "She and her collaborators made a series of tests with a bouquet of flowers of all colors which they photographed under various lighting conditions in order to study the sensitivity of the different film stocks." Riefenstahl afterwards instructed her cameramen to shoot the same subjects with each brand of film. "We shot landscapes in the sun with plenty of green and trees, then buildings and stonework, then pictures of people and heads, and so on," she noted. "We shot with and without yellow filters and assembled the bits for screening so that when we watched the screen nobody knew

The torch is carried along the shores of Corinth. *(Olympia)*

From the prologue to *Olympia*, photographed by Willy Zielke.

Javelin thrower. *(Olympia)*

The Barberinian Faun. *(Olympia)*

Ernst Jaeger and Leni Riefenstahl in Greece during the making of the prologue for *Olympia*.

which piece was on which film. The ten or twelve cameramen watching gave each film a rating." From these tests Riefenstahl found the Perutz film most suitable for trees and undergrowth; Kodak yielded the best results for photographing people; Agfa was good for statues and buildings. Thus, during the games the cameramen were issued the appropriate film stock according to the subjects they were to shoot.

To decide which events were to be photographed, Riefenstahl and her cadre of cameramen attended different sporting events in Germany prior to the Olympic Games. They viewed the events cinematically, giving careful attention to the motion and rhythm peculiar to each sport. By trial and error, they decided on camera angles, lenses, exposure, and the special equipment which might be required, repeatedly testing their apparatus under all kinds of weather and lighting conditions. "The program of the 16 days had to be visualized beforehand by a kind of imaginative camera," Riefenstahl recounted. "All its details had to be critically analyzed and thoroughly investigated, keeping in mind the requirements of filming. Every member of the staff had to be thoroughly acquainted with the sites of the streets on which the Führer would approach, the Olympic Village, the main stadium, the swimming stadium, the polo field, the hockey field, the sea, the Spree, the Deutschland Hall, the fencing halls, the courses of the Marathon race and the cycling races. No spot within the range of the Olympic events could be unknown to the camera-man."

The Marathon. *(Olympia)*

Jesse Owens. *(Olympia)*

The restrictions imposed on her filming by the International Committee and the nature of the Olympiad itself encouraged Riefenstahl and her crew to be inventive both technically and creatively. "Little by little, I discovered that the constraints imposed at times by the event could often serve me as a guide," she recalled. "The whole thing lay in knowing when and how to respect or violate these constraints."

In photographing the 100 meter finals of the decathlon she believed that event should be concluded with extreme closeups. But how could this be achieved without violating IOC rules? "There was no middle course between extreme proximity and following the movement at a constant distance," Riefenstahl wrote afterwards. "As there was no question of getting close to the runner, it called for the use of a telescopic lens. I withdrew to find a vantage point. It was at this moment that we began to employ the gigantic telescopic lenses that were to serve us from then on. It was the fusion of static shots, rhythmic shots and shots animated by technical movement that were to give the film its life, its rhythm. Thus, in the face of each problem, it was necessary to feel one's way, to make tests, and each test resulted in new ideas, some small and some big."

The marathon provided a special challenge for Leni Riefenstahl. She wanted her photographs to suggest the fatigue of the runners. During the training session several marathon contestants were equipped with Kinamo cameras harnessed to their chests in an attempt to record the runners "rhythmically pulling their feet off the ground with every step." "The result of the first trials was unusable," Riefenstahl recalled, "everything was blurred with camera shake. We tried again with different framing speeds and then took a bigger camera with 100 feet of film because the Kinamo's film lengths were too short. Eventually we ended up with a few short bits of footage which we cut into the sequence of the marathon run."

Leni Riefenstahl and her crew maintained a frantic pace during the two weeks of the Olympiad. Heinz Jaworsky recalled that Riefenstahl "would rush around from one cameraman to the other like a maniac and say—How are you doing, how are you doing? How about this and this? Screaming and hollering—oh, she was an absolute maniac, she was wild. But we [filmmakers] all are—either you are crazy in this business or you don't get anything done." Her crew "had to work with lightning speed in order to lose no valuable second. Dripping with perspiration they rushed to and fro untiringly with their heavy cameras." They were completely exhausted, Riefenstahl remembered, but "they had to use the greatest energy in order to concentrate on their work and to collect the most beautiful and outstanding material for their part of the film."

It was not unusual for Riefenstahl's working day to average sixteen hours. Seated at a large conference table at *Haus Ruhwald*, her headquarters, Riefenstahl and her cameramen would discuss the day's shooting in minute detail. Sometimes these discussions would last until the early hours of the morning. "We . . . tried to think of ways of shooting with maximum visual impact," she recalled. "Everyone made suggestions and I tried every idea, whatever it was. That's how we got such a varied approach." When someone fell asleep Riefenstahl would give a good-natured but firm rap on the table with the admonition: "Gentlemen, two weeks from now you can sleep. Right now we think about tomorrow."

After the shooting of *Olympia*, Leni Riefenstahl moved to the Geyer laboratory in Berlin to begin the arduous task of editing the 400,000 meters (1,300,000 feet) of film, nearly 6,000 individual pictures. Riefenstahl believes that "the true establishment of the form began with the editing." She edited *Olympia* single-handedly. "This was necessary, for each editor sets his own stamp on a film," she said in 1965. "Experience shows that if two or three different people edit a film, it is impossible for any sort of harmony to emerge. The nature of my films demands that they be edited by a single person, and that person must be the one who had the idea for the film, who was looking for precisely such a harmony. Harmony would not be born out of another's montage."

She approached the task with her characteristic *fanatismus*, screening the material over a period of two and a half months, working ten hours a day. "I spent eighteen months in the cutting room on *Olympia*. The cutting room was my entire life. The same happens with any director, but I was editing a million feet of film, nothing else mattered."

At the end of October, 1936, Riefenstahl selected material for the final montage. In our 1970 interview she drew an analogy between film editing and music composition: "Like a composer you must establish rhythm, sometimes going an octave deeper, then an octave higher, never bringing the best work at the beginning or the worst at the end. The making of montage is a sensitive art, more difficult than cinematography, and when I made the documentaries I could never find anyone who could edit to my satisfaction." Like Pudovkin she believes that "the film is not *shot*, but *built* up from the separate strips of celluloid that are its raw material." She has also likened editing to architecture: "The creation of a documentary is not unlike the building of a house. The film editor, like the architect, must have a feeling for the placement of each image."

In addition to the responsibility of editing *Olympia*, Leni Riefenstahl collaborated with Willy Zielke in the

Leni Riefenstahl and Walter Frentz in the Olympic Stadium. *(Olympia)*

making of the classical prologue to *Part I*. It required more than a year of work, although Riefenstahl did not direct or appear, as some have alleged, in any portion of the prologue. The prologue was the work of Zielke, created under the supervision of Leni Riefenstahl. "I couldn't imagine any other beginning," Riefenstahl recollected in her conversations with L. Andrew Mannheim. "It had to emerge from the dead ruins of Olympia without human figures. From the antique stones, I wanted to lead to antique Greek temples, drawing past them, as if in a dream, to the sculptures which, by an interplay of light and movement, were to appear like living faces in a vision of the past."

The premiere of *Olympia* at the UFA-Palast am Zoo coincided with the celebration of Hitler's 49th birthday, April 20, 1938. The members of the International

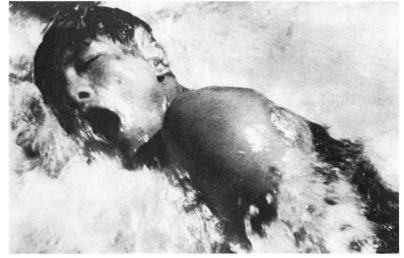

Shunpei Uto (Japan). *(Olympia)*

Photographer Hans Ertl. *(Olympia)*

171

Olympic Committee, German and Austrian Olympic winners together with high-ranking members of the Nazi Party, film notables and the ambassadors of the United States, Britain, France, and representatives of many foreign governments attended the showing. The Nazi press reported that at the end of *Part I* Hitler "still clapping, stood up and congratulated the artist on her success." During the half-hour intermission, Hitler received Riefenstahl in the foyer of the first level, and upon completion of *Festival of Nations*, about midnight, congratulated her for a second time.

German press notices were predictably ecstatic. Frank Maraun (pseudonym for Erwin Goelz) reported in *Der Deutsche Film* that the film was "one of the greatest works of art that the German film has produced up to now—filled with a spirit which we sense to be not only the spirit of *Olympia* but also to be the spirit of the German reality of today."

Olympia received the Reich film prize in May, 1938. At the close of August, 1938, delegates to the Sixth International Film Festival convened in Venice where Count Guiseppe Volpi proposed Riefenstahl's *Olympia* for the award of the most outstanding feature film of 1938. The American and British delegates protested, arguing that *Olympia* belonged to the documentary class and was therefore ineligible to compete in the feature film category. But in the final balloting the international committee awarded first prize, the Mussolini Cup, to *Olympia* and *Luciano Serra Pilota*, directed by Goffredo Alessandro. Walt Disney's feature-length cartoon, *Snow White and the Seven Dwarfs*, which the American representative Harold Smith had supported, received a special prize. Smith and Neville Kerney, the British delegate, were unconsoled and resigned from the festival jury.

Unfolding like a massive tapestry, *Olympia, Part I* begins with a prologue set in ancient Greece. Mist and night suggest the spiritual realm as the camera prowls across a grassy landscape littered with the stones of antiquity, remote and mysterious. In a series of tracking shots we dissolve from the Ionic colonnade of the Erectheum to a full view of the Parthenon, white and majestic against a clouded sky. The pensive music surges to a triumphant coda and then recedes as the statues of Greek gods and heroes pass before us, shrouded in mist or in mysterious silhouette: Medusa, Apollo, Aphrodite, Archilles, and the slumbering figure of the Barberino Faun.

The Discus of Myron serves as Riefenstahl's transition from the eternal realm of antiquity to the world of the present. The marble figure dissolves to an athlete of flesh and blood whose arm slowly revolves in a sweeping arc to hurl the discus. The music is intense and virile as we cut to other athletes viewed from various perspectives who throw the discus, javelin, and shot put in quick succession. The rhythm softens again as we dissolve to a pair of arms which gently toss the weight from one hand to another, and they in turn blend with the lifting movement of female arms, the shot put having become a large ball which is lightly tossed back and forth. The music is soothing and joyous as a girl dances with a hoop in slow motion above a sparkling sea, her nude form illuminated by the last rays of the sun. The tonalities grow darker as the forms of the Three Graces come together in silhouette to rekindle the Olympic flame. The music rises to a crescendo and for a few seconds the entire frame is dominated by a restless fire, a symbol of spiritual regeneration.

We dissolve to a full shot of the flame in a broken column tended by a young Greek who ceremoniously lifts the torch to the sky. Windt's heraldic music surges forward as the youth sprints down the rugged Olympian landscape, past stones and temples to the coast of Corinth. We see a runner superimposed against a roaring sea. An animated map of Southern Europe illustrates the progress of the torch through Greece, Bulgaria, Yugoslavia, Hungary, Austria, and Czechoslovakia, the music rising to a climax as the title "Germany" dissolves to a fluttering swastika banner and the tolling of the Olympic bell. As the mist recedes, we see an aerial perspective of the Olympic stadium in Berlin photogaphed from the *Hindenburg*.

The opening ceremonies in the stadium serve as a preliminary to the main events: the throwing of the discus (men and women); women's hurdles; the throwing of the hammer; the 100 meter race; the women's high jump; the 400 meter race; putting the weight; the hop, skip and jump; the long jump; the 1,500 meter relay; the high jump; hurdles; throwing of the javelin; the 1,000 meter race; pole vaulting; the 400 meter relay (women); the 400 meter relay (men); and the 1,600 meter relay. *Olympia I* concludes with the Marathon sequence which Riefenstahl considers her finest work as a film editor. In order to depict the physical agony of the runner in visual terms, Riefenstahl combines a traveling shot of a cornfield against a clouded sky, the face of a runner in extreme closeup, a traveling shot of trees, and the legs of an athlete pumping in slow motion as he approaches the stadium.

"I had the idea that one must try and show what the Marathon runner feels when he becomes tired," she recalled. "I showed his legs becoming heavier and his movements become machine-like and how everything passes by and then, as if in a dream, and with his last strength, he only hears the noise from the stadium which encourages him and supports his will. As we see his legs

172

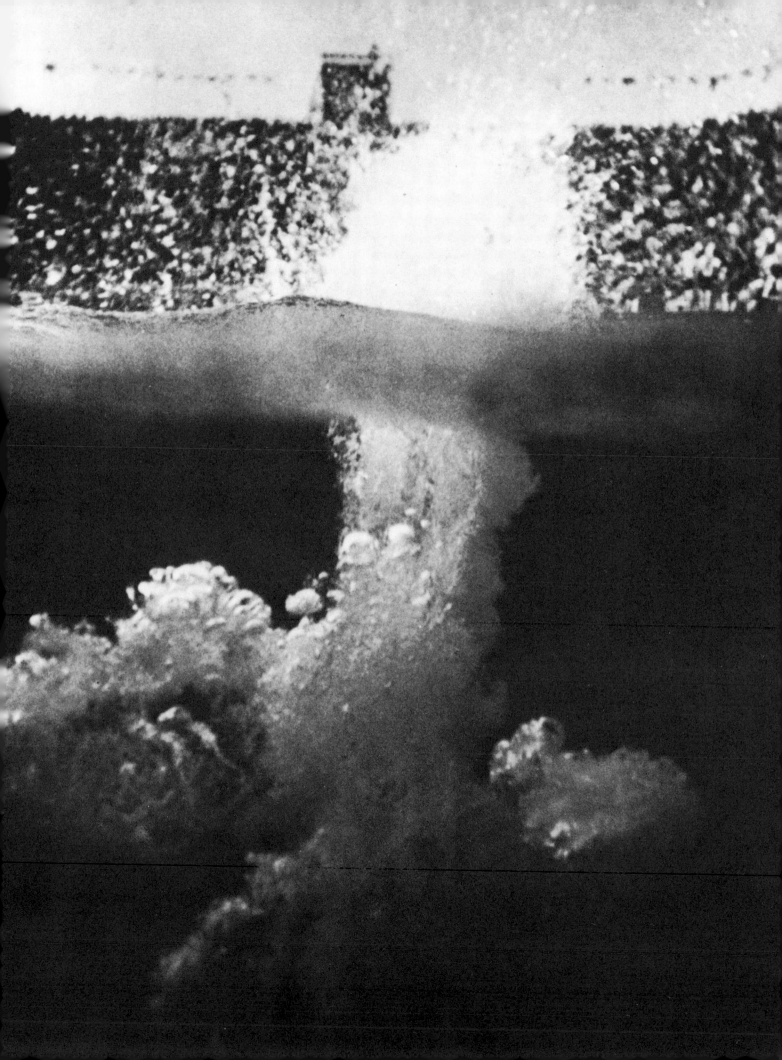

A telescopic lens in the Olympic Stadium. *(Olympia)*

in the dissolve we already hear the trumpet fanfare and the voices of the crowd, and that sustains him. I could only express his will in images which in turn were supported by Windt's music. As he runs in slow motion, the music becomes breathless. The music represents the will, the pictures show his exhaustion and through this contrast we experience unconsciously the agony of the Marathon runner."

Olympia I ends on a note of somber heroism. The screen tonalities are dark as the fluttering banners of the nations, illuminated by spotlights, are paraded in a massed formation on the floor of the stadium. These proceedings have a religious aura which reinforces Riefenstahl's translation of the Olympiad into a mythic ceremony. The soundtrack resounds with the voices of a great unseen choir as we track away from the stadium, a cathedral of light, and the tolling of the Olympic bell.

If the overriding tone of *Olympia I* is serious and at times ceremonial, *Olympia II, Festival of the People* is refreshingly warm-hearted and on occasion humorous. Only at the conclusion of the film does the mood once again become somber.

The six meter boat race. *(Olympia)*

Captain Stubbendorf (Germany), winner of the gold medal in the military riding competition. *(Olympia)*

Leni Riefenstahl: "The creation of a documentary is not unlike the building of a house. The film editor, like the architect, must have a feeling for the placement of each image." *(Olympia)*

Part II begins with a romantic montage of the Olympic Village and its forested environs at dawn. We see reflections in a sylvan lake, the morning mist, shimmering oak leaves, and the flutter of birds in a tree branch. Living in harmony with nature, the athletes run alongside the vaporous lake in the early morning. In the steamy sauna the Olympic *Übermenschen* are shown in repose, bathing, massaging, and perspiring. The poetic idyll concludes with the men diving from the platform of the sauna house into an opalescent lake.

The Olympic Village is presented in bright sunshine as the athletes stroll about the wooded grounds, exercise, shadow box, kick soccerballs, and rest. The events of *Part II* begin with a gymnastics display on the May Field. A few figures become a multitude as one shot dissolves into another to reveal row upon row of men and women performing calisthenics, their arms and bodies moving in a dance-like rhythm.

The Olympic venues represented in *Part II* consist of yacht racing at Kiel, an exciting montage of sails and sea; a fragment of the pentathlon (riding, pistol shooting and the cross country); hockey and polo; association football; the three-day competition; the 100 kilometer road race; the final of the double sculls, coxswainless fours and eights; the decathlon; the diving (women); the 200 meter

175

breast stroke; the 100 meter free style and the 100 meter free style (women).

The last section of *Olympia* is devoted to springboard diving. This aquatic and aerial ballet, choreographed by Riefenstahl at her editing table, is one of the most poetic examples of montage in the history of film. To the accompaniment of the music of Herbert Windt, a succession of divers spring into the sky, twisting and turning their bodies with consummate grace against a background of clouds and sun. The diving is shown at normal speed and in slow motion, and at one point a diver is lifted from the pool in reverse motion. Some are photographed under water, immersed in bubbles as they loop dexterously to the surface.

As the sky darkens, the divers soar into the clouds. Reason is suspended by the ecstasy of their silhouetted flight as they appear to strive for the infinite. Finally, the last diver disappears, zephyr-like, into a turbulent cloud bank. Riefenstahl's *Olympia* returns to its mythic, nebulous origins, the stadium having been transformed into a cathedral of light. They dying flame, the laureled staffs, and the fluttering Olympic banner are shown as a celestial choir and symphony echo the words and music of Paul Hoeffer's "Farewell to the Flag" and Beethoven's hymn, "The Flame Dies." A stream of smoke, symbolic of the Olympic idea, floats towards the heavens as shafts of light converge to form an immense star which appears to illuminate the universe.

(Opposite page) The spectacular diving sequence. *(Olympia)*

VI

Film in the Third Reich

1939-1945

Press Company cameramen photographing the German newsreel.

The outbreak of World War II in September, 1939, encouraged the production of a number of feature length documentaries of which *Der Feldzug im Polen (The Campaign in Poland)*, *Feuertaufe (Baptism of Fire)*, both released in 1940, and *Sieg in Westen (Victory in the West)*, released in 1941, were the most notable. These carefully crafted war documentaries, ingeniously compiled from footage shot by cameramen attached to the military units and underscored with music and commentary, strengthened the confidence of the German people in the nation's capacity to wage war, and their distribution abroad in various language versions conveyed the impression of an invincible military.

Der Feldzug im Polen presented highlights of the September blitzkrieg. "Hitler's infantry, panzer, and air units are depicted in an inexorable, cascading leap to greatness which, it appears, no power on earth could possibly stop," historian Jay Baird noted. *Feuertaufe* was no less awesome in its portrayal of the Luftwaffe during the invasion of Poland with electrifying photographs of the bombing of Warsaw from a myriad of perspectives. Its premiere at the UFA-Palast am Zoo was attended by Goering, Goebbels, and Generals von Brauchitsch, Beck and Milch. That the film was intended to influence foreign opinion is suggested by the fact that invitations were extended to all foreign military attachés and prominent foreigners residing in Berlin. On April 5, high-ranking Danes and Norwegians were invited to see *Feuertaufe* at the German Embassy in Oslo. As Lief Furhammer and Folke Isaksson observed in their *Politics and Film*, "This screening was a threatening diplomatic prelude to the invasion which was to come a few days later."

The *pièce de résistance* of the genre was *Sieg im Westen*, a cinematic record of the German sweep through the Low Countries and France, compiled from 2.7 million feet of material. Released in January, 1941, it made a strong impression on neutrals, including the United States.

Following the outbreak of war, priority was given to the weekly newsreel, officially designated *Die Deutsche Wochenshau* after its reorganization on June 19, 1940, which quadrupled in length from 350 to 1,200 meters with a running time of approximately three quarters of an hour.

Like the feature-length documentaries, the newsreels were designed for both domestic and foreign consumption and were produced at the rate of one thousand copies per week in fifteen language versions by the end of the first year of war. It became a principal source of information and propaganda about the war. The *Wochenshau* does not present "objective truth—for that

Dr. Goebbels is greeted by Dino Alfieri upon his arrival in Venice for the 1939 Film Festival.

Magda and Joseph Goebbels at the Venice Film Festival, August, 1939. *Robert Koch* was the chief German entry.

would have been pointless and was not within its power anyway," an official source proclaimed in 1940, "but using all decent means, it reveals that side of the truth that it is necessary to propagate in the interest of the German people." Attendance was encouraged in various ways. The contents of the weekly *Wochenshau* were previewed on the Reich Broadcasting System, which announced special features such as "birthday celebrations of the leaders—the arrival in Germany of workers from occupied countries—German schools in wartime—the appointment of a new commander to a castle of the National Socialist Order—new vocational training centers for disabled veterans."

In January, 1942, the Propaganda Ministry announced that mothers who saw their sons in a newsreel would be given a frame enlargement from the film. The

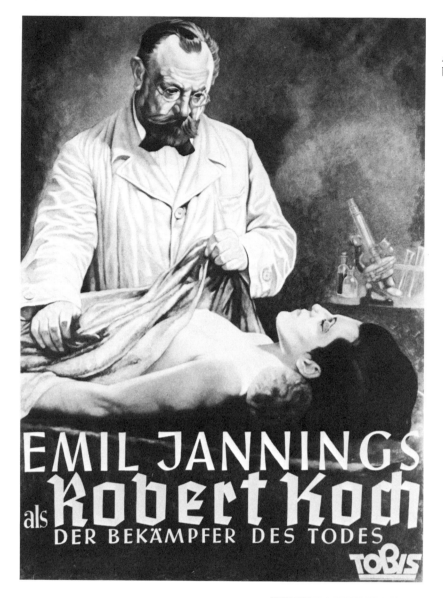

Advertisement for *Robert Koch*, directed by Hans Steinhoff, 1939.

D III 88, directed by Herbert Maisch, 1939.

180

demand proved to be so great that the Ministry was obliged to amend its offer; henceforth, photos would be issued only to mothers of soldiers who had died at the front.

Goebbels personally oversaw the production of the *Wochenshau*, as his diary entries for the war years attest. On March 4, 1941, he wrote: "Newsreel in the evening. A host of new and very impressive pictures from Bulgaria included. By dint of single-minded work, we are able to get it ready for this week. Hard going, when there is such a dearth of material." On April 6, 1941: "Newsreel in the evening. Rather vague and confused at first viewing, as always. But we shall make something of it." And finally, on July 8, 1941: "Work on the newsreel in the evening. Contains harrowing shots of the Bolshevik atrocities in Lvov. A red shocker! The Führer rings me up to say that it is the best newsreel we have ever made. I am very pleased." By January 1, 1942, newsreel production had risen to 2,400 copies, reaching a weekly audience of 30 million.

As Goebbels's diaries suggest, Hitler also took an interest in newsreels and documentary footage which he seems to have studied intensively. "For the sake of the future, it's important to preserve the news-films of the war," Hitler told his intimates in late 1941. "They will be documents of incalculable value. New copies of these films will have to be constantly printed, and it would even be best to print them on strips of metal, so that they won't disappear." In the future he hoped that newsreels would be made "by our very best film experts. One can get extraordinary results in that field. They can confine themselves to twenty-minute one-reelers, but these must be the result of intelligent work. The worst habit of all has been to restrict the films to thirty-foot strips, whatever the subject might be: an earthquake, a tennis match, a horse-race, the launching of a ship."

The motion picture became the most significant form of popular entertainment for the German people, both civilians and soldiers, following the outbreak of war. Attendance rose from 410,000,000 in 1938-39 to 850,000,000 in 1940, an increase of 70 percent since 1932. By 1940 Germany controlled some 7,000 cinemas.

Entertainment films mirrored the new situation. Biographical studies of historical figures as diverse as *Schiller* and *Bismarck*, directed by Herbert Maisch and Wolfgang Liebeneiner respectively, served the cause of nationalistic propaganda in the context of 1940-41.

The anti-British theme was represented in a number of films such as *Mein Leben für Irland* (*A Life for Ireland*); *Das Lied der Wüste* (*Song of the Desert*), a German rendition of Anglo-Arab conflicts in the aftermath of World War I; *Das Herz der Königin* (*The Heart of the Queen*), a somber retelling of the conflict between Mary Queen of Scots and Elizabeth with Zarah Leander as the Scottish queen; and *Der Fuchs von Glenarvon* (*The Fox of Glenarvon*), a portrayal of the 1921 Irish rebellion.

But the most significant anti-British film was *Ohm Krüger* directed principally by Hans Steinhoff from a screenplay by Harald Bratt and Kurt Heuser and based on themes suggested by the novel *Mann ohne Volk* by Arnold Krieger. Emil Jannings took the role of Krüger, the Boer leader, whose story is told in flashback. Franz Schafheitlin, Ferdinand Marian and Gustav Gründgens were appropriately villainous as Krüger's Anglo antagonists, Lord Kitchener, Cecil Rhodes and Joseph Chamberlain, while Hedwig Wangel played a rheumatic and alcoholic Queen Victoria. But it was Jannings, perhaps one of the greatest character actors of his age, who dominated the production with his overwhelming presence. Even the actor's strongest critics, among whom must be counted Louis Marcorelles, were moved by his performance in the final scenes of *Ohm Krüger* in which "Jannings, staggering blinded in his tent, only the whiteness of his eyes showing, becomes the symbol of a powerless humanity in the grip of fate." Blanketed and confined to a wheelchair, the graying and whiskered Krüger tells his Swiss nurse that one day a great nation will arrive to avenge the Boers for their ill treatment by the British.

Goebbels accorded *Ohm Krüger* his personal attention and appears to have relished his role as overseer of a project close to his heart. After a visit to Grünewald in early March, 1941, the minister described "the big studio as one enormous camp. Jannings is working on a wonderful scene. Then we see rushes from the film, which put all previous material in the shade. We spend a long time deliberating whether we should bring the film out in one part or two. I think one part because this will make for greater impact." And on March 16 he described *Ohm Krüger* as "A really great, thrilling work of art. The supreme achievement of the entire war. This is a film to go crazy about. Jannings is very happy. The film can only be released in one part." Ten days later Goebbels wrote that he and Reichsfilmdramaturg von DeWandowski, having looked "at three possible endings for *Ohm Krüger*," decided that "The one put together by me is the best and is accepted."

Goebbels screened the completed film to a large gathering at his home on April 2, 1941. "Great excitement," he writes. "The film is unique. A really big hit. Everyone is thrilled by it. Jannings has excelled himself. An anti-England film beyond one's wildest dreams. Gauleiter [August] Eigrunder is also present and very enthusiastic." The film premiered at the UFA-Palast am

Feuertaufe (Baptism of Fire), 1940.

Dr. Goebbels and Hermann Goering attend the Berlin premiere of *Feuertaufe*, the official film of the Polish campaign.

Lil Dagover and Heinrich George in *Friedrich Schiller*, directed by Herbert Maisch, 1940.

Zoo on April 4. "It is a success without equal," Goebbels wrote. "The audience reacts magnificently." On April 6 he recorded that "*Ohm Krüger* has set feelings ablaze. The critics' comments in the press are fantastic. A few ossified bureaucrats at the Foreign Ministry have taken offense. Otherwise the enthusiasm is universal."

Goebbels awarded Jannings the *Film Ring of Honor*, "For his great services to our German filmmaking art." And in the tense atmosphere which preceded the surprise attack on Yugoslavia and Greece on April 6, Goebbels had time to "drink tea with the Führer" and "chat about other things," including *Ohm Krüger*, which, according to Goebbels, he valued highly. "He tells me of the deep impression which the Boer War made on him as a boy. The characters in the film please him enormously."

Nazi Germany's mercurial relationship with the Soviet Union was also reflected in motion pictures. The films fall into three distinct periods: the anti-Comintern, 1933-1939; the interlude of Nazi-Soviet cooperation,

Advertisement for *Sieg im Westen* (Victory in the West), 1941.

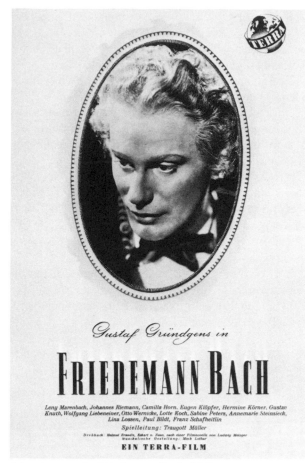

Advertisement for *Friedemann Bach*, 1941.

1939-1941; and the era of Barbarossa, 1941-1945. Between 1933 and 1939 the German film, echoing the sentiments of the state controlled press and radio, represented communists, both domestic and foreign, to be nothing less than the lethal antagonists of the National Socialist Reich. Feature films such as *Hans Westmar* (1933), *Um das Manschenrecht* (*For the Rights of Man*, 1934), *Friesonnot* (*Frisians in Peril*, 1935), *Mein Sohn, der Herr Minister* (*My Son, the Minister*, 1937) and *Kameraden auf See* (*Comrades at Sea*, 1938) reflected the spirit of the anti-Comintern.

In the immediate aftermath of the Nazi-Soviet Pact, the German screen reflected the spirit of *rapprochement* in feature pictures such as Carl Froelich's *Es war eine rauschende Ballnacht* (*It Was a Boisterous Ball-Night*), a fictionalized life of Tchaikovsky; Gustav Ucicky's *Der Postmeister* (*The Stationmaster*), based on a story by Pushkin; and Wolfgang Liebeneiner's *Bismarck*, which has the Chancellor explain to King William that the treaty with Russia will protect Prussia's eastern frontier.

But Hitler's desire for *Lebensraum*, living space in the East, expounded in *Mein Kampf* but suppressed during

the initial phase of the Soviet treaty, was revived after the fall of France. Hitler raised the possibility of an attack on Russia as early as July, 1940, and after the failure of the Molotov visit in November, he appears to have come to a firm decision regarding *Operation Barbarossa*, war against the Soviet Union. On June 22, 1941, Germany and its satellite states attacked the Soviet Union on a broad front extending from the Baltic to the Bosporus.

In the wake of Germany's surprise attack on the Soviet Union, Goebbels revised his film policy to reflect the changed conditions. Anti-Communist films such as *Friesennot* (*Frisians in Peril*), retitled *Dorf im roten Storm* (*Red Storm over the Village*) were reissued. Works

Advertisement for *Ohm Krüger*, directed by Hans Steinhoff under the supervision of Emil Jannings, 1941.

Emil Jannings and Hans Steinhoff during the making of *Ohm Krüger*.

in progress such as Viet Harlan's *Der grosse König (The Great King)*, which had been nearly completed at the time of the Soviet attack, required substantial reediting and additional reshooting. Originally, the Russian general, Chernichev, played by Paul Wegener, had been portrayed as a friend of King Frederick. But the revised version of *Der grosse König* employs voice-over narration to establish Chernichev's villainy, the King having discovered documents which prove Poland's complicity with France and England against Prussia.

Russia is represented as a duplicitous ally which intended to turn on Prussia at the opportune moment. When Frederick, played by Otto Gebühr, and clearly a Hitler prototype, is advised to make peace, he replies: "Capitulate? I take over the supreme command. We shall fight again! Whoever is afraid to accompany me may go home." The voice-over commentator continues, echoing a familiar Hitler pronouncement: "Frederick wages his wars not for the sake of war but from a historical necessity. Everyone knows that this great statesman would prefer to serve his people in peaceful work, that this great artist on the throne would prefer to stay with his beloved art than to carry out the cruel handicraft of murderous war."

Klaus Granzow, a member of the Hitler Jugend, found *Der grosse König* entertaining, but writing in his diary, *Tagebuch eines Hitlerjungen, 1943-1945*, expressed disappointment when his German teacher re-

Advertisement for *Über alles in der Welt* (The Greatest in the World), directed by Karl Ritter, 1941.

185

quired the students to compose an essay entitled, "A Great King—A Great Film!" According to Granzow, the teacher "wanted us to keep drawing parallels to the present, to the Third Reich, to this war and to the Führer. It was really difficult to do that and to work it out in such a way that one would still get an 'A.' "

Bismarck, like Frederick the Great, was also invoked to serve the present moment. *Die Entlassung (The Dismissal)*, directed by Wolfgang Liebeneiner and supervised by Emil Jannings for release in 1942, begins with Bismarck having created the German Empire, but as Jannings noted in an article, *"Bismarck in Dieser Zeit,"* "it is only a partial solution. He unified the German tribes, but he could not give them the space that was essential for their new, vigorous life. He bequeathed this heritage to posterity, and today we know that this task will also be carried out."

As German forces advanced farther into Russia, German studios prepared anti-Soviet features pertinent to the current crisis. History was freely manipulated to achieve dramatic truths. Karl Ritter's *G. P. U.* was released in August, 1942, as German armies made ready to attack Stalingrad. What *G. P. U.* lacked in subtlety, it achieved in sensation. A young White Russian woman, Olga Feodorovna (Marina von Ditmar), joins the G. P. U., the Soviet Secret Service, in order to avenge the deaths of her parents murdered by the Bolsheviks in 1917-18. When Olga discovers the man (Andrews Engelmann) who was responsible, she arranges his death by assassins of his own service. In the concluding sequence, German prisoners of the G. P. U. in Rotterdam are liberated by the timely arrival of Luftwaffe bombers.

In his public pronouncements Goebbels might describe Bolshevism as "a doctrine of the devil," but in private he did not hesitate to study examples of Soviet film propaganda, captured by German armed forces or obtained by agents in neutral countries. Shortly after his proclamation for total war in February, 1943, he advised his ministerial staff to see *The Fighting Leningrad* as an example of "what total war really means." The minister was particularly impressed by the fanaticism of the civilian population. "It will show you how they shovel snow before the gates of Leningrad, how old women labor with a heavy spade at forty below zero. A patrolling soldier armed with a gun walks up and down and sees to it that the work gets done. Those who collapse with cold and exhaustion drop to the ground, but no one takes notice of them." Perhaps Goebbels, although fanatical in his dedication to Hitler and victory (*"Adolf Hitler is der sieg!"*), may have recognized that Berlin might one day be a war front with images not unlike those which he had seen in *The Fighting Leningrad*.

"Our slogan should be now more than ever: 'Total War Is the Imperative Need of the Hour,' " Goebbels wrote on March 4, 1943. But the crisis of *Total Krieg* did not affect Goebbels' plan to celebrate the twenty-fifth anniversary of UFA, March 25, 1943, on a grand scale. The occasion was marked not by the release of a grim black-and-white documentary in the style of *The Fighting Leningrad*, but by the premiere of *Münchhausen*, a lavishly appointed color fantasy starring Hans Albers.

The stage of the UFA-Palast am Zoo was decorated with a huge banner, "Twenty-five Years of UFA," and clusters of swastika flags. The evening program, attended by several thousand select guests, began with a live orchestra performance of Beethoven's *Leonore* after which Dr. Ludwig Klitzsch, General Director of UFA, recounted the history of the studio since the end of World War I. Goebbels followed with a few words: "No one can deny that the German film is an international power in every respect: economically, technically and artistically. The German film has a great reputation in all countries of the world." The Minister was effusive in his praise for Alfred Hugenberg who sat nearby unsmiling: "You have created the great institution of the UFA. . . . For you, Mr. Hugenberg, the German film was the cause of the German nation. You were the first to liberate the UFA from the influence of the American film industry." Afterwards the old man from whom Goebbels had wrested the UFA six years before was ceremoniously decorated with the Order of the German Eagle. Drs. Klitzsch and Winkler received the Goethe Medallion while directors Wolfgang Liebeneiner and Veit Harlan were named professors. Although untainted by propaganda in an overt sense, *Münchhausen* served to inform audiences at home and abroad that film art had achieved a high standard under the aegis of the National Socialist Reich.

The wartime musical provided the German masses with a complete diversion from the crisis of war which had now been brought home to them by the Allied bombing from which even the UFA-Palast am Zoo was not spared. Goebbels had a particular preference for the Viennese musical which offered a *fin de siècle* atmosphere completely at variance to the realities of total war.

The most accomplished practitioner of the operetta genre was Willy Forst, a Viennese by birth and an actor by training who achieved distinction during the Third Reich as a scenarist and director as well. Possessing a subtle comic touch not unlike Lubitsch's, his *ouvre* of thirties films included *Maskerade* (1934), *Mazurka* (1935), *Serenade* (1937) and the charming *Bel Ami* (1939) in which he both directed and acted. Forst's *Operetta*, a 1940 release, recounted the rivalry between two Viennese theaters in which Strauss II, Franz von Suppé and Millocker each play a selection from *Die*

Director Karl Ritter.

Komödianten (Comedians), directed by G. W. Pabst, 1941.

Briggitte Horney in *Das Mädchen von Fano* (The Girl from
Fano), directed by Hans Schweikart, 1940.

Heinrich George and Eduard von Winterstein in *Andreas Schlüter*, directed by Herbert Maisch, 1942.

Fledermaus in a Viennese café. As one critic has noted, "Its atmosphere was the familiar one of spring, love, lilac, guitars and Viennese wine, of whistling baker-boys and housemaids who sing and waltz as they flick dusters over gleaming door-knobs, of dashing guardsmen who flirt with pretty milliners." Forst continued in the same blithesome tradition with *Frau Luna* (1941), *Wiener Blut* (1942), *Die Fledermaus* (1945) and *Wiener Mädel*, completed in 1945 as the military fortunes of the Reich moved from astonishing victory to crushing defeat.

Director Hubert Marischka, also of the "Viennese school," entertained with *Wir bitten zum Tanz (We Invite You to a Dance)* in 1941 with Paul Horbiger and Hans Moser in leading roles, while the Hungarian beauty Marika Rökk appeared the same year in Georg Jacoby's *Frauen sind doch bessere Diplomaten (Women are Better Diplomats)*.

Two of the most popular musical films with a military theme were *Wunchkonzert (Request Concert)*, released in December, 1940, and *Die grosse Liebe (The Great Love)*, released in 1942. Directed by Eduard von Borsody, *Wunchkonzert* was based on a popular German radio program which linked soldiers, sweethearts and families by way of musical requests. In the film version, a soldier and his sweetheart, separated for three years, are reunited by the Wunchkonzert broadcast. After the

188   Gerda Maurus, Leni Riefenstahl, Heinrich Schier and Carl Hoffmann witness the making of a film in Prague during World War II. By 1945, Prague had become a principal center of German film production.

Münchhausen with Hans Albers was made to celebrate the twenty-fifth anniversary of UFA in 1943.

UFA premiere, Goebbels wrote that "The film meets with a magnificent reception. I am all the more pleased because the idea for it came from me. Another job well done. The most pleasing thing is the extraordinary common touch which the film shows. It will kindle a spark throughout the German people. I stay on for a while to be with the artistes who are overjoyed at their success."

Die grosse Liebe, directed by Rolf Hansen and seen by twenty-seven million people, dealt with women separated from men at the front. Zarah Leander, the German Garbo, took the role of a Scandinavian revue star who falls in love with a German Luftwaffe officer on leave. Later, she sings for German troops in Paris. But as historian Richard Grunberger notes, Hansen's romantic fable characteristically omitted "any reference to the events or the background of the war." Grunberger writes that *Die grosse Liebe* makes "wartime separation seem to be a form of alchemy whereby the gold of marital love could be purged of all dross."

In June, 1944, the Allies landed in France as Soviet forces drove toward Central Europe. The German people were at last experiencing the full impact, if not the tragedy, of the war which Hitler had unleashed in 1939. As the frontier between Germany's war front and her home front became indistinct, mobile film vans were

Otto Gebühr, director Veit Harlan, Kristina Söderbaum and Goebbels at the premiere of *Der grosse König* (The Great King), 1942.

dispatched to German villages while bombed out areas were served by open-air cinemas, weather and military conditions permitting.

But despite the bombing raids, filmgoing remained the most popular recreation for German citizens in the metropolitan centers. Inevitably, black marketeers added

Theo Ortner's design for a German film theater (model), c. 1943.

admonishment, but also as a power rite to conjure up past victories. There is reassurance in the belief that fate will realize the wishes expressed in the rite." Veit Harlan's *Kolberg* was produced in this spirit. Goebbels believed that the story of Kolberg's resistance to the French in 1806 after Prussia's defeat by Napoleon suited the current crisis.

The minister accorded *Kolberg*, designated "Film der Nation," a ceremonious Berlin premiere on January 30, 1945, to mark the twelfth, and what would be the final, anniversary of Hitler's accession to power. As Gauleiter of Berlin, Goebbels identified with Joachim Nettelbeck, the tenacious Burgermeister who defies the defeatist military commander Lucadou to organize a citizens' militia suggestive of the *Volkssturm* of 1944-45 as Napoleon's forces lay siege to the fortress town. Unabashedly

Detail of Theo Ortner's murals for a German film theater, c. 1943.

cinema tickets to their inventory of precious commodities. In Berlin, queues would form in front of cinema houses in the early afternoon in order to reserve seats for the evening showings. And the once privileged German soldier was no longer given priority seating as the distance between the fighting front and the Reich capital diminished with the passing of each day.

"When a country goes to war, propaganda films revive the memories of past victories and glories and embellish them with tolling of bells, banners and other symbols worthy of the transcendental significance of the struggle," Lief Furhammer and Folke Isaksson write in *Politics and Film*. "The standard propaganda of the boastful historical film is there, not just as a pleasant memory or

propagandistic, the dialogue of *Kolberg* echoed Goebbels's own increasingly irrational pronouncements in the press and on the radio: "We would rather be buried in the ruins of our city than to give it up to the enemy." The day after *Kolberg*'s premiere, Soviet forces crossed the Oder River, the last natural barrier between their army and Berlin, fifty miles distant.

The final Soviet offensive against Berlin began a little before dawn on April 16, 1945. Devastated by air raids which had intensified since February, the Berlin of Walter Ruttmann's *Symphony of a City*, Volker von Collande's *Zwei in einer grossen Stadt (Two in a Big City)* and Wolfgang Liebeniener's *Grosstadtmelodie (Melody of a Great City)*, released in October, 1943, but based on photographic backgrounds taken before the apocalyptic air raids, had for all intents and purposes, disappeared. But on the eve of the Soviet attack, the population of the gutted and smoking metropolis by the Spree could still find solace in the darkness of a commodious *Lichtspielhäuser*, to be entertained by *Kameraden (Comrades)*, *Hallgarten Patrol (The Hallgarten Patrol)*, *Schwarzer Jäger Johanna (Black Fighter Johanna)* and comedies such as *Das Glück wohnt nebenan (A Merry House)*, *Ein Idealer Gatte (The Ideal Husband)* and *Esfing so Harmlos an (It All Started So Gaily)*, the last-mentioned feature, directed by Theo Lingen, having a particularly ironic ring.

During April, 1945, German audiences saw the final wartime edition of the *Deutsche Wochenshau* (No. 755/10/1945), issued at the end of March. Running eleven and a half minutes, this black-and-white sound film

Scenes from *Grosse Freiheil Nr. 7* (The Great Freedom No. 7), directed by Helmut Käutner, 1944.

A French cinema advertises German newsreels, c. 1942-1943.

German soldiers stationed in northern Norway attend a film at the "Lappland-Palast," 1943.

The final wartime edition of *Die Deutsche Wochenshau* was released at the end of March, 1945. Hitler awards the Iron Cross to twenty members of the Hitler Youth.

A member of the Hitler Youth describes his experiences in the final wartime edition of *Die Deutsche Wochenshau*, released at the end of March, 1945.

contained ten episodes including the work of a bomb disposal squad; civilians training to fire anti-tank grenade launchers; and members of the Hitler Youth on a visit to Hitler. A haggard Führer, attired in a vizored cap and great coat, is shown awarding the Iron Cross to twenty members of the Hitler Youth whom the voice-over narrator describes as "the loyal aids of our soldiers."

Heinrich George and Kristina Söderbaum in *Kölberg*, directed by Veit Harlan, 1945.

Although the narrator alleges that three of the youths recounted their exploits for the Führer, it is apparent that Hitler was no longer present during the brief filmed interviews. These newsreel pictures provided the German people with the last images of Hitler before the collapse of the Third Reich a few weeks later.

Although the advance units of Marshal Zhukov's tank force had reached the eastern suburbs of Berlin, German directors attempted to fulfill their 1945 production schedules. At the Barrandow studio in Prague, G. W. Pabst labored to complete *Der Fall Mollander* with Paul Wegener and Irene von Meyendorff, while on another stage Geza von Bolvary directed Marte Harell and Willy Fritsch in a color version of *Die Fledermaus*. At the Radlitz, also in Prague, Karl Anton oversaw the production of *Der grosse Fall*, starring Gustav Fröhlich. And in Berlin, the closing days of the Third Reich found Paul Verhoeven directing costumed extras in the Biedermier milieu of *Das kleine Hofkonzert*, Oscar Fritz Schuh making shots on the rococo set of *Ein toller Tag*, and Willi Forst standing behind the camera of *Wiener Mädeln*, a color extravaganza based on the life of waltz composer Carl Michael Ziehrer.

Goebbels met with representatives of the German press for the last time on April 21, 1945, addressing the group in the candle-lit film room of a mansion on the Hermann Goering Strasse, his own ministry having been bombed out. State Secretary Naumann recalled that Goebbels "spoke in deadly earnest about the coming end, that all attempts to turn the tide had failed, and concluded, 'May God be merciful to the German people, because I fear the worst. But gentlemen, you can be assured that neither I nor my family will be captured alive by the Russians.' " The minister's prophecy of suicide was fulfilled ten days later.

Michelangelo, Das Leben eines Titanen

MICHELANGELO, THE LIFE OF A TITAN

1940

CREDITS:

Production: Pandora-Film AG., Zurich-Berlin. Deutsch-schweizerische Gemeinschafts produktion. Released by Degeto-Kulturfilm GmbH. *Director:* Curt

Drohend und kriegerisch ragt der Palast der Signorie in Florenz. Ein Sinnbild seiner bewegten mittelalterlichen Geschichte.

Advertisement for *Michelangelo*.

Oertel. *Screenplay:* Curt Oertel. *Cinematography:* Curt Oertel and Harry Ringger. *Music:* Alois Melichar. *Speaker:* Mathias Wieman. *Released:* March 15, 1940. *Length:* 2558 meters. Released in 1950 by United Artists in a 70-minute English language version as *The Titan—the Story of Michelangelo*. Edited by Richard Lyford under the supervision of Robert J. Flaherty. Dramatic commentary spoken by Fredric March.

Michelangelo, Das Leben eines Titanen (Michelangelo, the Life of a Titan) represents one of the finest achievements in the genre of the cultural documentary, the special province of Curt Oertel. Oertel was born in Osterfeld, Thuringia, in 1890, the son of an art publisher. Before the First World War Oertel studied at the Munich *Staatlichen Lehr-und Versuchsnastalt für Fotografie* (State School and Laboratory for Photography). After 1918 he worked occasionally in the film industry, but also traveled on the continent where he studied works of art and architecture. During a trip to Egypt, he experimented in the photographing of ancient works of art, achieving dramatic effects with light, shadow and movement.

Oertel opposed the bold montage of Eisenstein and the avant-garde, believing that while the clash of images might excite the viewer momentarily, their impact was shortly forgotten. In lieu of stimulation, he preferred a "relaxed form of visual expression" which promised a longer after-effect. "The art of film must be planned carefully so that it relaxes the spectator, making him receptive to new experiences," Oertel wrote in the late 1930s. "Then the language of the screen image will emerge, filled with a secret force which I call the soul of the image."

From the early 1930s, it became Oertel's ambition to create works of cinematic art about art and artists. As a filmmaker, he saw himself as an intermediary between the work of art, statues, friezes, paintings, and the recording lens of the camera. He sought to deepen the effect of a work of art by breaking the subject into carefully composed shots. One of Oertel's finest works before *Michelangelo* was *Steinernen Wunder von Naumberg (Stone Wonders of Naumberg,* 1933). "No building could be more suitable for the realization of my ideas

The Slave, unfinished marble figure originally intended for the tomb of Pope Julius II. Accademia, Florence. *(Michelangelo)*

The tomb of Lorenzo, *Il Pensieroso*, with *Dawn* and *Twilight*.
Sacristy of San Lorenzo, Florence. *(Michelangelo)*

Photographing the colossal statue of *David* in the Accademia, Florence. Critic Heinrich Miltner wrote that Oertel "works with the noblest of materials, namely light." *(Michelangelo)*

than the Cathedral of Naumberg," he wrote afterwards. "The dramatic figures of the West Choir and the expressive statues of the founders, became my actors. . . ."

Oertel applied these same principles to *Michelangelo*, which he photographed in collaboration with Harry Ringger over a two-year period in 1938-1939, working primarily in Florence and Rome. The film was released in March, 1940, with a musical score by Alois Melichar and a dramatic commentary spoken by actor Mathias Wieman. Although the heroic figure of Michelangelo as conceived by Oertel may have accorded with the National Socialist ethos of the artist as genius, *Michelangelo* remains a landmark in the use of the film medium for artistic and educational purposes.

The story of Michelangelo is told through his works of art. Churches, ruins, palaces and tombs in Florence and Rome together with the portraits of popes, painters, merchants and princes recreate the world of the Italian Renaissance. Actors never appear. "Without seeing him we see what he was," John Mason Brown wrote. "With the aid of the narrative and especially due to the camera's chaperonage, we follow his life and sense the grandeur of his genius. The result is a masterpiece composed of masterpieces. In it a period writes its own history even as the art of an artist writes biography." Oertel relies on the visual metaphor to establish the world of the Renaissance: the closing of a paneled door, the passing of

One of Michelangelo's earliest works, the *bas relief* of the *Centaurs*. *(Michelangelo)*

clouds over a piazza, the reflection of Roman ruins in pools of water and, especially arresting, the death mask of Lorenzo the Magnificent, darkly saturnine.

"Lighting moves across the screen like an actor," another reviewer noted, the camera tilting "awry at an assassination," or the focus blurring "as if with pain when Michelangelo's nose is smashed in a brawl." And no less astonishing is Oertel's rendering of Savonarola's reign of fanaticism. Torches illuminate a darkening sky as "pagan" art treasures are heaped on the bonfire in front of the Palazzo Vecchio. But the persecutor, Savonarola, eventually becomes the persecuted, and in the final shot of the sequence we see Michelangelo's sketch of Savonarola's limp body hanging from a gibbet.

The marble masterpieces of Michelangelo appear to come to life as when Oertel photographs the towering figure of David: strong, defiant and proud. The countenance of the young warrior, captured in a series of

The face of *David*. *(Michelangelo)*

Director Curt Oertel and his assistants prepare to photograph Michelangelo's *David*, suggesting its transport in 1504 through the streets of Florence to its place before the Signoria. *(Michelangelo)*

197

Moses, centerpiece of the tomb of Pope Julius II. San Pietro in Vincoli, Rome. *(Michelangelo)*

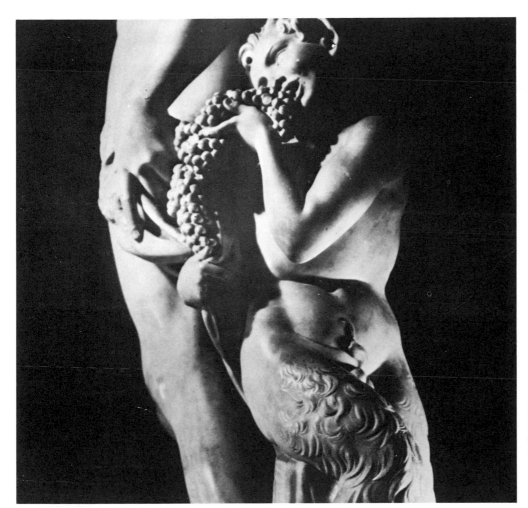

Detail of the satyr from
Bacchus. Muzeo Nazionale
del Bargello, Florence.
(Michelangelo)

remarkable closeups, alters with the change in light as the huge statue is wheeled through the streets of Florence to its pedestal in front of the Signoria.

In the Sistine Chapel, the camera follows the drama of man from the creation to the flood as it is unfolded by Sybils and prophets. Guided by torchlight, the viewer mounts a darkened staircase to the Medici tomb of San Lorenzo where Oertel exploits the camera's possibilities to the fullest with photographs of *Dawn* awakening to another day of pain, and *Twilight* weighed down by the burden of hopelessness. "As highlighted by Klieg lights, as surveyed through the camera's eye, as approached from unexpected angles or viewed in dramatic close-ups," Brown writes, "they leap and lunge into life even more amazing than that which we had prized as theirs."

The last scenes show the dome of St. Peter's, designed by Michelangelo, sparkling against a clouded sky. The film concludes with shots of an unfinished Pietá, the flickering of a candle, and a bare orchard to suggest the passing of the Titan. "Curt Oertel creates with the eyes of a sensitive artist who unconditionally gives priority to the visual and who avails himself of all devices of camera art such as the editing of picture and sound, music and dialogue," Heinrich Miltner wrote after the completion of *Michelangelo*. "He gives life to inanimate objects, transforming them into a powerful experience. As artist, painter, historian, writer, technician and director, Curt Oertel realizes his ideas, conquering new territories in the art of film."

A shorter, seventy-minute English language version of *Michelangelo*, edited by Richard Lyford under the supervision of Robert J. Flaherty, was released in the United States by United Artists in 1950. Flaherty believed that it would open new vistas for documentary films devoted to art and artists, as indeed it did. But while the film was widely praised, Oertel's role in its creation was almost unmentioned.

Otis L. Guernsey, Jr., reflected the sentiments of most Anglo-American critics when he wrote that in *Michelangelo* "the film medium has become a magic mirror which, though suffering from a physical handicap in its existence as a flat, black-and-white square of light, enhances in its own language the grand illusion which is the aim and achievement of all great art."

199

Der Postmeister

THE STATIONMASTER

1940

CREDITS:

Production: Vienna-Film GmbH und UFA. *Director:* Gustav Ucicky. *Screenplay:* Gerhard Menzel. Based on the novella by Alexander Pushkin. *Cinematography:* Hans Schneeberger. *Editor:* Rudolf Schaad. *Art direction:* Werner Schlichting and Kurt Herlth. *Costumes:* Alfred Kunz. *Sound:* Alfred Norkus. *Music:* Willy Schmidt-Gentner. *Released:* April 4, 1940 (Vienna), and April 10, 1940 (Berlin). *Length:* 2598 meters.

CAST:

Heinrich George (*the Stationmaster*); Hilde Krahl (*Dunja, his daughter*); Siegfried Breuer (*Captain Minskij*); Hans Holt (*Fähnrich Mitja*); Ruth Hellberg (*Elisawetha*); Margit Symo (*Mascha*); Erik Frey (*Sergej*); Franz Pfaudler (*Pjotr, Knecht*); Alfred Neugebauer(*Gotsbesitzer*); Leo Peukert (*Colonel*); Richard Häussermann (*Schneider*); Auguste Pünkösdy (*Wirobowa*); Oskar Wegrostek; Hugo Gottschlich; Anton Pointner.

Der Postmeister (The Stationmaster), based on the short story of Alexander Pushkin, was conceived during the early phase of Soviet-German rapprochement. Directed by Gustav Ucicky and photographed by the incomparable Hans Schneeberger against period settings created by Werner Schlichtung and Kurt Herlth, *Der Postmeister* is a film of extraordinary beauty and may be regarded as one of the most outstanding German films of the war period. Direction and photography were enhanced by the accomplished performances of Heinrich George in the title role, Hilde Krahl as his daughter Dunja and Siegfried Breuer as Captain Minskij.

The opening credits of *Der Postmeister* are accompanied by a song: "Russia sleeps its deep sleep from which it cannot be awakened. A knight with black eyes rides on his wild horse, and a garland of thorns lightens his bright forehead."

Siegfried Breuer. (*Der Postmeister*)

Heinrich George. *(Der Postmeister)*

One day Captain Minskij, elegantly attired in Circassian cap and military uniform, arrives at the posting station where an aged stationmaster lives with his daughter Dunja, a woman of extraordinary beauty and the source of his greatest pride. The captain is at first anxious to be on his way, but when Dunja appears he makes every effort to prolong his stay without arousing the suspicions of the girl or her father. The old man is easily deceived and, believing the captain to be seriously ill, advises a sweat cure which includes the ingestion of cucumber tea served at a scalding temperature. Bundled in blankets, the captain's protestations ("Imagine the sufferings of Holy Laurentius on the roast") are of no avail as the stationmaster proceeds with his cure and a steady stream of advice: "I always say that perspiration takes all the poison out of the system. You know, your Highness, I once had dysentery. Well, you have no idea how I perspired. Holy Saint of Novgorod, the water just ran down my whole body, right into the boots, but two drops spilled on the floor and a rat comes running, your Highness, and licks up these two drops. She trembles for a minute or so and then is dead. These two drops . . . all the poison was in these two drops. . . ."

Dunja succumbs to the officer's charm and upon his "recovery," agrees to accompany him to St. Petersburg with the promise of a better life. The old man gives his consent in the belief that Minskij intends to marry his

Heinrich George as the stationmaster. *(Der Postmeister)*

201

Siegfried Breuer as Captain Minskij. (*Der Postmeister*)

raged, he demands an explanation. Fearful of hurting the old man, Dunja persuades Minskij to stage a mock wedding followed by an elaborate banquet attended by officers and their paramours. Minskij agrees to this scheme, but Dunja, unhappily, must return as his mistress. Now consoled, the father returns home.

The despondent Dunja commits suicide, having secured Minskij's promise that the death notice communicated to her father will describe her as Minskij's wife.

Heinrich George, Hilde Krahl and Siegfried Breuer. (*Der Postmeister*)

Hilde Krahl. (*Der Postmeister*)

daughter. But in reality, the fickle captain seeks only a mistress.

In the Tsarist capital, Dunja is admired by other cavaliers. She forgets her father, but he has hardly forgotten her. When the old man decides to come to St. Petersburg, he learns that Minskij has yet to marry his daughter. There are ugly rumors and insinuations. En-

Advertisement for *Der Postmeister* with Hilde Krahl and Heinrich George.

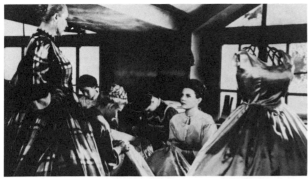

Hilde Krahl (seated). *(Der Postmeister)*

The old man mourns her death, but it is a mourning untroubled by the dismal truth. Until the end of his days, the old man tells travelers who stop at his station of his daughter Dunja and how she found happiness in St. Petersburg with her husband, Captain Minskij.

Released in Berlin on April 10, 1940, *Der Postmeister* served the needs of Soviet friendship, now vital to Hitler in the wake of his attack on Denmark and Norway which was launched at dawn the previous day. But after the passage of more than forty years, *Der Postmeister*, now separated from the political context which inspired its

Heinrich George and Ruth Hellberg. *(Der Postmeister)*

production, emerges as a highly meritable if not outstanding work of film art.

Sieg im Westen
Ein Film des Oberkommandos des Herres

VICTORY IN THE WEST

A Film on the German High Command.

1941

CREDITS:

Production: Produced by Noldan-Productions. *Cinematography:* Photographed at the front by cameramen of the Staff of the Commander-in-Chief of the Army, the Propaganda Company and troops of the Army Film Department. *Music:* Horst Sieber *(Der Entscheidung entgegen/Forcing the Decision);* Herbert Windt *(Der Feldzug/The Campaign). Released:* January 31, 1941 (UFA-Palast am Zoo).

After the fall of France in June, proposals were presented for a feature-length documentary of the western campaign in the format in *Feldzug im Polen,* which had dealt with the invasion of Poland. In October, 1940, Goebbels wrote in his diary that "Each branch of the Wehrmacht wants to make its own film about France. I put a stop to these ambitions and drew all the relevant plans together." The result was *Sieg im Westen,* produced under the aegis of Colonel Hesse, Wehrmacht Propaganda Chief, from 2.7 million feet of material shot by cameramen attached to the *Presse-kompanie* of the German army during the sweep through Belgium, Holland and France. In addition, the editors made extensive use of captured film, including "hitherto unreleased shots of the French forces manning the Maginot line" taken by the British, Belgian and French forces.

On December 20, 1940, Goebbels noted that "The new Wehrmacht film about the Western Campaign is ready except for some editing. Hesse wants to release it straight away. I continue to put a brake on things. Hesse is too hasty, a tendency which is also clear in his propaganda for Brauchitsch, which is doing more harm than good." Goebbels screened the film two days later.

His diary entries suggest approval but with reservations: "It has turned out to be entirely satisfactory. No clear line. And insufficient emphasis on the cooperation between the various branches of the Wehrmacht. I am against it being released straight away. The Führer agrees."

The final version was released on January 31, 1941, the eighth anniversary of Hitler's accession to power, with a ceremonious premiere at the UFA-Palast am Zoo attended by Goebbels, Keitel, Brauchitsch and the higher echelon of the Wehrmacht.

On the domestic front, *Sieg im Westen* was designed to stimulate national pride in the armed forces which had achieved a rapid victory with a relatively small loss of life, while its release in foreign countries under the sponsorship of German consuls and agents served the purposes of German diplomacy, principally as a warning to neutral nations and potential enemies. *Sieg im Westen* was shown to Premier Cvetković, Foreign Minister Cincar Marković and the Yugoslav defense chiefs on February 19, 1941, less than a month before the signing of the Tri-Partite Pact. In the following months, it was screened for government officials in Stockholm, Helsinki, Lisbon, Ankara and Teheran. King Boris of Bulgaria is alleged to have remarked to the German ambassador, Dr. Eugene Rümelin-Bülow, following the showing of the film in Sofia: "I should not like to meet your army under such circumstances." To which the ambassador replied, "There is no need to, your majesty." *Sieg im Westen* was also shown in Turkey where Franz von Papen, the German ambassador, issued invitations to the diplomatic community in Ankara, although the London *Times* wrote that "attendance was scanty and the film was boycotted by Americans."

German and English language versions of *Sieg im Westen* reached the United States in the spring of 1941 distributed by the German Library of Information in New York "without cost or question." A German Information memo described the film as "a spectacular documentary showing the full fury and power of a modern mechanized army." The memo briefly described the background of the film, noting that "Many lives were lost in recording these breath-taking war pictures." Its German advertisers were certain that "With the attention of America focused on preparedness and national defense, the preservation of this military document of actual mechanized warfare is both timely and important."

Life magazine (March 10, 1941) accorded the film a pictorial review, noting that "No Hollywood movie was ever more carefully script written and rehearsed than Germany's conquest of Western Europe. What is more astonishing is that the Germans then photographed it almost as thoroughly as if it were just a movie."

Advertisement for *Sieg im Westen*.

Its exhibition at the 96th Street Theater in the predominantly German-speaking community of Yorkville was occasioned by protest and picketing organized by The Friends of Democracy, the Non-Sectarian Anti-Nazi League and the German-American Congress for Democracy. In the following days, protests against the film reached the desk of Secretary Hull, who recommended Congressional action to further restrict the importation of Axis propaganda. Others thought differently, as a letter to *The New York Times* suggests: "The more the film is shown the easier it will be to convince certain people how they have been misled by isolationists. It will wake up America to the perils which are in store for us." Critic Bosley Crowther, writing in *The New York Times* on May 11, found it "an excellent compilation of actual war shots, carefully edited to omit the harrowing, and it is most effectively scored. But whether it will frighten anybody who doesn't want to be frightened remains to be seen."

Aerial perspective of German tanks. *(Sieg im Westen)*

The infantry maneuvers with machine-like precision. *(Sieg im Westen)*

Jerome S. Bruner and George Fowler analyzed the impact of the film on neutral America in a contemporary article for *The Journal of Abnormal Psychology and Social Psychology*. "The central theme of the film is the never-ending advance of the omnipotent and efficient German army," the authors wrote. "It is not a ruthless or bloody advance—indeed, no dead bodies are shown— but a methodical series of barrages, bombardments,

A Press Company cameraman at work. *(Sieg im Westen)*

206

troop movements, and stormings. Eternally the German soldiers move onward, athletic, happy, blond, often singing, but always determined. So easy and so organized are the victories that before many feet of film have flashed by, the onlooker finds mounting in himself a suspicion that no real resistance was put up."

Victory follows victory as shock troops and panzers force bridgeheads and bombard enemy strongholds. The siege of Fort Eben Emael is achieved after Wehrmacht units paddle across the Albert Canal under Belgian fire. The chronicle continues with the breakthrough at Sedan, the flanking of the Maginot Line, and preparations for the assault on Dunkirk. "The amount of destruction depicted is colossal," wrote Bruner and Fowler. "Everywhere there are bombed-out buildings, destroyed tanks and carrions, battered fortifications, smashed planes. To overcome the natural revulsion of such ravishment, the happy Nordic soldiers are made to appear almost angelic—fighting angels. Flower-throwing crowds greet

Perspective from the interior of a tank. *(Sieg im Westen)*

The unity of man and machine. *(Sieg im Westen)*

them wherever they conquer, babies are held up to be duly kissed, water is drunk out of homely containers. Though cities are destroyed, cathedrals are spared 'by strict orders of der Führer,' the advance goes on with battalions singing."

Through editing and narration, the disciplined power of the Wehrmacht is shown in direct contrast to the chaotic inefficiency of the enemy. "When enemy troops are shown, they appear as poorly dressed, morally depressed, unshaven prisoners of war marching stolidly to the rear while the German troops, immaculately clad and clean-faced, go forward," Bruner and Fowler note. "And the subtle monologue of the narrator is designed to make one believe the crushing onslaughts of this well-oiled juggernaut to be but the just desserts of the conquered people. Proof of the deservedness of the action is implied in shots of primitive-looking French and British colonial troops, beturbaned and smacking of another and less civilized world. About these prisoners no comments are made; they are shown, and that is all."

The film achieves a "cosmic sweep" by the inclusion of "frequent sequences taken from high flying planes." The spectator is allowed to share the cockpit of "the dive

208

bomber while a rail junction is annihilated." Animated maps further accentuate the "cosmic sweep" of the invaders. "For Germany the earth spreads itself as a great chessboard on which she alone can see the possible moves—the enemy never."

In his 1943 essay, "Propaganda and the Nazi War Film," reprinted in his psychological history of the German film, *From Caligari to Hitler* (1947), Siegfried Kracauer also described the adroit use of maps in *Sieg im Westen*. As Kracauer observed, maps served to harmonize with the aerial perspective of the film and the diving and panning movement of the camera. Maps stressed "the propaganda function of statements about strategic developments inasmuch as they seem to illustrate, through an array of moving arrows and lines, tests on some new substance. Resembling graphs of physical processes, they show how all known materials are broken up, penetrated, pushed back and eaten away by the new one, thus demonstrating its absolute superiority in a striking manner."

When Hitler is shown toward the end of the film, Bruner and Fowler observed that ". . . he is portrayed as a humanitarian though a mortal one, bringing peace to

Animated maps describe the rapid advance of the German Army and serve to reinforce the notion of its invincibility. *(Sieg im Westen)*

the 'gallant French' in the Forest of Compiègne. The Leader is careful to return a pencil to the person from whom he borrowed it, he jokes with his officers, but, as in the case of the soldiers, he is made to appear as a man of power and determination. One scene in which he is shown with Il Duce puts him at further advantage by juxtaposing his dignity with the opéra bouffe salutes of the Italian dictator."

As a result of an audience survey conducted among 260 Harvard and Radcliffe faculty and students plus a number of Cambridge and Boston townspeople on April 9, 1941, Bruner and Fowler concluded that "Three general reaction patterns seem to accompany successful resistance to feelings of futility in the face of terror propaganda—disgust, anger, or cool psychological distance." Bruner and Fowler found that interventionists

210

tended to resist feelings of futility more readily than isolationists. The researchers found that not a few respondents objected to *Sieg im Westen* because of its technical imperfections, especially the uneven lighting of shots. "Comments volunteered by one after another of our respondents taught us that many were not impressed by the film simply because it did not come up to Hollywood standards of what war brutality, viewed close-up, looks like." The survey concluded that "a third of the audience felt the futility of resistance against the Nazis during the film and not quite half of these persisted in these feelings after the film was over."

Kracauer's aforementioned essay, "Propaganda and the Nazi War Film," offered a perceptive analysis of the function of commentary, visuals and sound in *Sieg im Westen*. "The announcement of an action is immediately followed by its result, and long developments are supposed to have been consummated in the tiny period between two verbal units," Kracauer noted. "Thus a great deal of reality and enemy resistance disappears in the 'pockets' of the commentary, giving the audience a sense of ease of accomplishment and increasing the impression of an indomitable German blitz. Actually the blitz has flashed through an artificial vacuum."

Ingenius use was made of music in conjunction with photographs and commentary. As Kracauer noted, music "not only deepens the effects produced through these media, but intervenes of its own accord, introducing new effects or changing the meaning of synchronized units." As the British evacuate from Dunkirk we hear the mocking strains of "We'll Hang Our Washing on the Siegfried Line" while a jazz rhythm is heard over images of Algerian troops in a prisoner of war camp. "Music, and music alone, transforms an English tank into a toy," Kracauer noted. "In other instances, musical themes remove the weariness from soldiers' faces or make several moving tanks symbolize the advancing German army."

The detailed coverage of the construction and installations of the Maginot Line drawn from captured French films serves to accentuate the offensive quality of the German versus the defensive posture of the French. "By exhibiting that machinery to the full," Kracauer notes, "the Nazis wanted not only to heighten the significance of the German victory, but also to specify its unique character." The filmmakers ". . . wanted to show that the *deus ex machina* can never be the machine itself; that even the most perfect organization proves useless if it be regarded as more than a mere tool, if it be idolized by a generation-on-the-decline as an autonomous force. The whole presentation aims at implying that the Maginot Line was precisely that to the French, and that in consequence, the German victory was also a victory of life over death, of the future over the past." Thus, the commentator's statement when the fortress is shown at the end of the film carries a deeper meaning: "For the last time, the clockwork of this complicated defense machinery is in action."

Rembrandt

1942

CREDITS:

Production: Terra. *Director:* Hans Steinhoff. *Screenplay:* Kurt Heuser and Hans Steinhoff. Based on the novel *Zwischen Hell und Dunkel* by V. Tornius. *Cinematography:* Richard Angst. *Music:* Alois Melichar. Filmed in 1941 in the UFA studios at Tempelhof and Babelsberg and at the Cineton Studios in Amsterdam and the Haag. *Released:* June 17, 1942. *Length:* 2910 meters.

CAST:

Ewald Balser, Hertha Feiler, Gisela Uhlen, Elisabeth Flickenschildt, Theodor Loos, Aribert Wäscher, Paul Henckels, Hildegard Grethe, Wilfried Seyferth, Paul Rehkopf, Rolf Weih, Clemens Hasse, Helmut Weiss, Heinrich Schroth, Robert Bürkner, Karl Dannemann,

Ewald Balser as Rembrandt.

211

Unveiling of the controversial "Nightwatch." *(Rembrandt)*

Hans Hermann Schaufuss, Erika von Thellmann, Eduard von Winterstein, Walter Lieck, Hans Stiebner, Frida Richard, Walther Sussenguth, Lotte Rausch, Bruno Harprecht, Heinrich Marlow, Fritz Hoopts, Ernst Legal, Franz Stein, Viktor Janson, Ernst Rotmund, Otto Stoeckel, Franz Schafheitlin, Jack Trevor, O. E. Hasse, Werner Scharf, Michael Tacke, Lieselotte Walter, Hans Mierendorff, and others.

As a young man, Hans Steinhoff had interrupted his medical studies to join the theater, first as an actor and later as a director. He directed his first film, *Der falsche Dimitri (The False Dimitri)*, in 1922 but did not achieve prominence until 1933 with *Hitlerjunge Quex (Hitler Youth Quex)*. *Der alte und der junge König (The Old and the Young King)*, 1935, with Emil Jannings as Frederick the Great, established Steinhoff as a major directorial figure during the Third Reich. The chauvinistic *Robert Koch* (1939) and the anti-English *Ohm Krüger* (1941), presented "historical" biography in a contemporary frame of reference. Steinhoff's films often showed the individual in opposition to society, conscious of his obligation to the German collective spirit and German nationalism. Steinhoff died in an airplane crash near Luckenwalde in 1945. His last film, *Shiva und die*

One of the superb compositions designed by Steinhoff and his cameraman, Richard Angst. *(Rembrandt)*

Galgenblume (Shiva and the Flower of the Gallows), was unfinished at the time of his death.

Based on the novel *Zwischen Hell und Dunkel*, by V. Tornius, *Rembrandt* was perhaps Steinhoff's finest effort. It was photographed by the gifted Richard Angst, a veteran of the Fanck school, at Tempelhof and Babelsberg and at the Cineton Studios in Amsterdam and the Haag in 1941. The paintings of Rembrandt inspired the

Hans Steinhoff directing a scene from *Rembrandt*.

visual motif of the film. As Wilhelm Westecker wrote: "The paintings are the real scaffolding of the film. From the cheerful portrait of the artist's wife Saskia, Steinhoff creates a scene of domestic celebration when Rembrandt receives the commission to paint 'The Nightwatch.' "

It becomes the pivotal work around which Steinhoff interprets the story of Rembrandt the man and the artist.

"Hans Steinhoff has not taken the easy way in his presentation of the creative style and the psychological condition of the artistic genius," Westecker wrote. "Avoiding all cheap popularization, he gives the genius dignity and stature. And while the pictorial element is based strongly on Rembrandt's paintings, it is also indebted to other Dutch art. The picture steers a course between the monumentality of the paintings and the more subtle intermezzos of individual characters. Architect Walter Röhrig has created buildings which suggest the affluence of the Dutch burghers while Alois Melichar has composed an unobtrusive soft curtain of sound."

Steinhoff introduces Rembrandt at the height of his fame. The artist is persuaded to paint a group portrait, the Company of Captain Frans Banning Cocq, better known as the "Night Watch." When the portrait is completed, the Guild refuses to accept it and will not pay the agreed fee. During the dispute Rembrandt receives

Ewald Balser. *(Rembrandt)*

Aribert Wäscher (right). *(Rembrandt)*

Elisabeth Flickenschildt. *(Rembrandt)*

word that his wife Saskia is dying. After her death he loses his friends and his will to live. His house is auctioned and one by one his acquaintances from better days reject him.

At last he finds happiness with the simple maid Hendrickje Stoffels. It makes no difference to Hendrickje that Rembrandt will not marry her, but gossip and ecclesiastical disapproval disrupt their harmony, and she dies in premature childbirth. Rembrandt relapses into poverty and solitude. In the attic of the guildhall, he discovers his painting of the "Night Watch," humbly realizing that his life as an artist has not been in vain.

Rembrandt was first shown in June, 1942, during the Berlin *Kunstwochen* (Art Week). Westecker was certain that the film would "be a great success as an incisive portrait of one of the greatest geniuses of Germanic art. Since it approaches the genius of the artist less through the biography than through the art, it acquaints the people in a memorable way with the psychological conditions of artistic creation."

Comparison between motion pictures of the same subject is an inevitable feature of film criticism, although Steinhoff's *Rembrandt* with Ewald Balser in the title role is known to a smaller audience than the 1936 Alexander Korda production with Charles Laughton. But Balser's achievement was no less impressive than that of Laughton's. As Westecker wrote in his 1942

Ewald Balser. *(Rembrandt)*

commentary, Balser revealed enormous depth as an actor "in his transformation into the bent and aged Rembrandt of the later and famous self-portrait with the turban. He poignantly portrays the resigned wisdom of the artist who has outgrown all earthly needs and anxieties."

214

Münchhausen

1943

CREDITS:

Production: UFA. *Director:* Josef von Baky. *Screenplay:* Berthold Bürger [psuedonym for Erich Kästner]. *Cinematography:* Werner Krien (Agfacolor). *Special effects:* Konstantin Irmen-Taxhet. *Art direction:* Emil Hasler and Otto Gulstorff. *Music:* Georg Haentzschel. *Released:* March 5, 1943. *Length:* 3662 meters. A new version (100 minutes) has been prepared by the Friedrich-Wilhelm-Murnau Foundation in German, English and French with the title The Adventures of Baron Muenchhausen.

CAST:

Hans Albers *(Baron Münchhausen);* Brigitte Horney *(Catherine the Great);* Wilhelm Bendow *(The Man in the Moon);* Michael Bohnen *(Prince Karl of Brunswick);* Hans Brausewetter *(Frederick von Hartenfeld);* Marina von Ditmar *(Sophie von Riedesel);* Andrews Engelmann *(Prince Potemkin);* Kaethe Haack *(Baroness Münchhausen);* Hermann Speelmanns *(Christian Kuchenreutter);* Walter Lieck *(Runner);* Ferdinand Marian *(Count Cagliostro);* Leo Slezak *(Sultan Abd-ul-Hamid);* Gustav Waldau *(Casanova);* Ilse Werner *(Princess Isabella d'Este).*

Baron Münchhausen was commissioned by Dr. Goebbels to commemorate the twenty-fifth anniversary of UFA in 1943. Direction of the *Jubilaumsfilm* was entrusted to Josef von Baky, a young Hungarian of German background. Eberhard Schmidt, UFA production group manager, engaged novelist and poet Erich Kästner to fashion a screenplay about the legendary baron from Lower Saxony. But the choice of Kästner presented certain difficulties. His published work, novels, stories and poems, of which *Fabian* and the lyric, *"Kennst Du das Land, wo die Kanonen Bluhen?"* ("Do You Know the Land Where the Cannons Bloom?") were most characteristic, had fallen under official ban since 1933. Through the intercession of Schmidt and Dr. Fritz Hippler, the *Reichsfilmdramaturg* who worked closely with Goebbels in this period, Kastner was allowed to

Münchhausen (Hans Albers) and Catherine the Great (Brigitte Horney).

At the court of Catherine the Great. *(Münchhausen)*

Hans Albers. *(Münchhausen)*

write the screenplay under the psuedonym of Berthold Bürger.

Rudolf Erich Raspe established the literary tradition of Münchhausen with the publication in 1785 of a book which purported to be an account of the exploits of an actual person, Baron Karl Friedrich Hieronymus von Münchhausen, who lived in Göttingen from 1720 to 1797. The historical Münchhausen had travelled widely in the world, fought in the services of Catherine the Great, and for a time had been a prisoner of war in Turkey. When he retired to his castle in the Weser Hills, the baron would entertain his hunting and drinking companions with descriptions of his travels and adventures.

In the early nineteenth century Gottfried August Bürger elaborated on Raspe's account. Bürger told how

Baron Münchhausen on route to the Turkish camp.

the pigtailed, moustached and bowlegged Münchhausen pulled himself and his horse out of the mud with his own queue, and how he rode on a cannon ball to enter the enemy camp, but realizing that the Turkish enemy might hang him as a spy, jumped in mid-air to a Turkish cannon ball being fired in the opposite direction. In 1839 Karl Immermann wrote about the improbable figure in a long novel, *Baron Münchhausen*, and in the 1920s Carl Haensel reworked the legend for modern readers.

Although Kästner drew upon these sources, his filmscript may be considered yet another interpretation of the fabulous Münchhausen. Where Raspe and Bürger had portrayed Münchhausen as the *Lügenbaron*, the "Baron of Lies" from Lower Saxony, Kästner saw him as an easygoing if not frivolous rococo gentleman. Kästner's

Münchhausen (Hans Albers) and Sultan Abd-ul-Hamid (Leo Slezak).

Interior of the Sultan's palace. *(Münchhausen)*

Münchhausen's arrival at the Sultan's citadel.

debt to Bürger is subtly suggested by the selection of his *nom de plume*, while his choice of the surname Berthold may have been a gesture of homage to Brecht, whom the Nazis had forced into exile in 1933.

Preparation for the elaborate filming of *Münchhausen* began in 1941. Von Baky and his technical staff studied the special effects of numerous color productions, including Walt Disney's *Snow White and the Seven Dwarfs* (1938) and David O. Selznick's *Gone With the Wind* (1939), but particular attention was given to Alexander Korda's 1940 film, *The Thief of Bagdad*, which Goebbels

The Grand Canal. *(Münchhausen)*

Ilse Werner as Princess Isabella d'Este. *(Münchhausen)*

much admired and hoped to surpass in special effects and color artistry.

Prior to *Münchhausen* Germany had produced only three feature films in color, but by 1940 the Agfa laboratories had made substantial progress in the field of color cinematography. On March 25, 1941, Goebbels wrote: "We have now caught up with the Americans in this field, thank God. Filmwise, we are on the march."

The staging and editing of the trick effects was achieved under the supervision of Konstantin Irmen-Tschet, who worked over a ten-month period, while the stylized eighteenth-century settings, designed by Emil Hasler and Otto Gülstorff, were some of the most elaborate in the history of the German film. Museums and palaces loaned authentic Meissen services and silver and gold tableware for the fabulous banquet scene in the Russian palace, guarded, it should be noted, by SS men attired in period livery.

The colorful Venetian sequence was photographed in the summer of 1942. Railroad cars crossed the Brenner laden with "precious carnival costumes, robes for the doges, domino and harlequin costumes, tri-cornered hats and crimson sashes for the gondoliers, sedan chairs and flowers by the kilo." Correspondent Eberhard von Wiese described further the thousands of costumes "hanging row upon row in the warehouse while outside the sons and daughters of Venice, having been attracted by newspaper advertisements asking for extras, waited to slip into the garments of their ancestors." Von Wiese wrote that "although they didn't know much about Baron Münchhausen, they knew that a festival was in the offing, and that was sufficient to kindle their southern love for diversion. They willingly exerted themselves for an extraordinary purpose. Even the Italian police bowed to Münchhausen, barring a portion of the Grand Canal to public traffic for a single day."

And finally, von Wiese described the actual photographing of the Grand Canal sequence: "Josef von Baky gives the word, relayed by his Italian interpreter over the loud speaker, and the beautifully decorated flotilla of gondolas begins to move from the *Maria della Salute.* The red scarves and sashes of the gondoliers stand out

against their black garments while the dainty rococo ladies sit under brocaded canopies, framed by dignified patricians and youthful cavaliers. A rain of confetti pours from the bridges and palaces, and in the middle of this glittering scene, with the overtones of a fairytale, floats the gondola of the two lovers, Münchhausen and Isabella."

The cast was generally excellent although the mannerisms of Hans Albers as Münchhausen were thought by some to be more typical of a Frisian sailor than the elegant cavalier conceived of by Kästner. Nevertheless, Brigitte Horney in the role of the Tsarina, Ferdinand Marian as Cagliostro and Leo Slezak as the Sultan cannot be faulted.

The film begins with a gala eighteenth-century ball at the Bodenwerder castle presided over by the jovial but somewhat sinister Baron Münchhausen and his wife. There is a sudden lovers' quarrel between two of the young guests. The girl flees the party and jumps into her Mercedes. We have been viewing a costume party, and the period is very definitely the present.

The baron and his much older wife attempt to reconcile the pair. He tells them of the adventures of his "ancestor," the fabulous Baron Münchhausen, and the film goes into flashback, this time to the real eighteenth century.

Münchhausen and his servant Christian visit the baron's father, who is puzzled over Christian's invention of a rifle which can see and shoot a distance of 200 kilometers. After a series of surrealist sight gags, the pair

Gustav Waldau as Casanova. (*Münchhausen*)

Münchhausen (Hans Albers) converses with the daughter of the Man in the Moon (Marianne Simpson).

decides to go to Braunschweig at the invitation of the local prince to whom the Empress Catherine the Great has offered the command of a Russian regiment. The prince asks for Münchhausen's help in convincing his lovely mistress Louise la Tour to make the trip, and when this is accomplished the group sets off for Russia.

The dealings at the Russian court are devious. The magician Cagliostro tries to enlist Münchhausen in a plot against the empress, but without success. At a carnival the baron meets a young girl named Kätchen who is later revealed to be Catherine in disguise. Münchhausen becomes Catherine's new lover, kindling the jealousy of the former favorite, Prince Potemkin, who challenges the baron to a duel, injuring him slightly. Münchhausen goes to the strange house of "Doctor" Cagliostro to have his wound treated, and while there warns Cagliostro that he is about to be arrested. Although the magician knows this, he rewards the baron with the secret of eternal youth, and also gives him a ring that will make him invisible for one hour. As the secret police break into the house, the pair escapes, using magic.

Catherine soon tires of Münchhausen and sends him to Turkey in command of a regiment. He is inadvertently shot on a cannonball to Constantinople where he becomes a prisoner of the sultan. After a period of imprisonment he is reunited with his servant, Christian.

The baron is offered his freedom if he will convert to the Moslem religion. He explains to the sultan that this would be impossible because he would have to drink water instead of wine, but the sultan tells him he does not really have to abstain—and gives him a sample of his private stock of Tokay. Münchhausen insists that the Tokay he drank at the palace of the Empress Maria Theresa in Vienna was twice as good. This leads to a bet in which the baron promises to provide the sultan with a bottle of wine from Vienna in an hour. If he wins the bet he will have his freedom. Thanks to a wonderful runner, the bottle is produced, leading to a second wager. If the wine is indeed better than the sultan's, Münchhausen will be rewarded with the beautiful Princess Isabella d'Este, a prisoner in the harem. Münchhausen wins this bet too, but the sultan reneges on his promise, attempting to pass off another girl as Isabella.

Using the magic ring, the baron invades the harem, abducts the real princess, and sets sail for Venice. He learns that the girl's family had planned to marry her to an old man. She had fled the city but was abducted by pirates who sold her to the sultan. Her sudden return is no joy to her family, and her wicked brother Francesco has her kidnapped a second time and locked up in a convent. Münchhausen fights a duel with Francesco that results in the latter's clothes being cut to ribbons.

Münchhausen and Christian, with the d'Este family in pursuit, escape Venice in a giant balloon conveniently anchored in the Grand Canal. Their vehicle takes them to the moon. There, in a surrealist landscape, Christian ages and dies, because one day is equal to a year on earth—but Münchhausen is, of course, immortal. His gloom is dispelled by the presence of the daughter of the Man in the Moon. She can be in two places at the same time by separating her head from her body. But even her charms soon pale, and the baron returns to Germany.

The scene now shifts back to the present where Münchhausen tells the startled young couple that he and his distinguished "ancestor" are one and the same. Thoroughly frightened, they flee the castle. The baroness, having observed that her husband is attracted to the girl, tells him to follow his new love. Instead, he renounces the gift of eternal youth to grow old with her.

Münchhausen premiered at the UFA-Palast am Zoo on March 5, 1943, shortly before the destruction of this most famous Berlin theater.

Although Hitler did not attend the Berlin premiere, he was shown some scenes from the film at his headquarters. And when he was told that Kästner had authored the screenplay, he instructed Bormann to inform Goebbels that Kästner should have no further assignments. Upon receipt of Hitler's message, Goebbels wrote in his diary: "Through Bormann the Führer voices his opposition to the employment of former defeatist writers such as Bronnen, Gläser and Kästner. I order that they should no longer be employed in the cultural realm."

Was the film itself free of political overtones? Only in the framing story do we glimpse a tiny swastika standard on the fender of a Mercedes. Some critics, however, have discerned political allusions in Kästner's text. For example, when the devious Cagliostro suggests to Münchhausen that they go into partnership, the baron replies: "There is one thing we two will never agree upon. Principally, you want to rule, I want to live. Adventure, war, foreign lands and beautiful women: I want to use all of that but you want to abuse it." Or, when the sultan informs Münchhausen that his religion is the better one, Münchhausen answers: "Who can decide what is better where hardly anyone knows what is good?" And how should we interpret Casanova's declaration to Princess Isabella in the Venetian sequence: "The state inquisition has 10,000 eyes and arms, and it has the power to act justly or unjustly." Does Cagliostro represent Hitler, and should the comments of Münchhausen and Casanova be constructed as veiled criticisms of the National Socialist State?

It is possible that Kästner intended to give the speeches a contemporary significance, but if this is so, then what interpretation is to be given to Münchhausen's speech in which skepticism is expressed for theorists and reformers? "If you are born in Bodenwerder you cannot become a Turk. We can have only one home, just as we can have only one mother." Mindful of the rigorous censorship imposed on films and Goebbels's personal involvement in the production of *Münchhausen*, it would seem more likely that the passages refer to events in the film rather than the politics of the period.

Münchhausen exists in at least four versions. The first censored version (March 5, 1943) ran 133 minutes, but further excisions were thought necessary, and on June 17, the film was rereleased with a running time of 118 minutes. After World War II *Münchhausen* was condensed to 90 minutes, but its distribution abroad was restricted. A new 100-minute version prepared by the Friedrich-Wilhelm-Murnau Foundation and released by Atlas International holds the promise of bringing this most celebrated of German sound films, so often described but rarely seen, to a larger audience.

Kolberg

1945

CREDITS:

Production: Ein UFA-Farbfilm. *Director:* Veit Harlan. *Screenplay:* Veit Harlan and Alfred Braun. Cinematog-

raphy: Bruno Mondi. *Art direction:* Erich Zander and Karl Machus. *Sound:* Wolfgang Schleif. *Production supervisor:* Wilhelm Sperber. *Music:* Norbert Schultze. *Released:* January 30, 1945. *Length:* 3026 meters.

CAST:

Kristina Söderbaum *(Maria);* Heinrich George *(Nettelbeck);* Paul Wegener *(Loucadou);* Horst Caspar *(Gneisenau);* Gustav Diessl *(Schill);* Otto Wernicke

The people of *Kolberg.*

Advertisement for *Kolberg*.

(Werner, a farmer); Irene von Meyendorff *(Queen);* Kurt Meisel *(Claus);* Jaspar von Oertzen *(Prince Louis Ferdinand);* Hans Herrmann Schlaufuss *(Zaufke);* Paul Bildt *(Rektor);* Franz Schafheitlin *(Franselow);* Charles Schauten *(Napoleon);* Heinz Lausch *(Friedrich);* Josef Dahmen *(Franz);* Franz Herterich *(Kaiser Franz II);* Frau Schröder-Wegener *(Frau von Voss);* Fritz Hoopts *(Timm);* Werner Scharf *(General Teulié);* Theo Schall *(General Loison).*

By the summer of 1943, with German forces assuming the defensive on all fronts, Goebbels recognized that film might play an even more decisive role in the strengthening of public morale. On June 1, 1943, Goebbels wrote to director Veit Harlan, whom he had elevated to professor the previous March: "I hereby commission you to make the epic film *Kolberg.* The film is to demonstrate, through the example of the town which gives it its title, that a people united at home and at the front will overcome any enemy. I authorize you to request whatever help and support you deem necessary from all Army, Government and Party agencies, and you may refer to this film which I have hereby commissioned as being made in the service of our intellectual war effort." Writing in his diary, Goebbels reflected that he had great expectations for *Kolberg,* noting almost prophetically, "It will fit exactly the situation that we expect to be in when the film is ready to be shown."

The story of Kolberg's resistance to the French during the Napoleonic siege fascinated Goebbels, who saw a parallel between the events of 1806-07 and Germany's situation in 1943. Although the French had won the Battle of Kolberg and the city itself had been destroyed, the people had survived. Goebbels believed that the German population would be heartened by a film version of this event. There would even be a role for the minister, who was also *Gauleiter* and Reichs Defense Commissioner for Berlin, and, it should be noted, the most visible member of the National Socialist regime in this final phase of the war. Cinema audiences would see him as Nettelbeck, the tenacious mayor of Kolberg, who calls for the formation of a civilian militia as Goebbels had extolled the virtues of the *Volkssturm,* a civilian combat unit comprised of those ranging in age from 16 to 60, formed on October 13, 1944, the anniversary of the battle of Leipzig.

Goebbels insisted, however, that the role of the Prussian general Gneisenau be downgraded while the part played by Nettelbeck in the defense of Kolberg be enhanced in order to emphasize that it was the people and not the Army that would resist to the last. In an interview with the press in December, 1943, Harlan emphasized

Heinrich George as the Mayor of Kolberg.

this point, stating that *Kolberg* "is intended as a memorial to Gneisenau and Nettelbeck and to the people of Kolberg, but above all it is a memorial to the German people today."

The production of *Kolberg* consumed the remainder of 1943 and most of 1944, Harlan and his cameraman, Bruno Mondi, having exposed more than ninety hours of film. Delays were inevitable as the script required frequent revisions in light of the changing military situation. Elaborate sets were built at Neu-Stettin, scene of the actual battle, while interiors were created in Berlin. According to Harlan, who was allocated a budget

223

of 8.5 million Reichs Marks, 187,000 soldiers were withdrawn from active service to appear at various times in the crucial battle scenes of *Kolberg*. Additionally, some 4,000 sailors were commandeered to simulate the French attack across flooded fields while 6,000 men provided a cavalry in full regalia. The matériel requirements, considering the restrictions of "Total War," were very great. The UFA "'armory" replicated sabers, muskets, helmets, boats, and a wardrobe of 10,000 uniforms. Even the crown of Charlemagne was requisitioned for a needed scene. In an interview before his death in 1965, Viet Harlan reminisced:

The cost of the film was immaterial. Goebbels declared that this time the military would not be allowed to thwart him. On order of the Führer, the military would have to supply the necessary personnel and materials because the film was to be a colossal depiction. I had more power than the generals. . . . Both Hitler and Goebbels must have been obsessed by the idea that such a film would be more useful to them than, for instance, a victorious battle in Russia. Or perhaps they were waiting for a miracle because they could no longer believe in a logical kind of victory. They were more at home in the dream factory of film miracles than they were at the front. . . . I am not trying to ridicule this film in any way, nor am I trying to discount its humane values, but after all, everyone involved in making the film as well as anyone who later saw it knew exactly what purpose the film served. . . .

The minister arranged for a simultaneous premiere of *Kolberg* in Berlin and at La Rochelle, now under attack

Director Veit Harlan. *(Kolberg)*

Horst Caspar as Gneisenau. *(Kolberg)*

by Soviet forces, on January 30, 1945, the twelfth anniversary of Hitler's assumption to power. In a telegram Goebbels instructed the commandant at La Rochelle "to have a worthy opening performance to mark the close ties between those men fighting at the front and those at home who are displaying to the whole nation the virtues demonstrated in this film." But the magic of film could not prevent the inevitable. La Rochelle capitulated a short time later as Russian forces continued their advance into Pomerania. On March 4, 1945, Goebbels noted in his diary that Soviet tanks had reached the outskirts of Kolberg. And finally on March 20, 1945, he wrote that "Heavy attacks were made on our lines on the east bank of the Oder at Stettin; the enemy broke in on the east and south, reaching the Stettin-Altdamm railway. Altdamm itself was occupied by the enemy. Kolberg too fell into enemy hands."

Aside from the aforementioned screenings in La Rochelle and Berlin, conditions precluded an extensive distribution of *Kolberg* in regions still under Reich jurisdiction. Performances, however, were held in Breslau and Danzig, and when Soviet forces occupied Guben and Babelsberg in May, 1945, Harlan's staff was still in the process of editing a second negative.

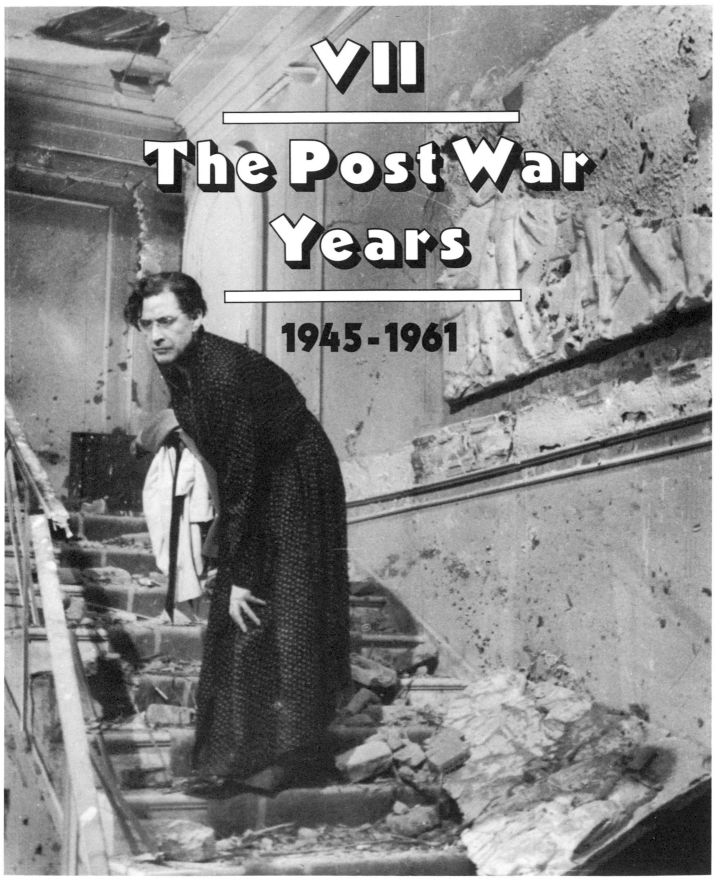

VII
The Post War Years
1945-1961

Hans Sohnker in *Film ohne Title* (Film Without a Title),
directed by Rudolf Jugert, 1948.

The nucleus of Germany's pre-war film industry, including two of the largest studios at Neubabelsberg and Johannestal outside Berlin and the Agfa film stock plant at Wolfen, fell within the Soviet zone of occupation. Soviet authorities rapidly reopened theaters, and by May 22, 1945, some thirty-six *Lichtspielhäuser* were functioning in the Soviet zone of Berlin, principally showing older, non-propagandistic German films. On November 17 the Soviets convened a meeting of German film personnel in the "Courier's Wing" of the Hotel Adlon on the Wilhelmstrasse in Berlin to discuss the rebuilding of an anti-fascist German film industry. The Adlon, save for the "Courier's Wing," had been reduced to ruins by a fire which had occurred in the first days of the Soviet occupation.

The Adlon meeting resulted in the formation of DEFA (Deutsche Film Aktiengesellschaft), the Soviet sponsored German Film Company. Colonel Tulpanov, representing the Soviet Military Administration, noted that the supreme obligation of the German film must consist in "aiding the democratic renewal of Germany, in educating the German people, particularly the youth, in a spirit of democracy and humanism in an effort to arouse respect for other people and countries." At the end of 1946, ten DEFA feature films were in production in addition to newsreels, special interest films and instructional shorts. By 1947 the embryonic company had metamorphosed into a state-sponsored organization employing no fewer than 1,300 people with administrative offices in the former UFA building in the Potsdamer Platz.

DEFA productions in this initial phase were set in a contemporary, post-war German background. The first, and in many respects the finest, of the *Trümmerfilms* ("rubble" films) was *Die Mörder sind unter Uns (Murderers Are Amongst Us)*, directed by Wolfgang Staudte. It told the story of a former *Wehrmacht* captain, now a respectable entrepreneur and family man, who is revealed to have overseen the liquidation of an entire Polish village. There were other notable DEFA productions in the years 1946-1948. In *Irgendwo in Berlin (Somewhere in Berlin)*, director Gerhard Lamprecht, remembered for his 1931 masterpiece, *Emil and the Detectives*, presented the poignant story of a soldier returning home to his family. Employing a documentary style, Milo Harbig's *Freisland (Free Land)* focused on the problem of land reform in the Soviet Union. *Razzia (Round-Up)*, directed by Werner Klinger, described the battle of the Berlin police against the black market, while Kurt Maetzig's *Ehe im Schatten (Marriage in the Shadows)* dealt with the tragic deaths of the Gottschalks.

Colonel Tulpanov, representative of the Soviet Military Administration, at a DEFA meeting in 1946.

In its initial phase, British zonal policy was satisfied to educate and entertain German audiences in accordance with the Allied policy of de-Nazification, making extensive use of German motion pictures untainted by National Socialist propaganda. By presenting the "right" films, the Film Section hoped "to make the Germans in time say to themselves, 'The people in this film seem happy; they are free; they seem to have all they want. Why can't we be like that?' The screen is being designed to act as a signpost which will point the way to future progress."

The second phase of British policy focused on the tasks of reviving the German film production, building up a non-theatrical film movement, the fostering of film societies and the establishment of a Film Censorship Board and the reestablishment of a German film industry on a democratic basis. In the name of democracy, both British and American authorities forbade combines or cartels and separated the functions of production, distribution and exhibition. In reality, this calculated fragmentation of the industry served to prevent the development of a serious competitor to the well-organized Anglo-American interests.

Hamburg emerged as the principal center of film production in the British zone. The absence of studios required that much of the shooting be done in the open air. Raw film stock remained scarce and expensive, restricting the number of copies of each film, and technical equipment and apparatus remained in short

By the end of 1946, ten DEFA feature films were in production.

Ilse Steppart and Paul Klinger in *Ehe im Schatten* (Marriage in the Shadows), directed by Kurt Maetzig, 1947.

supply. The process of de-Nazification of actors and technical staffs impeded production still further.

In July, 1946, the British granted a production license to a Berlin company, "Studio 45," founded by Ernst Hasselbach the year before. Later in 1946, zonal authorities licensed a second company, C. C. C. (Central Cinema Company), while in Hamburg licenses were issued to Helmut Käutner (Camera Film) and Walter Koppel (Real Film).

The problems of film production in the British zone of Berlin were nearly as great as those in Hamburg, a fact attested to by H. H. Wollenberg, former German film correspondent for *Sight and Sound*, in the summary of a conversation between Hasselbach and Paul Ickes: "Shooting has to be done mainly at night in view of the frequent electricity cuts. The artists and technicians are thus confronted with a very strenuous task, but all have responded extremely well and have no other desire but to work in films again. The principal consideration in choosing a story is the lack of material for sets and costumes, and the final selection of subjects is largely determined by these conditions. The technical studio equipment, however, is more or less adequate. The first production schedule included only two films, both of which have now been completed."

William B. Kelly, the United States Consular representative in Hamburg, noted in August, 1948, that "The British point to the popularity of the simpler, more realistic types of film, particularly those now being produced by the Italians and, to some extent, the French." And while filmmakers in the American zone depended on German actors who had been prominent in the Third Reich and Weimar, British policy favored the newer stars. Kelly conceded that British zonal policies had not been without success: "From the high quality of the films thus far produced, for example, *Wege im Zwielicht (Twilight Paths)*, *Arche Nora (Nora's Ark)*, *In jenen Tagen (In Those Days)*, and *Menschen in Gottes Hand (People in God's Hand)*, it would appear that this policy may result in the creation of a new postwar set of German stars."

Welt im Film (World on Film), the official Anglo-American newsreel, provided zonal audiences with information about Germany and the outside world. Produced in Munich by a joint Anglo-American newsreel board and funded equally by the British and United States governments, *Welt im Film* presented foreign news received from British and American sources, news of the British zone and news of the American zone in equal proportion. More in the nature of a short documentary or cinematic "newsmagazine" than the conventional newsreel of the period, *Welt im Film* subordinated topicality for perspectival reporting in the context of the

Allied goal of "educating German public opinion on sound democratic lines."

Although stories were chosen by Anglo-American control officers, much of the actual operation of *Welt im Film* was conducted by a German production staff chosen because of their previous experience. According to the *British Zone Review* of September 27, 1947: "Priority is given to matters of national interest to the Germans, to world news, and finally to sports items, both German and foreign, if the latter has an international significance. Political developments, economic plans and stories connected with the food and fuel situation are of constant interest. Sports items are always popular, and so are reports of scientific inventions, whether German or foreign. The German thirst for overseas information is very real."

German cameramen, many of whom had served on the war front, proved their agility and courage once again as they scurried about the zones with tripod and portable batteries to photograph unusual scenes—an oil well bursting into flames or shots of impoverished German boys raiding a coal train. "These men do a splendid job, and the material they produce will compare with the work of any newsreel team anywhere," reported the *British Zone Review*. "It is of high quality and well up to the high standards of pre-war German camera work."

The revival of the *Kulturfilm*, that uniquely German contribution to the documentary genre which had flourished before World War II, was encouraged by the convocation of the first *International Kulturfilmtagung* in Hamburg from May 6-16, 1949. Organized under British auspices, representatives from Austria, Australia, Denmark, France, Britain, Sweden, Switzerland, Spain, Italy, America, Finland and Holland met with German delegates from the three Western zones to consider the future of the *Kulturfilm* in the context of German film production. Lectures, seminars and discussions were punctuated by the showing of over 200 films from seventeen countries, including works from Poland and the Soviet Union.

In the aftermath of the war, *Kulturfilm* production had practically ceased. And while old UFA *Kulturfilme* were reissued, the profits were impounded and therefore could not be applied to current production, an unfortunate circumstance. The *Internationale Kulturfilmtagung* nonetheless called for a release of more of the older *Kulturfilme*, the granting of a tax relief for the production of films of cultural value and the reimposition of the pre-war requirement that a *Kulturfilm* be included in each program—all positive steps in the furthering of this genre.

The conferees debated the differences between the *Kulturfilm* and the documentary. While the *Kulturfilm*

Hildegard Knef and Viktor de Kowa in *Zwischen Gestern und Morgen* (Between Yesterday and Tomorrow), directed by Harald Braun, 1947.

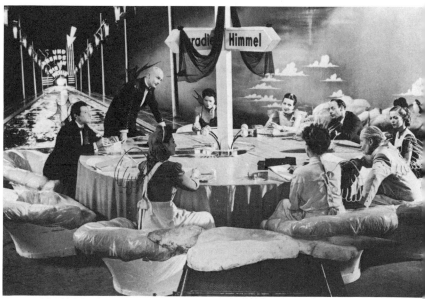

Der Apfel ist ab (The Apple has Fallen), directed by Helmut Käutner, 1948.

was inclined to be romantic and subtly poetic in photographic style, emphasizing the beauty of the landscape or the works of man, the documentary, as defined by John Grierson, emphasized realism in the service of social, political and economic reform, a tendency reflected in such notable British films as *Song of Ceylon, Night Mail* and *Housing Problems*. In contrast to the creators of the German *Kulturfilm*, the British documentarians were overtly propagandistic.

Irene von Meyendorff in *Film ohne Titel*.

Dr. Viege Traub, Hans Sohnle, Robert Herlth, Josef von Baky; seated: Helmut Beck, Eugen Klagemann and Hermann Warm in 1950.

Directors of the *Kulturfilm*, however, continued to search for the timeless rather than the transitory. *Leidensgeschichte (Passion of Our Lord)*, directed and photographed by Alfred Ehrhardt, was one of the most notable *Kulturfilm* achievements of the immediate post-war period, sponsored by Film Section in the British Zone in 1949. The altar of Schleswig Cathedral, carved in 1521 by Hans Brueggemann, was used to tell the story of the death, resurrection and ascension of Jesus. The figures of Jesus, Mary, and the flagellators come to life as the camera "moves from tableau to tableau, accentuating detail, co-ordinating and illuminating, till the intensity of feeling and the fine craftsmanship which created these carved figures, aided by the artistic integrity of the film direction, bring the whole story to life." There is no spoken commentary, only the music of Cibolt's "Elevazione" and Bach's "Johannes Passion." A British reviewer of the period was moved to write: "I left the cinema with a real sense of loss, knowing that most of us who live in the twentieth century can only admire, but are not privileged to share, the unquestioning and passionate faith which alone could create such a masterpiece 'for the Glory of God.' " Such was the power of the German *Kulturfilm*.

Film policy in the American zone was guided by the Office of War Information Overseas Motion Picture Bureau (OWI). During the spring of 1945, German theaters, production facilities and film collections were systematically confiscated by the OWI which sought to impress upon the German people their responsibility for the war. Factual films, newsreels and short documentaries of concentration camps compiled by Signal Corps photographers were shown to German audiences in the American Zone during the first weeks of the occupation. The OWI regarded film as a tool for the reeducation of the Germans and not as a medium for entertainment. Appropriate feature films which reflected "the American scene and democracy in a wholesome fashion" would be introduced in time—*Young Tom Edison*, *The Gold Rush* and *It Started with Eve* were in the process of being dubbed into German—but only after the documentary film had achieved a measure of psychological "cleansing" in keeping with the goals of de-Nazification.

In general, the American programs, running approximately one hour and fifteen minutes, were characterized by a certain dullness. The ponderous and didactic quality of the American programs did not take into consideration the desire of the German public to be entertained and to escape from the awful realities of daily life in the post-war era. Germans were especially curious to see certain American films, such as *Gone With the Wind*, which had been censored during the Nazi era. But its exportation was deemed inappropriate in light of the American philosophy of educating the German accord-

Advertisement for the 1952 Berlin Film Festival.

ing to democratic precepts. As Bosley Crowther noted: "*Gone With the Wind* would encourage the latent Scarletts and Rhetts, and it would cast a most dubious reflection upon the integrity of Americans."

During the spring and summer of 1945 American authorities presented the War Department's *Why We Fight* series, *The Fighting Lady, Attack! The Battle of New Britain* and other information films but soon converted to a program of an entertainment feature, an informational or educational subject and a specially edited newsreel. These efforts were organized by director Billy Wilder, now Colonel Wilder, who served as head of the film unit of the American Information Control Division between May and September, 1945. He found the Germans "thirsting for information about America and the rest of the outside world."

Wilder's initial contacts with the Soviet film authorities were cordial, in part, he believed, because they had mistaken him for William Wyler, the director of *Mrs. Miniver* and *The Little Foxes*, which the Soviets seem to have much admired. With his indefatigable Viennese humor, Wilder "took the bows very graciously, if sheepishly, and was never more grateful for the similarity of our names. . . . We might not have got along so well if the Russians had realized that I had a hand in the writing of *Ninotchka*," a film which had satirized the Soviet regime.

On a more practical level, Wilder's experiences in Berlin, a city which he had known intimately before 1933, gave him the idea for "A true and realistic, not a prettied up account" of life in the capital which he described as a modern "Sodom and Gomorrah." He wanted to show how thoroughly beaten the Germans were while pointing to future possibilities in the context of a story "about a romance between a GI and a German girl." Wilder hoped to subtly convey "some very definite ideas." Such was the genesis of *A Foreign Affair*, a sentimental farce set against the ruins of Berlin which Wilder directed and co-wrote with Charles Brackett for release in 1948.

In July, 1946, Eric Pommer, the former UFA producer, was appointed Film Officer of the State Department's Information Control Division which was shortly afterwards transferred to the War Department. As chief of the Motion Picture Branch of the Information Service Division of the Office of the Military Government for Germany (OMGUS) with headquarters in Berlin, Pommer advised the American military government on policy for all motion picture matters. In addition, he had responsibility for the reconstruction of the German film industry in the American zone of Germany. To achieve this goal he worked with the four-power occupational forces serving as liaison officer with the British, French and Soviet motion picture organizations and as a member of the Tripartite Film Board in Wiesbaden. He was confident that Germany would "be a very interesting film country again."

The appointment was not without political significance. As *Film Daily* reported in September, 1946: "Germany is generally regarded as the political key to Europe and the motion picture program will play a top role in this country's future plans."

In contrast to the achievements in the Soviet and British zones, filmmaking in the American zone revived slowly. Production licenses were issued only after a thorough investigation of the applicants' political background. All members of the cast and crew were carefully scrutinized for political acceptability within the parameters of de-Nazification. According to critic and historian H. H. Wollenberg, "Pommer relegated applicants to three 'sheep' categories." The black sheep were removed from consideration while the white were looked upon with suspicion. Pommer preferred the gray, which in his opinion, could be "thoroughly cleansed."

The quantity of production was small—only thirteen features were produced in the American sector in 1948—but the quality, the traditional trademark of a Pommer film, remained high. Pommer did not hesitate to concern himself with the smallest details of film production. A man of immense talent and enormous energy, it was not uncommon to observe him, as Stuart Schulberg did, going "from the complexities of a 4-Power film control meeting in Berlin to an analysis of strong nuances in a script conference, and then to a cutting room where, exasperated by an editor's inability to time a cut, take over the moviola and the splicer."

The first German production to receive an American license was *Und über uns der Himmel (The Sky Above Us)* directed by Josef von Baky from a script by Gerhard Grindel. Released in December, 1947, correspondent Thomas F. Hawkins described it as "the most beautiful record yet made of Berlin as it now is. Shots of the gloomy, ugly miles of ruins are impressive, and against this background unrolls the life of the people, the black market, the hunger and the hopelessness of youth who do not know which way to turn."

Von Baky offered the story of a returning veteran, played by Hans Albers, who becomes a black marketeer. When his son who is blind regains his sight, he repudiates the black market luxury which his father has achieved while others live in misery. Photographed by Werner Krien, it contained "individual scenes which only Germans who know the city [Berlin] could make so true to life," Hawkins notes in his review. "There is the shot of an old German fishing for food from garbage pails; I see the same scene in real life, three or four times

Alfred Bauer, director of the Berlin Film Festival, Archbishop Alfred Bengsch and James Stewart.

a day along the street where I live." In another shot an old woman "having crawled from bed, cuts into the last hunk of dried-out bread in an effort to still hunger. The old man tells her he will sell his ring and buy food in the black market—which he does next day, but is caught in a raid and loses both ring and food."

Other notable German films created during Pommer's tenure as chief of OMGUS in 1947 and 1948 were: *Lang ist der weg (Long Is the Road)*, *Zwischen Gestern und Morgen (Between Yesterday and Tomorrow)*, *In Jenen Tagen (In Those Days)* and *Film ohne Title (Film Without Title)*. There were many other films which bear the imprint of the man who, more than two decades before, had made possible the Golden Age of the German film.

In December, 1948, Pommer relinquished his position as chief of OMGUS to Arthur Mayer, former owner of the Rialto Theater in New York. "I've done the job I set out to do in Germany," Pommer stated, "and my usefulness there has come to an end." According to his son John, Eric Pommer considered his work in Germany with the Military Government to be the most significant achievement of his entire career. Although an American citizen since 1944 and a resident of Los Angeles, Pommer returned to Germany periodically during the next decade, producing films independently, the most important of which was *Kinder, Mütter und Ein General (Sons, Mothers and a General)*, directed by Laslo Benedek in 1955.

In his memoir, *Merely Colossal*, published in 1953, Mayer recalled the nature of his mission: "We were, or so I was told, to recreate the German film industry along modern, progressive lines and help, through the production and circulation of documentaries, 'to inculcate democratic ideas, the respect for human rights and the development of individual responsibility.' "

Mayer was very different from Pommer in terms of temperament and background. Unlike his renowned predecessor, Mayer had little empathy for Germany and had no particular desire to see the German film industry become a viable force in European or world cinema. While the European-born Pommer was both artist and businessman, Mayer was almost solely an organizer and entrepreneur with a distinctly American perspective. De-Nazification edicts as they pertained to the employment of Germans in the film industry were handled more stringently.

Under Mayer's aegis OMGUS continued to emphasize documentary production as a way "to reorient the Germans into the intellectual life of the Western world." Stuart Schulberg, brother of the novelist and screenwriter, Budd, organized and supervised the United States Documentary Film Unit which produced *Zeit im Film*, a newsreel in the style of *March of Time*. Schulberg additionally produced a series of feature-length documentaries.

Mayer's tenure as Chief of the Motion Picture Branch of Military Government terminated in 1949 with the establishment of the West German Federal Republic. At the time of his departure the impresario appears to have doubted the success of his mission, convinced as he was that he had done "little to advance the cause of democratic institutions" in Germany.

234

Hildegard Knef and Erich von Stroheim in *Alraune*, directed by Arthur Maria Rabenalt, 1952.

If the American effort to educate through film had been only a partial success as Mayer suggests, four years of American occupation and control achieved the goal of subordinating the German industry to the United States, giving the American film a predominance in Germany which it exercises to this day. From the beginning American films dominated the United States zone of occupation. By 1948-1949, approximately 70 percent of the pictures exhibited in the American sector were of Hollywood origin. By way of contrast, programs in the British zone comprised 60 percent German, predominantly pre-1945 productions which had been approved for viewing. And while the British encouraged the distribution of German films in the United Kingdom, the powerful Motion Picture Export Association (MPEA) representing the Hollywood industry remained adamant in its opposition to the importation of German films into the United States on the grounds that America was not interested in receiving films produced by former Nazis.

It was argued, also, that German films, in general, had not reached their former quality and were treating subjects which, on the whole, were peculiarly German and therefore not of great interest to a wide audience in foreign countries. It was a curious perspective when one considers that in this same period the Italian neo-realist films, concerned with themes peculiarly Italian, were enjoying a wide success in the United States. Many American critics regarded *Open City, Paisan* and *The Bicycle Thief* to be nothing less than the reinvention of the cinema.

The MPEA regarded a revival of the German film industry as a threat which it was prepared to resist with all manner of influence. German movie production, which had been so effectively dismantled, must not be allowed to dominate foreign markets, or, for that matter, its own home market, now secured by the world-wide film imperium of the United States.

The role of Film Branch was to have long-term consequences for the post-war German film. While the currency reform of 1948 reinvigorated the economy of the Western sector, German filmmakers did not share in the increased prosperity. As Mayer admitted at the close of his tenure as administrator, "They were considerably handicapped by our vigorous enforcement of denazification and decartelization regulations. The great majority of the former leading actors, authors, directors, and technicians of the German film industry who had not been purged, rendered impotent by years in concentration camps, or exiled, had paid lip service to the Hitler regime." Some of those who were denied permission to work in the reconstructed West German industry found employment in the East. Others resumed their careers in foreign industries or took up new occupations at home.

These restrictions, however well-intentioned, hindered the reconstruction of the German film industry at mid-century.

The decisions of the Decartelization Branch were no less consequential. "Writing a film *finis* to UFA" was a primary goal of the decartelization measures. Resentful of its historic control over the production and distribution of films, the Film Branch enacted new regulations which disposed of UFA properties to individuals who had been cleared by denazification. To insure against the revival of a UFA-like cartel, no exhibitor was allowed to acquire more than three theaters. While these measures were theoretically democratic, the result was less than ideal. The Americans relinquished control of a German industry which rested on a foundation of sand.

The decade of the 1950s proved to be a time of crisis and transition for the West German film industry. The first year of the new decade found the German industry in dire financial straits, having lost not only its international market but the greater share of its domestic market. Some 150 new firms were licensed in the immediate postwar period, but banks refused to make loans and private credits were difficult to obtain. Many were forced to depend on sponsors such as Arthur Brauner and Ilse Kubaschewski, entrepreneurs who were less concerned with the art of filmmaking than turning a good profit. Some Germans began to have second thoughts about the desirability of a system based on "complete independence" without "state interference." And while the Federal Republic and the separate states were eventually moved to support the industry by guaranteeing deficits, commercial considerations weighed heavily in their decision to grant subsidies.

Producers and directors proceeded with the greatest caution. Most were reluctant to experiment with new themes and develop new talent. The German film appeared to have reached an artistic and commercial *cul de sac.* "West German producers turned to operettas and insufferably sentimental 'local color,' " Friedrich Luft observed in a 1957 article. "Only a rare picture saved the intelligent movie-goer from constant embarrassment. In the East Zone there were biographies of Communist heroes, such as *Thälman, A Fighter for His Class; Advice of the Gods*, an exposé of capitalism; and *The Lost Village*, which showed Americans mistreating a West German community."

Film critic and historian Enno Patalas described the paralysis of the German industry in a perceptive appraisal written in 1956. According to Dr. Patalas, the German situation was "the inevitable result . . . of the absence of stability and certainty—something that has characterized almost every enterprise in postwar West

Curt Jürgens in *Des Teufels General* (The Devil's General),
directed by Helmut Käutner, 1955.

Maximilian Schell in *Kinder, Mütter und ein General*
(Children, Mothers and a General), directed by Laszlo
Benedek, 1955.

236

John Saxon and Helmut Käutner during the making of *The
Restless Years*, the German director's first venture into
American production, 1958.

Germany." But Patalas took exception to the argument that economics accounted for the inferior quality of the German film, noting that *In jenen Tagen* and other *Trümmerfilme* ("rubble" films) had been produced on a meager budget with limited resources. Patalas believed that the problem was spiritual as well as economic. He attributed the failure of the German film to the fact that its current offerings did not represent the reality of life, but presented, instead, "a reflection of reality broken up in the prism of collective wishes and projections of anxiety."

Adopting a neo-Kracauerian viewpoint, Patalas analyzed the contemporary German film's "psychological dispositions" and "the deep, concealed layers of collective temperament." The author believed that "weakness, passivity, resignation, had become the hallmarks of "the 'serious' German films of these years." *Illusion in Moll (Illusion in a Minor Key)*, *Meines Vaters Pferde (My Father's Horses)*, *Regina Amstetten*, *Ein Leibesgeschichte (Love Story)*, *Geliebtes Leben (Beloved Life)* were offered as examples of films which lacked "inner tensions," contained "weak characterizations" and were marked by the absence of an "inner dynamic force."

"Intelligence and initiative seem suspect in the German cinema, and only the rogue is allowed to display cleverness or common sense," Patalas wrote. "The 'positive' hero has to be carried away by his 'beautiful' feelings, by the 'stirring of his blood,' by his 'unerring instincts'. . . . Regardless of changing commercial considerations, the basic mood of German film production has remained constant over the last few years. Both the macabre pessimism of the so-called *Trümmerfilme* . . . and the thread-bare optimism of more recent pictures reflect the same thing: a desire for rest, for release, for freedom from responsibility." In Willi Forst's 1951 film, *Die Sünderin (The Sinner)*, for example, the heroine (Hildegarde Knef) prostitutes herself in order to finance an operation for her lover (Gustav Fröhlich). The operation fails and the lovers commit suicide by putting veronal in their champagne.

Escape from reality was likewise reflected in a group of films which glorified country and provincial life: *Grun ist die Heide (Green Is the Heath)*, *Rosen bluhen auf dem Heidegrab (Roses Blooming on the Heath Grave)*, *Wenn die Abendglocken lauten (When the Evening Bells are Tolling)*, *Tausend rote Rosen bluhen (A Thousand Red Roses Blooming)*, while the *Heimatfilme* (homeland films) presented the evil of city life in contrast to the life of the village. But German life, Patalas concluded, "especially life within society continued to be represented less as a challenge to be met than as a fate to be accepted."

At the same time, the new optimism generated by economic prosperity fostered a non-political attitude in the newly constituted West German Republic not unlike the period in Weimar history from 1924-1929. Patalas saw a dangerous parallel: "When social and economic foundations collapse, the non-political individual is only too likely to resign his autonomy and submit himself blindly to authority." Rolf Hansen's *Sauerbruch/Das war mein Leben (Bitter Spring/That Was My Life)*, released in 1954, and *Der letzte Sommer (The Last Summer)*, directed by Curt Braun in the same year, were prime examples of this tendency.

Escape from reality was no less evident in the military genre films which date from 1954. *08/15*, directed by Paul May with a plot reminiscent of *From Here to Eternity*, focuses on Corporal Asch who undergoes the trials and tribulations of the military but emerges a model soldier. The military comedy reappeared in *Der Hauptmann und sein Held (The Captain and His Hero)*, a satire about service bureaucracy directed by Max Nosseck, while the military's opposition to Nazism was portrayed in Alfred Weidemann's *Canaris*, Helmut Kautner's *Der Teufels General (The Devil's General)*, Laslo Benedek's *Kinder, Mutter und ein General (Sons, Mothers and the General)*, G. W. Pabst's *Der letzte Akt (The Last Act)*, Falk Harnack's *Der 20 juli (It Happened on July 20th)* and Harald Reinl's *Solange du Lebst (As Long as You Live)*.

Like many of West Germany's younger critics writing at mid-century, Dr. Patalas was encouraged by cinematic achievements outside the commercial film establishment, such as Herbert Seggelke's in Munich and Harold Senft's in Wiesbaden; both experimented in the field of abstraction. *In Jedem Land zu dieser Zeit (In Any Country at the Present Time)*, produced in 1952 by a group of students at the University of Munich under the supervision of Dr. Hedwig Traub, explored through the medium of avant-garde tradition the theme of "a student's homelessness in an emptied world and his isolation in the dimension of art which he has constructed for himself as a refuge."

Also working in the avant-garde and at the same time showing the influence of the Soviet silent classics was the Viennese Herbert Vesely, whose *Nicht Mehr Fliehen (Fly No Longer)*, produced by Filmaufbau in 1954, choreographed movement and sound on a twelve-tone score composed by Gerhard Ruhl. Photographed by Hugo Holub, the film conveyed Vesely's sense of the moral and emotional futility of postwar Europe and postwar Germany. Patalas described its theme as "the awareness of *absurdity*—in the sense that Camus has conveyed it in literature: the crucial situations of human beings confronted with the atomic bomb. But it is not in the least literary. Its structure is nearest to a lyric poem in

Bernhard Wicki and Erik Schumann in *Unruhige Nacht* (The Troubled Night), directed by Dr. Falk Harnack, 1958.

its lack of 'logical' development and narrative." *Nicht Mehr Fliehen* was critically acclaimed after its premiere at the 1955 Berlin Festival. These independent films, produced on modest budgets but evidencing technique and artistry of the highest order, may be looked upon in retrospect as the medieval stage in the development of a German film which would attain its renaissance in the 1970s.

The 1960s proved to be the darkest decade in the history of the postwar commercial German cinema. In 1959 West Germany produced about 106 films, declining to 98 in 1960 and 75 in 1961. Many production companies closed while survivors such as Constantin, Gloria, Atlas-Film, Rialto Film Preben Philipsen, CCC-Film and Studio Hamburg struggled to maintain their share of the theatrical film market, now seriously eroded by American competition and the growth of television. In 1961 the revenue accruing to distributors from German-made films fell to 92 million marks ($23 million) from 130 million marks ($32.5 million) in 1960, while Germany's share of the domestic market dropped from 41 percent to 32 percent. Profits from the export of German films declined to one million marks ($250,800) from 26 million marks ($6.5 million), which amounted to roughly one-third of the foreign sales of the French and Italian industries combined. In their 1962 annual report German producers attributed the losses to economic factors but noted that "artistic reasons should not be minimized in any way."

Writing in 1961, Geoffrey Donaldson could say that sixteen years after the fall of the Third Reich "one fails to discern any indications of a renewed vitality, of any new ideas. In reviewing the prolific West German film output since 1945, one searches in vain for anything mildly resembling a movement comparable to the French Nouvelle Vague [New Wave]." Nor could the German cinema point to a director of the stature of Satyajit Ray in India, Ingmar Bergman in Sweden or Torre Nilsson in Argentina, or a producer in the mold of Carl Anders Dymling who had encouraged Bergman.

Germany's most notable producer remained the commercially oriented but artistically vacant Arthur Brauner, founder and principal shareholder of CCC-Film (Central Cinema Company). Brauner attempted to capitalize on foreign stars, often "B" class players such as Debra Paget and Linda Christian, and "name" directors, most notably including William Dieterle, William Thiele, Curtis Bernhardt, Douglas Sirk and Fritz Lang who had retired from the American screen but might be exploited for the benefit of a decrepit West German industry. They achieved a measure of success in the postwar German industry and influenced younger directors, notably Rainer Werner Fassbinder, but on the whole their record was unsatisfactory, and in the case of Lang, who chose to reenter the German cinema after an absence of more than a quarter of a century, saddening.

Much was expected of Fritz Lang, who returned in 1958 to direct a new version of *Das indische Grabmal* and *Der Tiger von Eschnapur* to be produced by Arthur Brauner on location in India. In reviving the fictional India of unscrupulous Maharajas, colorful temple dancers and adventurous tiger hunts, Lang appears to have believed that the screenplay written by his former wife, Thea von Harbou, who had died four years before, would be as valid in 1958 as it had been in 1920. As a German film critic poignantly suggested, film manuscripts, unlike wine and cognac, do not improve with age. Stored in vaults, their pages mold and decay. And such was the fate of *The Tiger from Eschnapur* and *The Indian Tomb*, film scenarios shaped for another age.

Die Brücke (The Bridge), directed by Bernhard Wicki, 1959.

Bernhard Wicki during the making of *Die Brücke* (The Bridge), 1959.

Der Spiegel described Lang's two-part film as a "monstrous memorial" to the man who had created *Die Nibelungen* and *Metropolis*. Lang's second and final feature, *Die Tausend Augen des Dr. Mabuse (The Thousand Eyes of Dr. Mabuse)*, based on his successful *Mabuse* films of 1922 and 1932 but more a pastiche of his earlier films in the detective-spy genre, was released in 1961. In directing a third version of *Mabuse*, Lang believed "that it might be interesting to show a similar criminal almost thirty years later and again say certain things about our time—the danger that our civilization can be blown up and that on its rubble some new realm of crime could be built." But neither the film nor the remembered eminence of its director contributed, as some German *cinéastes* had hoped, to the renaissance, let alone a revival, of the German film.

"A kiss—a shot—and then nothing" was the epithet employed by one German critic to describe the quality of the German films being shown during the 1963-64 season. Commercially oriented filmmakers reworked the *krimis*, criminal stories drawn from Edgar Wallace and "westerns" based on the literature of Karl May and James Fenimore Cooper. Some American players like Lex Barker, remembered for his Tarzan roles, found employment and a transitory fame in these low-budget, medium-grade German entertainments. Horst Wendlandt of Rialto Film, a company which specialized in the western genre, defended his productions with the statement: "I'm only trying to do what Americans have been doing for years, providing good entertainment. I'm not a dreamer. The public appeal comes first. No experiments. I'm only making films of which I know in advance that they will appeal to the public. I'm a realist."

Der Schatz im Silbersee (The Treasure of Silver Lake) and *Winnetou*, directed in 1962 and 1963 by Harald Reinl, a former co-worker of Dr. Fanck and Leni Riefenstahl, and *Flusspriaten des Mississippi (Mississippi Pirates)*, directed by Jürgen Roland in 1963, were three notable examples of the German western, but most lacked artistic value. As critic Robin Bean observed: "They look authentic enough; the mountains, streams, plains and even the Red Indians are very familiar; but what is lacking in three out of the first four is imagination and style. Often the impression is that the directors have sat through many American films and then set out to copy them."

The poverty of the German situation was appraised by producer Gottfried Reinhardt in 1964: "The Germans are unwilling to look at themselves or their customs. Their interest in making so-called westerns in Yugoslavia is a sad commentary on the imagination and the courage of what was once a great film industry."

Die Mörder sind unter uns

THE MURDERERS AMONG US
1946

CREDITS:

Production: Deutsche Film AG., DEFA, Berlin. Distributed by Sovexport-Film GmbH (Berlin, Russian Zone). *Director:* Wolfgang Staudte. *Screenplay:* Wolfgang Staudte. *Cinematography:* Friedl Behn-Grund and Eugen Klagemann. *Production director:* Herbert Uhlich. *Music:* Ernst Roters. *Released:* October 15, 1946 (East Berlin); April 10, 1947 (Baden-Baden); July 23, 1948 (Bochum). *Length:* 2400 meters.

CAST:

Hildegard Knef, E. W. Borchert, Erna Sellmer, Elly Burgmer, Arno Paulsen, Marlise Ludwig, Hilde Adolfi, Ursula Krieg, Robert Forsch, Albert Johannes, Wolfgang Dohnberg, Ernst Stahl-Nachbaur.

"The remains of Stettiner railway station loomed up out of the desert of rubble like a prehistoric skeleton," Hildegarde Knef wrote in her memoir *The Gift Horse*. "It formed both the foreground and background to our first day of shooting on the first postwar German film: *The Murderers Among Us*."

The Murderers Among Us was produced by DEFA, the Soviet-sponsored film monopoly, and directed by Wolfgang Staudte from his own screenplay. Knef's description of the Stettiner railway station sequence suggests the fine line between fact and fiction which characterized the postwar *Trümmerfilme*, motion pictures photographed among the ruins of German cities. "The extras hung like bunches of grapes around the furiously snorting locomotive, intent only on protecting their places on the crowded footplates and handles." These Germans had only to portray their recent experiences. And for the leading members of the cast and crew it was no different. Knef described how the co-photographer, Friedl Behn-Grund, who had lost his leg on the last day of the war, "limped across the plowed-up platform spreading sweetness and light, squeezed in behind the antique camera wiping away the tears which rolled

The ruins of Berlin provide the background for *Die Mörder sind unter uns*, Germany's first postwar feature film.

down his rosy cherub's cheeks and furtively massaged his stump, which had not yet healed and still caused him great pain under the crude wooden peg attached to it."

That the result was achieved under difficult circumstances would be an understatement. Knef remembered how the cast and crew "spent most of the shooting time either beating off hordes of rats or repairing spluttering arc lights, failing cameras, dead microphones, and flimsy film which broke every few meters. There were no distributors to harass us, no reporters to hold us up, no concerns about money or star-images; we waited patiently, thankful to be able to shoot the first film." The crew survived on Russian food packages which occasionally contained bacon and flour. Knef believed that she was more fortunate in one respect. As a member of the Schlosspark Theater, where she also worked as an actress, Knef was entitled to partake of the weekly "soup evening" provided by the American zonal authorities.

Staudte's screenplay is a tale of pursuit not unlike Lang's *M*, a film which the director had originally wanted to call *The Murderer Among Us*. Brückner, a former Army captain who was responsible for the liquidation of an entire Polish village, is the pursued. He attempts to take his place in the society of postwar Germany as a respected citizen and family man. But Brückner's role in the Polish atrocity is known to Doctor Hans Martens, a subordinate, who involuntarily participated in the mass execution. Believing that an individual act of retribution against Brückner will relieve him of guilt, Martens pursues the captain into the ruins, but Susanna who loves Martens and was herself a victim of Nazi persecution, intervenes. She persuades him to give up his private revenge. Brückner's guilt must be decided by a court of law. In the final and perhaps most effective sequence, Brückner repeatedly shouts, "I am not guilty," against kaleidoscopic shots of the war.

The Murderers Among Us premiered at the Admiral's Palace on October 15, 1946. British representatives boycotted the performance, however, when it was discovered, somewhat ironically, that Wilhelm Borchert who played Dr. Martens had been a nominal Nazi in the early years of the regime, a fact which he concealed from the Allied officials. Borchert was subsequently arrested by United States authorities and sentenced to three months in jail.

At the premiere Knef sat between Erich Pommer and

241

Hildegard Knef and Wilhelm Borchert. *(Die Mörder sind unter uns)*

Wolfgang Staudte and received her "first lesson on the subject of premières and the infinite variety of tortures they hold in store." Writing in her memoirs:

At one point the sound track broke down, at another the film decelerated, the picture faded, the voices grew sadder and sadder and finally sank into the cellar as the film broke altogether. Scenes which I'd treasured in my memory as bearable had been cut; others, which I'd forced myself to forget, seemed to run twice. The balcony had been taken over by a company of influenza victims who settled down to an orgy of sneezing and coughing, one man got up in the middle and went out slamming the door behind him, another fell audibly asleep, and a woman in the first row dropped her handbag, and it was a long time before she found it between the feet of the spectators sitting behind her. They applauded as the lights went up, and a photographer said, "I'm Walter Sanders from *Life* magazine." He leaped around me, clicking tirelessly. Erich Pommer drove me to the Schlosspark Theater, and I was thankful when the curtain went up at 7:30, and I could lollop about the stage lisping outrageously.

The film gained international notoriety, but its distribution in the West was limited. It was received with some hostility in Britain, although Richard Winnington wrote a favorable review in April, 1948, noting that "It is in the real sense of the word post-war and that can be said of few films to-day. It is German and reflects German consciousness into which it is surely incumbent on us to gain every form of insight. . . . *The Murderers Among Us* carries the UFA heritage of camera angles, heaviness, neurosis, sentimentality and deviations into dim and fleshy cabarets. It is somber, slow, intense, tragically moving and in common with the post-war Italian films as true as it can be to the surrounding reality. It would seem that only the impoverished and the defeated can focus the camera lens on life." Winnington praised "the sound track with its rediscovery (for us) of silence and the spare and apt music of Ernst Roters is a joy and a relief."

The Murderers Among Us reached the United States in August, 1948. Reviewers were either indifferent or hostile. *The New York Times* found it "A confused and rambling study of dissolutionment in post-war Germany . . . presented in heavily stylized fashion." Staudte was reproached for being "mostly interested in camera effects" while his technique was criticized as "stilted and old-fashioned."

Staudte emerged as East Germany's most important filmmaker, directing socially conscious films in the Soviet zone until 1953 when he permanently relocated in the Federal Republic. While undeniably gifted, he was never to achieve a success comparable to *The Murderers Among Us*. Unseen by generations of filmgoers, *The Murderers Among Us* documents a crucial period in German history and is deserving of a reappraisal in a retrospective showing.

Berliner Ballade

THE BERLINER

1948

CREDITS:

Production: Comedia-Filmgesellschaft, Berlin-Munich. Released by E. Dietz-Filmverleih GmbH (West Berlin/Munich/Frankfurt)-Norddeutscher Filmverleih, Adolf Bejöhr (Hamburg/Düsseldorf). *Director:* Robert A. Stemmle. *Screenplay:* Günter Neumann. *Cinematography:* George Krause. *Production director:* Werner Drake. *Music:* Werner Eisbrenner and Günter Neumann. *Released:* December 31, 1948. *Length:* 2499 meters.

CAST:

Gert Fröbe, Tatjana Sais, Aribert Wäscher, Ute Sielisch, O. E. Hasse, Werner Oehlschläger, Hans Deppe, Erwin Biegel, Herbert Weibbach, Rita Paul, Marianne Prenzel, Brigitte Mira, Ruth Zillger, Georgia Lind, Jeanette Brons, Herwart Grosse, Alfred Parpart, Kurt Weitkamp, Franz Otto Krüger, Otto Matthies, Franziska Dörr, Walter Strasen, Georg August Koch, Franz Pollandt, Walter Schramm, Walter Bluhm, Karl Hannemann, Veronika Mayer, Auguste Frede, Kurt Muskato, Alf Kuck, Georg Völkel, Edgar Pauly, Walter Bechmann, Kurt Gethke, Ilse Trautscholt, Reinhold Bernt, Karl Schönböck, Eric Ode (speaker), and others.

In their sardonically humorous satire, *Berliner Ballade (The Berliner)*, director Robert A. Stemmle and scenarist Günter Neumann describe the troubles that beset the average, law-abiding citizen in postwar Berlin. Critic John Adams noted that "because of the ambiguities and stylistic changes, the film may be read as an expression of the German trying to wake up to the realities of post-war life and to the deceptive qualities of dreams and ideologies. The hero of the film is 'Everyman' whose very lack of heroic qualities debunks pretentious idealism and provides a realistic basis for the action."

Otto, a homely and bedraggled war veteran, tries to return home but is delayed by red tape, a woman and zone barriers. He finds that his old apartment is occu-

Advertisement for *Berliner Ballade.*

Photographing in front of the Reichstag building. *(Berliner Ballade)*

Ute Sielisch and Gert Fröbe. *(Berliner Ballade)*

Gert Fröbe and Ute Sielisch. *(Berliner Ballade)*

pied by a black marketeer and a woman who runs a lonely hearts club. They permit him to occupy a bedroom with only two walls and no ceiling. In the days that follow, he has various troubles as a factory worker, a waiter, and nightwatchman. The social, political, and economic struggle in Berlin is made all the more confusing by the fact that women outnumber men. But gradually he becomes aware of the changes and problems which face postwar Germany. He dreams of enormous cakes laden with whipped cream which are served to him by a beautiful pastrycook who becomes his feminine ideal. When he meets her in reality, they rush to get married. But harmony is illusory and Otto, having been wounded in a fight and thought dead, is prepared for burial. He awakens in time to say that the average man cannot be killed, and that fear, egotism, indifference and hate must be buried in his stead.

During an international conference, a diplomat's cigar accidentally incinerates the globe. *(Berliner Ballade)*

Rooted in the tradition of German cabaret entertainment, *Berliner Ballade* employs numerous symbolic almost Chaplinesque devices such as a diplomat's cigar which at a conference of statesmen falls from the man's hand and incinerates a globe of the world. In another sequence, the administering politicians engage in endless talk, entering and re-entering the conference hall in quick motion photography. The songs, "When Will We Fight Against Fighting" and "A Thousand Hearts Search for Love," served to accentuate the cabaret origins of *Berliner Ballade*.

Georg Krause photographed the film against the ruins of war-torn Berlin. Gert Fröbe, who had performed in many of Neumann's cabaret sketches, was cast as the bewildered German "Everyman," while Aribert Wäscher and Tatjuna Sais appeared as the dubious tenants. Ute Sielisch played the pastry girl who marries the hero. The film was released in the United States in 1952 as *The Berliner* with a "desperately droll running commentary written and recited by the comedian Henry Morgan." *Berliner Ballade* represented a remarkable achievement, the product of a company, Comedia-Filmgesellschaft of Munich and Berlin, which had started production after 1945 with a furniture van and one camera.

Advertisement for the Italian release of *Berliner Ballade*.

Advertisement for *Berliner Ballade*.

Des Teufels General

THE DEVIL'S GENERAL

1955

CREDITS:

Production: Real Produktion. *Director:* Helmut Käutner. *Screenplay:* Georg Hurdalek and Helmut Käutner. Based on the play by Carl Zuckmayer. *Cinematography:* Albert Benitz. *Running time:* 124 minutes. Released: 1955.

CAST:

Curt Jürgens *(General Harras);* Victor de Kowa *(Schmidt-Lausitz);* Karl John *(Oberbruch);* Eva-Ingleborg Scholz *(Fraulein Mohrungen);* Marianne Koch *(Dorthea Geiss);* Albert Lieven *(Oberst Eilers);* Erica Balque *(Anne Eilers);* Werner Fuetterer *(Baron Pflungk);* Harry Meyen *(Lt. Hartmann).*

Beginning in 1954 the German film took up the theme of Germany during the Second World War and the resistance to Nazism among the officer class. *Canaris,* directed by Alfred Weidenmann, *Kinder, Mutter und ein General (Sons, Mothers and a General),* directed by Laslo Benedek, *Der Letzte Akt (The Final Act),* directed by G. W. Pabst, and *Des Teufels General (The Devil's General),* directed by Helmut Käutner, were manifestations of a new interest in the German resistance to the National Socialist regime. Writing in the mid 1950s, German film historian Enno Patalas took a more critical view of the perspective adopted by the aforementioned filmmakers:

It is interesting that all these films emphasize the "positive" aspects of the situation: nobility and honesty assert themselves against the external circumstances of war and Nazism, but there is no consideration of the absolute negation that war symbolizes. And it seems significant that an ordinary citizen is never permitted to take the leading part in these resistance

Curt Jürgens and Victor de Kowa. *(Des Teufels General)*

Curt Jürgens and Victor de Kowa. (*Des Teufels General*)

films. Superiors (authority) take the center of the stage, and the audience knows why—it feels itself exonerated. The emphasis on indecision, on people whose anti-Nazism becomes overt only when the war is evidently lost, confirms a general feeling that it was impossible until too late to show which way things were going.

Patalas' neo-Kracauerian analysis may have some validity. Civilians and even students also resisted. But the weight of historical evidence suggests that the only significant and potentially effective resistance to Nazism occurred within the ranks of the military forces. Unlike the resistance movements in other European countries, the German resistance was required to act within the confines of a totalitarian system.

Karl Zuckmayer wrote *The Devil's General* during his exile in America. In December, 1941, the playwright had read a brief notice in the American press about the death of Ernest Udet, Chief of the Air Force Supply Service of the German Army. According to these fragmentary reports, Udet had died during the test of a new weapon and had been honored with a state funeral. "That was all," Zuckmayer recalled. "There were no commentaries, no surmises about his death. Fatal accident; state funeral."

In the months that followed, Zuckmayer thought often about Udet. He remembered his earlier pre-war association with the anti-Nazi major. They had seen one

Curt Jürgens. (*Des Teufels General*)

247

Victor de Kowa. *(Des Teufels General)*

another for the last time in 1936, meeting inconspicuously at a Berlin café. On that occasion Udet had advised him to "Shake the dust of this country from your shoes. . . . Clear out of here and don't come back. There is no more decency here." When Zuckmayer inquired what he intended to do, Udet had replied, almost casually, that he was dedicated to flying: "I can't disentangle any more. But one of these days the devil will fetch us all." They did not discuss the question further. "We drank," Zuckmayer recalled, "and when we bade each other goodbye, we embraced."

Zuckmayer completed the manuscript shortly after World War II. *The Devil's General* premiered in Zurich in 1946, and the first German performance occurred in Frankfurt in November, 1947.

Working in close collaboration with scenarist Georg Hurdalek and veteran camerman Albert Benitz, Käutner adapted Zuckmayer's text to the language of film. The film opens in November, 1941. Unexplained crashes have occurred during the test flights of new aircraft and sabotage is suspected. General of the Luftwaffe Harras, who has often criticized the Nazi regime, Hitler, and the decision to invade Russia, becomes the focus of the investigation spearheaded by SS General Schmidt-Lausitz, whose ambitious chief, Heinrich Himmler, seeks to gain control of the Luftwaffe.

Harras is arrested and briefly imprisoned as a "softening up" exercise. After his release, Harras learns that his best friend has been killed in one of the new planes and decides to test the aircraft himself. Oberbruch, his comrade from the First World War and the officer in charge of test flights, tries to prevent this and confesses to Harras that he is responsible for the sabotage. Schmidt-Lausitz and the SS arrive to occupy the landing field, but Harras, disillusioned by the cause which he has served, resigns himself to death. Eluding the SS, he takes up a plane which he crashes into the airport. The SS leader cynically issues the report that General Harras was "fatally injured in the performance of his duties for the Fatherland."

Curt Jürgens, whom critic A. H. Weiler described as "an actor of regal bearing and a classic profile," was an inspired choice for the role of General Harras, the disenchanted Luftwaffe General, "a man too weak to put the public good before his private passions, the picture of a Fascist Faust," while Victor de Kowa played the brutal SS leader, Schmidt-Lausitz, with overtones of Mephistopheles. Karl John, Albert Leiven and Carl Ludwig Diehl were no less brilliant in supporting parts.

Der Hauptmann von Köpenick

THE CAPTAIN FROM KÖPENICK

1956

CREDITS:

Production: A Gyula Trebitsch production for Real-Film, Hamburg. *Director:* Helmut Käutner. *Screenplay:* Helmut Käutner and Carl Zuckmayer. Based on the play by Carl Zuckmayer and an actual incident. *Cinematography:* Albert Benitz (Technicolor). *Editor:* Klaus Dudenhoefer. *Art direction:* Herbert Kirchhoff and Albrecht Becker. *Costumes:* Erna Sander. *Music:* Bernard Eichhorn. *Running time:* 93 minutes. *Released:* 1956. Released in the United States by Distributors Corporation of America (1958).

CAST:

Heinz Rühmann *(Wilhelm Voight, Cobbler);* Hennelore Schroth *(Mathilde Obermuller);* Martin Held *(Mayor Obermuller);* Erich Schellow *(Captain von Schlettow);* Ilse Furstenberg *(Marie Hoprecht);*

Heinz Rühmann. *(Der Hauptmann von Köpenick)*

Leonard Steckel *(Adolph Wormser, Tailor);* Walter Giller *(Willi Wormser);* Maria Sebaldt *(Auguste Viktoria Wormser);* Willy A. Kleinau *(Friedrich Hoprecht);* Friedrich Domin *(Prison Director);* Wolfgang Neuss *(Kallenberg);* Reinhard Kolldehoff *(Drunk Soldier);* Willy Rose *(Police Sergeant).*

The saga of Wilhelm Voigt, the cobbler and ex-convict who masqueraded as the Captain from Köpenick for the purpose of acquiring a passport, was given definitive screen treatment by Helmut Kaütner in 1956. But Kaütner was by no means the first director to attempt a motion picture version of the popular story. In 1906, the year of the incident, no fewer than three films, each titled *Der Hauptmann von Köpenick*, were produced by German firms. Siegfried Dessauer directed Hermann Picha as Voigt in a 1926 silent, and five years later Max Adalbert appeared in a sound version directed by Richard Oswald. In 1941 Oswald remade the film in Hollywood with Albert Bassermann in the title role.

Kautner was encouraged to direct *The Captain of Köpenick* after an experience in the studio commissary during the production of *The Devil's General.* He recalled that at lunch "the generals would sit together at one table, the noncoms at another, the regular soldiers at

Martin Held as Mayor
Obermuller. *(Der
Hauptmann von Köpenick)*

another! And, mind you, these were not army men but
extras hired for a day's work. To a German, the uniform
makes him different." Käutner hoped that his new version of *The Captain of Köpenick* would serve as a
warning against the rebuilding of the German Army.

Working in collaboration with Carl Zuckmayer, who
had written a play about the incident in 1928, Käutner
broadened the satire to include German society with its
emphasis on rank above every human quality. Careful
consideration was given to the choice of the indomitable
imposter, Voigt. Curt Jürgens and Hans Albers were
preferred by Käutner's producers, but the director insisted on Heinz Rühmann. It was a fortuitous choice.
Recalling the earlier characterizations, Zuckmayer
wrote:

Rühmann, under Käutner's splendid direction, gave Wilhelm
Voigt, the Prussian Eulenspiegel, a deeper significance and did
complete justice to the role. Laughter and tears always remained in close proximity. When he dismisses the soldiers on
the stairs of the city hall after his successful "Köpenickiad" and
says: "For each man a beer and a bock sausage"—which is one
of the funniest parts of the action—he simultaneously trans-
mits enough profound sadness to make the viewer shiver in the
awareness of the futility of any escape from human destiny.

Veteran cameraman Albert Benitz was engaged to
photograph the film over a thirty-eight-day period
against turn-of-the-century settings created by Herbert
Kirchoff and Albrecht Becker in the Hamburg studios of
Real-Film. "Carl Zuckmayer, Käutner and I sat down
together for many days studying scenery designs, discussing the manuscript, crossing out, expanding and talking
about interpretations," Rühmann recalled. "Most of all

Heinz Rühmann as Wilhelm Voigt. *(Der Hauptmann von Köpenick)*

Martin Held. (*Der Hauptmann von Köpenick*)

we tried to work out one thing: the progression of the uniform, because both, Cobbler Voigt and the uniform, follow their own path. Both downward."

The story opens in the shop of the court tailor Wormser, who has measured Captain von Schlettow for a uniform. But when the captain leaves the service, Wormser sells the garment to the mayor of Köpenick, a lieutenant in the reserves who is preparing to go on maneuvers. While hurrying to help him dress, the mayor's wife tears a hole in it. The uniform is returned to Wormser where it is mended and worn by the tailor's daughter to a costume ball. During the evening champagne is spilled on the uniform, and the next day it is delivered to a second-hand clothes dealer.

Wilhelm Voigt, a cobbler by trade, finishes a fifteen-year prison sentence and returns to his home town of Köpenick, eight miles from Berlin. He is anxious to work but learns that he cannot get a job without residence papers, and residence papers cannot be obtained without a job. Frustrated, Voigt decides to leave Germany, hopeful that he will be able to return some day. But when he breaks into a police station to forge his own passport, he is arrested and sentenced to a twelve-year prison term.

Voigt has time to reflect on the fact that the badge of authority is invariably accepted as the real thing, and in Wilhelmian Germany the uniform is the guarantor of privilege. During his confinement he memorizes the military *Field Service Regulations*, becomes an expert on militarism, and upon his release buys the captain's uniform, complete with helmet, boots and saber. Leaving the men's room of the Berlin railway station, he commandeers a squad of soldiers, marches to the town hall of Köpenick and with proper military bearing arrests the mayor. Voigt seeks only a passport, but when he learns that Köpenick is too small to warrant a passport bureau, he requisitions the town treasury and disappears. As the world learns of the hoax, the "captain" offers to restore the funds in return for the coveted passport. Even the German Kaiser is amused, commenting appreciatively, "See, that's discipline. You won't find that anywhere on earth." Voigt is pardoned by the emperor and is at last issued his passport.

In his recent autobiography, Heinz Rühmann recalled that he and Käutner "had discussed everything so thoroughly that when the shooting began we were so familiar with the material that Helmut and I knew what we wanted without any more discussion." The actor had special praise for Kautner: "What a brilliant director Helmut Käutner was! And author. And actor. And cabaret writer. We had not worked together since *Kleider machen Leute* [1940]. But now with Hauptmann, I experienced him again. He was highly talented, had enormous empathy, and directed his actors with a gentle hand. . . ."

The German Federal Republic designated *The Captain from Köpenick* "Best Feature Film of International Quality" in 1957. It was additionally awarded "Best Screenplay," while actor Heinz Rühmann received the "Best Actor" award for his portrayal of the captain.

Heinz Rühmann (right). (*Der Hauptmann von Köpenick*)

Die Bekenntnisse des Hochstaplers Felix Krull

THE CONFESSIONS OF FELIX KRULL

1956

CREDITS:

Production: A Kurt Hoffmann Film distributed by DCA. Produced by Filmaufbau, GmbH. *Director:* Kurt Hoffmann. *Screenplay:* Robert Thoeren with the co-operation of Erika Mann. Based on the novel by Thomas Mann. *Cinematography:* Friedl Behn-Grund. *Music:* Hans-Martin Majewski. *Running time:* 107 minutes. *Released:* 1956. Released in the United States as *The Confessions of Felix Krull.*

CAST:

Horst Buchholz *(Felix Krull);* Liza Pulver *(Zaza);* Ingrid Andree *(Zouzou);* Susi Nicoletti *(Madame Houpfle);* Paul Dahlke *(Professor Cuckoo);* Ilse Steppat *(Maria Pia);* Walter Rilla *(Lord Killmarnock);* Peer Schmidt *(Marquis de Venosta);* Paul Henckels *(Schimmelpreester).*

Thomas Mann was keenly interested in the motion picture, "this phenomenon of our time," and on at least one occasion expressed the desire to write a book-length study of the motion picture, but the commitment to his fiction, coupled with the unplanned exigencies of exile, precluded the fulfillment of this project.

In 1933, however, Mann set down some of his ideas about film in a perceptive essay in which he wrote that the film "is not art, it is life, it is actuality." He likened the film to "raw material" which "has not been transmuted." Mann believed furthermore that the film had nothing to do with the drama. He described it as a "narrative in pictures." Mann wrote: "That these faces are present to your sight does not prevent their greatest effectiveness from being in its nature epic, and in this sphere, if any, the film approaches literary art." He found it "much too genuine to be theater," for "The stage setting is based upon delusion," whereas "the scenery of the film is nature itself, just as the fancy stimulated by the story creates it for the reader." Mann believed that

Thomas Mann and his wife Katja during a visit to Lübeck in 1955. *(Die Bekenntnisse des Hochstaplers Felix Krull)*

the film possessed "a technique of recollection, of psychological suggestion, a mastery of detail in men and in things from which the novelist, though scarcely the dramatist, might learn much."

Mann had been disappointed with the 1923 screen version of *Buddenbrooks*, his great autobiographical novel which Gerhard Lamprecht had directed from a screenplay by Alfred Fekete and Louise Heilborn-Körbitz. "Instead of narrating, only narrating, and letting the characters speak for themselves," Mann wrote in his appraisal, "what has been made of it is a poorish play of merchant life in which not much remains of the book save the names."

Not until after World War II was it possible for the works of Thomas Mann, proscribed by the Nazi regime in 1936, to be considered for motion picture adaptation by German filmmakers. In 1953 *Königliche Hoheit (Royal Highness)*, a delightfully comic and optimistic novel with the atmosphere of a fairytale, was brought to the screen by Harald Braun; three years later Kurt Hoffmann directed *Die Bekenntnisse des Hochstaplers Felix Krull (The Confessions of the Swindler Felix Krull)*; a new version of *Buddenbrooks*, directed by Alfred Weidenmann, appeared in 1959; and in 1964 Rolf Thiele directed *Tonio Kröger* based on Mann's most popular novella.

In 1982 Hans W. Geissendorfer brought *Der Zauberberg (The Magic Mountain)* to the screen in an impressive and costly production which features Christoph Eichhorn as the young hero, Hans Castorp, Flavio Bucci as Ludovico Settembrini and Rod Steiger as Mynheer Peeperkorn. Although unseen at this writing, intelligent criticism suggests that Geissendorfer remains

Horst Buchholz in scenes from *The Confessions of Felix Krull*.

Concluding scenes from *The Confessions of Felix Krull*.

faithful to the literary source in his creation of characters, dialogue and costuming. The film is a triumph of décor, its principal set being a meticulously detailed lung sanatorium of the period 1907-1914 situated near the summit of the symbolic "magic mountain."

As early as the 1920s Mann had believed that "a bold treatment of [*The Magic Mountain*] might have produced a wonderful spectacle, a fantastic cyclopaedia, with a hundred digressions into all points of the compass: visions of all the worlds of nature, sport, research, medicine, politics, all grouped round an epic core. What might not have been made simply of the chapter 'Snow' with its Mediterranean dream poem of humanity!" Although "a very good Berlin producer" considered a film version, the project did not materialize. Mann reflected that "Such a production made too great material and intellectual demands."

Mann had started *The Confessions of the Swindler Felix Krull* in 1911 but had set the work aside to write *Der Tod in Venedig* (Death in Venice). He resumed the novel in 1951, starting on the same manuscript page where he had left off more than forty years before. The result was a masterful portrait of the artist as criminal, a comment on the "Duality of existence, a double life," as critic Henry Hatfield noted, and "of the relation between duplication and duplicity" enriched with personal anecdote, irony and humor and set against *fin de siècle* society. The book enjoyed an immense popularity upon publication in Germany in 1954, and the following year Robert Thoeren, in cooperation with Erika Mann, the novelist's daughter, prepared a scenario for director Kurt Hoffmann.

In Germany around 1900, 20-year-old Felix Krull avoids the imperial draft board by feigning epilepsy and then proceeds to Paris to seek his fortune. In a short time the disarmingly seductive scoundrel is being pursued by an insanely masochistic poetess, an amorous dancer, a jealous Scottish nobleman and a vigorous farmer's daughter with an unquenchable infatuation. Felix then vies with the Marquis de Venosta for the love of the frivolous Zaza. The Marquis' family want to send him on a world cruise, but since this would interfere with his pursuit of Zaza, he persuades Felix to impersonate him on the trip. In Lisbon Felix meets Professor Cuckoo whose wife and daughter soon become additional conquests for Krull. When the real Marquis becomes involved in a scandal, Felix is blamed and jailed. His departure from Europe is arranged by the professor and the Marquis' family, who also provide him with a traveling companion, Zaza.

While Hoffmann's debonair adaptation may be faulted for its absence of Goethean subtlety present in the original work, his film is nonetheless a felicitous rendering of the picaresque tale and one of the best adaptations of a Mann work. Horst Buchholz played the confidence man, mixing the attributes of Don Juan and Leporello. No less accomplished were Lisa Pulver as Zaza, the dancer; Ingrid Andere as Zouzou, the daughter of the professor; and Susi Nicolette as the sensuous Madame Houpfle. Paul Dahlke played Professor Cuckoo in a broad comic style.

Die Brücke

THE BRIDGE

1959

CREDITS:

Production: A Fono-Film Production (Dr. Herman Schwerin) in cooperation with Jochen Severin. *Director:* Bernhard Wicki. *Screenplay:* Michael Mansfeld and Karl-Wilhelm Vivier. Adapted from the novel by Manfred Gregor. *Cinematography:* Gerd von Bonin. *Editor:* Kurt Desch. *Music:* Hans-Martin Majewski. *Released:* 1959.

CAST:

Volker Bohnet *(Hans Scholten)*; Fritz Vepper *(Albert Mutz)*; Michael Hinz *(Walter Forst)*; Frank Blaubrecht *(Jurgen Borchert)*; Karl Michael Balzer *(Karl Horber)*; Volker Lechtenbrink *(Klaus Hager)*; Guenther Hoffmann *(Sigi Bernhard)*; Cordula Trantow *(Franziska)*; Wolfgang Stumpf *(Stern, the teacher)*; Gunther Pfitzmann *(Cpl. Heilmann)*; Heinz Spitzner *(Captain Froehlich)*; Siegfried Schurenberg *(Lt. Colonel)*; Ruth Hausmeister *(Frau Mutz)*; Eva Vaitl *(Frau Borchert)*; Edith Schulze-Westrum *(Frau Bernhard)*; Hans Elvenspoeck *(Herr Forst)*; Trudy Breitschopf *(Frau Forst)*; Kalus Hellmold *(Herr Horber)*; Inge Benz *(Sigrun)*; Edeltraut Elsner *(Barbara)*.

Trained as an actor, Bernhard Wicki had appeared in more than thirty films before he directed his first motion picture, a feature documentary, *Warum sind sie gegen uns? (Why Are You Against Us?)* in 1958. The success of this film confirmed Wicki in his decision to make the

The youthful defenders of the bridge. *(Die Brücke)*

transition from acting to directing. "An actor is limited by his role in self-expression," he once reflected. "On the other hand, a director has an opportunity to state his feelings and observations and expressions." Wicki achieved his goal the following year, directing *Die Brücke (The Bridge)* from the autobiographical novel by Manfred Gregor.

Gregor had been one of a group of German adolescents recruited for battle against the advancing American armies during the very last days of the war in Europe. The author had worked on the novel for many years, writing six versions, but none satisfied him. He finally freed himself with the seventh after reading Norman Mailer's novel about World War II, *The Naked and the Dead.* Mailer's novel provided Gregor with the form which had eluded him in the composition of his earlier drafts.

The story opens in a small German town on April 27, 1945. Seven German schoolboys have been called up for military service. In the first half of the film Wicki develops the character and background of the boys, particularly Jurgen, the son of a rich landowner who has already fallen in battle, who is eager to inherit his father's epaulets; Walter, the son of the brutish local *Kreisleiter,* who is something of a bully but is intensely devoted to his mother; Karl, the son of the town's beauty-parlor proprietor, who discovers that the girl he loves is his father's mistress; and Klaus, who is innocently in love with a pretty schoolgirl. The other boys are Sigi, Albert and Hans.

The boys are eager for battle, and after receiving their uniforms, most of which have been stripped from corpses, they are convoyed to the front to meet the advancing American forces. But after talking with their teacher, Herr Stern, a kindly colonel intervenes and orders them to guard the bridge to their village which has no military importance; the *Wehrmacht,* in fact, has already prepared for its demolition. The corporal posts them at the bridge, but he is killed before he can tell the boys that the bridge is of no consequence and will soon be destroyed.

Their quiet vigil ends when an American fighter plane strafes the bridge, killing one of their classmates, Sigi. They are goaded into a reckless attack on American tanks which arrive moments later. The boys disable two tanks with hand grenades and cause the others to turn back, but at a terrible price. Four of their number are dead. When the German demolition squad appears and blows up the bridge, Albert realizes that his companions gave their lives in vain. The crazed youth shoots the demoli-

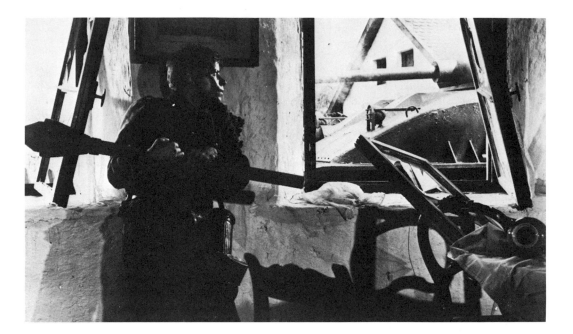

tion sergeant whose squad returns the fire and kills one more boy, Hans.

Unnerved by all that has transpired, Albert staggers back into town and collapses on the doorstep of his home. The film closes with the director's laconic comment: "The events in this story happened in 1945. Two days later the war in Europe ended."

The Bridge was judged the best film of the year by the Berlin critics and won honors in Italy, Japan, Belgium, Austria, Uruguay, Mexico, the Soviet Union and the United States. In early 1963 *The Bridge* was shown during the Moscow Film Week, where it received the praise of *Sowjetskij Ikran (Soviet Screen)*. "It seems a paradox, but it is a fact the only courageous person is the one who shows himself a coward for several minutes and suggests going home," the Soviet reviewer noted in an extensive analysis of the film. "Courageous because it is courageous to think and not to obey; it is courageous to understand and not merely to carry out commands."

Released in the United States by Allied Artists in 1961 with a spoken prologue by the American news commentator Chet Huntley, *Die Brücke* received the Hollywood Press Association's Golden Globe Award and was nominated for an Academy Award as the best foreign film. Many critics regarded it as the most significant German film since Käutner's *The Devil's General*.

Upon completion of *Das Wunder des Malachias (The Miracle of Father Malachias)*, Wicki enjoyed a brief Hollywood career under the auspices of Darryl Zanuck, who commissioned him to direct the German sequence in *The Longest Day* (1962). In Rome he directed a second Fox film, *The Visit*, starring Anthony Quinn. Returning to Hollywood, he was assigned by Zanuck to

Morituri, a World War II melodrama photographed on locations off the California coast.

Directing in Hollywood represented a new challenge to Wicki. "In Europe the director is completely responsible for his picture—he works with the author, cuts it, even chooses his score," Wicki commented during the final stages of his work on *Morituri*. "Here the producer means much more; let's say their work is at least divided. Therefore, it is difficult for me to comment before I have started my work." Wicki admired the craftsmanship of Hollywood and the artistry of its cameramen, but had strong reservations concerning the restrictive role of the film industry unions. Upon completion of *Morituri*, a film which disappointed many of his admirers, Wicki returned to Europe. He continues to direct, but *Die Brücke*, thus far, remains the greatest achievement of his *ouvre*.

259

VIII
Emergence of the New German Cinema

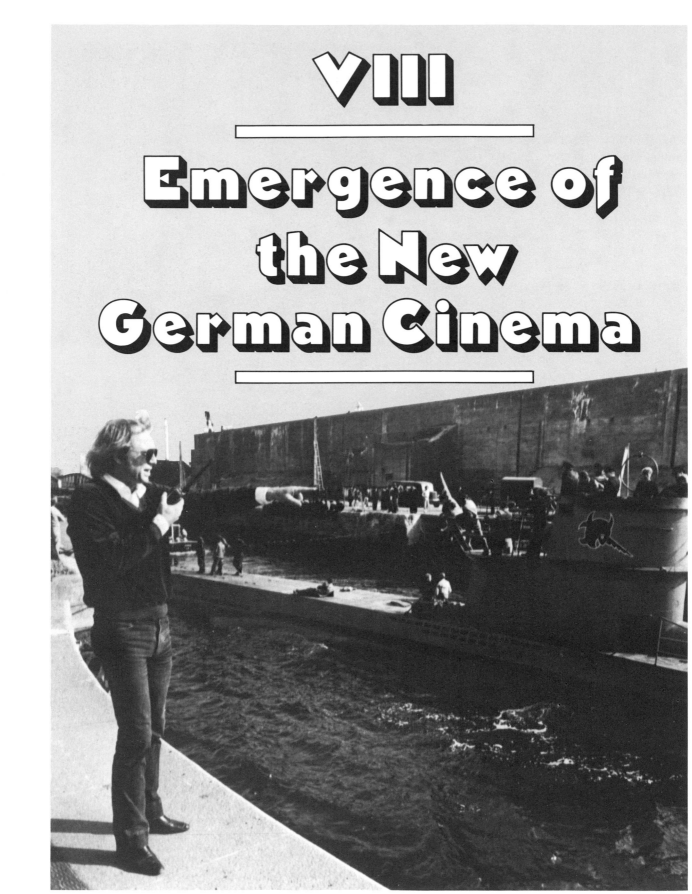

Wolfgang Petersen directing *Das Boot* (The Boat), 1981.

By 1962 West German production had declined to sixty-three features with the Federal Republic ranking fifth in world production. The vast majority of these German films were of mediocre quality with no possibility of competing in the export market dominated by the United States. American competition remained a continuing challenge for the German film in the 1960s. Of the 391 films which played in 6,300 German cinemas in 1963 only 44 were German whereas 115 were American, or 29.5 percent of the total. Attendance meanwhile had dropped dramatically, from 818 million admissions in 1956 to 453 million in 1962. During this same period some of Germany's most notable talents, Romy Schneider, Curt Jurgens, Maximilian and Maria Schell and Horst Bucholz, began appearing in Italian, French and American movies.

As early as the mid-1950s critics like Dr. Patalas had believed that youth represented the salvation of the German cinema. Perhaps the young German filmmaker might inaugurate a movement comparable to the French "New Wave." A step in this direction was achieved on February 28, 1962, during the German Festival for Short Films when twenty-six filmmakers signed the *Oberhausen Manifesto* which boldly declared the old German cinema dead: *"Papas Kino ist tod* (Papa's movies are dead)."* The signers of the manifesto emphasized the importance of short films which had recently received favorable attention at festivals and proved "that the future of the German film lies with those who have proved that they are speaking a new film language." They correctly calculated that in Germany as well as in other countries the short film had "become a school and experimental field for the feature film." Addressing themselves to the economic and artistic problems, the Oberhausen group asserted its claim "to create the new German feature film." According to the Manifesto, "This new film needs freedom. Freedom from the conventions of the industry and from commercial interference from the establishment." The group declared that it had "definite intellectual, formal and economic ideas about the production of a new type of German film. We are prepared to undertake financial risks."

These highly individualistic young Germans, represented by such figures as Alexander Kluge, Edgar Reitz, Hans Rolf Strobel, Herbert Vesely and Will Tremper, came from diverse backgrounds in journalism, law, art and the humanities. Their short, unstructured films, produced on meager budgets and photographed in a quasi-documentary style, reflected their philosophy that the German film should concern itself with contemporary German problems: the materialism of postwar society, the morality of the bourgeoisie, the alienation of

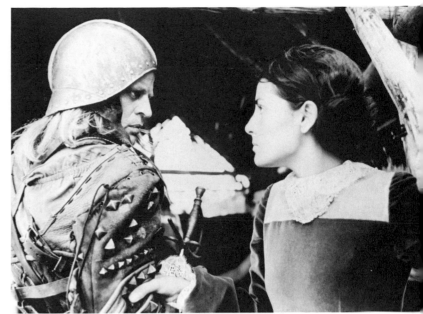

Klaus Kinski and Helena Rojo in Aguirre, der Zorn Gottes (Aguirre, the Wrath of God), directed by Werner Herzog, 1972.

Peter Kern in *Ludwig—Requiem für eienen Jungfraulichen König* (Ludwig, Requiem for a Virgin King), directed by Hans-Jürgen Syberberg, 1972.

youth and the "moral wreckage" of the Nazi era. Predominantly left wing, they sought to teach rather than entertain. Some of the young filmmakers did not hesitate to make partially autobiographical films in the belief

Helmut Käutner in *Carl May*, directed by Hans Jürgen Syberberg, 1974.

Winifred Wagner und die Geschichte des Hauses Wahnfried, 1914-1975 (Winifred Wagner and the History of the House of Wahnfried, 1914-1975), directed by Hans-Jürgen Syberberg, 1975.

that one's personal problem was also the world's problem. And when their films ended inconclusively and pessimistically, the young filmmakers argued that such is the course of life. Strongly influenced in many instances by Czech and Polish models, styles ranged from the experimental to the naturalistic. Although detractors referred to the offerings of the young German filmmakers as "*Bubis Kino* (Little Boys' Movies)," their films, while often bearing the imprint of the novice, gradually acquired the stature of an alternative cinema, a development which would have important implications for the course of the German film in the next decade.

Appraising the accomplishment of this first group of young German filmmakers in 1967, Will Tremper, regarded by many as the Father of the *Bubis Kino*, believed that it was a mistake "to think that with one step, as the New Wave did in France, the German film industry can rise out of the ashes of the past." In reality, "all that can be achieved after a year or so of activity by the young filmmakers is that the standard of films is raised a little. At the moment there is almost a battalion of young filmmakers, and from these will emerge two or three geniuses. But these two or three won't make a summer."

Many of the young German filmmakers were strongly political. Disdainful of "artistry" and "entertainment," they believed that the film should serve as a forum for the dissemination of ideas and philosophies which challenged the established order. Ulrich von Thüna warned that "The continuing politicization of short films (and political here means Marxist, naturally) is combined with a curious lack of any aesthetic quality among the followers of Eisenstein and Godard." Von Thüna predicted that for "the immediate future the happy combination of social significance and aesthetic innovation one finds in a man like Alexander Kluge will be rare indeed."

The filmmaker cautioned those who set little store in aesthetics to remember words of "old father Goethe: 'The form needs to be digested as well as the content; in fact, it is much harder to digest.'" These celluloided polemics, while applauded by audiences of revolutionary-minded students and intellectuals, were, in general, rejected by the great majority of German filmgoers. As Theo Hinz noted in an appraisal of the *Bubis Kino*, "The movement was economically a disaster and ground to a halt." Hinz rightly considered the 1960s "more a time of stumbling than taking giant steps forward."

The transformation from *Bubis Kino* to the *Neue Deutsches Kino*, or New German Cinema, occurred in the late 1960s, evolving steadily in the early 1970s to achieve a maturity at the close of the decade. Wim Wenders, Rainer Werner Fassbinder, Werner Herzog and Volker Schlöndorff stood in the forefront of *die Neue Welle*, the German "New Wave." Schlöndorff characterized the group when he described Wenders as the "guru of Munich sensitivities. He and his followers shy away from politics. Fassbinder is the Puccini faction. He can make any kind of movie you ask. Herzog is also a one-man faction, of the existential school of [Martin] Heidegger."

Other directors who achieved prominence during the decade included Hans-Jürgen Syberberg, Reinhardt Hauff, Wolfgang Petersen, Margarethe von Trotta and Christian Ziewer. As Schlöndorff suggested, the directors of the New German Cinema defy classification. They have no common aesthetic. Their interests vary widely, and while many reside in Munich, they are not close personally. Their themes and styles range from myth and abstraction with an emphasis on image, camera angle, lighting and sound, to the most austere form of documentary reporting. But as the German *Neue Welle* continued to unfold, most have returned to more traditional modes of cinematic expression. As in all revolutions, the conservative tendency inevitably asserts itself. By the early 1970s the greater number of the *Obermünchhauseners*, as some critics derisively described the Munich contingent of the *Oberhausen* group, had turned from the avant-garde to television and commercial film production.

Younger German directors have been more inclined to study the successful efforts of Francis Ford Coppola, Hal Ashby, Martin Scorese, Steven Spielberg and Peter Bogdanovich, representatives of the new American cinema who have demonstrated that the personal film can also be entertaining *and* commercial. The offerings of Karl Reitz (*Zero Hour*), Erwin Keush (*The Baker's Bread*), Richard Hauff (*Paule Paulaender*), Volker Schlöndorff (*Katharina Blum*) and the films of Fassbinder, Wenders and Herzog were examples of the tendency toward commercial production with serious overtones.

A curious if not ironic development was the compromise effected between the young Germans and their chief *bête noir*, the American film and its creators, past and present. Classic American films of the 1930s and 1940s have exercised a strong influence on the style of the directors of the New German Cinema. Particularly admired were the Hollywood films of Billy Wilder, Douglas Sirk, Fritz Lang, Orson Welles and Alfred Hitchcock, shown in 16 mm format in art house theaters. "All my films have as their underlying current the Americanization of Germany," Wim Wenders had noted. "I saw the German films of the 30's, for instance, only after having seen a thousand American films. I see my own films as American." Evidence of American derivativeness in the New German Cinema was particularly pronounced in some of the last works of Fassbinder, particularly his *Marriage of Maria Braun* and *Lili Marlene*.

The contribution of the Arsenal Cinema in West Berlin should also be noted. Developed by the *Freunden der Deutschen Kinemathek* (Friends of the German Cinema), the Arsenal presented contemporary and retrospective programs comparable to the London National Film Theater, while the *International Film Series*, sponsored by the Literarisches Colloquium at the University of Berlin, presented weekly programs with personal appearances by Alain Robbe-Grillet and Marguerite Duras of France, Tony Richardson and John Schlesinger of England, Milos Forman of Czechoslovakia and Pier Pasolini of Italy. Television documentaries about the history of Hollywood such as Hans C. Blumenberg's production for Westdeutscher Rundfunk in Cologne and Christa Maeker's documentary reports on John Wayne and James Cagney were also influential.

While the German "New Wave" surged forward, motion picture attendance in the Federal Republic continued to decline. The competition of television was a primary factor, but the quality of the German film must also be taken into consideration. Most of the new German films and their directors, Fassbinder, Wenders and Herzog, for example, were treated with apathy by the German public. Their films, especially in the early years of the "New Wave," were often critical of bourgeois society and irreverent in their treatment of German

Peggy Aschcroft, Elisabeth Bergner, Lil Dagover, Käthe Haack, Johanna Hofer, Elsa Wagner and Francoise Rosay in *Der Fussgänger* (The Pedestrian), produced and directed by Maximilian Schell, 1973.

Hans W. Geissendörfer.

history. These films were seen by a relatively small audience composed of the young intelligentsia and *cinéastes*. "You have to remember that for years Germany had no film tradition," Wenders intoned in 1977. "Now it's beginning to come back. We're building an audience and it will continue to grow if we have support."

In the parlance of West German film production, support must be translated into subsidy. By 1977, 80 percent of the funding of a typical German feature was accomplished through a subsidy of one kind or another.

The subsidy system has proved a mixed blessing. While the subsidy has no doubt encouraged the production of noteworthy films which might not have reached the screen in a free market, subsidies also allowed the production of some of the most abstruse and undisciplined films in the whole history of the German cinema. The attitude of Niklaus Schilling, who left Switzerland to make films in Germany, was not untypical: "I never think about the audience when I write a script. I only write for myself. Of course, I'm not *unhappy* if the audience likes it, too." It is ironic that the young German *auteurs* working in the 1960s and early 1970s saw no relationship between the quality of the classic American, British and German films which they so admired and the disciplined studio system which had made their production possible. The pedagogic impulse bloomed and fortunately faded. In general, German filmmakers today have adopted a more realistic attitude with respect to their art and their audience. They have demonstrated that education and entertainment are not inseparable and that communication with a large audience does not violate artistic integrity.

Minister of the Interior Fritz Genscher, Dr. Wilke (Bureau of Chancellor), Maximilian Schell and Rut Brandt, wife of Chancellor Willy Brandt, attend the premiere in Bonn of *Der Fussgänger* (The Pedestrian), 1973.

The subsidy system has had the predictable effect of discouraging political films which do not accord with the established authority. "I can't have money from the government to make a political film," Werner Schaeffer,

264

Werner Herzog directing a sequence from *Nosferatu*, 1979. "I know I have seen things that have never been seen" Herzog once said, "and it is these things that I want to make visible."

director of *Kälte Heimat (Cold Homeland)*, noted. "In 1975 I wanted to make a film like *The China Syndrome*, a film about nuclear reactors. But not in the Hollywood way, in the *German* way. I worked for about two and a half years for this film, and in the end I couldn't make it." Schaeffer is no doubt correct when he asserts that the situation tends to encourage self-censorship. The filmmaker gravitates to subject matter which he believes will be approved. "There are many German directors who do this," Schaeffer asserts. "[They focus on] a problem in history, something in literature . . . something *safe*. I never write scripts for the ministry." Schaeffer is at least partially correct, although it is unfair to suggest that the literary and historical subject represents a "safe harbor" for filmmakers. In the hands of an authentic talent these films may be as pertinent for our time as a contemporary polemic on disarmament or the sexual revolution. I believe some of the richest and most enduring achievements of the New German Film have been drawn from historical and literary subjects, as selected works by Herzog, Syberberg, Fassbinder, Giessendorfer and Adlon amply suggest.

No one is completely satisfied with the subsidy system, but at the same time there appears to be no acceptable alternative. A return to the "free market" under present

Director Volker Schlöndorff

circumstances is impossible. Doubtless 80 percent of German film production would disappear were it not for the availability of a subsidy.

As the decade of the 1970s closed, German filmmakers had cause for optimism. Dieter Menz, a prominent film exporter and a director of the German Export Union, could write in 1980 that the "chances for Ger-

265

Fritz Hakl and David Bennent in *Die Blechtrommel* (The Tin Drum), directed by Volker Schlöndorff, 1979.

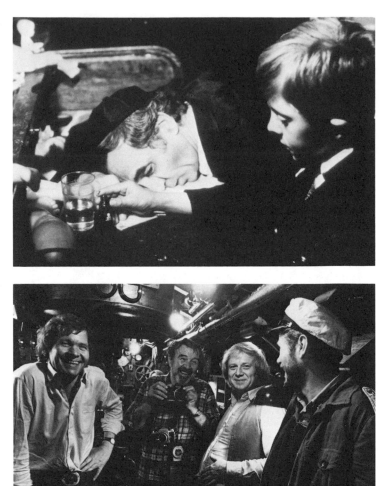

Usch Barthelmess-Weller, cameraman Jürgen Jürges (center) and Werner Meyer (far right) during the production of *Die Kinder aus No. 67* (The Children of No. 67), 1980.

Novelist Lothar Günther Buchheim, cameraman Jost Vacano, director Wolfgang Petersen and Jürgen Prochnow during the making of *Das Boot* (The Boat), 1981.

Director Percy Adlon in 1982.

Director Edgar Reitz.

man films with audience appeal and quality were never so good as today. Interest in German films has grown distinctly in Spain, France, Sweden and Brazil. It may grow in the U.K. after the success of *The Tin Drum* and the German film week."

Menz believes that Germany's aim must be Europe. Director Volker Schölendorff, who is also a member of the board of the Export Union, is of a similar opinion, believing that while "the American market is the most important one in the world and should of course always be tried . . . it is also the most difficult market, especially for German pictures. Hence, it can be of commercial interest only in rather isolated cases. The real commercial chances lie in Europe, in England, France, Italy, the Benelux countries and Scandinavia."

Will the 1980s become the decade of the German cinema? The artistic and commercial success of *The Tin Drum, Nosferatu, The Marriage of Maria Braun, Das Boot* and *The Neverending Story* suggest that the German film may have at last achieved an international acceptance approximating the period which followed World War I. Production rose from 57 films in 1978 to 65 in 1979 while the number of cinemas increased from 3,110 to 3,196 during the same period. Paid admissions grew by 4.3 percent or 142 million persons.

But there is a negative side to recent developments, and it is principally one of economics. German films garnered only $7.5 million in rental fees world-wide in 1980, a relatively small figure when one considers that a single motion picture, Disney's *Jungle Book*, earned $11.5 million in the United States during the same year. Ironically, the renaissance of the German film was made possible from an economic standpoint by the success of American films in Germany, and, needless to say, American critics such as Andrew Sarris and Vincent Canby, writing for publications as diverse as *The Village Voice* and the new York *Times* in the mid-1970s, did much to make the New German Film an international success.

Yet another challenge has been the equipment revolution. In 1972 the German Film Amateur Association, numbering about 5,000 members, produced 2,000 short films which were shown privately to members in 231 clubs. As *Der Spiegel* noted, "the biggest film production in the world has no role in the cinemas." These enthusiastic amateurs, working with Super-8 equipment, were

Günther Lamprecht, Giesela Uhlen, Gottfried John, Anton Schirsner, Hanna Schygulla and Elisabeth Trissener in *Die Ehe der Maria Braun* (The Marriage of Maria Braun). directed by Rainer Werner Fassbinder, 1979.

spending most of their leisure and money on equipment, film stock and Super-8 transcriptions of film classics which could be procured at local camera shops, bookstores and art galleries. Some enterprising entrepreneurs created mini-television studios where space could be rented for the production of more professional films.

The videocassette recorder (VCR) represents still another phase of the equipment revolution and offers the greatest threat to the German film in a theatrical context.

Germany has already adopted the practice of simultaneously releasing films in theaters and on cassette. German cinema owners regard this develoment warily but express more concern about the showing of cassette versions of popular motion pictures in bars and other public places which offer amenities unavailable in a film theater.

The continued development of the German film will depend on something more than a favorable economic climate, refined technologies and the training of personnel in the use of this new technology. Much will depend upon the filmmakers themselves and the quality of their lives. Technique, proficiency in the handling of appa-

Charles Aznavour (Naphta) and Flavio Bucci (Settembrini) in *Der Zauberberg* (The Magic Mountain), 1982.

Rod Steiger (Mynherr Peeperkorn) and Marie-France Pisier (Clawdia Chauchat) in *Der Zauberberg* (The Magic Mountain), directed by Hans W. Geissendörfer, 1982.

ratus, even artistic talent is not enough. If the German film renaissance is to be sustained, its makers must have experience beyond the confines of the course of study offered by institutes, academies or the film departments of universities. The great filmmakers created great films because they brought a knowledge of life to the films as Goethe, Flaubert and Dostoyevski brought the richness of original experience to their literature. Germany's early film history is abundant with such examples. If we still find *The Cabinet of Dr. Caligari, The Last Laugh, Metropolis, Pandora's Box* and *Such Is Life* extraordinary works of art, it may be due in large measure to the fact that the men who made these films led extraordinary lives.

In 1995 the German film will celebrate its one hundredth anniversary. The technical advances achieved by the centennial year will no doubt seem revolutionary by the standards of the mid-1980s. Our predictions concerning the technologies of 1995 will probably be surpassed by more far-reaching technologies, undreamed of innovations, as momentous as the transition from silence to sound, from black and white to color. But regardless of the technologies which will have been developed to aid him in the creation of images and sounds, the *Regisseur* will still be a human being, and the quality of his life will determine the quality of his motion picture art.

Aguirre, der Zorn Gottes

AGUIRRE, THE WRATH OF GOD

1972

CREDITS:

Production: A Werner Herzog Filmproduktion. *Director:* Werner Herzog. *Screenplay:* Werner Hergoz. *Cinematography:* Thomas Mauch. *Editor:* Beate Mainka-Jellinghaus. *Music:* Popol Vuh. *Running time:* 95 minutes. *Released:* 1972.

CAST:

Klaus Kinski *(Don Lope de Aguirre);* Cecilia Rivera *(Flores, his daughter);* Ruy Guerra *(Don Pedro de Ursua);* Helena Rojo *(Inez de Atienza, his wife);* Del Negro *(Br. Gaspar de Carvajal);* Peter Berling *(Don Fernando de Guzmán);* Armando Polanha *(Armando);* Dany Ades *(Perucho);* Edward Roland *(Okello).*

Werner Herzog: "I have never made a film about a figure for whom I have not felt compassion—not even Aguirre." *(Aguirre, der Zorn Gottes)*

"Werner Herzog is a cinema magician who is constantly discovering new ways to entice the moviegoer, to involve him even more deeply in what unfolds on screen," Gambaccini wrote in his appraisal of the German director. "Watching a Herzog film is the nearest thing to transcendence one is likely to encounter in a movie theater." Herzog has been aptly described as the most mystical and most lyrical of the younger generation of German filmmakers. There is something of the visionary poet in Herzog, who has said: "We are surrounded by worn-out images, and we deserve new ones. I see something on the horizon that most people have not yet seen. I seek planets that do not exist and landscapes that have only been dreamed."

Aguirre, der Zorn Gottes (Aguirre, the Wrath of God) was based on the account of a sixteenth-century monk, Brother de Carvajal, who accompanied the Spanish explorers into the jungle of the Amazon in search of Eldorado. Herzog and his crew worked on the Wyaga and Namai Rivers of Peru and Colombia between January and March, 1973. The director's working method was as unorthodox as the subject matter of his film was bizarre. Actors were informed of the storyline but were never shown a script. "Herzog is very secretive about how he works," actor Dany Ades notes. "He doesn't let anyone know what he is after." But despite the chaos of his methodology, which may have been necessary when

Klaus Kinski as Don Lope de Aguirre. *(Aguirre, der Zorn Gottes)*

one considers the chaotic environmental conditions under which he labored, the result is astonishingly beautiful.

The opening of *Aguirre* must be accounted one of the most visually arresting sequences in the whole history of cinema. We are shown a long train of Spanish soldiers descending a steep mountainside "like a rivulet of quicksilver melting into nature's green vastness." Shrouded in the gray mist of early morning, the scene has a graphic monumentality reminiscent of Lang's *Die Nibelungen*. This dreamy beginning, superbly photographed by Thomas Mauch, establishes the appropriate background for the unfoldment of Herzog's strange story of insatiable greed and the absolute corruption of absolute power.

On Christmas Day, 1560, explorer Gonzalez Pizarro (Alejandro Repulles) splits up his expedition which is searching for the legendary city of gold, El Dorado, in Peru. Don Pedro de Ursua (Ruy Guerra) is assigned to travel down a river when the jungle becomes impenetrable. Father Carvajal (Del Negro), Don Lope de Aguirre (Klaus Kinski) and others use rafts for their journey. Ursua's wife (Helena Rojo) and Aguirre's daughter (Cecilia Rivera), aged 15, accompany them. When one raft is caught in a whirlpool and its passengers are killed by Indians, Ursua decides to turn back. Aguirre assumes

Helena Rojo as Inez de Atienza, the wife of Aguirre. *(Aguirre, der Zorn Gottes)*

Benediction at the shore of the Amazon. *(Aguirre, der Zorn Gottes)*

The Amazon. *(Aguirre, der Zorn Gottes)*

Klaus Kinski and Helena Rojo. *(Aguirre, der Zorn Gottes)*

Klaus Kinski in the final scene of *Aguirre, der Zorn Gottes*.

command and makes Guzmán (Peter Beiling) the emperor of El Dorado as they claim the land they see for Spain.

Fever and hunger take their toll while cannibals lurk nearby. Guzmán's gluttony causes his murder, after which Aguirre has Ursua hanged. "Herzog assuages the viewer with the savage beauty of the landscape," Derek Elley wrote, "inserting sudden jabs of violence and paranoia like so many pinpricks." Later, during a raid on an Indian village, Rojo disappears into the jungle. Only Aguirre survives, escaping from fevers and deadly arrows, his daughter and most of the men having died. Herzog's "kaleidoscope of the fabulous and the bizarre" concludes with Aguirre, now insane, dreaming of a new dynasty for himself.

"We are enveloped by *Aguirre* as we would be if we were immersed in water," Elley noted in his review of the film. "In fact, Herzog uses the Amazon River to lend a definite liquid flow to his film, and the audience drifts along with it in midstream. *Aguirre* has the power to make one thoroughly rethink what it *means* to be a filmgoer."

Ali: Angst essen Selle Auf

ALI: FEAR EATS THE SOUL

1974

CREDITS:

Production: Tango-film, Rainer Werner Fassbinder, Filmverlad des Autoren GmbH und co KG. *Director:* Rainer Werner Fassbinder. *Screenplay:* Rainer Werner Fassbinder. *Cinematography:* Jürgen Jürges (Eastmancolor). *Editor:* Thea Eymèsz. *Art direction:* Rainer Werner Fassbinder. *Music:* Archive material. *Running time:* 94 minutes. Released in the United States by New Yorker Films; in Great Britain by Cinegate.

CAST:

Brigitte Mira *(Emmi);* El Hedi Ben Salem *(Ali);* Barbara Valentin *(Barbara, the barmaid);* Irm Kermann *(Krista);* Rainer Werner Fassbinder *(Eugen, her husband);* Karl Scheydt *(Albert);* Elma Karlowa *(Frau Kargus);* Anita Bucher *(Frau Ellis);* Gusti Kreissl

272

(Paula); Walter Sedlmayr (Herr Angermeyer, the grocer); Doris Mattes (his wife); Liselotte Eder (Frau Münchmeyer); Marquard Bohm (Herr Gruber); Katharina Herberg (girl in bar); Rudolf Waldemar Brem (customer in Bar); Peter Moland (chief in car workshop); Margit Symo (Hedwig); Peter Gauhe (Bruno); Helga Ballhaus (Yolanda); Elisabeth Bertram (Frieda); Hannes Gromball.

Rainer Werner Fassbinder once described his eighteenth film, *Angst essen Selle Auf (Fear Eats the Soul)*, as "a film about love, which in a way is impossible but is still a possibility." While Fassbinder reworked this theme in many of his motion pictures, rarely did he achieve the poignancy and restraint which marks the dialogue and imagery of *Angst essen Selle Auf*.

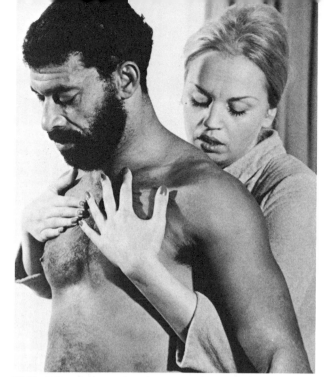

El Hedi Ben Salem and Barbara Valentin. *(Ali: Angst essen Selle auf)*

Barbara Valentin and El Hedi Ben Salem. *(Ali: Angst essen Selle auf)*

Brigitte Mira (right). *(Ali: Angst essen Selle auf)*

Brigitte Mira and El Hedi Ben Salem. *(Ali: Angst essen Selle auf)*

273

The story line of *Angst essen Selle Auf* is narrated with slight variation by a character in an earlier Fassbinder film, the austere and perplexing *American Soldier*. *Angst essen Selle Auf* opens on a rainy night as Emmi, a sixtyish charwoman, widowed and lonely, steps into a café catering to Arab workers. While Emmi sips her cola, Ali, a handsome Moroccan laborer half her age approaches and they converse. Because the Moroccan speaks an imperfect German, a language which he must know in order to survive, Fassbinder renders the title as *Angst essen Selle Auf* instead of the grammatically correct, *Angst isst die Seele auf*. After they have danced, Ali offers to see her home. Emmi invites him into her tidy flat, and when she learns of his poor lodging, she asks him to stay the night.

Emmi loves the Moroccan and they eventually marry, but her grown children react with cruel intolerance. When her son, played by Fassbinder, angrily kicks in the television screen, Emmi comments with calm reserve, "You were always hot-headed. Remember the cat?" She is ostracized by her co-workers and shunned by the tradesmen.

To escape the enveloping hostility, the couple go abroad for a short holiday. Upon their return, family and friends, neighbors and merchants show a greater tolerance toward Emmi and Ali, but their motivation is selfishness rather than love. The meanness of her family and the community has the effect of driving Emmi and Ali apart. Fear begins to eat at their souls, and when they return to the café where they first met, Ali collapses on the dance floor, violently ill from a perforated stomach ulcer. The doctor tells her that "foreign workers suffer from a particular strain." The love of Emmi and Ali is rekindled, but it is understood that the Moroccan does not have long to live.

El Hedi Ben Salem (right) and supporting players. (*Ali: Angst essen Selle auf*)

Stunde Null

ZERO HOUR

1977

CREDITS:

Production: Edgar Reitz-Filmproduktion, Munich/Solaris-Film, Munich/WDR, Cologne. *Director:* Edgar Reitz. *Assistant director:* Winifried Hennig. *Screenplay:* Peter Steinbach and Edgar Reitz. *Cinematography:* Gernot Roll. *Editor:* Ingrid Boszat. *Art direction:* Winifried Hennig. *Costumes:* Gerlinde Gies. *Sound:* Vladimir Vizner. *Music:* Nicos Mamangakis. *Production director:* Martin Häussler. *Released:* March 8, 1977. *Running time:* 108 minutes. Released in France as *Le Point Zero*.

CAST:

Kai Taschner *(Joschi);* Anette Jünger *(Isa);* Herbert Weissbach *(Mattiske);* Klaus Dierig *(Paul);* Günter Schiemann *(Franke);* Erika Wackernagel *(Frau Unterstab);* Erich Kleiber *(Motek);* Thorsten Nenties *(little boy);* Bernd Linzel *(Karl-Heinz).*

Edgar Reitz was a founding member of the Film School in Ulm where he lectured on filming and film direction from 1962 to 1968. Between 1959 and 1966 he produced numerous short films, including *Geschwindigkeit (Speed)* which was shown at the Cannes Film Festival in 1962. *Mahlzeiten* (1966), his first full-length film, was awarded the prize of "Best First Film" in Venice in 1967. Some of Reitz' most important films are *Cadillac* (1968), *Geschichten vom Kübelkind* (1970), *Das Goldene Ding* (1971), *Reise nach Wien* (1973), *In Gefahr und Grosster Not Bringt der Mittelweg den Tod* (1974) made in collaboration with Alexander Kluge, and *Stunde Null* (1977).

Born in the village of Morbach in the Rhineland in November, 1932, three months before Hitler came to power, Rietz experienced the Third Reich as a child. But as he grew, he "became aware of a world at pains to erase the memories of this era. Nobody had been a Nazi, and everyone pretended he had not been part of the history of that time."

Unlike *Reise nach Wien (Journey to Vienna)*, which

Kai Taschner and Anette Jünger. *(Stunde Null)*

attempts to recreate the atmosphere of the Nazi era, *Stunde Null (Zero Hour)* "concentrates entirely on the unhistorical moment between war and peace: July, 1945." The film opens shortly after the collapse of the Third Reich. Joschie, formerly a member of the Hitler Youth, has a new dream: America. Once an admirer of the German Air Force, he now wears an American flying jacket. He has become acquainted with American soldiers and is impressed by their victory. When the Americans leave, having relinquished their territory to the Russians in accordance with the Allies' treaty, Joschie sets out for Möckern, a village near Leipzig, on a motorbike stolen from the German Army. He also has a map of the village cemetery marked with the spot where some retreating Nazis buried their valuables. Joschie intends to find this treasure and join the Americans.

The cemetery is opposite the railwayman's cottage on the outskirts of the village. Old Mattiske, who used to operate the level crossing, lives here and repairs bicycles for his living. For a few packets of Lucky Strikes, Mattiske agrees to let Joschie stay with him. Together with Frau Unterstab and Paul, who has lost a leg in the war, Mattiske awaits the arrival of the Soviet Army. No one knows what is going to happen. Franke, a former Nazi, puts up anti-fascist posters just to be on the safe side. In a greenhouse Paul has made a hiding place for Isà, a young refugee whom Frau Unterstab has taken in.

Thorsten Nenties. *(Stunde Null)*

275

One day Matek, a Pole, arrives with a carousel which he sets up. Afterwards Mattiske, Frau Unterstab, Paul and Matek celebrate the occasion together. While they drink wine, Joschie and Isa uncover treasure in the cemetery. They carefully hide the horde of Nazi medals and jewelry, having resolved to escape to the American lines. Joschie's enthusiasm for the Americans knows no bounds.

Suddenly the Red Army arrives, jolly soliders with cows and horse-drawn carts instead of tanks. They merrily gather around the carousel, ride Joschie's motorbike and a small boy's bicycle and, after a further search, discover Isa's hiding place in the greenhouse. When Isa shouts for help, Joschie tries to rescue her and fires a warning shot. Within seconds, war breaks out once again. The men are lined up against the wall, but the soldiers do not shoot. They accept Matek's explanation that Joschie fired the shot out of love and put down their guns.

Joschie and Isa travel in the direction of the American zone, walking for hours before reaching their destination. Finally an American jeep pulls up alongside them. The soldiers search Joschie's pockets, confiscate the valuables and flying jacket and drive off with Isa. Joschie is left standing alone on the country road.

"The people I have described in the film were part of the Third Reich," Reitz noted. "My memories seem to contradict the judgments made about this generation of parents. It still remains a mystery to me how the Ger-

Anette Jünger and Kai Taschner. (*Stunde Null*)

Anette Jünger and Kai Taschner. (*Stunde Null*)

Thorsten Nenties. (*Stunde Null*)

276

many of Hitler could have come about; the murderous brutality on a political level and, at the same time, the feeling of well-being and homeliness in one's private life. Thus, I, too, have developed the love-hate relationship typical of my generation in Germany. The war is not over yet." Reitz likened his perspective to that of the little boy with the bicycle in *Stunde Null:* "He will only understand much later what his curious eyes are seeing at the moment."

Der Amerikanische Freund

THE AMERICAN FRIEND

1977

CREDITS:

Production: Road Movies Filmproduktion-Les Films Du Losange-Wim Wenders Produktion-Westdeutschen Rundfunk Produktion. *Director:* Wim Wenders. *Screenplay:* Wim Wenders. Based on the novel *Ripley's Game* by Patricia Highsmith. *Cinematography:* Robby Muller (Eastmancolor). *Music:* Jurgen Knieper. *Film editor:* Peter Przygodda. *Released:* 1977. Running time: 127 minutes.

CAST:

Bruno Ganz *(Jonathan Zimmermann);* Dennis Hopper *(Tom Ripley);* Lisa Kreuzer *(Marianne Zimmer-*

Dennis Hopper as Tom Ripley, the American friend. *(Der Amerikanische Freund)*

Bruno Ganz as Jonathan Zimmermann. *(Der Amerikanische Freund)*

mann); Gerard Blain *(Raoul Minot);* Nicholas Ray *(Derwatt);* Samuel Fuller *(The American);* Peter Lilienthal *(Marcangelo);* Daniel Schmidt *(Igraham);* Jean Eustache *(Friendly man);* Lou Castel *(Rodolphe).*

Adapted from the novel *Ripley's Game,* by Patricia Highsmith, *Der Amerikanische Freund (The American Friend)* functions on one level as an adventure thriller in the tradition of *film noir* with Hitchcockian overtones. The exciting scenes aboard the Europa Express, for example, recall moments in *The Thirty-Nine Steps* (1935), *The Lady Vanishes* (1938) and *Strangers on a Train* (1951), also adapted from a Highsmith novel. On a second tier, *The American Friend* may be appreciated as a psychological study of two men, Tom and Jonathan, recalling once again *Strangers on a Train* in which Hitchcock probed the relationship of Bruno and Guy. But it is on the level of allegory that *The American Friend* achieves its deepest significance, Wenders having fashioned a superb parable of postwar Germany's seduction by the culture and mores of America.

Tom (Dennis Hopper) and his German accomplice (Bruno Ganz) aboard the train. *(Der Amerikanische Freund)*

Tom Ripley is the symbol of this America. He is a dangerous man, crassly materialistic, amoral by nature and instinctively exploitative. Tom develops a certain sympathy for his German friend, Jonathan, the *petite bourgeoise* family man from Hamburg who believes himself to be dying of leukemia. Jonathan represents the weaker partner in what proves to be a doomed transatlantic alliance.

When Tom Ripley, a dealer in forged art, learns that Jonathan Zimmermann, a Hamburg picture framer with whom he deals, is dying of an incurable blood disease, he promises him a sum of money to kill a man. Jonathan is at first hesitant, but finally acquiesces in the belief that after his death the money will provide for his wife and child. But the first murder leads to a second which Jonathan and Ripley commit together aboard a train. Curiously, the mayhem serves to deepen the friendship between the lonely American and the sickly German. They return to Tom Ripley's Hamburg hideout only to be confronted by a contingent of Mafia-style gunmen intent on revenge. But Tom and Jonathan manage to escape, accompanied by Jonathan's wife Marianne. Their bizarre flight, undertaken in a Mercedes ambulance belonging to the crooks and an old Volkswagon sedan, ends on a forlorn seacoast near Hamburg. Having resolved to break with the American, Jonathan speeds away with Marianne at his side. Tom makes a pathetic attempt to follow them on foot. Jonathan recklessly

accelerates, running the car up a concrete embankment before it stops. Slumped at the steering wheel, Jonathan falls unconscious, having succumbed to his illness.

As suggested above, *The American Friend* was strongly influenced by the tradition of the American *film noir* as it evolved in the 1940s and 1950s. Wenders has studied the work of Samuel Fuller, Nicholas Ray, both of whom appear in cameo roles in *The American Friend*, Douglas Sirk, Alfred Hitchcock and others. The impress of their work on his technique is pronounced.

Wenders' study of the *film noir* school may be a strength, but it is also his principal weakness. He has learned a great deal from a study of the old masters. But reverence for the past has given his art a derivative quality which is impossible to ignore.

The derivativeness of Wenders' film art is strongly indicated by his use of music in *The American Friend* and in *Hammett*, which he directed in Hollywood. Wenders prefers a continuous score, strongly melodramatic in the tradition of 1940s filmmaking, but with the absence of subtlety. In a Wenders film, a menacing chord punctuates each dramatic situation with monotonous regularity. The intrusion of these pretentious sounds in imitation of Bernard Herrmann, Miklos Rozsa and the studio symphony orchestras of another era serves to underscore the borrowed quality of his technique while distracting from the dramatic visuals or the performance of his players. Wenders would be better served by silence, natural sound or the imaginative use of music.

Lisa Kreuzer and Bruno Ganz. *(Der Amerikanische Freund)*

The production of films in imitation of another director or school of filmmaking is a course best abandoned. In literature, the influence of Goethe on Thomas Mann was profound, but the writings of Mann were unique. Orson Welles is alleged to have made a careful study of John Ford's *Stagecoach* before he embarked on the production of *Citizen Kane*, but the films of Welles bear the imprint of Welles.

After a period of apprenticeship, it is customary for the student painter to leave the studio of his master, and so the apprentice filmmaker, while inspired by the examples of his teachers, must eventually forsake the study of past works and create independently, drawing upon inner resources and life experience.

Unser Hitler, ein Film Aus Deutschland

HITLER, A FILM FROM GERMANY

1977

CREDITS:

Production: TMS-Film GmbH (Munich), Westdeutscher Rundfunk (Cologne). *Executive Producer:* Bernd Eirchinger. *Director:* Hans-Jürgen Syberberg. *Assist-*

Heinz Schubert as a toga-clad Hitler speaks from the grave of Richard Wagner: "I was and am the end of your most secret wishes, the legend and reality of your dreams. . . ." (*Unser Hitler, Ein Film aus Deutschland*)

A scene from *Unser Hitler* with Brechtian overtones.

Syberberg's *Unser Hitler* explores the psyche of the German nation.

ant directors: Gerhard von Halem and Michael Se-devy. *Screenplay:* Hans-Jürgen Syberberg. *Cinematography:* Dietrich Lohmann. *Camera assistant:* Werner Luring. *Special effects:* Theo Nischwitz *Editor:* Jutta Brandstaedter. *Assistant editors:* Helga Beyer and Lydia Pieger. *Art direction:* Hans Gailling. *Costumes:* Barbara Gailling and Brigitte Kühlenthal. *Properties:* Peter Durst. *Puppets:* Barbara Buchwald and Hans M. Stummer. *Unit manager:* Ike Werk. *Production assistant:* Annie Oleon. *Production manager:* Harry Nap *Released:* 1977. *Studio and processing:* Bavaria Atelier GmbH. Presented and distributed in the United States by Francis Ford Coppola. *Running time:* 7 hours, 30 minutes.

CAST:

Heinz Schubert, Peter Kern, Helmut Lange, Rainer Von Artenfels, Martin Sperr, Peter Moland, Johannes Buzalski, Alfred Edel, Amelie Syberberg, Harry Baer, Peter Luhr, André Heller.

Since the 1930s Hitler has appeared in a variety of film genres. He has been represented in documentaries ranging from the educational to the propagandistic; he has been seen in dramatized biographies and television docudramas based on memoirs and histories; and, over the years, he has appeared as a *dramatis personae* in countless fiction films. In his 1977 film *Unser Hitler, Ein Film aus Deutschland* (*Our Hitler, A Film from Germany*), Hans-Jürgen Syberberg approached Hitler and the Nazi phenomenon in a unique manner. "I never

would make a film about a man called Adolf Hitler but rather about the people who decided to have a Hitler," Syberberg explained. "I wanted to show that it can happen in a democracy. I also wanted to try to go through the darkest part of our history and still leave people with a love for the culture of the country where this man came up. And I try to do it with Hitler, not Beethoven or Goethe, which is so easy. Then maybe I have done something for my country as well as for the people who sit through seven hours of my film. Art is always intensifying you own life."

Strongly influenced by the Brechtian *Lehrstruck*, a play that teaches, Syberberg described his work as "an aesthetic scandal" which combined "Brechtian doctrines of epic theater with Richard Wagner's musical aesthetics." Syberberg characterized his seven-hour film as "a monologue—my monologue." Financed by British, German and French television, *Our Hitler* represented four years of research and preparation followed by seven weeks of shooting at Bavaria Studios near Munich.

Syberberg was motivated to make a film about Hitler for two reasons. First of all, because the Nazi Führer embodied utopia. "He offered the future like Jesus, like socialism, as a cruel god with sacrifices and obedience," Syberberg noted in a 1980 interview. "And in a perverse way, he delivered it. And the people followed him. That's the cruel thing to realize."

Syberberg was drawn to Hitler in the second place "because Hitler was the greatest filmmaker of all times." Making his point with hyperbole, Syberberg asserted that Hitler created World War II for the same reason that he commissioned Leni Riefenstahl to photograph the Nuremberg Party Congress, viz., "in order to view the rushes

Eintopf in the Chancellery, the patriotic "utility Irish stew," which Germans were encouraged to eat at least twice a week. (*Unser Hitler, Ein Film aus Deutschland*)

Hans-Jürgen Syberberg and his daughter Amelie. (*Unser Hitler, Ein Film aus Deutschland*)

Heinz Schubert in the role of Himmler. (*Unser Hitler, Ein Film aus Deutschland*)

A mannequin stares at Edison's "Black Maria" studio, symbolic of the century's greatest myth-making instrument, the motion picture. (*Unser Hitler, Ein Film aus Deutschland*)

privately every evening for himself, like King Ludwig attending a Wagner opera alone. It is very interesting that the only objects that remain of the Third Reich are fragments of celluloid; nothing else exists—not the architecture of Albert Speer, nor the borders of the big German Reich of which Hitler dreamed—only the celluloid record of his existence, of the war."

Syberberg regarded Hitler as the culmination of tendencies born in nineteenth-century German art, litera-

"Part illustrated lecture, part symphony, part circus sideshow, part fever-dream," wrote the American critic, J. Hoberman, *"Our Hitler* is a prolix, extravagant, staggering work. It is exhilarating, exhausting, infuriating, and devastating." *(Unser Hitler, Ein Film aus Deutschland)*

Ludwig of Bavaria, an innocent progenitor of National Socialism. *(Unser Hitler, Ein Film aus Deutschland)*

ture, philosophy and music, particularly the music of Richard Wagner. "Perhaps the legends of history are more truthful than the reality," he elaborated. "Perhaps through an understanding of such myths one can better pierce the center of ideas than through an understanding of the actual history. My film is not actually a film about Hitler as an historical person. Very often I don't follow the actual historical incidents and events." Instead, the director concentrated on the banality of everyday life during the Third Reich. Forsaking the conventional, his film became something other than the story of Hitler, Germany, Western Europe or the conflict between East and West. In Syberberg's words, "It's a film about human conditions in the twentieth century and the turning point of our times, fixed to Hitler as an historical model."

He made a conscious effort to avoid "the easy moralizing of Hollywood." Nor did he wish to show the killing of people or to entertain and profit from the subject of Hitlerism. "To make money with Hitler is not Nazism," Syberberg stated emphatically, "but it is something similar."

Syberberg did not see Hitler as "a devil who seduced the German people," but rather the contrary: It was the German people who sought Hitler. "It is unfortunately true that the most interesting aspect of crime is the criminal, not the victim," Syberberg noted. "Without a doubt, what is most interesting is the motive and psychology of the criminal. My film is an examination—a psychoanalysis, if you will—of the victimizer. If one wants to understand the empire of Julius Caesar, one must examine his life and way of thinking—not that of Spartacus. It is easy to understand the revolt of slaves but difficult to comprehend the evil of tyrants."

Running seven hours and thirty minutes, the film is divided into four parts: "The Grail," "A German Dream," "The End of the Winter's Tale," and "We Children of Hell." Syberberg achieved his cinematic

Syberberg: "It is easy to understand the revolt of slaves, but difficult to comprehend the evil of tyrants." (*Unser Hitler, Ein Film aus Deutschland*)

"monologue" with a variety of props, back projections of Berchtesgaden, the chancellory, the Black Maria of Thomas Edison, a cardboard cutout of Dr. Caligari and an assortment of ghoulish puppets in the likenesses of Hitler, Goering, Goebbels, Himmler and Eva Braun. A dozen actors appear in various Nazi guises. Hitler is represented as Charlie Chaplin in *The Great Dictator*, a house painter, Hamlet meditating on a skull marked "Jew," as Napoleon Bonaparte and most effectively as a toga-clad Führer who enunciates the thesis of the film from the misty grave of his idol and spiritual progenitor, Richard Wagner.

Syberberg purposely avoided the use of archival film showing parades and demonstrations. He did want to present the image of Hitler which Leni Riefenstahl created in *Triumph of the Will*.

The dramatic vignettes are interwoven with radio announcements of the Reich Broadcasting System and the music of Wagner, Beethoven, Mozart and Haydn. Against a dreamy mountain landscape, we hear announcers report from the various fronts. Rarely, if ever, has a film about the Nazi era made such effective use of radio transcriptions. Through their use of the radio the Nazis attempted to synthesize German culture with the National Socialist idea, and Syberberg's film is a reminder that it was the radio that served as a daily source of news and entertainment, politics and culture, death and dreams for millions of Germans during the almost six years of war.

While unquestionably innovative, *Our Hitler* has certain weaknesses. It is overly long and imposes an unnecessary hardship on audiences. Abridgement would not have destroyed but only strengthened the epic pretensions of the work. The film does not testify to the power of editing and the virtue of brevity. The motion picture is capable of making an overwhelming point in ten seconds. It does not require ten minutes.

While Syberberg claims to admire the work of Eisenstein and Stroheim, his film is curiously unreflective of their technical achievements as filmmakers. The aforementioned directors were great visualists as is Syberberg on occasion, but they never lost sight of the fact that the essence of motion picture art is *movement*. *Our Hitler* is static to a fault, and as an exercise in cinema it represents a retrogression rather than a progression in the development of the medium. The strengths of *Our Hitler* lie elsewhere.

To the question that Martin Bormann is alleged to have asked in the closing days of the Third Reich: "When all is said and done, the Führer is the Führer: Where would we be without him?" Syberberg would amend the question: "Where would Hitler be without us?" And this is the thesis of Syberberg's film, the Hitler

in ourselves. Was not Hitler's evil but a reflection of man's evil? Syberberg believes that we must unburden ourselves of the myth that Hitler exploited the people; rather the reverse, the people exploited *him*, seeking through Hitler the fulfillment of their noblest and darkest desires.

Syberberg contends that Hitler is the creation of twentieth-century democratic man and must be seen as the culmination, not of reactionary, but of progressive tendencies. The title, *Our Hitler*, may suggest that Hitler is a phenomenon to be shared by all people and all nations, a reflection of the darker image of mankind.

Nosferatu

1979

CREDITS:

Production: Michael Gruskoff. *Executive producer:* Walter Saxer. *Director and producer:* Werner Herzog. *Assistant directors:* Remmelts and Mirko Tichacek. *Screenplay:* Werner Herzog. *Cinematography:* Jörg Schmidt-Reitwein (Eastman Color). *Editor:* Beate Mainka-Jellinghaus. *Production design:* Henning von Gierke. *Special effects:* Cornelius Siegel. *Costumes:* Giesela Storch. *Music:* Popol Vuh and Florian Fricke. Richard Wagner: *Rheingold;* Charles Gounod: *Sanctus* (Messe Solennelle) Vok. Ansambl Gordela. *English dialogue:* Tom Schachtman and Martje Grohmann. Released in the United States by 20th Century-Fox. *Running time:* 105 minutes.

CAST:

Klaus Kinski *(Count Dracula);* Isabelle Adjani *(Lucy Harker);* Bruno Ganz *(Jonathan Harker);* Jacques Dufilho *(Captain);* Roland Torpor *(Renfield);* Walter Ladengast *(Dr. Van Helsing);* Dan van Husen *(Warden);* Jan Groth *(Harbormaster);* Carsten Bodinus *(Schrader);* Martje Grohmann *(Mina);* Ryk de Gooyer *(Town Official);* Clemens Scheitz *(Town employee);* Lo van Hensberger *(Councilman);* John Leddy *(Coachman);* Margiet van Hartingsveld *(Maid);* Tim Beekman *(Coffinbearer).*

Werner Herzog has a deep sense of film history, a trait which he shares with Wim Wenders and other film directors of the New German Cinema. The artistry of the German silent film has had a pronounced influence on all his work. Because of his refusal to recognize the achievements of German filmmakers in the period 1933-1945, Herzog looks to the creators of the silent film for inspiration and artistic guidance. This reverence for German silent film found expression in a uniquely Herzogian gesture when Lotte H. Eisner, the renowned critic, historian and archivist of the German film, became ill in the 1970s. Elderly and frail, her death seemed imminent. "I just walked straight to Paris," Herzog recalled. "It was some sort of protest. She was going to die and we couldn't allow it. I am not superstitious, but somehow I knew that she would be all right and standing when I got there." His presentment concerning her recovery proved correct.

Nosferatu was created in homage to Friedrich Wilhelm Murnau whose 1922 version of the Dracula story occupies a prominent place in the pantheon of the German film. Herzog feels a strong kinship for Murnau, whose career Eisner chronicled in a definitive biography. "He is my favorite director in German film history, and I like him much more than, for example, Fritz Lang," Herzog reflects. "Fritz Lang is too geometrical in his thinking. Murnau's *Nosferatu* is the most visionary of all German films—it senses what was going to happen, it has an undefined sense of fear and danger."

Herzog was also attracted to *Nosferatu* for other reasons. Always fascinated by the bizarre, *Nosferatu* appealed to the sensibility of this self-styled "Bavarian of the late Middle Ages" whose works are permeated by dreams, nightmares and visions. Photographed by Jörg Schmidt-Reitwein on locations in Holland and Czechoslovakia, *Nosferatu* is a superlative probing of the relationship between man and nature. Werner Herzog has in fact described himself as a director of landscapes, and as Diane Jacobs noted some years ago: "If people of earlier centuries believed the land was alive, Herzog proves that it is so. His landscapes become characters themselves, with their own dialogue. In *Nosferatu*, the evening skies are not so much troublesome as troubled."

Herzog was no less fascinated by the character of Dracula, whom he interpreted differently from Murnau. "In Murnau's film the vampire is without a soul, he is like an insect, a crab," Herzog observes. "My vampire plays against his appendages—his long claws, his pointed fangs. He is so suffering, so human, so sad, so desperately longing for love that you don't see the claws and fangs any more."

And while Herzog captures the tone and tempo of Murnau's film and, on occasion, duplicates some of Murnau's compositions, such as Harker's arrival at the Transylvanian inn, it would be unfair to suggest that he limited himself out of respect for Murnau's film. From

Nosferatu, Herzog's homage to Murnau.

Jonathan Harper (Bruno Ganz) and Count Dracula (Klaus Kinski). *(Nosferatu)*

Jonathan Harper (Bruno Ganz) on route to Castle Dracula. *(Nosferatu)*

Klaus Kinski. *(Nosferatu)*

Werner Herzog: "Murnau's *Nosferatu* is the most visionary of all German films."

the opening shot of skeletal remains in a darkened catacomb to the final vision of Jonathan Harker, recipient of the vampire's curse, galloping toward the horizon, Herzog's concern with composition never impedes the fluidity of the total work. Running 105 minutes, *Nosferatu* is an outstanding example of economical editing in an era when many directors seem unable to separate the superfluous from the essential.

Isabelle Adjani and Klaus Kinski. *(Nosferatu)*

Victims of the plague. *(Nosferatu)*

The Vampyre (Klaus Kinski) and his victim (Isabelle Adjani). *(Nosferatu)*

Die Blechtrommel

THE TIN DRUM

1979

CREDITS:

Production: Franz Seitz and Anatole Dauman. A German-French co-production; An Artemis Film (Federal Republic of Germany), Argos Films (France). *Director:* Volker Schlöndorff. *Screenplay:* Jean-Claude Carriere, Volker Schlöndorff, Franz Seitz, which the collaboration of Günter Grass. Based on the novel by Günter Grass. *Cinematography:* Igor Luther. *Editor:* Suzanne Baron. *Production design:* Nicos Perakis. *Music:* Maurice Jarre. *Released:* 1979. *Running time:* 142 minutes. Released in the United States by New World Pictures.

CAST:

David Bennent *(Oskar)*; Mario Adorf *(Alfred Matzerath)*; Angela Winkler *(Agnes Matzerath)*; Daniel Olbrychski *(Jan Bronski)*; Katharina Tahlbach *(Maria)*; Heinz Bennent *(Greff)*; Andrea Ferreol *(Lina Greff)*; Fritz Hakl *(Bebra)*; Mariella Oliveri *(Roswitha Raguna)*; Tina Engel *(Anna Koljaiczek, young)*; Berta Drews *(Anna Koljaiczke, old)*; Roland Beubner *(Joseph Koljaiczek)*; Ernst Jacobi *(Gauleiter Lobsack)*; Wener Rehm *(Scheffler, the baker)*; Ilse Page *(Gretchen Scheffler)*; Kate Jaenicke *(Mother Truczinski)*; Wigand Witting *(Herbert Truczinski)*; Marek Walczewski *(Schugger-Leo)*; Wojcech Pszoniak *(Fajngold)*; Otto Sander *(Meyn, the musician)*; Karl-Heinz Titelbach *(Felix)*; Emil F. Feist and Herbert Behrent *(Circus performers)*; Bruno Thost *(Corporal Lankes)*; Gerda Blisse *(Miss Spollenhauer)*; Joachim Hackethal *(Father Wiehnke)*; Zygmunt Huebner *(Dr. Michon)*; Mieczyslaw Czechowicz *(Kobyella)*; and the participation of Charles Aznavour as Sigismund Markus.

Völker Schlöndorff's adaptation of Günter Grass's satirical novel, *Die Blechtrommel (The Tin Drum)*, did more to reestablish the prestige of the German film than any single work produced since 1945. First published in 1959, the novel describes the course of German history from the turn of the century to after World War II and is

David Bennent as Oskar. *(Die Blechtrommel)*

narrated by little Oskar, who at the age of three vows that he will grow no further, not "by so much as a finger's breath." He prefers to remain "the precocious three-year-old towered over by grownups but superior to all grownups, who refuses to measure his shadow by theirs, who is complete both inside and outside, while they, to the very brink of the grave, are condemned to worry their heads about development. . . ."

While the novel enjoyed a considerable success in Germany and abroad, no one believed that the strange story could be transferred to the medium of film. Franz Seitz was one of the few producers in the German industry to appreciate the cinematic possibilities of *The Tin Drum*. For ten years Seitz tried without success to interest various directors, including Roman Polanski and Walerian Borowczyk. In April, 1977, he asked Völker Schlöndorff to read the novel. "I was very impressed with the book," Schlöndorff recalled, "but like everybody else I thought it was not feasible as a film. Who's going to be interested in a dwarf and his problems? But then I was having lunch with Bertrand Tavernier, who said, 'It's not about a dwarf, it's about a child—a child remaining a child while everybody else grows up.' " Schlöndorff was intrigued by the notion of "the child's refusal to participate in society, to bear or share responsibility," which

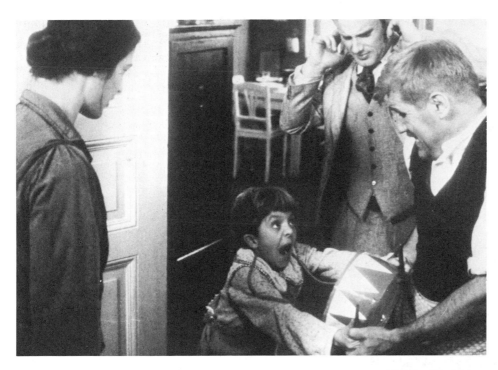

Angela Winkler, David Bennent, Daniel Olbrychski and Mario Adolf. (Die Blechtrommel)

seemed to him "to represent the whole attitude of our younger generation in Europe. He protests and rejects by those shattering screams of his and by his beating the drum."

Schlöndorff "was less interested by the whole Nazi aspect," believing that "Everything's been said and said again about the rise and fall of Hitler but never so forcefully as by Günter Grass who said, 'Nazism is the infantalism of an epoch and a society.' " Schlöndorff was also concerned with "the child's discovery of the grown-ups' and his relation to sexuality." As Schlöndorff noted, "Oskar was very definitely attracted to women but didn't want to play the part of the man. He wanted the privileges but none of the responsibilities for women."

Scenarist Jean-Claude Carriere, working in collaboration with Schlöndorff and Seitz, designed shots appropriate for a child's viewpoint. "A child's perspective is not a matter of a lens but how he sees people behave," Schlöndorff reflected. "You could call it the Benji perspective!" Schlöndorff was then introduced to eleven-year-old David Bennent, the son of actor Heinz Bennent, who had appeared in three previous Schlöndorff films. He knew immediately that he had found his Oskar, "the eternal three-year-old drummer." The script required that he range in age from infancy to a man of twenty who could still be three. "When I first met him," Schlöndorff noted, "I was convinced only he could do the picture— not because of his size but because of his eyes. He looked as if he had witnessed all the tragedy and folly of mankind but still had a child's face." A year of research and rewriting followed, with Schlöndorff reading and

Fritz Hakl and Angela Winkler. (Die Blechtrommel)

rereading the novel to Bennent, whose reactions were incorporated into the evolving photoplay. "David was a kind of pillar, and the film was built around him," the director recalled.

Schlöndorff assembled a German and Polish cast with Angela Winkler as Oskar's mother, Agnes; Daniel Olbry-

289

David Bennent. *(Die Blechtrommel)*

chski, the star of Andrzej Wajada's *Landscape After Battle* and *The Young Girls of Wilko*, as her poetic cousin and lover, Jan Bronski; Mario Adorf as Oskar's callous and opportunistic father, Matzerath; and Charles Aznavour as the gentle Jewish toy merchant, Sigismund Markus, who reveres Oskar's mother.

While Schlöndorff was largely successful in his ability to recruit Polish actors, he was unable to secure the permission of the Polish government to film in Gdansk (Danzig), the setting of the story and the novelist's native city. *The Tin Drum*, it seems, had never been published in Poland because of a sequence which depicted the rape of civilians by Soviet soldiers. Schlöndorff was disappointed but with the aid of production designer Nicos Perakis meticulously recreated interiors, façades and backgrounds to suggest pre-war Danzig.

Schlöndorff was confident from the first day of shooting: "I never came to the set not knowing where to put the camera or the people. This had never happened to me before," he remembered. "I had always been very worried about such things."

The story opens in a potato field late one October afternoon in 1899 with Oskar's grandmother-to-be giving sanctuary beneath her large and numerous skirts to a man fleeing the police. The charge is arson, and the man, who according to family legend has fathered a child while hiding beneath the skirts, flees to America where he becomes a success in the fire insurance business.

The scene shifts to the delivery room of a Danzig hospital where Oskar recalls the moment of his birth in 1924. Like a pagan diety, fully conscious in his mother's womb, he debates whether to leave the security of the womb for the vicissitudes of the world. The glow of a naked light bulb dangling from the ceiling of the operat-

ing room provides Oskar with his first impression of the world. As he passes out of the womb, "outwardly wailing and impersonating a meat-colored baby," he overhears that he will be given a tin drum on his third birthday.

The promise is fulfilled at a family gathering three years later. Oskar decides that he has all that he will ever want and resolves that he will never grow up. To legitimize his situation, "to provide a plausible ground for [his] failure to grow, even before the doctor should offer his explanation," he throws himself down the basement staircase on "a sunny day in September," his third birthday. The "accident" is accepted by the family as the explanation for his arrested development.

Oskar and his tin drum become inseparable. He is regarded "as a quiet, almost too well-behaved child" until a schoolteacher attempts to take the drum away. Oskar issues a piercing, primal scream which devastates the classroom and unnerves the teacher. Later, in a doctor's office his voice shatters glass jars containing

Circus performers on the ramparts of Normandy. *(Die Blechtrommel)*

fetuses and reptiles which swim about the floor in streams of formaldehyde.

The years pass. Hitler comes to power and Oskar's grocer father, Matzerath, a loyal German, becomes a Nazi. When Germany attacks Poland, Oskar and Jan Bronski, his presumptive father, find themselves trapped in Danzig's post office. Bronski is executed, but Oskar manages to escape from the rubble with his tin drum in tow.

During the war he joins a troop of midgets who entertain at the front. The midget leader of the group warns Oskar that the big people will soon take over the fairgrounds, and so the little people should protect themselves. As the fortunes of the Reich ebb, the distinction between the real and the surreal become increasingly blurred. That Oskar and his Lilliputian compatriots should picnic on the concrete bunkers at Normandy acquires a certain logic. Germany's collapse is signalled by the arrival of Soviet soldiers who invade the Mat-

Gerda Blisse and David Bennent. *(Die Blechtrommel)*

zareth household. The Nazi leader endeavors to divest himself of his Nazi past, but chokes to death when he attempts to swallow the symbol of that past, his party badge. Oskar observes the hypocrite's death with a wide-eyed demonic gleam.

Standing at the open grave of Matzerath, Oskar at last resolves to grow up. But the decision has come too late. His little brother, approaching stealthily, administers the fatal shove. Oskar is dead, but it is merely a moment in the cycle of history. As one critic perceptively noted, "Oskar . . . has created a son in his own image and with his own uncommon powers—presumably because the brutalities and the dislocations never end and still another surviving witness will be required."

It is at this point that Schlöndorff ends his film, although Grass's novel continued the story of Oskar into the postwar period. Through a force of will he grows into a hunchback and performs in a nightclub called the Onion Cellar which invites customers to peel onions and cry as an expiation of their sins. In a mental institution attended by Bruno his keeper, Oskar writes his autobiography, which is told in retrospect.

Die Kinder aus No. 67

THE CHILDREN OF NO. 67

1980

CREDITS:

Production: Road Movies Filmproduktion GmbH, Munich. *Directors:* Usch Barthelmess-Weller and Werner

Meyer. Screenplay: Usch Barthelmess-Weller and Werner Meyer. *Cinematography:* Jürgen Jürges. *Editor:* Helga Borsche. *Art direction:* Maciej Putowski. *Costumes:* Gisela Storch. *Sound:* Gerhard Birkholz. *Music:* Andi Brauer. *Production director:* Reneé Gunelach. *Released:* 1980. *Running time:* 103 minutes. *Length:* 2814 meters.

CAST:

Bernd Riedel *(Erwin);* René Schaaf *(Paul);* May Buschke *(Miriam);* Jürgen Frei *(Willi);* Ralf Rackwitz *(Heiner);* Andrea v. Lieven *(Lotte);* Laila Renz *(Lucie);* Dirk Lüerss *(Emil);* Sabine Kolbatz *(Martha);* Martina Weiske *(Walli);* Stefan Bossenberger *(Peter);* Jörg-Dennis Schmidt-Voss *(Gerdchen);* Birgit Nauendorf *(Tina);* Franziska Krumwiede *(Fränzi);* Sebastian Steinke *(Hotte Tetzmann);* Thomas Weiske *(Bäckerlehrling Gustav);* Heike Falkenberg *(Pummel);* Elfriede Irrall *(Mutter Brackmann);* Tilo Prückner *(Vater Brackmann);* Thomas Ahrens *(Steineklopfer Gunter);* Johanna Karl-Lory *(Witwe Weyermann);* Barbara Morawiecz *(Frau Marnasse);* Claus-Dieter Reents *(Herr Franke);* Udo Samel *(Lehrer Köwel);* Gotthard Kuppel *(Lehrer Zemski).*

Directed by Usch Barthelmess-Weller and Werner Meyer from a novel by Lisa Tetzner, *Die Kinder aus No. 67 oder Heil Hitler, Ich hätt gern'n paar Pferdeäppal (The Children of No. 67, or Heil Hitler, I'd Like Some*

René Schaaf and Bernd Riedel. *(Die Kinder aus No. 67)*

Peter Franke, Bernd Riedel and Tilo Prückner. *(Die Kinder aus No. 67)*

Horse Droppings) is a masterful recreation of a time and place: the Berlin-Mowabit working class district shortly before and after Hitler's ascendancy to power. While Tetzner "pursued very didactic pretentions," the filmmakers were drawn to the material for its "story of two twelve-year-old boys, Paul and Erwin, [who] have their special way of deciding between right and wrong, important and unimportant."

The filmmakers quote Maxim Gorki to the effect that " 'Things must be written for children just as they are for adults, only better.' " "A good children's film can also be a film for adults because every adult has her/his own childhood history," the directors note. "We are formed not only by our parents, but also by our surroundings and the political circumstances in which we grew up. Since the children of the past are today's parents and grandparents, this film contributes to the remembering of that past in two ways: in the historic and in the personal dimension. . . . [But] to learn from the past does not only mean to learn from history, but also from one's own development. To get in touch with one's own childhood, trying to find out which feelings, fantasies

and wishes got lost on the way to becoming an adult—perhaps this would be a way to becoming an adult—perhaps this would be a way to question rigid modes of behavior and standards, discover unused potentials and find new approaches." In the view of Barthelmess-Weller and Mayer, it is not the task of a feature film to transmit factual knowledge or to render an historical analysis, but rather "in showing empathy for people and their experiences the film can create an awareness of everyday events in order to sharpen one's view and consciousness of the historical and social interconnections."

In *Die Kinder aus No. 67* the filmmakers "attempt to give children and young adults access to topics and problems which arise where social and political events and the personal meet. How people lived together shows us the nature of the National Socialist regime." They "tried to build up the film in such a way that there is always a story-line which leads the younger audience through the film and lets them participate in the lives of Erwin, Paul, and the children of No. 67. The film also contains all that information which becomes visible when reconstructing that era, even if the younger viewers are not yet able to grasp its meaning. There is hardly a young person who has heard of August Bebel and thus will not understand what Lotte means when she says to her father, 'Why don't you burn your stupid Bebel?', after he had burned the newspaper *Vorwärts* after the first wave of persecutions."

The directors gave particular attention "to the personality and peculiarity of each child," believing that "the

The Brackmann family: Elfriede Irrall, Tilo Prückner and Bernd Riedel. *(Die Kinder aus No. 67)*

role should be suited to the acting child's personality, not the opposite." Their previous film experiences with children gave the directors "a clear idea of the differences between children of various social milieus: special body language and social behavior. These essential features cannot be found among children of middle class surroundings." As a consequence, they looked for actors only among working class children.

To establish rapport with the children and to familiarize them with their roles, the directors informed them about the Nazi era and showed them photographs of the period and during a four-day stay at a youth hostel allowed them to wear their film costumes. At first they planned to live together as a "film family," sharing a residence in Berlin-Kruzberg. "The children would have been enthusiastic about it," the directors recalled, "but we would have been unable to give them the kind of care which they had at home and would have needed during the strenuous shooting." Before filming, they discussed and played all the scenes in order that the children could "establish a total connection between all events," which, of course, would not be photographed chronologically. "Furthermore, it was an important chance for us to examine our work on the script." During these preparations the directors encouraged the children to conceive stories by themselves, which they photographed and edited with Super-8 equipment. This experience allowed them to understand the problems of the cameraman and the requirements of the director.

Paul Brackmann and Erwin Richter are friends who belong to the gang of children from one of the back courtyards of apartment building No. 67. When they are not at gang meetings or doing chores for their families, Paul and Erwin are out trying to earn some money. Their greatest wish is to possess a real leather football.

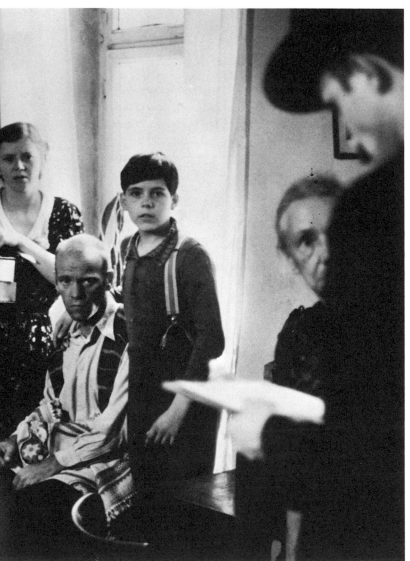

The Richter family: Martina Kravel, Peter Francke and René Schaaf.

Erwin (Bernd Riedel) and Paul (René Schaaf) in the final scene of *Die Kinder aus No. 67* (The Children of No. 67).

While the children are preparing for a big masquerade in the courtyard, Paul's family becomes destitute. Unable to pay their rent, the Richters are threatened with eviction. The gang responds by declaring the masquerade a benefit party. During the celebration Erwin announces that the proceeds are enough to pay the Richters' rent.

After Hitler's accession to power in January, 1933, the gang from the courtyard of No. 67 disbands. Most of the children, including Paul, join the HJ (Hitler Youth) or BDM (Federation of German Girls). Inevitably, the friendship between Erwin and Paul is broken. Erwin becomes more isolated after the arrest of his father, who has agitated against the Nazis. But it is Erwin who has the final word as we see him clutch Paul's brown collar in a gesture of anger and defiance.

Direction and cinematography are uniformly excellent. The quasi-documentary camera of Jürgen Jürges captures the dank, claustrophobic atmosphere of the tenement milieu, superbly detailed by art director Marciej Petowski. *The Children of No. 67* is very much a film about the art of filmmaking. The directors achieve movement within the frame or create movement through a tightly structured montage. Avoiding the polemical, the filmmakers accomplish their education, entertainment and artistic tasks through a refreshing understatement.

Directors Werner Meyer and Usch Barthelmess-Weller with Tilo Prückner, Andrea von Lieven, Elfriede Irrall and Bernd Riedel during the production. *(Die Kinder aus No. 67)*

Das Boot

THE BOAT

1981

CREDITS:

Production: A Bavaria Atelier/Radiant Film Production. Produced by Günter Rohrbach. *Director:* Wolfgang Petersen. *Assistant director:* Maria-Antoinette Petersen. *Screenplay:* Wolfgang Petersen. Based on the novel by Lothar-Günther Buchheim. *Cinematography:* Jost Vacano. *Miniature photography:* Ernst Wild. *Miniatures and technical effects:* Hans Nothof, Gerhard Neumeier, Erwin Schnetzer, Oliver Nothof, Alfred Schallmeier. *Art direction:* Gotz Weidner. *Production design:* Rolf Zehetbauer. *Special effects:* Karl Baumgartner. *Costumes:* Monika Bauert. *Music:* Klaus Doldinger. *Sound:* Mike Le-Mare,

Jürgen Prochnow (The Captain). *(Das Boot)*

Klas Wennemann (Chief Engineer), Jürgen Prochnow (The Captain) and Herbert Grönemeyer (Lieutenant Werner/correspondent). *(Das Boot)*

G.B.F.E. *Film editor:* Hannes Nikel. *Naval advisors:* Achim Krug, Karl Böhm. *Released:* September 17, 1981 (Munich). Released in the United States by Columbia Pictures (1982). *Running time:* 150 minutes.

CAST:

Jürgen Prochnow *(The Captain);* Herbert Grönemeyer *Lieutenant Werner/Correspondent);* Klaus Wennemann *(Chief Engineer);* Hubertus Bengsch *(1st Lieutenant/Number One);* Martin Semmelrogge *(2nd Lieutenant);* Bernd Tauber *(Chief Quartermaster);* Erwin Leder *(Johann);* Martin May *(Ullmann);* Heinz Hönig *(Hinrich);* U. A. Ochsen *(Chief Bosun):* Claude-Oliver Rudolph *(Ario);* Jan Fedder *(Pilgrim);* Ralph Richer *(Frenssen);* Joachim Bernhard *(Preacher);* Oliver Stritzel *(Schwalle);* Konrad Becker *(Bockstiegel);* Lutz Schnell *(Dufte);* Martin Hemme *(Brückenwilli).*

Das Boot (The Boat) was directed by Wolfgang Petersen from Lothar-Günther Buchheim's semi-autobiographical novel of the same title, first published in Germany in 1973. As a war reporter, Buchheim had gone on several submarine missions under the command of Heinrich Lehmann-Willenbrok, who became the basis for "Der Alte," the captain of the U-96. A great part of his original report was destroyed during an air raid, but the memories haunted him and twenty years later he wrote *Das Boot.* Buchheim's realistic portrayal of the U-96 made a deep impression on Petersen who regarded it as "the most radical, the best, and possibly the most difficult material ever written about the war." Petersen also stated he "wanted to give people a different perspective of Germans as normal human beings. We suffer a little under the fact that we are always presented in films as the bad guys. That was always a problem for my generation. It's important for the younger Germans to be accepted as people so that others can see that we are not always terrible and cruel."

Bavaria had purchased the rights to *Das Boot* and a production was planned in 1974, but when the costs were considered too great, the film was postponed. Sometime afterwards, and to the dismay of Petersen and Buchheim, Bavaria entertained the idea of Americanizing the production with John Sturgis directing Paul Newman as the U-Boat commander. Another proposal would have allowed Don Siegel to direct with Robert Redford in the role of the commander. While Buchheim found Siegel's adaptation of his work more acceptable, he refused to allow his story to be transformed into a cliché-ridden adventure film. Petersen, who was making

Erwin Leder as Johann, the chief machinist. *(Das Boot)*

The U-96 sails out of the occupied French port of La Rochelle to begin a patrol of the North Atlantic. *(Das Boot)*

The claustrophobic interior of the U-96. *(Das Boot)*

The U-96 is equipped with torpedos. *(Das Boot)*

Interior of the U-96. *(Das Boot)*

Wolfgang Petersen directing at La Rochelle, France. *(Das Boot)*

Swarz und Weiss Wie Tage und Nachte (Black and White Like Day and Night) during these negotiations, remembered his feelings: "Sometimes I think I was a little bit jealous hearing them planning *Das Boot.* I was thinking it was a pity we couldn't make it because it's our story." When the talks with Siegel reached an impasse, production manager Günter Rohrbach interceded with Bavaria on behalf of Petersen.

Das Boot consumed nearly four years of production. Engineers and studio technicians created three models of various sizes in addition to two full-scale replicas, one for filming at sea and another for studio interiors. After locating plans for the Type VII-C in the archive of the Chicago Museum of Science and Industry, a submarine was replicated by a manufacturer which had not built U-Boats since 1945. At Bavaria Studio the fifty-ton U-Boat was then mounted on a sixteen-foot-high machine dubbed "the Wippler," which enabled the crew to simulate every imaginable movement of the boat on the high seas, including the violent rocking brought on by enemy depth charges and the powerful jolts of deep sea plunges.

Designer Rolf Zehetbauer had equipped the set with removable walls, but Petersen, intent on capturing the claustrophobic atmosphere of the U-Boat, chose to leave

Jürgen Prochnow and Herbert Grönemeyer in the final scene of *Das Boot.*

them in place during the filming. "It was constructed like a weapon—a torpedo," Petersen recounted. "It was not constructed for human beings." Indeed, the original Type VII-C was 150 feet long but scarcely wider than a man's outstretched arms. The danger and hardship were felt most of all by Petersen's cameraman, Jose Vacano, who was obliged to wear a crash helmet, elbow pads and knee cushions during his filming in the steely, cylindrical labyrinth. Some of Vacano's finest effects were made with a hand-held Arriflex while a special gyroscope mount was devised to steady the picture during the battle scenes. Cast and crew were confined to these close quarters for 150 days.

Location photography was achieved in the North Sea over a three-month period. For these scenes, engineers designed a thirty-five foot version of the U-96 with the capacity to dive and cruise on the high seas. A single pilot manuevered the boat with the aid of a small television monitor. When the vessel surfaced, the captain and his crew were represented by puppets twelve inches high. Two additional models, one eighteen feet long and the other eight feet long, were fabricated for underwater photography, while scale models of a tanker and destroyer were employed for the dramatic battle sequence. Petersen left no stone unturned to achieve realism. Torpedoes were handcrafted from illustrations in war manuals; the crew's food was treated to look moldy and unappetizing; and every article of clothing was researched down to the shoelaces.

Petersen exposed over one million feet of film to create the 150-minute theatrical version of *Das Boot*, which premiered in Munich on September 17, 1981. Other material appeared in a six-hour television mini-series in 1985. Costing 11 million dollars, *Das Boot* proved to be the most expensive German production since World War II. But by the early spring of 1983, *Das Boot* had grossed twelve million dollars from its American distribution alone, making it the second highest grossing foreign film, surpassed only by *La Cage aux Folles.*

Petersen was both heartened and surprised: "Who could have imagined it would do so well [in America]? And what a thrill it was! When you've grown up on a diet of American films, as I did, it's a fantasy come true when Hollywood producers start calling you and offering you work." The director was no less gratified when the Academy of Motion Picture Arts and Sciences nominated him for awards in two categories, Best Director and Best Screenplay Adaptation. Petersen also received a Best Director nomination from the Directors Guild of America.

While Petersen strove for realism in *Das Boot*, small liberties were taken to intensify the drama. Perhaps the

299

most objectionable was the opening sequence at the Bar Royale prior to a launching of U-96 at La Rochelle. An inebriated captain makes a spectacle of himself. During the wild bacchanal, table settings are thrown to the floor and a gun is fired. The theatricality of the sequence is in jarring contrast to the sober realism of the submarine scenes which followed. One Rudi Toepfer who served as a lieutenant aboard U-406 (code name Sparrow) during World War II believed that "A German officer would never have behaved like that. . . . Certainly, when an Iron Cross was awarded it was a big event and everyone got quite tipsy. But an officer would never get that drunk and make a fool of himself in public."

Toepfer also took exception to the excessive profanity which at that time was uncommon even among the lowest classes. And later, aboard the U-96, Toepfer doubted that the captain would have drawn his pistol when his chief petty officer becomes hysterical. "I don't believe my captain ever carried a pistol," Toepfer recalled. But the former lieutenant was generally satisfied with Petersen's portrayal of the separateness of the submarines, represented in the argument between the captain, forthright and honest, and the fanatical Nazi Party member, a product of the Hitler and the men who served in the German military," Toepfer noted. "Many of us felt that the party had allowed too many ignorant people into its leadership."

While Toepfer found the sinking of the British tanker realistic, with its depiction of a flaming hull and men jumping overboard into a fiery sea, he did not believe that a torpedo would have been wasted to "break the back" of a sinking ship. But the empathy shown by the German submariners for the British crewmen who plead to be taken aboard the U-Boat, an impossibility under the circumstances, corresponded to the terrible reality. Toepfer remembered that "There were instances early in the war when we threw supplies to enemy lifeboats." And when the German crew, having torpedoed a British tanker, listen to the sound of the doomed vessel, groaning and creaking, as it disappears down to an unfathomable grave, their heartfelt expressions convey the tragedy of war as it has only rarely been experienced in motion pictures.

Petersen conveys the extreme danger of submarine service, hardly exaggerated when we recognized that of the 40,000 Germans who served in submarines during World War II, only 10,000 survived. Depth charges resound with frightening force while rivets from the metal hull exploded like bullets, whizzing across the passageway as the submarine descends beyond the 300-foot maximum stipulated by the ship's designers to 800 feet.

Petersen has described *Das Boot* as "a war story from the German viewpoint. It shows the waste, the demoralization of men. The tragedies are not just the men who are killed, but those who survive only as psychological cripples." *Das Boot* is universal and transcendent and must rank with *All Quiet on the Western Front*, *Grand Illusion*, *Paths of Glory* and *The Bridge on the River Kwai* as one of the century's greatest war films.

Céleste

1981

CREDITS:

Production: Polemele Film GmbH, Munich. Distributed by Filmverlag der Autoren, GmbH, Munich. *Executive Producer*: Eleonore Adlon. *Director*: Percy Adlon. *Screenplay*: Percy Adlon. Based on the book *Monsieur Proust* by Céleste Albaret. *Cinematography*: Jürgen Martin. *Editor*: Clara Fabry. *Art direction*: Hans Gailling. *Costumes*: Barbara Gailling. *Sound*: Rainer Wiehr. *Music*: César Franck, performed by the Bartholdy-Quartet. *Released*: 1981. *Running time*: 107 minutes. *Length*: 1941 meters.

CAST:

Eva Mattes (*Céeste*); Jürgen Arndt (*Monsieur Proust*); Norbert Wartha (*Odilon*); Wolf Euba (*Dr. Robert Proust*); Joseph Manoth; Leon Bardischewski; Horst Raspe; Andi Stefanescu; Rolf Illig.

While the lives of musicians and painters have often been put on celluloid, great films about great writers have been the exception rather than the rule. The chief business of the writer is writing and this occupation with all its attendant agony, while recognized to be essential in the creation of literature, has generally been regarded as uncinematic. Filmmakers prefer to deal with incidents from the love life of the writer (*The Barretts of Wimpole Street*), a celebrated scandal (*The Green Carnation* and *The Trial of Oscar Wilde*) or the writer in dramatic conflict with the established order (*The Life of Emile Zola*), and ignore the process of writing. Presumably, the books are written off screen, although a director may include a brief scene of the writer at a lamp-lit desk, attired in a velvet jacket and scarf, but the creation of the written work is always incidental to other activities.

A notable exception to this traditionally superficial

Eva Mattes as Proust's devoted housekeeper, Céleste.

treatment of the writer is *Céleste*, directed by Percy Adlon, who based his film on the memoir of Céleste Albaret, the housekeeper of Marcel Proust between 1913 and 1922. Andrew Sarris described Adlon's work as "one of the most profound tributes one art form has ever paid to another."

Céleste was photographed by Jürgen Martin and a crew of ten over a five-week period in 1981 at a cost of DM 800,000, a low budget even by German standards. Because Adlon could not afford a studio, principal photography was achieved within the confines of a private house in Munich which substituted as Proust's Parisian apartment. The film was shot with original sound, including the sequence of the string quartet. *Céleste* was finished in April, 1981. "I had no distributor, no reputation as a filmmaker and no experience with cinema promotion," Adlon recalled. "My wife, Eleonore, and I arranged for a screening at our own expense during the Cannes Festival after the film had been refused by the official *'semaine de la critique.'* " For several days the Adlons stood at the festival house, distributing information leaflets about *Céleste* to filmgoers. "And then we heard that some connoisseurs of Proust planned to attend in order to have a good time laughing at this 'German Proust.' But on the day of the showing, no one laughed. We received a standing ovation and invitations from fifteen festivals all over the world. It was like a dream."

Within the cork-paneled rooms of Proust's apartment we are shown the act of writing with all its attendant joys and sorrows, viewed from the perspective of the master's

Jürgen Arndt as Marcel Proust. *(Céleste)*

301

devoted servant, Céleste Albaret, played by Eva Mattes. The routine of life is presented with fascinating detail: Céleste's careful preparation of *café au lait* and croissants, the author's basic sustenance in the final years, the fumigation of Proust's bedroom (a few pinches of Legras powder lit by a candle) as a preventative against asthma, the changing of the bedclothes, the airing of the room, the disinfecting of the mail, the warming of the shirts, the delivery of hot water bottles and the pasting together of his notes to form a concertina-like page of manuscript, the director piling incident upon incident to give us the equation of Proust's life.

Adlon captures the rhythm of a life in which "time contained no hours—just a certain number of definite things to be done every day," as Céleste Albaret recounted in her memoir. "Everything else depended on his work; on some concern or need connected with his writing; or on a whim, the satisfaction or the disappointment over an evening out, a meeting, or a visit; or on the fatigue, beneficial or harmful, of going out, or of writing, with all the inevitable consequences to his sensibility and his illness."

Only on rare occasions does Adlon take us outside the apartment. In a magnificent retrospective we visit the Grand Hotel at Cabourg with its magnificient esplanade. It is the summer of 1914 and the occasion of Proust's final visit. A big bull's-eye window frames the sunset "with the sea glittering below." And in another retrospective we return to Céleste's childhood village, Auxillac in the Lorzère, where she recalls the burning of a barn and how her mother, a week later, lost her baby. "In spite of this tragedy, I caused M. Proust much amusement

Eva Mattes, Jürgen Arndt and the Bartholdy-Quartet. *(Céleste)*

Céleste (Eva Mattes) and Odilon (Norbert Wartha) patiently reconstruct Proust's manuscript. *(Céleste)*

telling him that my father, who'd lost everything, had to borrow a neighbor's hat to go to mass on Sunday, and the hat was too small." Proust's descriptions of an evening out, "how this man was ridiculous or that woman had been in splendid form all evening—and what she was wearing," are narrated by Jürgen Arndt in the role of Proust against the background of the hermetically sealed apartment.

Percy Adlon entered film from a background of music, a circumstance which further enriches *Céleste*. The director reconstructs the occasion when Proust arranged for the Poulet quartet to play the music of César Franck in the drawing room of his apartment. The musicians assembled at one o'clock in the morning. "They played Franck's Quartet, and he listened to it lying down with his eyes closed," Céleste Albaret wrote. "After the interval, M. Proust asked the musicians, if they weren't too tired, to play again, not the whole quartet but a certain part of it" The scene is nearly the same in the film. "'It has been a great expense, Céleste,'" Proust told his housekeeper afterwards. "'And all the trouble and fatigue! But I had to. It was necessary.' He didn't say 'for my work.' There was no need."

In the final sequence we witness the death of Proust, pale, bearded and gaunt. When his breathing has stopped, Céleste silently steps forward and snips a lock of hair which she gives to his brother Robert and then a lock for herself. The film concludes with Céleste happy in the knowledge "that she has been privileged and that everything has ended as it was meant to end," as Stanley Kaufmann wrote in his review of the film.

Céleste was Percy Adlon's first theatrical film. Born in

Jürgen Arndt and Eva Mattes. *(Céleste)*

Director Percy Adlon in 1981. *(Céleste)*

Céleste (Eva Mattes) rushes to Proust's sickroom.

Odilon (Norbert Wartha), Robert (Wolf Euba) and Céleste (Eva Mattes) attend the dying Proust (Jürgen Arndt). *(Céleste)*

1935, he grew up in Ammerland Starnberger See. He studied German literature, theater, acting and art history. He has adapted and narrated works of literature for German radio and directed documentaries for television: *Tomi Ungerers Landleben (Tomi Ungerer's Rural Life)*, *Mann und Frau im Gehause—Über Gisela und Alfred Andersch (Man and Wife in the House They Built—About Gisela and Alfred Andersch)*, *Portraits of Emigrant Germans*, *The Dancer Heinz Bosl*, *The Woman Bilek*, *The True Liliom—Portrait of a Survivor*, *Widows—Notes on a Problem Suppressed* and *Entertainment on Travel—Karajan Orchestra Orderly*. In 1979 he won the Grimme Prize for his film on Robert Walser, *The Guardian and His Poet*, and in 1980 for his television play, *Herr Kischoff*. In 1982 he directed his second theatrical film *Funf Letze Tage (Five Last Days)*, based on the lives of Sophie Scholl and her brother Hans who were executed for their opposition to Hitler.

Percy Adlon is a refreshingly original artist who studies his subject with the eye of the documentarist, but what he sees is filtered by a mind intensely poetic.

Auxillac in the Lozère, Céleste's childhood home. *(Céleste)*